IDEAS OF

IDEAS
OF REVELATION

An Historical Study

A.D. 1700 to A.D. 1860

BY

H. D. McDONALD

B.A., B.D., Ph.D.(Lond.)

LECTURER IN HISTORICAL THEOLOGY
LONDON BIBLE COLLEGE

LONDON
MACMILLAN & CO LTD
NEW YORK · ST MARTIN'S PRESS

1959

MACMILLAN AND COMPANY LIMITED
London Bombay Calcutta Madras Melbourne

THE MACMILLAN COMPANY OF CANADA LIMITED
Toronto

ST MARTIN'S PRESS INC
New York

PRINTED IN GREAT BRITAIN

FOREWORD

'Whoever would take the religious literature of the present day as a whole, and endeavour to make out clearly on what basis Revelation is supposed by it to rest, whether on Authority, on the Inward Light, Reason, Self-evidencing Scripture, or on the combination of the four, or some of them, and in what proportions, would probably find that he had undertaken a perplexing but not altogether profitless inquiry.'

These words, written by Mark Pattison almost exactly a century ago, are in his usual ironical vein. But, ironical or not, the Anglican bishops who have been discussing the authority of the Bible at the 1958 Lambeth Conference, will no doubt testify that they are as applicable to-day as they were when they were first written. And the very fact that the Lambeth Conference has raised this question as one of the major items on its agenda is evidence that modern Christians by no means regard it as an 'altogether profitless inquiry'; on the contrary, Christians of all kinds are becoming increasingly concerned with it. No great rashness is needed to predict that in the coming decades one of the most debated theological questions will be how the Bible is to be understood and approached if it is to be a vehicle of revelation for our time.

Mark Pattison's contribution to the discussion in his day was to write a history of how the matter had been viewed between 1688 and 1750. Dr McDonald has sought to make a similar contribution, though his work is on a larger scale and brings the history of the discussion down far enough to include the views of F. D. Maurice. If Dr McDonald's writing avoids the ironical vein of Pattison's, it is based on the same exhaustive study of the original sources, and Dr McDonald seems to have a special gift for singling out the telling quotation which sums up in memorable form the quintessence of a writer's argument.

If we can ever learn anything from history, this book should help us to do so, so far as its subject is concerned, the sense in which the Bible is, or yields, revelation. For the most part the reader is left to draw the moral for himself, but there are not lacking definite hints that Dr McDonald has his own ideas on the contemporary relevance of his researches, and these hints the reader will find it worth his while to follow up.

D. E. NINEHAM

UNIVERSITY OF LONDON
KING'S COLLEGE
1958

PREFACE

THE subject of Revelation is of special interest to-day. Recent writers have been concerned with such subjects as the fact and focus of the divine self-disclosure. This pre-occupation with the problems of revelation is, however, no new thing, for it is the purpose of the following pages to show that the ideas which in recent years have come to prominence are the very ideas which were forced into the foreground in a past period. It will be necessary to mark out this era and to show how these several different views of revelation came about.

Much which has of late appeared on the subject is, we believe, not as original as it is stated. Claims and charges are made which we think would never have been made if writers had come to their subject aware of the historical background of their own particular view. The fact is, of course, that there is no helpful volume to supply this information. There are Histories of specific Christian Doctrines, as, for example, the Atonement and the Person of Christ, but there is little on the subject of Revelation as such. This is an omission which it is the purpose of the present volume to remedy. Apart from the last two or three pages, the remainder constitutes a thesis approved for the Degree of Doctor of Philosophy in the University of London.

The work should have a special interest for serious students of theology. But it should appeal also to the informed general reader who is concerned to know how Christian men have regarded Divine Revelation.

A work of this nature has demanded a good deal of withdrawal to the seclusion of the study and for this reason the author would like to acknowledge the co-operation of his wife and family who did not lay claim to his presence and help when they were rightly demanded.

A special word of thanks must be recorded to the Rev. Professor D. E. Nineham, Professor of Biblical and Historical Theology, King's College, University of London, who read through each section as it was completed. His criticisms and suggestions were of the greatest help and many of them have been acted upon. Professor Nineham has continued his kindness by writing a 'Foreword'.

I am further indebted to two of my friends and colleagues of the London Bible College for their help: to the Principal, Rev. E. F. Kevan, M.Th., B.D., for his unfailing interest, and to the Rev. J. C. J. Waite, B.D., for reading through the page proofs.

Grateful acknowledgement is also made to a number of publishers for permission to use copyright material: to the Epworth Press for Edwin Lewis's *A Philosophy of the Christian Revelation* and C. R. North's *The Old Testament Interpretation of History*: to the Lutterworth Press for Auguste Lecerf's *An Introduction to Reformed Dogmatics*; Alan Fairweather's *The Word as Truth*; and Wilhelm Niesel's *The Theology of Calvin*: to the S.C.M. for Emil Brunner's *Revelation and Reason*: to the Princeton University Press, for R. Bretall's *A Kierkegaard Anthology*: to Wm B. Eerdmans for Louis Berkhof's *Systematic Theology* (Introductory Volume, 1932), E. J. Carnell's *A Philosophy of the Christian Religion*, and E. J. Young's *Thy Word is Truth*: to Messrs Faber and Faber for Donald Baillies' *God Was In Christ*; Reinhold Niebuhr's *The Self in the Dramas of History*, and J. V. Langmead Casserley's *The Christian in Philosophy*.

A final word of thanks is due to the publishers for their kind co-operation during the process of publication.

H. D. McDonald

London Bible College

CONTENTS

CHAPTER I

THE BOUNDARIES OF AN AGE

The purpose of the following pages is to single out various views of revelation which came to the fore within the period of history from 1700 to 1860. In addition, an endeavour will be made to find a starting point, and to trace out the developments of each separate doctrine.

Questions concerning how and why and where God has revealed Himself must ever be of fundamental importance. Yet, as the student of historical theology will have observed, the problems raised by the idea of a disclosure of God were not early discussed. Centuries of theological debate, created by other needs, were to pass before attention was focused upon the subject of revelation as such.[1] It is living issues, after all, which call for immediate investigation. Abstract problems, unrelated to pressing needs, do not claim the attention of the generality of men. In the history of Christian doctrine it has been the urgent problems which have claimed the concern of the Church at large. Theological debate has sprung out of the necessities of experience or been entered upon to meet a challenge to the faith.

(i) *The Interest of the Age*

In the post-apostolic period problems specifically theological became central. Questions concerning the relation of the one God to the world and of Christ to the one God had to be solved. Following from and arising out of these discussions were the great Christological controversies which for many years agitated the Church. Attention was here fixed upon the inner nature of Christ's Person. In the process of these debates the Church elaborated its creeds and fenced itself off from those anathematized as heretics. The ecclesiastical and hierarchical system developed as a result.

[1] The discussion by Irenaeus on the subject of Inspiration may be quoted as an exception. But an exception to the general truth stated above it most certainly was.

Ecclesiology was therefore the dominant interest of the mediaeval period. The Church regarded as the gift of God and the guardian of truth claimed to be the arbiter in the affairs of the soul. The Church was believed to be a divine institution in which alone men and women could be guaranteed eternal life. This conception taking priority and pre-eminence, was defended with all the weapons of warfare, legitimate and illegitimate, spiritual and carnal. Both intellect and instrument were called upon to maintain the autocracy of the papacy believed to be established by divine decree.

This notion was, however, soon to be dispelled. An interest, at once spiritual and personal, was to turn men's attention from the institution to the individual. The whole stately edifice of ecclesiasticism which had been built up by tools provided by Aristotle was shattered by the dynamic discovery of Luther. Now became central the soteriological question concerning the significance and sufficiency of Christ's work and the right of each man to stand alone, *coram Deo*, and secure the saving benefits of the only Redeemer. How can a man be just before God? such was the pressing issue of the period. The answer of the Reformation was that a man is declared righteous by faith.[1] And this answer, vindicated in the actuality of experience, was believed to be validated in the writings of the New Testament.

From the question of justification by faith, circumstances, particularly in England, were to force upon men another interest. From the problem of personal salvation attention was turned to the problem of divine revelation. The Deists of the early eighteenth century refused to allow that God had given any special message to man beyond those indications of Himself set upon the original creation. It was, therefore, the denials of the Deists which raised the issue. 'Books on evidences had been written before this time, but it is to the rise of the Deists that we owe nearly the whole of our evidence literature.'[2]

Difficulties of a new kind were being raised. The intellectual atmosphere at the turn of the eighteenth century called for a fresh

---

[1] It must, of course, be allowed that the problem which became a personal one for Luther was an inevitable one arising out of the prevailing Zeitgeist. Harnack has a discussion on how far Luther's significance is rightly to be understood as a rediscovery of the Pauline doctrine of justification by faith. A. Harnack, *History of Dogma*, vol. 7, p. 206 f.

[2] J. Hunt, *Religious Thought in England* (1873), vol. 3, p. 97.

type of literature. It was the realization of this that made Robert Boyle found his lectureship and so anticipate the problems which the discoveries of the Royal Society might raise.

The first of the Boyle Lectures was delivered in 1692 by Richard Bentley under the title, *The Folly of Atheism and Deism even with respect of the Present Life*. Thus was begun that extensive literature for which the period is noted, all dealing with evidences of Christianity, or to be more exact, using the title given by the same Bentley to his Boyle Lectures in 1693, *The Christian Revelation*.[1]

The idea of revelation was, therefore, the dominant one of the period. Put generally it may be said that it was the purpose of the orthodox apologists to prove the need for a special revelation to

[1] This series of lectures was never published. It is of interest to note how many of the Boyle Lectures (or Sermons) for the first half of the eighteenth century treat of the subject of Revelation. In 1699 the preacher was Dr Samuel Bradford, later Bishop of Carlisle, and then of Rochester. He discoursed on *The Credibility of the Christian Revelation from its Internal Evidences*. His approach was that God authenticates His revelation to all who are in the right attitude to receive it. The one who is willing shall know of the doctrine. He shall be taught of the Father. This knowledge of the Father comes by 'studying the works of creation, by the suggestion of conscience, and by the inward teaching of the Divine Spirit'. Bradford goes on then to expound those doctrines of Christianity involved in the knowledge of the Father.

In 1700, Blacknell, afterwards Bishop of Exeter, was the lecturer. His first sermon on Luke 16. 30, 31, entitled, *The Sufficiency of a Standing Revelation*, appears to cover the whole series. Blacknell argues that the Scriptures are that 'Standing Revelation', and that the authority and genuineness of its several books are sufficiently established. So complete is the evidence that it is 'an unreasonable request to ask for more'. In 1710 Dr Josiah Woodward preached on *The Divine Original and Incomparable Excellency of the Christian Revelation*. His argument is that Christianity must be true because it is founded upon Scripture and the Scripture must be true because it is God's Word. The general tone of the lectures had already been set in 1705 by Dr Samuel Clarke who followed his series of the previous year with the subject, *The Unchangeable Obligation of Natural Religion and the Truth and Certainty of the Christian Revelation*.

William Denham's *Physico-Theology* (1711) and (1712) also bears upon the subject. So also does Benjamin Ibbot's *Free Thinking* of the years 1713 and 1714. It is indeed Ibbot's purpose to maintain the reality and sufficiency of the Christian revelation. Dr John Leng, who was later to become Bishop of Norwich, explicated the *Natural Obligation to believe the Principles of Religion and Divine Revelation* in 1717 and 1718. In 1721 and 1722 Brampton Gurdon dealt with *The Pretended Difficulties in Natural Religion no excuse for Infidelity*. Dr Burnet's subject for 1724/5 was *The Demonstration of True Religion*. William Berriman took the years 1730, 1731, 1732 to explain the sufficiency of *The Gradual Revelation of the Gospel for the time of Men's Apostasy*. In the lectures of 1739, 1740, 1741 Dr Leonard Twells spoke about miracles and prophecy. Henry Stebbing sought in the years 1747, 1748, 1749 to rout the Deists. His title was *Christianity Justified upon the Scripture Foundation, being a Summary View of the Controversy between Christians and Deists*. After the half-century had passed the Boyle Lectures seemed to excite little attention. During the next fifty years six of the lecturers only put their work in print.

those who questioned it, as it was the desire of those, who for want
of a better designation may be called the Evangelicals, to show the
sufficiency of it to those who sought it.

Had the two, however, worked together head and heart might
have been satisfied. But trouble arose because those who essayed
to meet the enquiries of the mind did not always remember that
man was more than mind. On the other hand, those who endeavoured to bring the saving revelation to the heart were inclined
to forget that man had a head as well as a heart.

In this way the protagonists of each view were at odds. Opposing
doctrines were brought into conflict. And on each side there were
those ready to press the idea accepted by this group or that to its
logical conclusion. Some fell naturally into a position of compromise. The consequence was that a variety of views can be dis-
entangled from the literature of the period each giving a different
understanding of the doctrine of revelation.

The period, then, is characterized by a deep interest in the subject
of revelation. This indeed is its distinctive feature.

Yet certain as this fact seems to be, there has been no serious
attempt, as far as we can discover, to trace out the various views of
revelation which came into prominence at the time. Certain
aspects of the period are, of course, well known, and brief summaries of the general concepts can be found. On the whole,
however, specific note has not been taken of the ideas with which
we are concerned. Histories of Christian Doctrine pay scant
attention of the views of revelation which characterized the era.[1]

(ii) *The Confines of an Era*

It is regarded as a truism to-day that there are no breaks in
history; that the past is not isolated from the present, and that the
present is creative of the future. This being so there will be,
necessarily, a certain artificiality about all suggested divisions of
history. For the convenience of study, however, there must be a
cleaving of the centuries into periods. Yet each era must reveal
its own special characteristics. At the same time, it must be
observed, that the views which become dominant in any one period

---

[1] Harnack's *History of Dogma* ends at the Reformation. The works of Dorner
and Hagenback are mainly concerned with German theology. Fisher's, *History
of Christian Doctrine* passes lightly over the period. Something of more detail,
but not from the point of view that we have adopted can be found in Hunt's,
Religious Thought in England (3 vols., 1873).

are those very tendencies which stirred in the underground of that which precedes. It is these creative undertones, understood by men of deep insight, which indicate the pattern of the dawning era.

It has been observed, however, that from the point of view of Christian doctrine history can be divided according to the prevailing theological interest: and the interest of our period was certainly focused on the problems of revelation. But these very questions were themselves raised by the deistic claim that reason was of itself sufficient and that no special word from God was needed. It was in this way that the deists initiated the period known in history as 'the Age of Reason'.

It is usual to place its start at the beginning of the eighteenth century and the whole of that century is then generally so designated. The Bampton Lectures of the year 1805, given by Edward Nares, Rector of Biddenden, Kent, were published under the title, *A View of the Evidences of Christianity at the Close of the Pretended Age of Reason*. Nares considered himself to be placed at the end of an epoc, an era which 'has ostentatiously indeed been denominated the Age of Reason'.[1] Throughout the previous years, the Christian revelation, he asserts, has been assailed with every weapon which reason could rally to the battle, 'the heavy artillery of learning and criticism, as well as the lighter weapons of wit and ridicule have been repeatedly brought into the field.'[2]

Although Nares places himself at the end of the Age of Reason and thus marks the beginning of the nineteenth century as that end, for the purpose of our investigation it is extended down to 1860, for the reason that discussion concerning revelation was still to the fore. However might be the reactions to rationalism in the first half of the nineteenth century, the period can still broadly be referred to as the *Saeculum Rationalisticum*. We thus find Herbert Spencer in the middle of the century becoming enthusiastic in denouncing reason's tyranny. 'Reasoning', he says, 'has come to excite an amount of faith greatly in excess of that which is its due.' There has arisen, 'an awe of Reason which betrays many into the error of supposing its range unlimited'. 'By extinguishing other superstitions,' he adds, 'Reason makes itself the final object of superstition.'[3]

---

[1] Edward Nares, *A View of the Evidences of Christianity, etc.*, p. 17.
[2] Op. cit., p. 11.
[3] *Principles of Psychology*, pt. vii, ch. 2.

Yet it must be acknowledged that there were, particularly in England in the second half of our period, other influences which were challenging the dominant rationalism. Coleridge's insistence on a more spiritual philosophy, for example, was a vigorous protest against the sufficiency of mere reason: as was the Christian idealism of F. D. Maurice. This philosophy of opposition was itself bound to create its own understanding of revelation.

There were other influences, too, which were calling in question the omnipotence of reason. In the realm of a more theoretic philosophy the ideas of Kant were being understood. Kant's significance for theology was to put God outside the range of reason. In his book, *The Critique of Pure Reason*, Kant reduced to impotence the whole array of theistic proofs, and there as 'a grim, inexorable iconoclast', as Heine expresses it, he left men with no reasoned God at all. He then, however, in his *Critique of Practical Reason*, endeavours to find an argument for the existence of God based upon man's moral need. He thus 'as with a magic wand, revives the corpse of deism which theoretic reason has slain'.

While Kant thus emphasized the limitation of knowledge to the phenomenal, Sir William Hamilton insisted upon its relativity. Neither philosopher, it is true, sought to weaken belief in God, but rather to put such belief on a foundation that lay outside the power of reason to undermine. Yet the conclusion of each philosophy was the creation of a new agnosticism: it is to express and confess with Tennyson,

> 'We have but faith: we cannot know;
> For knowledge is of things we see.'

(iii) *The Change of an Emphasis*

The middle of the nineteenth century has been noted as marking a new stage in theological discussion, and this fact makes more explicit the reason why the date 1860 has been chosen as the close of a period.[1] It is distinctly the start of the modern scientific age which initiated the conflict between religion and science. Here indeed lies the contrast between the two periods. The former was concerned with specific problems of a special revelation, while the latter was concerned with the serious question whether there was

[1] Cf., V. Storr, *The Development of English Theology in the Nineteenth Century from 1800 to 1860*, and L. E. Elliot-Binns' *English Thought*, 1850–1900.

any revelation at all. Two influences brought about this change which threw into such sharp contrast the two periods.

1. The Influence of Darwin

In 1859 Darwin's *Origin of Species* made its appearance. As gradually the implications of the work became evident, it was seen that theology was being forced out of its isolation, and that it could no longer maintain a divorce between sacred and secular knowledge. The view was taken that the new apologetic, unlike the old, cannot be concerned with such items as the reasonableness, the content and the sources of a special revelation *per se*. A challenge had been issued to the very existence of theistic belief itself. Whereas the earlier apologetic made it its task to prove the necessity and value of a special revelation to those who believed that God need not and could not make any such, it was the task of the newer to indicate the evidences for an actual God Who could reveal Himself to those who believed that there was nothing above, beyond or other than the system of nature which alone is self-evident and self-explanatory.

However true it may be that Darwin's work was the climax of a movement, it certainly is to be marked as the commencement of an era.[1] Reinforced by the philosophies of Comte, Bain and Spencer, and by the researches of Tyndall and Huxley, and by the historical studies of Buckle and Taine, the movement reached its dogmatic position and took up a hostile attitude to theology. From now on the battle between science and religion was joined, and the next few decades saw it waged with not a little fury on each side.

The theory of Darwin was eagerly grasped as providing unbelief with its decisive weapon. 'The plain truth is', declares Wildon Carr with evident enthusiasm, 'that the evolution theory has antiquated all theodicies.'[2] Intoxicated with its early success the new view confidently announced mechanism, not merely as a scientific method, but as a body of doctrine adequate to explain the whole universe. Banished now were all notions of teleology and axiology. The whole domain of life was subjected to the rigor of mechanism and the hypothesis of vitalism which had been allowed in the early

[1] Cf., 'Doubtless the greatest dissolvent of contemporary thought of old customs, the greatest precipitant of new methods, new inventions, new problems, is the one effected by the scientific revolution that found its climax in the *Origin of Species*.' J. Dewey, *The Influence of Darwin on Philosophy*, p. 19.
[2] *The Changing Background of Religion and Ethics*, p. 75.

years of the century as necessary to account for the behaviour of living organisms was abandoned.

'The scientific interpretation of natural phenomena', declares Wildon Carr again, 'has made the interest of God more remote, God's existence more problematical, and the idea of God unnecessary. Mathematics and physics are making it increasingly difficult to assign a place for God in our co-ordinations and constructions of the universe, and the necessity of positing a first cause or of conceiving a designer, a necessity which seemed *prima facie* obvious to a pre-scientific generation, does not exist for us.'[1] This certainly was what many of those who lived in the immediate post-Darwin period believed.

Darwin, then, initiated a new climate of opinion. His doctrine was eagerly accepted.[2] Anyone rash enough to call this thesis in question was brushed aside as *impos animi*, or, as a man *hors de saison*. His notion of natural selection was held to play havoc with the spiritualistic understanding of the world. Natural theology had no possible foundation.[3]

It was, strangely enough, in the year 1859, the year of Darwin's *Origin of Species*, that there appeared the *Political Economy* of Karl Marx. Whereas Darwin was over-awed by the misery in nature, Marx was overwhelmed by the misery in society. Darwin sought to explain the riddle by the principle of the development of organic nature, while Marx proclaimed his famous dialectic of

---

[1] *The Changing Background of Religion and Ethics*, p. 71.
[2] Cf., Du Bois Reymond's feeling for Darwin's view. He compares it to the feeling of a drowning man to whom a plank was pushed out. 'When', he adds, 'the choice is between a plank and destruction, the advantage is on the side of the plank.' *The Seven Enigmas*, pp. 78, 79.
[3] Cf., Fiske's *Outlines of Cosmic Philosophy*. 'From the dawn of philosophical discussion, Pagan and Christian, Trinitarian and Deist, have appealed with equal confidence to the harmony pervading nature as the surest foundation of their faith in an intelligent and beneficent Ruler of the Universe . . . . One and all . . . they challenge us to explain, on any other hypothesis than that of created design, these manifold harmonies, these exquisite adaptations of means to ends, whereof the world is admitted to be full, and which are equally conspicuous among the phenomena of life. Until the establishment of the Doctrine of Evolution, the glove thus thrown, age after age, into the arena of Philosophical controversy was never triumphantly taken up. It was Mr Darwin first, by his discovery of natural selection, supplied the champions of science with the resistless weapons by which to vanquish, in this their chief stronghold, the champions of theology. . . . It needs but to take into account the other agencies in the organic evolution besides the one so admirably illustrated by Mr Darwin, it needs but to remember that life is essentially a process of equaliberation, both direct and indirect, in order to be convinced that the Doctrine of Evolution has once and for all deprived natural theology of the materials upon which until lately it subsisted.' Op. cit., vol. 2, pp. 366–9.

history and announced his doctrine of the evolution of human
society. The concurrence of these two works was dramatic. The
immediate disciples of Darwin believed that the new empirico-
scientific world-view had banished for ever all notions of deity,
purpose and miracles. Marx and his adherents considered themselves to have discovered the key to inevitable social progress and
to have swept aside the theological superstititions of basic social
moralities. Gone for ever, it was announced, was the old dualistic
notion of two orders of existence, a natural and a supernatural. In
such a context there was no place for another world; no existent
and active God. Any idea of revelation was, therefore, sheer
illusion. Nature was all and there was nothing else. Renan thus
states it to be a fact that none could dare be temerarious enough to
deny, 'Il n'y a pas de supernatural.'

From the middle of the nineteenth century there was, therefore,
a totally different view of the world, which is characteristically
modern. This Weltanschauung is essentially antisupernaturalistic.
The religious interpretation of the world had given place to the
scientific. A. M. Fairbairn spoke of this Zeitgeist as a 'heathen
revival'.[1] He does not use the term as one of reproach but as an
endeavour to indicate its main feature. 'Its characteristic is
naturalism, the expulsion from thought, not merely of the supernatural, but of the ideal, of the transcendental and spiritual, and a
return to a nature sensuously interpreted. This naturalism is so
marked as to constitute the differentiating element of our intellectual movement. The thought of the Christian centuries, even
where it has been least Christian, has still been penetrated by the
ideal and theistic elements. Theism has been, as it were, its
common basis.'[2] The Renaissance indeed was a classical not a
pagan revival. Even deism, although it moved away from Christ,
did not discard God. By relieving Him of the care of the universe
it gave Him little to do. Still God was necessary for thought, and
reward for keeping His laws essential for the life of reasonable
religion.

The concept of evolution as such was not, of course, new.
Hobbes, Voltaire, Rousseau and Kant, to mention but a few, had
already taught that man arose out of a prior animal state. But with
these thinkers the notion was philosophical, and, as such, did not

[1] *Studies in Theology and Religion*, p. 80.
[2] Ibid.

make any great impact upon general thought. Darwin, on the other hand, was believed to have given to the speculative ideas of the philosophers a basis in scientific fact. From now on it was hailed as the only scientific account of the world and consequently naturalism was the apparent logical conclusion. There therefore arose a host of writers who conceived it to be their special prerogative to show how impossible it was to believe in any God or any revelation at all. The progress of science, it was declared, had rendered all such beliefs invalid, since, as T. H. Huxley contended in his *Lecture on the Physical Basis of Life*, 'the extension of the province of what is called matter and causation' means 'the concomitant gradual banishment from the region of human thought of what is called spirit and spontaneity'. So great a difference then did Darwin make in the interpretation of the world, that whereas the advocates of essential Christianity between the years 1700 and the middle of the nineteenth century were concerned to show that God had given a special word, those who followed had to prove that He was there to speak any word. This means that the earlier writers considered it their business to maintain the value of a special revelation. With the later apologists interest turned to the vindication of the reality of a general revelation.

2. *The Introduction of the Historical Method*

Just as Darwin was thought to have given to evolution a basis in scientific fact, so the introduction of the so-called historical method was held to justify the criticisms which the deists maintained against the Bible.[1] The deists, observes Professor Norman Sykes, 'hit upon some of the agreed conclusions of the higher critics of the nineteenth century.' Yet they did so 'by chance rather than by scientific research'.[2]

---

[1] Collins maintained that the religion of Israel was a combination of Egyptian and Chaldean theologies. He dated the book of Daniel in the Maccabean period and considered the greater portion of the Old Testament to be a reconstruction by the scribe Ezra. Toland anticipated the Tübingen School of Baur by proclaiming that there were in the early Church, two parties, the Ebionites or Judaizers, and the liberal party of Paul, which somehow became fused into a unity. On the Continent, Lessing turned attention to the New Testament. In a posthumous work, entitled, *A New Hypothesis concerning the Evangelists regarded merely as Human Writers* (1788), he raised the question of the origin of the Gospels; his critical work was carried on by Herder and Reimarus. Reimarus is referred to by A. M. Fairbairn as the last representative of the 'dying Deism'.

[2] N. Sykes, *The English Religious Tradition*, p. 61.

It was because the criticism of the Bible was associated with deism that the conclusions of Bishop Colenso were greeted with such antagonism, although his views, in comparison with later critical writers were modest indeed. The Church felt bound, in the earlier period, to reject the valuation of the Scriptures associated with deistic scepticism. It was only in the second half of the nineteenth century, and especially after the publication of the *Essays and Reviews* in the year 1860, that the opinions which the deists expressed gained a firm foothold in the Church itself.

It is, of course, true that the beginnings of historicism are to be found prior to the middle of the nineteenth century. This understanding of history as something dynamic, was itself a reaction from the account of it as artificial and sterile which had earlier prevailed. The earlier writers were indeed completely indifferent to the significance of history. Their view was merely the prolongation of the Enlightenment's repudiation of the historical in the interests of the rational.

An impetus towards this newer appreciation may be found in Leibniz's exposition of the law of continuity in the theory he set forth of the gradation of the monads. 'Nature', he declared, 'never makes leaps.'[1] The whole universe is to be viewed as a living thing 'like a garden full of plants and like a pond full of fish'.[2] There is therefore nothing sterile or static in the universe. There is the appearance of chaos and confusion, but appearance only.

But of the individual monads which make up the totality of existences, each is complete in itself, occupying itself with itself alone. Each is *Einmalige* (singular). 'The monads', he writes in an euphistic manner, 'have no windows through which anything may come in and go out.'[3] At the same time the whole army of monads cannot exist without contact. They are therefore brought into union by his principle of pre-existing harmony.

In Leibniz, then, two principles, namely that of continuity and that of connection are seen. By Lessing these twin fundamental ideas were taken as providing the key to the understanding of history. Lessing brought into being 'a deeper sense of the meaning of the historical'.[4] In his *Education of the Human Race* a break is made with the Enlightenment. The rationalist, it has been

---

[1] *The Monodology*, tr. R. Latta, p. 376.
[2] *Discourse on Metaphysics*, tr. G. R. Mackintosh, p. 266.
[3] *The Monodology*, p. 219, cf., *Discourse on Metaphysics*, p. 252.
[4] A. K. Rogers, *A Students' History of Philosophy*, p. 410.

observed, could not find any middle ground between the truth of a religion based upon reason alone, and its falsity, and therefore its beginning in fraud and priestcraft. Lessing refused to accept the antithesis. For him absolute truth was outside the range of man's ability: but so, too, was absolute falsity an impossibility. This meant for Lessing that God sought to educate men by a progressive revelation, moving from the less adequate to the more effective. God was not, therefore, outside the world in solitary isolation. He is within the movement of history and the events of experience, as the immanent God, energizing and unifying. With Lessing the emphasis which Spinoza had earlier given to the immanence of God as ἕν καί πᾶν, and which failed of immediate influence, was now made effective. Even Lessing in his famous dictum that 'Accidental truths of history can never yield proof of necessary truths of reason', far from denying the cogency of history, was actually seeking, as Karl Barth has shown, to evaluate its true significance.[1]

This understanding of history was extended by Herder. Not only, as in Lessing, was the concept of development to be applied to religion, but all life grows and develops. Thus we find Herder turning his attention to the folk origins of national cultures. It was in this way that the Leibnizean hypothesis of external connection was exchanged for an inner principle of development.

Together, the notion of connection and continuity were to change the whole understanding of history. All life began to be regarded as the unfolding of the one divine ζωή. History is all of a piece. No single event stands apart from the rest. No hiatuses are to be observed, since past and present are bound together in a living union. History reveals, it was claimed, an evident development, a process from a lower to a richer and fuller life.

By such ideas theology was necessarily influenced. The clear-cut distinction between natural and revealed religion was now abandoned. This meant that no single people and no special history

[1] Cf., *Die protestantische Theologie im 19 Jahrundert*, p. 209 ff. See also, *Church Dogmatics*, vol. 1, i, p. 166. 'Lessing recognizes perfectly well a proof of Christianity by history.' But it must be 'the proof of the Spirit and power'; i.e., history proves us no truth, so long as it is 'accidental truth of history', truth merely told us by others but not as such 'felt' and 'experienced' as such by us, experienced in the way the 'paralytic feels the beneficent shock of the electric spark'. 'Religion is not true because the evangelists and apostles taught it, but they taught it because it is true. By its inner truth must Scriptural traditions be explained, and all the Scriptural traditions in the world cannot give it inner truth if it does not possess it,' op cit., ad loc.

could be claimed as the specific sphere of the divine activity. All religions developed from one common origin. There were cruder religious ideas suited to the underdeveloped state of the religious instinct. But, as the *sensus numinis* grew, so too did religion; from the natural to the spiritual, from the tribal to the universal. In all religious groups the one true religion finds expression more or less.

It is in this context that Kant is to be found refusing to set Christianity over against other religions as the only true one. He distinguishes between the various religious creeds and religion *per se* in a manner characteristic of the earlier Lessing. 'There is', writes Kant, 'only *one* true religion, but there can be many varieties of religious creeds . . . . It is, therefore, more appropriate to say: this man is of the Jewish, Mohammedan, Christian creed, than he is of this or that religion.'[1]

It is against the background of such views of the divine immanence that we will have occasion later to refer to the understanding of revelation by men like Coleridge and Maurice.

With Hegel the new historical sense adumbrated by Leibniz and advanced in Lessing found its most thorough philosophical expression. Here the concept of development was raised to provide the key to the riddle of existence. Man was conceived to be but a part of the one divine life, a temporary manifestation of the one divine spirit. In this context all was supernatural because everything is but a transitory expression of the Eternal Absolute. To such a conclusion was the historical method driven under the influence of an idealistic philosophy.

A new twist was given to historicism after the middle of the nineteenth century. The principle of continuity was now reinforced by the Darwinian biological theory. Historical occurrences must be conceived consequently as the outcome of mechanical processes. All life can be explained as the product of natural laws. Thus some writers sought for the creative causes of historical events in man's physical environment, and endeavoured to base history upon anthropogeography. Others looked to the social environment for an explanation. Spencer, Comte and a host of like-minded writers conceived of society as somehow itself a higher organism which, like other living things, is subject to biological laws and will

---

[1] *Religion within the Bounds of Pure Reason*, p. 108. Cf., 'The distinction between natural and revealed religion is impossible . . . Christianity is not the one religion, the only one, but simply the most complete species of the genus', W. Bousset, *What is Religion?*, pp. 8, 9.

eventually come to perfection in the struggle for existence by natural selection and heredity. Consequently, whereas for the earlier idealism all was supernatural, for the new materialism all was natural.

(iv) *The Contrasts within the Period*

The discussions of the previous section will have revealed that the age under consideration was dominated by two main influences, the deistic and the idealistic. In the earlier period there was the deistic emphasis upon the remoteness of God, while the later part, in which idealism was in the ascendancy, accent was on the nearness of God. This means that the first was generally rational-istic and the second broadly mystical. The contrast is not, of course, absolute, as will be seen later, since, as always, however sharply it may be drawn, there is still the tendency for an opposi-tion quickly to appear.[1] A comparison between Clarke and Coleridge will confirm the general truth of this statement.

Objectivity and abstraction are, then, the characteristics of the first half of the eighteenth century. Operating with Aristotelian categories of thought, the reasoning by which its theology was maintained was discursive. God was detached from the individual consciousness and viewed as a mere transcendent Object. He was removed beyond the bounds of the universe. He was to be sought, not in the depths of man's consciousness, but in the heights beyond man's vision. God, in this conception, is the Altogether Other; the great Exception not the close Example. The divine was so separated from the human in the rational theology of the time, that there was no God near enough to be worshipped. There were abstract con-ceptions of Him conjured out of its own grandiose dialectic. God was consequently objectified, externalized and intellectualized. The result was that the theology of the period was the product of a sort of conceptual self-hypnosis.

On the other hand, and by contrast, the sort of view that de-veloped as a reaction was a type of philosophical mysticism. Here God was sought, not above but below, not without but within. He

---

[1] Cf., 'It is no accident that in the *saeculum rationalisticum* the heyday of Deism and of the Wolfian philosophy saw the rise of a series of strongly emotional religious movements, of Pietism, Moravianism, Methodism in Protestant Europe, and in Catholic Europe of the devotion (presenting marked affinities with these) of the Sacred Heart; while, outside the Churches, close upon the heels of Voltaire there came Rouseau.' C. C. J. Webb, *Problems in the Relations of God and Man*, p. 73.

was not detached from the human consciousness. He is the Eternal Subject, occupying the innermost shrine of man's spirit to be discovered by an intuitive awareness. Emphasis is here placed upon the 'kinship' between man and God; upon the divinity of man and the humanity of God.

The rational theologians tended towards the mechanical. The order in the objective world was made the basis of the large quota of religious knowledge to be gained from general revelation. While the Church, as heir to the special revelation made to the Jews, was conceived to be the custodian of those extra doctrines which were to be believed. Thus faith was regarded as intellectual assent to the revelation, objective as a concept and stereotyped into a dogma, which were to be accepted as of binding authority.

For men like Coleridge and Maurice, on the other hand, the external was rejected as a tyranny. Man's own spirit was the sphere of the divine operation, and faith was a coming to the awareness that in the depths of his soul man is akin to God. This discovery of God within one's own being, is revelation: this is the ultimate authority for the individual man.

Some writers would characterize Eastern theology as mystical and the Western as rationalistic. The East followed the lines of the Platonic thought and tended to emphasize the inward.[1] The West, on the other hand, more influenced by Aristotle, was inclined to accentuate the objective. There is, of course, some justification for this wide generalization, but it is so general as to have no real value. The truth is that in Western theology itself there is the same tendency, at one time to stress the objective, and at another time the subjective. This fact can be illustrated by the doctrines of the atonement which can be, and, indeed, have been divided into objective and subjective views.

The relationship between subject and object is an issue of fundamental importance. Whenever the correct balance between the two is upset some element of the full truth must be lost. This observation holds good in all realms of knowledge, and theology is not an exception.

[1] Cf. Berdyaev's rejection of 'creationism' and acceptance of Origen's 'pre-existence' doctrine. 'The traditional opinion, according to which each human soul is created by God at the moment of physical conception, is such a lamentable one that we need not stop to consider it . . . . The pre-existence of the soul (sc. spirit) in the spiritual world is an indispensible truth, for the soul (sc. spirit) is, not the child of time but of eternity.' N. Berdyaev, *Freedom and the Spirit*, p. 326.

'Theology is certainly a human enquiry, whether or not it be more, whatever its assurance of a more than human reference and validity in the objects with which it deals or the methods by which it deals with them. It is to be expected, therefore, that theology, too, will share in that error which is common to humanity, and that sometimes such error will be the result of a disproportion of the subjective and objective factors in its special kind of knowledge.'[1]

[1] James Brown, *Subject and Object in Modern Theology* (The Croall Lectures given in the University of Edinburgh, 1955), p. 12.

CHAPTER II

THE MANIFESTATION OF
AN ANTITHESIS

The period, then, which has been marked out reveals, in the main, two sharply opposed views of revelation. These may be described, broadly, as objective and subjective.

It was against the background of deism that the first view was elaborated, and it is in this context it must be understood. It was essentially a rationalistic doctrine of revelation basing itself upon the Aristotelian principle of the sufficiency of reason. It demanded assent to certain doctrinal propositions. As a theory of revelation, it was psychologically unsound because it failed to take account of the other constituents of man's psychical nature. As a polemic against deism the orthodox arguments became nugatory. The battle waged against the deistic opponents, indeed, could never be decisive for the origin and weapons of both were the same. Each was the product of that estimate of the natural man characteristic of the Enlightenment with its fundamental principle of 'sound common sense'. So closely akin, in this respect, were the deists and their opponents, that the former could refer to Archbishop Tillotson as their spiritual father. On the fly-leaf of Toland's, *Christianity not Mysterious*, there is a quotation from the Archbishop which serves as a text for all that follows. Tindal has some fourteen extended passages from Tillotson's works in his, *Christianity as Old as Creation*. In one place he refers to the renowned ecclesiastic as 'the incomparable Tillotson'.[1] Anthony Collins, likewise contends that Tillotson is the one 'whom all English free-thinkers own as their head'.[2] On the other hand the general position of Tillotson is the same as that adopted by the orthodox in the next century.

This fact means that each side was hindered from dealing a decisive blow on the other. It is for this reason that the arguments of the orthodox apologists were for the most part nullified, and the

---

[1] *Christianity as Old as Creation* (3rd edition), p. 197.
[2] *Discourse of Freethinking*, p. 171.

battles which they waged against the deists, in their defence of revealed religion were so much 'sound and fury, signifying nothing'.

It was inevitable that the era should give birth to a doctrine of protest. The inevitable reaction soon set in. There thus developed, in opposition, a doctrine of revelation which sought its origin and authority within each individual soul. Attention was directed to the inner life of man. It was consequently an understanding of revelation as something subjective in contrast with the objective view of the anti-deistic apologists. Here we have an idea of revelation as something based upon the inner experience of the individual. Whereas the objective doctrine has affinities with Aristotle, this view is more akin to Socrates.

There are broadly two movements in philosophical thought running through history which may be called the Aristotelian and the Socratic. The first of these was more concerned with the external world. It began with physical facts and based its inferences by way of abstraction upon the data they provide. Much was made of the logic of analogy. This was the view which dominated Mediaevalism and found a supreme advocate in Aquinas. The orthodox apologists were in line with this conception. They consequently made much of external proofs and were more concerned with propositions than with persons; more interested in the niceties of exact logic than in the necessities of human lives.

Socrates, on the other hand, gave attention to the individual, to the truth already held. He began with self-consciousness. The second view of revelation which took its rise as a doctrine of protest is in line with this philosophic emphasis. It would find its certainty, neither as a formal result of the principle of analogy nor as a conclusion to a chain of syllogistic reasoning, but as a fact already given in self-conscious experience. It was therefore argued that the array of proofs so carefully marshalled by the writers on 'evidences' can bring no assurance to the doubting mind. There is in the obscure retreat of the human heart an *aliquid inconcussum*, an unshaken somewhat, independent of and undisturbed by the finest and fiercest intellectual arguments. The attitude of those who advocated this view is well expressed in a letter by Principal John Cairns to George Gilfillan in 1849. Gilfillan had written expressing the wish for some great minds to appear to confound the arrogant pretences to knowledge claimed by unbelievers.

Cairns replies: 'I cannot share your longing for intellectual giants to confound the Goliaths of scepticism — not that I do not think such persons useful in their way, — but because I think Christianity far more impressive as a life than a speculation, and the West Port evangelism of Dr Chalmers far more effective than his Astronomical Discourses.'[1] Cairns allows that such apologists are 'useful in their way', but many of those who adopted the view that the orthodox doctrine was sterile and that vital Christianity is a datum or revelation made immediately to a spiritual faculty of the soul were far from granting that it had any value at all. It was the inward assurance of God's immediate presence which provided for these writers the *point d'appui*. Here was a certainty which no metaphysical speculation could injure, for this *aliquid inconcussum* was for them akin to the *Cogito, ergo sum*, of Descartes. Faith bore its own signature and the assurance of its authenticity was within. That this understanding of revelation did justice to the important psychological element of affection is undoubted, thereby correcting an obvious deficiency of the propositional doctrine. But the view thus elaborated is itself, none the less, theoretically and spiritually insufficient.

A reading of the period, then, reveals an antithesis between the objective and subjective estimates of revelation. The doctrine of revelation as a body of divinely mediated truths to which assent was to be given was advanced against the deists and maintained against the 'Enthusiasts'. The idea of revelation within the immediacy of experience gave exclusive emphasis to the subjective side. This doctrine developed as a conscious repudiation of the propositional view. Each suffers, therefore, from the defects of onesidedness.

(i) *The Philosophical Background*

DESCARTES

Put into a more immediate context these opposing views can be seen to derive from the dualism left by, and the antitheses latent in the philosophy of Descartes. When Descartes was, as he tells us, 'shut up in a stove',[2] it was out of that day's meditation there was

[1] Professor MacEwen, *Life and Letters of John Cairns*, p. 307, cf., John Cairns, *Principal Cairns*, p. 84.

[2] *The Discourse of Method* (tr. John Veitch), p. 10. Veitch translates the passage '. . . a whole day in seclusion'. A footnote explains, 'in a room heated by means of a stove.' Bertrand Russell (*History of Western Philosophy*, p. 581),

begun a fresh departure in philosophic thought. Repudiating the grand system of doctrine set up on the authority of the Church, Descartes, with no tradition behind him, had to find the starting-point for his philosophical reconstruction 'within himself'. The *Discourse of Method* was the 'trumpet-note for the resurrection of the human mind from the death of formalism'.[1] Descartes says that his 'design was singly to find ground of assurance'.[2] He believed he had found this in what has come to be called the principle of 'Cartesian doubt'. Let all else be considered unreal, the existence of the 'I' which doubts must remain an undisputable fact. 'But immediately upon this I observed that, whilst I thus wished to think that all was false, it was absolutely necessary that I, who thus thought, should be somewhat: and as I observed that this truth, I think, hence I am, was so certain of such evidence, that no ground of doubt, however extravagant, could be alleged by the sceptics capable of shaking it. I concluded that I might, without scruple, accept it as the first principle of the philosophy of which I was in search.'[3]

Descartes gives to the concept of self as a 'thinking thing' a connotation wider than the modern psychological use of the term. A thinking being is one which 'doubts, understands, (conceives), affirms, denies, wills, refuses, that imagines also, and perceives'.[4] It is from this, *Cogito, ergo sum*, that Descartes builds up a new superstructure of knowledge, moving from man to God.

For Descartes there was first of all stress upon 'clear and distinct ideas' as the only justifiable assurance of certainty. Reason, he says, 'is by nature equal in all men.'[5] Thus 'we ought never to allow ourselves to be persuaded of the truth of anything unless on the evidence of our reason, and it must be noted that I say of

comments, 'Descartes says it was a stove (poêle), but most commentators think that this is impossible. Those who know old-fashioned Bavarian houses, however, assure me that this is entirely credible.'

[1] J. P. Mahaffy, *Descartes*, p. 70.
[2] Op. cit., p. 23.
[3] *Discourse of Method*, p. 27.
[4] *Meditations*, p. 89. Cf., *Principles of Knowledge*, 1, 9. 'The ordinary translation of *cogitare*, to think (*denken*) is liable to occasion misunderstanding since *denken* in German (and the same is true of *think*, in English, at least in philosophical terminology) signifies a particular kind of theoretical consciousness. Descartes himself elucidates the meaning of cogitate by enumeration: he understands by it to doubt, affirm, deny, understand, will, abhor, imagine, feel a sensation, etc. For that which is common to all these notions we have in German scarcely any word but *Bewesstein* (consciousness).' W. Windelband, *History of Philosophy*, p. 391.
[5] *Discourse of Method*, p. 3.

reason, and not of our imagination or our senses'.[1] Then, secondly, Descartes makes the individual consciousness the secure beginning of the process of knowledge. An application of this principle of knowledge by doubt, is found in Butler's, *Analogy*. 'The very act of doubting religion', writes Butler, 'implies some evidence for that of which we doubt.'[2]

This double aspect of the Cartesian Philosophy is noted by Hegel, who, however, does not follow through its implications. To Descartes, observes Hegel, 'nothing is true which does not possess an inward evidence in consciousness, or which reason does not recognize so clearly and conclusively that any doubt regarding it is impossible.'[3] These two principles, once stated, soon diverged and became hostile. The necessity for clear and distinct ideas gave rise to the demand for mathematical certainty. On the other hand, by seeking a basis in the individual consciousness there developed a feeling for, what may be called, mystical assurance. Thus it came about that two views which were to influence the understanding of revelation were brought into opposition: an antithesis was set up between reason and feeling, between external and internal, between object and subject, between deductions from the facts of experience and inductions from the realities within experience.

(a) Reason and Feeling

The side of the Cartesian philosophy which bore immediate fruit was the insistence upon the supremacy of reason. Religious truths must be demonstrated after the strictest Euclidean fashion. Windelband declares that, 'it was in this direction that the influence of the Cartesian philosophy proved strongest in the following period. In all the changes of epistemological investigation until far into the eighteenth century, this conception of mathematics was a firmly established axiom of all parties.'[4] Not only upon Continental writers, but, as Professor Mahaffy contends, in no less measure upon English thinkers is the influence of Descartes to be noted: 'the theological arguments of Clarke on the Attributes, and of Butler on the doctrine of the future life, are framed on the model of Descartes.'[5] But apart from these specific instances, the

[1] Op. cit., p. 32.
[2] *Analogy* (New edition), p. 266.
[3] S. W. F. Hegel, *History of Philosophy*, vol. 3, p. 227.
[4] W. Windelband, *History of Philosophy*, p. 395.
[5] J. P. Mahaffy, *Descartes*, pp. 202–3.

whole apologetic of the anti-deistic apologists was dominated by
the idea that the exactitude of the mathematical method should be
applied to metaphysical speculations and theological doctrines. The
object was to construct a train of reasoning so compact that there
should be no flaw in the train. It goes without saying that for the
deists the principle of clear and distinct ideas was absolute. The
rule is: 'whatever is evidently repugnant to clear and distinct Ideas,
or to our common notions is contrary to reason.'[1] In these words
Toland, for example, considers reason to be not only the ultimate
ground of knowledge, but, besides, the only test of certainty.
Tindal, too, makes it 'His grand design to prove, that there neither
hath been, nor possibly can be Revelation at all: And the main
Principle on which he builds is this; That the Light of common
Reason is abundantly sufficient without it'.[2]

There is no need to ransack the literature of the orthodox
apologists to see that the same idea there prevailed. A. A. Sykes
declares it to be his purpose 'to treat of Religion both Natural and
Revealed, as to deduce it from its first Principles, and to show that
they are both strictly Rational'.[3] Later in the same book, he avers
that, 'the Light of Reason is not that uncertain, weak, insufficient,
inconstant thing, that is by some pretended: nor ought it to be
treated as something carnal and dim.'[4] In language no less strong,
Bishop Browne asserts that the orthodox are no whit behind their
opponents, the deists, in 'the use of reason in religion'.[5] Dr Clarke
considers that the doctrines disclosed by special revelation, when
taken together, present a scheme more 'confident and rational . . .
than any of the wisest of the Ancient Philosophers ever did, or
the cunningest of the Modern unbelievers, can invent or con-
trive'.[6]

In the same vein Bishop Butler, although he allows that there
must be in the scheme of Revelation much that the human understanding cannot grasp, will not 'vilify reason', since reason alone
is competent to judge of the credibility and consistency of revelation. Emphasis was thus placed upon the cogency of the theistic

---

[1] J. Toland, *Christianity not Mysterious* (1696), pp. 23–4.
[2] J. Conybeare, *A Defence of Revealed Religion*, pp. 4, 5.
[3] A. A. Sykes, *The Principles and Connection of Natural and Revealed Religion,
Distinctly Stated*, Preface, viii.
[4] Ibid and p. 385.
[5] P. Browne, *Answer to Toland*, p. 120.
[6] *A Discourse Concerning the Unalterable Obligation of Natural Religion, and the
Truth and Certainty of the Christian Religion* (9th edition), p. 370.

proofs and the ability of reason to reach certain conclusions regarding God's existence and attributes.

Turning to the other side of the Cartesian doctrine, namely, the teaching that the basis of certainty is to be found within the individual consciousness, it was inevitable that sooner or later theology would be affected thereby. Descartes asserted that 'nothing is true which has not this inward evidence in consciousness'.[1] Nature itself could only be assured on the grounds of an existent God Who could not deceive; it followed therefore that no argument for God's existence could be based thereon. The proof must rest, not upon things without, but upon things within, upon ideas rising out of the individual consciousness. Here was a change of emphasis, which under the influence of men like Coleridge and Maurice gave impetus to the notion of revelation as the feeling of God's indwelling presence. No longer was appeal to be made to the concinnity of nature but to the immediate consciousness of God native to the individual soul.

Certainly F. D. Maurice realized this creative significance of Berkeley's philosophy. He regarded Berkeley 'as the strongest and honestest thinker among our English metaphysicians' yet, although he 'missed the circumference', 'found the "centre" in the heart.'[2] In his, *Christianity not founded on Argument*, H. Dodwell contends for 'a constant and particular Revelation imparted separately and supernaturally to every individual'.[3] It is a revelation of this nature which alone is effective. It was by a flash of divinely given insight that Peter made the Great Confession. When once it comes there is no need any further for subtle sophistries and conceited casuistries. Here is absolute certainty, not built upon the credit of ancient literature, for each possesses his own contemporary proof. What need now to 'apply to Libraries for a more compotent Information and Discovery'?[4] Each has his own divine literature written upon the tables of his heart, which time cannot destroy, nor change render useless. 'Now,' asks Dodwell, 'what a very different prospect this, and Ground of Security from the empty Notion of mere manuscript Authorities and Paper-Revelations?'[5]

Opposed thus were two views of revelation each of which could

---

[1] S. W. F. Hegel, *History of Philosophy*, vol. 3, p. 232.
[2] *Life of F. D. Maurice* (by his Son), vol. 1, pp. 82, 83.
[3] *Christianity not founded on Argument*, p. 58.
[4] Op. cit., pp. 59, 70.
[5] Op. cit., p. 60.

find its source in Descartes: the one basing itself upon reason and
the other on feeling.

(b) Objective and Subjective

By his sharp distinction between extension and thought,
Descartes accentuated an antithesis between the object and the
subject. As a result 'in its quest for truth the seventeenth century
discovered two main kinds of certainty, one objective and external,
the other subjective and internal'.[1] With Descartes, then, 'the
subject and object, always interconnected in man's actual experience, were thus severed from each other in the very starting-
point of philosophy.'[2] This antithesis between the two gave rise to
the tension which later developed into the antagonism between the
religion of authority and the religion of the spirit. A time came
when, in Protestant theology, any reference to objective proof was
wholeheartedly repudiated. A point was reached when Sabatier
can say: 'The two methods are so radically opposed that to accept
the latter (the subjective) is at once to mark the former as insufficient and outworn.'[3]

For the anti-deistic apologists stress was laid upon external
proofs. On the other hand 'in finding the ground and type of all
certainty in his own existence, Descartes was shutting himself up
within his own subjectivity',[4] and, as a consequence, gave rise to
the subjective criterion. The assumption of the externalists was
that revelation consisted in a system of supernatural notions and
inspired doctrines authenticated by clear and discernable objective
evidence. The assumption of the subjectivists was that all external
proofs were unnecessary and useless. For those who emphasized
this side of the Cartesian dualism 'the living centre, the luminous
focus, of the Gospel is the inner and immediate sense of the divine
sonship'.[5]

The literature of the period reveals how great was the attention
given by the externalists in collecting and collating evidences. To
them the world existed, 'out there', as God's world, since He

[1] B. Willey, *The Seventeenth Century Background*, p. 76. Cf., 'The two orders
of certainty, objective and subjective, correspond to Descartes's division of
reality into Extention (matter) and Thought (mind, soul).' Ibid.
[2] Baron von Hügel, *The Reality of God*, p. 188.
[3] *Religions of Authorities and the Religion of the Spirit*, (E.T.), p. 15.
[4] J. Baillie, *Our Knowledge of God*, p. 152.
[5] Prof. Lobstein, *Introduction to Protestant Dogmatics* (tr. A. M. Smith),
p. 159.

could not deceive us. It is a divine creation and bears upon itself evidence of God's image and superscription. Let men behold the ordered mechanism, the intricate combination of cosmic order, let them but see the delicate arrangements of the several parts, and they must believe. It was the firm conviction of the apologetic writers that when the evidences were marshalled and indicated, assent could not be withheld.

Before the eighteenth century dawned Joseph Glanvill wrote: 'When God himself would represent his own Magnificence and Glory, he directs to his Works.'[1] Nature, he says later, 'is no Holy Mount, which ought not to be touched; yea, we are commanded, To search after Wisdom and particularly this, when we are so frequently called to celebrate our Creator for his Works.'[2] In the same spirit Paley began his *Natural Theology*, by making effective the illustration of the watch found on the heath, giving it a sense of originality.[3] The finder of such a watch, observing the delicate arrangements of its works, the intricate union of its several parts under the control of an over-arching purpose, must, Paley asserts, be led unerringly to the idea of a maker. The conclusion is not invalidated if one had never seen a watch constructed, or if the precise duties of each part is not understood. The watch is not explained on the suggestion that it is the product of metallurgic laws. The world, like the watch, presents evidences of design, and the question 'is not shaken off',[4] by supposing an endless succession. To believe it just came to be without art or skill is manifestly absurd. 'This is Atheism: for every indication of contrivance, every manifestation of design, which existed in the watch, exists in the world of nature.'[5] The Atheist is the one who fails to see the design or acknowledge the Designer. It was along this line of 'Evidences for Christianity' that the whole apologetic of the orthodox was conducted with

'The repetitions wearisome of sense
Where soul is dead, and feeling hath no place.'[6]

[1] J. Glanvill, *Essays on Several Important Subjects in Philosophy and Religion*, Essay 1, p. 15.
[2] Op. cit., p. 38.
[3] The watch illustration is used by Tucker, *The Light of Nature*, 1, 523; 2, 82; Bolingbroke, *Works*, 3, 188; Clarke, *Works*, 1, 6; Burnet, *Sacred Theory of the Earth*, 1, ch. 4.
[4] *Natural Theology*, p. 12.
[5] Op. cit., p. 14.
[6] Wordsworth, *Excursion*, 4, 620.

The same exclusive emphasis on the objective element is made
by the anti-enthusiasts. The position taken up by Knott in the
Bampton Lectures of 1802 was maintained by John Bidlake nine
years later. One of the most extraordinary works of the period
comes from George Lavington, Bishop of Exeter, entitled, *The
Enthusiasm of the Methodists and the Papists Compared*. The book
called out a reply from John Wesley himself. Wesley not unjustly
charges Lavington with stabbing 'Christianity at the heart, under
cover of opposing enthusiasm'.[1] It was Lavington's conviction that
any emphasis upon the inner and individual would disturb the
stately edifice of doctrine which the Church declared to be revealed.
It was in such a 'climate of opinion', to quote a phrase from Glanvill,[2] made popular by W. N. Whitehead, that the works of Butler
and Paley came to be regarded highly and were studied with a
reverence born of their assumed finality.

This reference to Glanvill recalls us back to this author who nigh
a century and a half earlier classed 'enthusiasm' with Atheism as
'another dreadful Enemy . . . a false conceit of inspiration'.[3] Its
worst feature being its disparagement of sober reason. The enthusiast 'having heard great things of the Spirit's immediate
Motions and Inspirations cannot well fail of believing himself
inspired, and of entitling all the excursions of his Fancy to the
immediate Acting of the Holy Ghost'.[4]

The subjective emphasis took longer to gain position and
popularity, but its significance lies in its wholehearted repudiation
of all external evidences. F. D. Maurice, for example, grounds
revelation in the being of the individual which is divine in its inner
essence. He can thus say of Renan that although he took 'the
supernatural out of the Gospels, he cannot take it out of his own
life'.[5] It is his charge against Dean Mansel that, because he
'differs from St Paul and St John he must deal unfairly with the
witness in our hearts'.[6] External evidences are merely learnt off;
the conclusion is reached: all is clear. Young men are made to
'take Paley's evidences for granted as if they were divine'.[7]

[1] Wesley, *Works*, vol. 13, p. 22.
[2] *The Vanity of Dogmatizing*, p. 227.
[3] *Essays on Several Important Subjects in Philosophy and Religion*, Essay 4,
p. 17.
[4] Op. cit., p. 18.
[5] *Life of F. D. Maurice* (by his Son), vol. 2, p. 463.
[6] *What is Revelation?* p. 444.
[7] Op. cit., p. 453.

Thomas Erskine allows that a just appreciation of the created universe and its providential arrangement should lead men to the necessity of conforming their lives thereto. But the fact is it never does. Men are content to speculate as long as they are not challenged to alter their lives: 'men are in general so much occupied with the works that they forget their great Author: and their characters are so opposed to his, that they turn away their eyes from the contemplation of that purity which condemns them.'[1] Inevitably natural theology becomes a subject for metaphysical speculation. It can be evaluated without enthusiasm: 'it would be difficult to find a devoted natural religionist.'[2] It creates no sense of need; it gives no feeling of urgency; it has no moral constraint. Mere abstract principles can be admired, and will be, as long as they remain so. It is when they take breath, when they become the incarnate realities of a human life, that they become challenging. A corrupt politician may speak loudly in the admiration of the abstract idea of integrity, but when the idea takes the form of a man and a course of action, then it is transformed from a principle to be lauded into a person to be lashed. Then it becomes obvious that the proclaimed love of the abstract principle was sheer illusion, for the man who really loves the abstract principle, cannot but love it when it is embodied and exemplified. Man can easily profess high esteem for harmless generalities. They will 'admit the abstract ideas of a God of infinite holiness and goodness: and will even take delight in exercising their reason or their taste in speculating on the subject of his being and attributes; yet these same persons will shrink with dislike and alarm from the living energy which these abstract ideas assume in the Bible'.[3]

S. T. Coleridge sweeps aside the whole array of external proofs. On Paley he is specially severe, for it is Coleridge's teaching that Christianity is spirit and life. 'Hence,' he writes with vigour, 'I more than fear the prevailing taste for books of Natural Theology, Physico-Theology, Demonstrations of God from Nature, Evidences of Christianity and the like. EVIDENCES OF CHRISTIANITY! I am weary of the word. Make a man feel his WANT of it: rouse him, if you can, to the self-knowledge of his NEED of it, and you can safely trust it to its own Evidence — remembering only this the

---

[1] *Remarks on the Internal Evidence for the Truth of Revealed Religion*, p. 48.
[2] Op. cit., p. 51.
[3] Op. cit., p. 79.

express declaration of Christ Himself: No man cometh to Me, unless the Father leadeth him.'[1]

Such then was the message of those who valuated revelation in its subjective action. It is because the divine message appeals to the heart and there authenticates itself that it does not call for mental gymnastics. The divine author 'must have known that not one out of a hundred who ever heard of it could ever have leisure or learning to weigh its external evidences'.[2]

(c) Inference and Intuition

It will have become obvious that the Cartesian dualism created the opposition which more recent philosophical theology has discussed under the question: Does the knowledge of God come by Inference or by Intuition? The rationalists and objectivists necessarily maintain the former. Professor A. Lecerf insists that 'with the first successors of Descartes we find ourselves still in the full floodtide of rational dogmatism'.[3] Arising therefrom there will be denial of all ontological arguments. Stebbing consequently emphatically declares that 'there are no innate ideas of God, so likewise we can have no proof of such a being *a priori*'.[4] Emphasis is thus placed upon the sufficiency of external evidence. Bishop Browne, in a later book, takes up a point made in an earlier, and announces as 'a sure and incontestable Truth, that we have no immediate proper Idea of God at all, or of his Attributes as they are in themselves; or anything else in the world'.[5] Analogy is therefore the only acceptable method for the attainment of divine knowledge. This idea is not to be set aside as 'strange and new'. It is as old as the Fathers.

On the other hand Bishop Berkeley rejects analogical knowledge and insists upon immediate revelation. He refers to Browne as a 'minute philosopher' who lived 'not long since'. In his book with that title, one of its characters, Euphranor, confesses that the idea of divine knowledge gained by means of analogy is new to him. Crito tells that he entered into an investigation as to 'what foundation there is in the Fathers and Schoolmen' for the view. He con-

---

[1] *Aids to Reflection* (new edition), p. 272.
[2] Thomas Erskine, *Remarks on the Internal Evidences for the Truth of Revealed Religion*, p. 186.
[3] A. Lecerf, *Introduction to Reformed Dogmatics*, p. 45.
[4] H. Stebbing, *An Enquiry into the Evidences of the Christian Religion*, p. 10.
[5] *The Procedure, Extent and Limits of the Human Understanding*, Intro., p. vi.

cludes that the idea 'owes its original to those writings which have been published under the name of Dionysius the Areopagite'.[1]

By insisting upon certainty within the individual consciousness, Descartes gave rise to the 'so-called immediate and inward revelation which in modern times is so highly regarded'.[2] Those who follow this line contend that the awareness of God wells up from within. Mansel had condemned any assertion of the immediate knowledge of God. F. D. Maurice retorts that this doctrine which has 'fallen into oblivion in the last century',[3] is what earnest and religious men require. However Mansel may limit the soaring spirit of man, however he may clip the wings of the soul to hinder its flight to realms divine he cannot obliterate the human feeling of God, nor banish the truth that the real meeting-place between God and man is the inner arena of the human spirit. In a note dedicating the *Theological Essays* to the poet Laureate, Alfred Lord Tennyson, Maurice says: 'I maintained in these Essays that a Theology which does not correspond to the deepest thoughts and feelings of the human being cannot be a true Theology.'[4] It is from this standpoint that Maurice rejects, what he calls, all 'notional' views of revelation. He argues that there is a manifesting of God in every striving for good, in every fight against evil. 'God manifests Himself in every act distinguishing the man from the evil which has possessed him.'[5] Revelation is, in fact, the unveiling to man of his divine origin; the casting out of the foreign spirits, the awakening of man to his own divine humanity. Revelation is not, therefore,

---

[1] *Minute Philosopher*, p. 164. This claim by Berkeley is, I think, justified by the historical facts. It is the purpose of the pseudo-Dionysian writings of the fifth and sixth centuries to effect a synthesis between the prevailing neo-Platonist philosophy and orthodox Christianity. This fact is seen more especially in the work entitled the Divine Names. The true Godhead according to 'Dionysius' is super-personal and undifferentiated. The Scriptural titles for God refer to the whole nature of the godhead. But as the godhead is itself beyond knowledge the undifferentiated names cannot give adequate understanding of God as He is in Himself. 'The Scriptures lead man along the affirmative path as far as he is able to go, but such conceptions of the Divine nature they give are to be regarded in the form of metaphor and analogy. In His essential nature, God is above and beyond all beings, sensible and spiritual . . . . All perfections of creatures can be attributed to God to a superlative degree, but, as the cause always remains superior to the effect, the Supreme Cause can only be described in analogical fashion.' S. J. Curtis, *A Short History of Western Philosophy in the Middle Ages*, p. 22. Cf. C. E. Rolt, *Dionysius the Areopagite on the Divine Names and the Mystical Theology*, (S.P.C.K., 1920), Introduction.

[2] S. W. F. Hegel, *History of Philosophy*, vol. iii, p. 226.

[3] *What is Revelation?*, p. 134.

[4] *Theological Essays*, Preface.

[5] *What is Revelation?*, p. 77.

regulative injunctions, but redemptive inspiration. The former is powerless, since it is like announcing elaborate instructions on good swimming to a drowning man. Those who specify revelation as merely regulative axioms are asked: 'Has not Methodism vanquished you, and Puritanism vanquished you before?'[1]

Julius Hare goes so far as to contend for this inwardness of revelation amongst the heathen and specifically amongst the Jews. There was a feeling after and a desire for God as the living one to be trusted. To the patriarchs of Israel God was intimately near. He lit the light of faith in the heart of Abraham. 'It was by a direct, special revelation of Himself, that God awakened the life of faith in Abraham.'[2] True faith is not belief in a Book, it is not assent to propositions but a 'living personal relation' with God. The upholders of 'notional faith' usually regard those who testify to this 'living personal relation' as 'enthusiasts' and 'fanatics'. Some may, indeed, have overstepped the bounds of propriety, failing to wed caution to their zeal, but their real offence, in the eyes of their critics, 'was the witness they bore in behalf of a living as opposed to a notional Faith.'[3] For Coleridge, Christianity is an affair of the heart. His position is that of St Bernard, 'We must retire inward, if we would ascend upward.'[4] Coleridge, says Dr Marsh, 'boldly asserted the reality of something distinctively spiritual in man, and the futility of all modes of philosophizing in which this is not recognized, or which is incompatible with it.'[5]

(d) Facts and Values

The man whose interests lie in the rational, the objective, the inferential, will of necessity be concerned with 'facts'. To him, as to Plato, poetry will be anathema. His concern will be with cold proofs. Such a man will talk, as Locke does, about the *Reasonableness of Christianity*. To him the mysterious will be suspect. That which is another's glory is to him repugnant. Thomas Browne had written with obvious exhilaration, 'I love to lose myself in a mystery, to pursue my Reason to an O altitudo! . . . I can answer all the Objections of Satan and my rebellious reason with the old

[1] Op. cit., p. 87.
[2] *Victory of Faith*, p. 145.
[3] Julius Hare, *Victory of Faith*, p. 73.
[4] Quoted in Marsh's *Preliminary Essay*, p. xxv. (This essay by the Rev. D. J. Marsh, President of the University of Vermount, U.S.A., was published with the first American edition of Aids to Reflection, 1829.)
[5] Ibid., p. xxxi.

resolution I learned from Tertullian, *Certum quia impossibile est.*[1] '*Credo quia impossibile est,*' retorts Locke, 'might be a good rule for a sally of zeal, but would prove a very ill rule for men to choose their opinions or religion by.'[2] The man of reason concerned with facts cannot be carried away from the world of hard facts.

The subjectivist will be more concerned with the appreciation of facts, than with their investigation. He will be more of a poet. Thus we find Locke a master of prose and Coleridge an authority on poetry. In the Cartesian philosophy, therefore, there is latent this further opposition 'which has become so troublesomely familiar to us since, between "values" and "facts"; between what you *felt* as a human being or as a poet, and what you *thought* as a man of sense, judgement, enlightenment'.[3] How sharply opposed these two became later is well known. It was the boast of the scientists of the new age that they had successfully eliminated all values from their consideration. On the other hand, theologians like Ritschl made it their glory to state religion merely in terms of value apart from any basic facts.

(ii) *The Religio-Philosophical Background*

THE CAMBRIDGE PLATONISTS

A further accentuation of these antitheses can be traced to a group of thinkers known to us as the Cambridge Platonists or Latitudinarians. From a more pronounced religious standpoint these writers of the seventeenth century provide a background for the oppositions which came into sharp focus in the next era. The most prominent members of the Cambridge Platonists were Whichote, More, Cudworth and John Smith. Their supreme significance, it is agreed, was to stress the rationalistic appreciation of Christianity. Whichote refers constantly to reason as 'the candle of the Lord'. Allied to the Cambridge men were preachers like Tillotson and Stillingfleet. Their views on reason, however, differed. For Tillotson it was a ratiocinative process; the latitudinarians, on the other hand, conceived of it in the Platonic fashion as a means whereby direct contact could be made with spiritual reality. 'In the Cambridge Platonists the spirit of Plato aids the spirit of Descartes in the task of reducing the imagery of religion

---

[1] *Religio Medico*, i, p. 9.
[2] *Essay on the Human Understanding*, 4, 18, sect. ii.
[3] B. Willey, *The Seventeenth Century Background*, pp. 87, 88.

to clear and distinct ideas.'[1] Whichote advocated a liberal policy towards men of good will whatever their persuasion. 'Let all uncertainties lie by themselves in the catalogue of disputables; matter of future enquiry.'[2] Cudworth was undoubtedly the most renowned of the group, as he was the most exclusively ethical in his teaching. He conceived of good and evil as grounded in the reality of things and cognizable by reason. They are objectively existent and 'the knowledge of them comes no doubt to the human mind from the divine; but it is from the Divine Reason in whose light man imperfectly participates, not merely from the Divine Will of each. Ethical, like mathematical, truth relates properly and primarily not to sensible particulars, but to the intelligible and universal essences of things, which are as immutable as the Eternal Mind whose existence is inseparable from theirs: ethical propositions therefore, are as unchangeably valid for the direction of the conduct of rational beings as the truths of geometry are.'[3]

It is in John Smith, the clearest speculative thinker of the Cambridge Platonists, that we find, not only the rationalistic element strongly stated, but the feeling antithesis very definitely implied. The very first property of religion, Smith contends in his *Discourses*, is to widen and enlarge a man's mental capacities. 'A good man, one that is actuated by religion, lives in converse with his reason; he lives at the height of his own being.'[4] In common with the other writers, Smith evinces an evident belief in the ability and dignity of reason. However their interpretation differed from that of their contemporaries: their emphasis upon the sublime quality of reason was of supreme significance. It was to give impetus to that rationalism which prevailed throughout the Age of Reason.

There was, however, another message, found especially in Smith which led to another conclusion. This is confirmed by the fact that Coleridge acknowledges his indebtedness to the Cambridge Platonists. There are numerous passages in the *Discourses* where Smith repudiates the rationalistic and objective views. Divine truth, he tells us, 'is not to be discerned so much in a man's brain,

---

[1] Op. cit., p. 151. Cf., 'The Cambridge Platonists were in fact more influenced by Descartes than by Bacon,' C. E. Raven, *Rational Religion and Christian Theology*, vol. 1, p. 109, Gifford Lectures, 1951. They were not slow, of course, as Raven goes on to point out, to observe his weakness.

[2] *Moral and Religious Aphorisms*, p. 547.

[3] H. Sidgwick, *History of Ethics* (5th edition), pp. 170, 171.

[4] *Discourses* (4th edition, edited by H. G. Smith, 1895), p. 376.

as in his heart.'[1] 'It is but a thin, airy, knowledge that is got by mere speculation.'[2] In this way Smith undermines the rationalism which he has already asserted. The knowledge 'ushered in by syllogisms and demonstrations' is of least value. In language that could well have been taken from Pascal, and which can be paralleled in Coleridge, Dodwell and Maurice, he proclaims religion to be 'a heavenborn thing, the seed of God in the spirits of men'.[3] It is from the hidden depths of the individual soul that divine knowledge springs. 'Therefore to seek our divinity in books of writings, is to seek the living among the dead: we do but in vain seek God many times in these, where His truth too often is not so much enshrined as entombed: — no; *intra te quaere Deum*, seek *God within thine own soul*.'[4]

In a section in the *Discourses* entitled, 'Of Legal and Evangelical Righteousness,' Smith condemns the legalism of Judaism with its notion of salvation by obedience to precepts as 'an external and lifeless thing'.[5] He contrasts this with the gospel which 'is not so much a system and body of saving divinity'.[6] Should it be turned into an external administration 'credenda propounded to us to believe',[7] it becomes as killing as the law itself. The old covenant 'was only externally promulgated, wrapt up, as it were, in ink and parchments, or, at least, engraven upon tables of stone, whereas this new covenant is set forth in living characters engraven upon the vital powers of men's souls'.[8]

In the *Discourse*, 'Of the Existence and Nature of God,' a note characteristically modern is struck. Smith asserts that it is his purpose not 'so much (to) demonstrate THAT (God) is, as WHAT He is'.[9] Although 'God has copied Himself out in all created being' it is still true that certainty is not found by the mere contemplation of the external world, but the world within. Within the individual is to be found, not simply an image of the divine, but 'the Deity itself'. It will follow then that 'whenever we look upon our soul in a right manner, we shall find a Urim and Thummim there, by which we may ask counsel of God Himself, who will have this always borne upon its breastplate'.[10] There is, he asserts, that which is the best and truest knowledge of God, which is not discoverable by the

---

[1] *Discourses*, p. 300.　　　　[2] Op. cit., p. 4.
[3] Op. cit., p. 390.　　　　　　[4] Op. cit., p. 3.
[5] Op. cit., p. 323.　　　　　　[6] Op. cit., p. 339.
[7] Op. cit., p. 328.　　　　　　[8] Op. cit., p. ibid.
[9] Op. cit., p. 329.　　　　　　[10] Op. cit., p. 128.

labour and sweat of the brain, but 'that which is kindled *within* us by a heavenly warmth in our hearts'.[1]

For the godly man this is the highest assurance. No external evidences and no elaborate arguments are needed by those whose hearts are thus 'strangely warmed'. The one so assured 'will find satisfaction within, feeling himself in conjunction with truth, though all the world should dispute against it'.[2]

Although it was the purpose of the Cambridge Platonists to rescue religion from all meaningless additions and to set forth its essentials in clear and distinct ideas, it is, at the same time, equally true that the aim of all these writers 'was to "call men off from dogmas and barren speculations" . . . affirming values where the orthodox affirmed facts'.[3]

[1] Op. cit., p. 3.   [2] Op. cit., p. 13.
[3] B. Willey, *The Seventeenth Century Background*, p. 138.

CHAPTER III

THE SUPREMACY OF THE RATIONAL

The antithesis, then, which revealed itself in the preceding period, and which was accentuated by the work of the Cambridge Platonists, developed, in our era, into the rationalism of Deism, on the one hand, and the enthusiasm of the Quakers, on the other. Here can be seen two opposite views of revelation, the rational-objective and the mystico-subjective. It is against the background of both these that the 'orthodox' apologists justified their understanding of revelation.[1] It is this fact which accounts for the seeming contradictions which pervaded their writings. Against the deists, who resolved revelation into truths of natural reason, they had to humble reason from its exalted position: against the enthusiasts they had to exalt it from its humble position.

The battle which had been earlier fought out in the field of politics was now transferred to the sphere of religious thought. The deists conceived of reason as an absolute sovereign, whereas their opponents would make it a limited monarchy. In the eyes of both, the enthusiasts were rabid republicans, if not absolute anarchists. The contradictions inherent in the orthodox literature of the eighteenth century are due to their effort to find an argument against these two, Dogmatism and Enthusiasm. Even before the century had begun Glanvill gave expression to the opposition. In his *Essays on Several Important Subjects in Philosophy and Religion* (1675) he castigates the Enthusiasts because they argue 'for the Universal Inability of Reason in the things of Religion'.[2] Against them, he replies: Reason is 'in a sense, the Word of God ... written upon our Minds and Hearts; as Scripture is that which is

---

[1] The term 'orthodox' is used in a broad sense throughout these pages to describe those who were active in the defence of the accepted doctrines of the Church. They were content with the established order and stood against innovations in theology. They were, for the most part, apologetic and evidence writers. Cf., V. Storr, *Development of English Theology in the Nineteenth Century*, p. 79; J. H. Overton, *The English Church in the Nineteenth Century*, p. 24.

[2] *Essays on Several Important Subjects, etc.*, Essay 5, p. 16.

written in a Book'.[1] Depraved in some sense the reason may be, but, his conclusion is: 'Follow reason, for no article of faith can contradict it, and every article of faith must agree thereto.'

On the other side, in his *Vanity of Dogmatizing*, Glanvill seeks to weaken the sovereignty of reason. The Preface tells us: 'It is levied against Dogmatizing, and attempts upon a daring Enemy, Confidence in Opinion.' On Aristotle he is especially severe. His works comprise, 'a huddle of words, and terms insignificant.'[2] He asserts that Aristotle drew a veil over nature and upon theology has had a damaging effect, so that Luther's censure is neither unjust nor uncharitable. 'While Aristotle is made the centre of things there is little hope.'[3] He thus concludes, 'It is shallow, unimproved intellects which are the confident pretenders to certainty.'[4] Since, then, both rationalism and enthusiasm had a specific doctrine of revelation, it is important that the ideas of each should be drawn out so as to understand the significance of the orthodox reply.

REVELATION AS INFALLIBLE REASON

THE DEISTIC DOGMATISM

(i) *A Summary of the View*

One of the most important influences of the Renaissance was to give man complete confidence in himself as a rational being. The human individual was believed to possess a faculty capable of searching into the ultimate mysteries. In this way, as Berdyaev says, the 'Renaissance once more discovered the natural man, the old Adam of the pre-Christian world, for whom Christianity had substituted the new Adam or the spiritual man'.[5] The Erasmic view of man as a creature of reason issued in the Deistic, Enlightenment and Illumination ideas of which 'the distinctive mark was the conscious rejection of all external, authoritative infallibilities'.[6] The general view that developed therefrom was that religion consisted in a few simple truths which were of its very essence, and, which were available to all men, since all possessed the sovereign faculty of reason. 'The Enlightenment', observes Professor Tillich, 'fore-

---

[1] Op. cit., p. 20.
[2] Op. cit., p. 150.
[3] Op. cit., p. 166.
[4] Op. cit., p. 15.
[5] N. Berdyaev, *The Meaning of History*, p. 131.
[6] J. Oman, *Grace and Personality*, pp. 3, 4.

shadowed by Erasmus' fight with Luther, and by theological humanism ... believed in the possibility of inducing the great majority of individuals to follow the demands of an integrated personal and social life by education, persuasion and adequate institutions.'[1]

It was in this context that man's estimate of himself as a rational being became absolute. He was able to penetrate to the last secrets of the universe. There was no island of knowledge he could not explore. The most thorough application of this doctrine of reason's sovereignty is seen in the deistic movement which opened the modern era of rationalistic criticism of the Bible.

Descartes, as has been shown, gave philosophical justification for this high estimate of man's ability. His view-point was adopted by the theologians of the seventeenth century. To Glanvill, a Fellow of the Royal Society and Rector of Bath Abbey, Descartes is the 'great', the 'renowned', the 'unparalleled'. He thus announces that 'reason is certain and infallible'.[2] Nothing, he insists, has done more harm to religion than the disparagement of reason.

The apologists in our period, as staunch Churchmen, were interested in defending institutional religion. This conception went back to Bishop Hooker. In his *Ecclesiastical Polity*, Hooker introduced a doctrine of conformity based upon an ecclesiastical theory. He sees God as the supreme keeper of law and order. He thus considers all human law to have as its purpose the curbing of man's outward actions for the sake of the common good.[3] As the angelic host reveal their perfection by their unhesitating obedience to the divine will, so submission to the 'saving legislation' which God gave to the Church is the ordained way of salvation. The state has therefore the duty to maintain the authority of the Church, since the two are but different aspects of the one reality. This point is made in Book 8 of the *Polity*. 'We hold', he says, 'that there is not any man of the Church of England but the same is also of the commonwealth, nor any man a member of the commonwealth, which is not also of the Church of England ....'[4]

There is, according to this thesis, a law of society, namely,

---

[1] P. Tillich, *The Protestant Era*, Preface, p. xxxv.
[2] *Essays on Several Important Subjects, etc.*, Essay 5, p. 20.
[3] *Ecclesiastical Polity*, vol. 1, 10, 1, 2.
[4] Op. cit., vol. 2, bk. 8, ch. 1, 2. These words may not be Hooker's own. Isaak Walton in his *Life of Hooker* prefixed to vol. 1, refers to Hooker as 'the happy author of five (if not more) of the eight books of the Laws of the Ecclesiastical Polity'.

'consent to some general bond of association,' and, in addition, certain divine imperatives to fill up 'the defects of those natural ways of salvation'. The Church therefore unites within itself 'a law of reason and a law supernatural'.[1] Here God's saving legislation is looked upon as the supernatural addition to the natural laws of society.

Accepting this conception of the Church as coextensive with the state and the distinction between natural and supernatural laws, the deists went on to deny the need for these asserted divine extras. They consequently argued that the natural laws of society, unfolded by reason, were sufficient, and that they themselves were true Christians.

It was, however, as has been earlier indicated, to Archbishop Tillotson that the deists looked as their head. Tillotson was the foe of all irrationalism. Mysticism and enthusiasm were anathema to him. He laid stress upon the sufficiency of reason, first to comprehend natural religion and then to judge of revealed. He begins his series of sermons on, 'The Miracles Wrought in Confirmation of Christianity,' with the observation 'Whosoever impartially considers the Christian Religion, cannot but acknowledge the Laws and Principles of it to be reasonable'.[2] By giving special insistence to the subject and scope of natural religion, and by putting strong emphasis upon the adequacy of human reason, Tillotson gave the impression that Christianity was a matter of mere common sense. All immediacy in religion was regarded as either a futile enthusiasm or a fatal superstition. To say with Tertullian, *Certum est quia impossibile*,[3] is to utter the utmost blasphemy, for reason is God-given and whatever is not of reason is not of faith. It was thus evident that: νοῦς ἐστί βασιλεὺς ἥμιν οὐρανου τε καί γῆς.[4]

Tillotson, of course, still gave allegiance to the prevailing view of revelation as the disclosure of certain divine truths. But he regarded these extras as a sort of republication of natural religion. They served, with their promises of rewards and threatenings of punishments, to enforce those obligations of which all men, as reasonable beings, were aware. For Tillotson this meant that nothing could be received as revelation which contradicted the natural truths of reason. It is clear that Tillotson was anxious to

[1] *Ecclesiastical Polity*, vol. 2, bk. 1, 15, 2.
[2] *Sermons*, vol. 2 (3rd edition, 1727), p. 494.
[3] *De Carne Christi*, 5.
[4] Plato, *Philebus*, 28.

stress the importance of the Christian revelation. But he still maintained that both natural and revealed religion were grounded on reason.

He illustrates from the story of Abraham. It was, he asserts, only after he had 'reasoned with himself', and based his conviction on the omnipotence of God, that the patriarch's readiness to act passed from the realm of credulity to that of faith. This understanding of faith will be seen to be in line with that of revelation. There is no faith, Tillotson declares, where there is no sufficient reason. Faith implies conviction, and conviction, in its turn, is based upon rational evidence. Teaching like this, it will be obvious, undermined the old view in which special revelation was allowed to contain mysteries which reason could not fathom.

Tillotson, indeed, goes to extremes in condemning those who, in their zeal for revealed religion, overthrew natural. He is convinced of the binding obligations of natural religion. This principle is carried so far that Tillotson places the natural duties of nursing mothers above the laws of revealed religion.

'This I foresee will seem a very hard saying to nice and delicate mothers', he writes, 'who prefer their own ease and pleasure to the fruit of their own bodies, but whether they will hear or whether they will forbear, I think myself obliged to deal plainly in this matter, and to be so faithful as to tell them that this is a natural duty, and because it is so, of a more necessary and indispensable obligation than any positive precept of revealed religion, and that the neglect of it is one of the great and crying sins of this age and nation.'[1] Statements like this, with the whole drift of Tillotson's teaching, seems to justify Charles Smyth's remark that, 'The content of his preaching was little more than a prudential morality, based rather on reason than on revelation, and appealing deliberately to sober common sense.'[2]

Already before the eighteenth century had begun, the notion that true religion was the intellectual discovery of certain fundamental axioms had been set forth by Lord Herbert of Cherbury. Leyland with some reason refers to Herbert as the first of the

---

[1] *Works*, vol. 4, p. 452 (edition, 1741).

[2] In the light of what is here said it will be easy to understand the high place accorded to Tillotson by both the deists and their orthodox opponents. A very different estimate is given by Whitfield and Wesley. During his stay in Georgia in 1740 the former declared that Tillotson knew no more of Christianity than Mahomet. He sought to justify his statement in two pamphlets in which it is asserted that 'all natural men speak well of his works', and that the archbishop

deists. In his book, *On Truth as it is distinguished from Revelation, Probability, Possibility, and Falsehood*, Herbert seeks to discover what he regards as the essentials of true religion. He draws up a list of five articles,[1] or 'common notices', as he calls them. These are innate, and therefore discoverable by all men everywhere. Because they are disclosed directly to the mind they are the only necessities and the only certainties. When all religions are stripped of their priestly additions, then, Herbert declares, we are left with the absolute requirements, 'the only true catholic religion.'

Herbert does not, indeed, deny the possibility of a revealed religion. There are some truths which have been revealed, but these do not possess the same certainty as those 'derived from the faculties'. These revealed truths depend for their authority upon the revealer. They are not certain truths of the mind. Herbert specifies certain criteria by which external revelation is to be tested, but these are so strict that there is no authority left for any revelation except those cases of immediate disclosure to the individual himself. This last point justifies Herbert's own assertion that on 'one fair day in summer', when the sun shone clear and no wind stirred, it was revealed to him that it would benefit the world if his book, *De Veritate*, were published.

This idea was later reasserted by Charles Blount in a volume of papers published in 1693 under the title, *The Oracles of Reason*. Blount denied that there was any other revelation beyond that which man's unaided reason could discover. If such a revealed religion existed it would of necessity need to be universal, since 'no Rule of Revealed Religion was, or ever could be made known to all Men'.[2] There must, therefore, be no such thing. He contends that 'what is not universal and equally known to All Men, cannot be needful for Any'.[3]

---

had 'no other than a bare historical faith'. It was the restraining influence of Lady Huntingdon which kept Wesley from making an open attack upon Tillotson and Bishop Bull in his Oxford University sermon of 1741. The position he intended to take was found among his papers after his death, and is now number CXXXIV of his published sermons.

[1] The five fundamental truths of religion, according to Herbert are: (1) Belief in the existence of a Supreme Being; (2) The duty of worship; (3) The Obligation of virtue and piety as service due to the Supreme Being; (4) Necessity of repenting of sins and forsaking them; (5) Rewards and punishments in this life and the next.

[2] A supposed Letter from A. W. to Charles Blount, Esq., 'Of Revealed Religion as opposed to Divine Revelation', published in *Oracles of Reason*, No. 14.

[3] Ibid.

(a) Reasonableness of Christianity — Locke

It is John Locke, however, who took up a position fruitful alike for the deists and their opponents. This point is illustrated by the references to Locke made by different writers. E. S. Waterhouse, for example, considers Locke to have been a 'powerful supporter' of the deistic position.[1] G. Fisher, on the other hand, maintains, 'Of the writers on the anti-deistic side, there was none abler or more eminent than John Locke (1632–1704).'[2] The fact is that each of these writers is correct in his estimate. Under the influence of the deistic onslaught, Locke felt that the interests of orthodoxy would be best served by 'rationalizing' theology and thus make it less vulnerable. This was the purpose of his *Reasonableness of Christianity*. The result was, that in seeking to make Christianity 'easy' of acceptance, Locke really robbed it of its worth, and consequently his work which was meant to be a sword against deism became a powerful weapon in its hands.

Standing as he does on the threshold of the new century, his work is at once the conclusion of the ideas which revealed themselves in the seventeenth as well as the starting-point of the enquiries which occupied the eighteenth century. Locke's 'influence pervades the eighteenth century with an almost scriptural authority'.[3]

It has been usual to speak of Locke as the founder of rational theology in England. This is not strictly exact since he says no more than the most orthodox theologians in the preceding period. He was, however, more thorough in the application of accepted principles. He pressed the claims of reason so as to leave no room for the background of traditional superstitions and unfathomable mysteries. Locke was, in fact, so complete in his reasoning that he was often carried logically far beyond the position that he desired to establish.

In his *Reasonableness of Christianity*, he assures us that belief in Jesus as the Messiah is the only thing needful. To believe this is to believe all that God has demanded as necessary. While Locke allows that revelation discloses truths beyond the compass of reason, there are still passages in which he comes near to the true deistic position. 'Reason must', he says, 'be our last judge in

[1] *The Philosophical Approach to Religion*, p. 151.
[2] *History of Christian Doctrine*, p. 374.
[3] *Spectator*, No. 387, quoted by B. Willey, *The Seventeenth Century Background*, p. 269.

everything.'[1] Like Whichote he refers again and again to reason as 'the candle of the Lord'. True religion cannot be out of reach of the common man, for plain men form the generality of mankind: the majority 'have not leisure for Learning and Logick'. The one who asserts that God has given a long catalogue of things to be believed will run into infinite absurdities. God has made no such demand, for He is a compassionate Father. To man 'He has given Reason, and with it a Law. That could not be otherwise than what Reason should dictate; unless we should think, that a creature (reasonable) should have an unreasonable Law'.

In the fourth edition of his *Essay Concerning Humane Understanding*, which appeared in 1700, there was added a chapter, on 'Enthusiasm', in which Locke approximates more closely to the true deistic standpoint. This chapter now forms an integral part of the fourth book, and with the one preceding, entitled, 'Faith and Reason,' gives a fair indication of the drift of his argument.

It is first laid down, in a manner followed later by Mansel, that the boundary between Faith and Reason should be drawn. Those ideas 'beyond the discovery of our natural faculties and above reason, are, when revealed the proper matter of faith'.[2] Nothing contrary to reason can be accepted on the supposed authority of revelation; 'if anything shall be thought revelation which is contrary to the plain principles of reason and the evident knowledge the mind has of its own clear and distinct ideas, there reason must be harkened to as to a matter within its providence.'[3] Revelation itself must have the approval of reason; it is not a matter of faith. Faith 'can never convince us of anything that contradicts our knowledge'.[4] The sum of the matter is, 'Whatever God hath revealed is certainly true; no doubt can be made of whether it be a divine revelation or no, reason must judge; which can never permit the mind to reject a greater evidence to embrace what is less evident, nor allow it to entertain probability in opposition to knowledge and certainty.'[5]

It is the folly of Enthusiasm that it asserts revelation without reason. It takes feeling for seeing, and can itself be no proof. Locke reiterates that 'Revelation must be judged by reason',[6] indeed reason alone is the true judge. No prophet is a mere complex

[1] *The Reasonableness of Christianity*, sect. 14.
[2] *On the Human Understanding* (New edition, 1894), p. 587.
[3] Ibid.   [4] Op. cit., p. 586.   [5] Op. cit., p. 588.
[6] Op. cit., p. 595.

of unreasoned emotions. 'God when He makes a prophet does not unmake the man: he leaves all his faculties in their natural state, to enable him to judge of his inspirations, whether they be of divine origin or no. When He illuminates the mind with supernatural light, He does not extinguish that which is natural.'[1] In another passage in the same chapter there are statements which come still nearer to deism, and may be regarded as the occasion for some writers putting him in their company. 'Reason', says Locke, 'is natural revelation, whereby the Eternal Father of Light and Fountain of all Knowledge, communicates to mankind that portion of truth which he has laid within reach of their natural faculties. Revelation is natural reason enlarged by a new set of discoveries communicated by God immediately, which reason vouches the truth of by the testimony and proofs it gives that they come from God.'[2]

The eighteenth century, then, opened with an unbounded confidence in reason, and the 'immediate offspring of Locke's book was Toland's, *Christianity not Mysterious*'.[3] By exaggerating some of the statements of Locke's, *Essay*, and applying them in his own way, under cover of Locke's authority, Toland led on naturally to the true deistic position, in which revelation is regarded as infallible reason.

(b) Christianity not Mysterious — Toland

In the Preface of Toland's book the basic assumptions of deism are stated. Toland, it should be observed, did not regard himself as a deist. He certainly did not deny the possibility of revelation. He boldly contends that it is the rejection of his views which is the occasion of so many becoming 'Deists and Atheists'.[4] He is to be regarded as a disciple of Locke who consistently applied the philosopher's logic. Toland's fundamental assumption is that all that is essential in Christianity must be understandable. It is, therefore, impossible for reasonable men to receive mysteries on the proclaimed authority of the Early Fathers,[5] particular Doctors pronounced orthodox,[6] a general Council or an infallible pope.[7] Toland announces the sincerity of his purpose with the information that reason and its uses have been 'the happy instruments'[8] of

---

[1] Ibid. [2] Op. cit., p. 591.
[3] B. Willey, *The Seventeenth Century Background*, p. 280.
[4] *Christianity not Mysterious* (3rd edition, 1696), p. 176.
[5] Op. cit., p. 2. [6] Op. cit., p. 3. [7] Op. cit., p. 4. [8] Op. cit., Preface, p. ix.

his own conversion. The reference is to his renunciation of Roman Catholicism and his acceptance of Protestantism.

The gospel contains nothing obscure, for 'religion must necessarily be reasonable and intelligible'.[1] He thus makes the equation: 'Religion is always the same like God its author,' and, 'Truth is always and everywhere the same.'[2] It is no objection to urge that reason is depraved. Toland denies that it is. The rationality of the divine image has not been impaired. Revelation, Toland argues, is a removal of the veil. It is a disclosure of the true meaning of religion, which reason must appreciate and approve. Faith and knowledge are thus identified and faith is consequently defined as 'a firm persuasion built upon substantial reason'.[3] Toland avows it to be an article of his faith that he can believe only that which is reasonable. Reason, he asserts, tends to 'confirm and elucidate' revelation. He will dispense with the varied opinions of sects and parties and consider only 'those of Jesus Christ and his apostles'.[4] The element of mystery, he boldly declares, must be eliminated from Christianity because it is not only an easy refuge for the unthinking, but a real stumbling-block in the way of its acceptance.

To be sure, mysteries have crept into Christianity, but the advice that 'we must adore what we cannot comprehend' is impossible. Some assert that the Scriptures contain mysteries: they would have us 'believe what the literal Sense imparts, with little or no Consideration for Reason, which they reject as not fit to be employed about the revealed Part of Revelation. Others assert, that we may use Reason as an Instrument, but not as a Rule of our Belief. The first contend some mysteries may be, or at least, seem to be received by Faith. The second that no mystery is contrary to Reason but above it. Both of them from different Principles agree that several Doctrines of the New Testament belong no further to Enquiries of Reason, than to prove them divinely revealed, and that they are properly Mysteries still. On the contrary, we hold that Reason is the only Foundation of all Certainty: and that nothing Revealed whether as to its Manner or Certainty is more exempted from its Disquisitions, than the Ordinary Phenomena of Nature. Wherefore, that there is nothing in the Gospel contrary to Reason, not above it; and that no Christian Doctrine can properly be called a Mystery.'[5]

[1] Preface, p. xxvii.　　[2] Preface, p. xx.　　[3] Op. cit., p. 138.
[4] Op. cit., Preface, p. ix.　　　　[5] Op. cit., pp. 5, 6.

Scripture itself must be subjected to the test of reason since it is the reason which must judge of what is figurative and what is literal; 'otherwise, under the pretence of Faith in the Word of God, the highest Follies and Blasphemies may be deduced from the Letter of Scripture; as that God is subject to passions, is the author of sin, etc.'[1] Seeming contradictions are to be patiently worked out in the assurance that they are not ultimately real. The purpose of the gospel is to dispel ignorance and eradicate superstition, herein lies the evidence of its own rationality. Toland considers that the Mystery Religions disguised 'naked religion' under all sorts of rituals which became the selfish concern of priests. He investigates the meaning of the word 'mystery', and concludes, rightly, that it connotes the disclosure of a secret. Things hidden from the philosophers of Greece and the people of Israel are now plain to those instructed of God. It is absurd to think of Paul saying that the Gospel is the mystery 'made known unto all the nations' if it is still incomprehensible.

No wise man would assert that a substance like water was above reason because he has never enquired into its parts and properties. This means for us: 'First, that no Christian Doctrine, no more than any ordinary Piece of Nature can be reputed Mystery, because we have no adequate or complete Idea of what belongs to it. Secondly, that what is revealed in Religion as it is most useful and necessary, so it must and may be easily comprehended, and found as consistent with our Common Notions as what we know of Wood, or Stone, or Water or the like. And, thirdly, that when we do as familiarly explain such Doctrines as what is known of Natural Things, (which I contend we can) we may then as properly be said to comprehend the one as the other.'[2] The real essence of things, is after all, unknown to us.

The question remains, How were mysteries introduced into Christianity? Broadly, according to Toland, the process was, what we may describe as, firstly natural, and then, secondly, deliberate. To begin with, the converts from Judaism 'who continued mightily fond of their Levitical Rites and Feasts',[3] retained their rituals. These, being at first tolerated by the stronger brethren, soon became part of Christianity itself and apostolic sanction sought for them, Then, too, the Gentile converts, 'not a little scandalized at the Plain Dress of the Gospel,'[4] brought with them

[1] Op. cit., p. 34.   [2] Op. cit., p. 80.   [3] Op. cit., p. 159.   [4] Ibid.

the pomp and secret mysteries of their old religion. The Christians, eager to win them, did not oppose their additions. Philosopher and 'wise man' saw it worth their while becoming Christians, and they soon made unintelligible puzzles out of what was originally plain. To crown the process, when the Emperor Constantine became a Christian, 'multitudes then professed themselves of the Emperor's Persuasion, only to make their Court and mend their fortunes thereby, or to preserve those Places and Preferments whereof they were possessed.'[1] All the paraphernalia of the heathen temples were thus sanctioned and sanctified for the service of the Church and multitudinous accretions were added to the primitive simplicity of the gospel, which was already overlaid with Jewish and Gentile excesses.

Over against this more natural process went the deliberate. Toland puts it like this: 'Now their own advantage being the Motive that put the Primitive Clergy receiving Mystery, they quickly created themselves, by its existence, into a separate and politick Body.'[2] In this way there grew up grades and distinctions in their ranks till at length they claimed the sole right of interpreting the Scripture. Thus they became apart from, above, and authoritative for the rest. Ceremonies are, therefore, the source and cause of mystery. Let them but be eliminated, and reason be free to exercise its native ability, and then, so Toland assures us, we will come to the pure essence of Christianity, the true understandable revelation of God — the revelation of reason.

Collins presses Toland's ideas to their logical conclusion. Whereas Toland sought to dissociate himself from deism, Collins had no such hesitancy. The very titles of Collins' five major works gave all a fairly accurate indication of his position. The first, *An Essay on Reason*, appeared in 1707. This was followed two years later by *Priestcraft in Perfection*. His most important work, *The Discourse of Freethinking* came out in 1713, eleven years later came his, *Grounds and Reasons of the Christian Religion*. His last work, *Scheme of Liberal Prophecy*, is dated 1727. In *The Discourse of Freethinking*, Collins argued for the identity of revelation and reason. In no way was reason to be restricted, for by it alone can truth be discovered and error detected. For Collins the adoption of rationalistic principles meant the abandonment of supernaturalistic

[1] Op. cit., p. 162.
[2] Op. cit., p. 170.

religion. It was at this point he left himself open to an attack which his many enemies were not slow to press home. Amongst his more formidable foes are to be found Bentley and Swift.

It was a strange irony which called down upon Collins' head the biting sarcasm of Dean Swift. Collins in his *Discourse of Freethinking* had made the injudicious jest that certain 'zealous divines' should be shipped abroad to convert the heathen. Their absence would result, not only in the spread of Christianity elsewhere, but in freedom from faction at home. Among the divines designed for this export, Collins names Swift. The Dean of St Patrick's, Dublin, was not the man to take such a remark lightly; soon the 'freethinker' was made to feel as diminutive as one of the Lilliputians of the *Gulliver's Travels*. Swift's retaliation came in the form of a tract entitled, *Mr Collins' Discourse of Freethinking put into plain English, by way of Abstract for the Poor*.

In the tract Collins' arguments were restated but the result was a fantastic burlesque. The Bible is set over against the statements of the 'Freethinker', and it is easy to draw the conclusion that the 'Freethinker' is both knave and fool. One example of Swift's method will indicate how crushing was the result. 'The Bible says the Jews were a nation favoured by God; but I who am a freethinker say that cannot be, because the Jews lived in a corner of the earth and freethinking makes it plain that those who live in corners cannot be favourites of God.'[1]

(c) Christianity as Old as Creation — Tindal

It is in Tindal's, *Christianity as Old as Creation* that we have 'the culminating point of the whole deistic controversy'.[2] A sermon preached by Dr Sherlock, Bishop of Bangor, before the Society for the Propagation of the Gospel gave Tindal the title for his book. The bishop argued that the religion of the Gospel is the true original religion of reason and nature. The gospel of repentance assured a restoration to that position from which man by transgression fell. Thus 'the Gospel was the Republication of the Law of Nature, and its Precepts declarative of that original Religion, which is as old as Creation'.[3] It is Tindal's starting declaration that the only true religion is that discoverable by reason. The notion

[1] Swift's *Works*, vol. 2 (edition, 1859), p. 185.
[2] L. Stephen, *English Thought in the Eighteenth Century*, vol. 1, p. 134.
[3] *Christianity as Old as Creation* (3rd edition), p. 60.

that there are two, one a natural and the other a revealed, is rejected at the outset. Natural and revealed religion are in fact but different aspects of the one rational religion. The two are alike in the manner of their communication. 'The one being the Internal and the other the External Revelation, the same unchangeable Will of a Being, which is alike at all times infinitely wise and good.'[1]

From the beginning God has given a rule or law of conduct, and what He has given can be neither imperfect nor incomplete. It being God's will that 'all men should come to a knowledge of the truth', it follows that He, at all times, must have given the means whereby they should find those laws which they should profess and practise. Christianity is, therefore, true, because it must be regarded, and only in so far as it is regarded, as a republication of natural religion.

The laws of conduct are based upon the unalterable principle of things. Thus the revelation of nature is absolutely perfect so that external revelation can add nothing to it. The gospel must thus be grounded in the same eternal necessity. If this were not so God could be condemned as arbitrary. 'If He once commanded things without reason, there can be no reason why He may not endlessly change His commands.'[2] No special revelation can be claimed as enlarging or ennobling the revelation of nature, since this would call in question the perfection of what has been given by nature. The voice of nature issues its convincing demand that God should be worshipped. The method of such worship is left to man's convenience. Man alone has 'issued out commands which have no Foundation in Reason'.[3] The benevolent God, Tindal argues, has granted to men senses to make them aware of that which is hurtful or helpful to their bodies. It cannot be supposed that He has less regard for their souls. Adopting a hedonist ideal, he concluded that reason is given 'to discern what Actions make for and against Happiness'.[4]

It is by fulfilling their duties that men are 'made partakers of the divine nature'. No written book could contain the precepts and prescriptions for every need. And certainly no atonement is required by God for men's transgressions. 'A mediatory conception of God', he says, 'led the heathen to think that He delighteth in the butchery of innocent Animals; and that the stench of burnt Flesh

---

[1] Op. cit., p. 2.   [2] Op. cit., p. 52.
[3] Op. cit., p. 101.   [4] Op. cit., p. 18.

should be a sweet-smelling Savour to his nostrils as to atone for the Wickedness of Men.'[1] Tindal asks, in words akin to Socinius: 'How sins freely pardoned could want any expiation? or how after a full equivalent paid and adequate satisfaction given all could be mercy and pure forgiveness?'[2] All that is required of men is summed up in the Sermon on the Mount, although Tindal makes the audacious claim that its precepts are better expressed by Confucius.[3] The epitome of true religion is, therefore, 'Do all the good we can, and thereby render ourselves acceptable to God in answering the end of creation.'[4]

He sees rituals and ordinances, 'the Borders and Fringes' of religion, raised by human authority to the status of essentials. Thus is the indifferent made the binding. But all that is needful is to follow reason, for therein lies true religion. 'As long as Men believe the Good of Society is the supreme Law, they will think it their Duty to be governed by that Law: and believing God requires nothing of them than what is for the Good of Mankind, will place the whole of their Religion in benevolent Actions, and to the utmost of their Abilities copy after the divine Original; but if they are made to believe that there are things which have no relation to their Good, necessary to Salvation; they must suppose it their Duty to use such means as will most effectually serve this Purpose; and that God, requiring the End, requires all those means as will best secure and propagate it.'[5] There is nothing left but to trust reason and 'every attempt to destroy reason by reason is a demonstration that Men have nothing but Reason to trust to'.[6]

Where reason is set aside the way is left open for a host of impostures all claiming to umpire in the life of man. No book can be regarded as infallible because of the human means of transmission; 'the Probability of Facts depending on human Testimony must gradually lessen in Proportion to the Difference of Time when they were done.'[7] Tindal refers to several 'orthodox paradoxes', like the doctrine of the Trinity, which are beyond the common people. He insists that the accumulating of external marks like 'uninterrupted Tradition, incontested Miracles, Confessions of Adversaries, Numbers of Proselytes, Agreement among themselves',[8] are not sufficient to establish a particular religion. Prophecy cannot be

[1] Op. cit., p. 78.
[2] Op. cit., p. 419.
[3] Op. cit., p. 310.
[4] Op. cit., p. 18.
[5] Op. cit., p. 133.
[6] Op. cit., p. 158.
[7] Op. cit., p. 163.
[8] Op. cit., p. 211.

appealed to, since, he contends, the Apostles' expectation for an immediate return of Christ was proved false.

Variant readings, and according to Bentley there are 30,000 in our 'present best editions',[1] make the Bible unreliable. To say that most of these are insignificant is no sufficient reply, since in a book in which most things are regarded as of the greatest moment it is impossible to accept so much as of no importance. The truth of a doctrine cannot be established by all the 'plain texts' adduced in its favour. In Augustine's time all the 'plain texts' were on the side of predestination: it is now contended that they are on the side of Free-will. Nor, indeed, can the commands of the Bible be observed in present society. Who, for example, will refrain from eating black-puddings because of the injunction to abstain from blood?

Tindal repudiates a Book religion, because, he argues, the greater part of humanity has no knowledge of it; while those who have, owing to the imperfections of language cannot understand it. Following Locke[2] he urges that an attested copy of an original only is permitted as evidence in law: 'and a Copy of a Copy never so well attested, and by never so many credible Witnesses will not be admitted as Proof in Judicature.' No refuge can be sought in appointed teachers, for to place the necessities of salvation in the hands of the local clergy is only to set up a pope in every parish. Then, too, the Reformers' doctrine of the *testimonium Spiritus sancti internum* only leads to an unhealthy subjectivism. Difficulties and alterations in theological views, Tindal takes as evidence that there is no secure special revelation. 'There are twenty several Opinions concerning Justification all drawn from the Scriptures by men only of the Augustine Confession; and there are sixteen several Opinions concerning Original Sin; and as many Distinctions of the Sacraments as there are Sects of Men that disagree about them.'[3]

Having in Tindal the best exposition of the deistic dogmatism it is unnecessary to follow their literature any further. What followed was but a less vigorous reiteration of *Christianity as Old as Creation*. How the orthodox met the challenge of Tindal will be seen later: it is estimated that one hundred and fifty replies to him were forthcoming.[4] Fortunately most of these, which were mere repetitions

---

[1] Op. cit., p. 294.
[2] *Essay on the Human Understanding* (2nd edition), pp. 276–7.
[3] *Christianity as Old as Creation*, p. 261.
[4] *Bibliography of British History*, ed. by Pargellis and Madley (1714–89), p. 150.

of the greater works, have long since passed into oblivion. The fact is, as C. E. Moore rightly observes: 'The arguments of the deists were never successfully refuted. On the contrary, the striking thing is that their opponents, the militant divines and writers of numberless volumes of 'Evidences of Christianity', had come to the same rational basis as the deists. They referred even the most subtle questions to the pure reason, as no one now would do. The deistic movement was not really defeated. It largely compelled its opponents to adopt its methods.'[1]

(ii) *Criticism of the View*

Leaving, then, until a later chapter an investigation of the mode and method of the orthodox reply, we purpose here to make some criticism of the deistic presuppositions.

To begin with, the basic notion of the whole deistic movement was the Cartesian doctrine of the equality of reason in all men. 'Reason', observes Toland, 'is the Foundation of all Certainty.' It is not just an instrument of the self, but the very essence of the self, consequently, reason does not operate merely to make discriminate judgements but is the only source of religion and virtue. Setting out from this premise, the deists believed that sure and certain knowledge was truly attainable by all without too much effort. They thus proclaimed that since the world is the creation of a deity of absolute rationality, then men made in His image are also supremely rational beings who can follow God's plan in the created universe. 'The intellect cannot question the truth of what it apprehends as necessary; and the only necessity it recognizes is the necessity of what is intelligible.'[2]

A. Starting then from this premise that reason is equal in all men the logical results for deism must be an unhealthy individualism. Each man is king in his own domain; each recognizes no other authority but the findings of his own unstained and unstunted reason. There is no objective standard, for the criterion of truth lies in the knowing subject, not in the object to be known. By exclusive emphasis on the divine transcendence, deism repudiated any idea of the divine immanence which, in some sense, can be held to interrelate the individual units.

On the other hand, by separating man from God, deism made

---

[1] *Christian Thought since Kant*, p. 24.
[2] W. de Burgh, *Towards a Religious Philosophy*, p. 138.

the relation between man and man a purely pragmatic one. There was no real binding link. This deistic conception is in line with the Leibnizian doctrine of monads each separate and self-sufficient. Leibniz had insisted that the individual entities which make up the totality of the universe is each complete in itself. Each monad is 'big with the future', thus having its explanation within itself. For the deists, then, the single individual, with his 'clear and distinct ideas' was his own authority. He has no connection with and no responsibility to, another. The deistic position was a mere doctrinaire one, only possible on the basis of a complete misunderstanding of the human individual.

In the rejection of the Leibnizian doctrine there is no need to go to the other extreme and advocate the Humian denial of an existing self. Nor, on the other hand, need it be maintained that the individual is the result of the interplay upon some neutral 'stuff' of social forces. Personality is not created by the environment. Because it develops in a social content it does not follow that it is produced by it. It is true that human beings do become aware of their own personalities by association with others. But it is also true that there is a 'self' which becomes aware; an 'I' that takes notice. 'Because we arrive at the knowledge of our own personalities through contact with others,' observes Dalgairns, 'it does not follow that personality itself is constituted by the sharp shock which comes of knocking our own self against another self.' The paradox exhibited by the fact of personality is, that, while it has a centre all its own, a private world of thought and feeling which others cannot penetrate, yet, because we are persons, we can transcend our isolation. As Professor John MacMurray remarks, 'The more universal a person becomes in his self-transcendence, the more unique does he become in his individuality.'[1]

The deists failed to grasp the fact stated by Aristotle in his definition of man as a 'political animal', or as we might say to-day, a 'social being'. In a recent book Reinhold Niebuhr has pointed out that each individual is 'unique', and that the 'internal dialogue of the self' is beyond the penetrating analysis of any 'depth psychology'. There is an internal self which cannot be invaded by the most formidably armed host of psychoanalysts. At the same time, just because man is a social being, the self cannot be complete in isolation. 'The self is engaged in a perpetual dialogue with other

[1] *Adventure*, ed. by B. H. Streeter, p. 193.

selves in which its dependence upon others becomes apparent.'[1] The more real an individual knows himself to be the more related does he recognize that he is. Even Leibniz, who had insisted so strongly upon the separateness of the monads, could not leave it at that; he thus reintroduced a principle of unity by the back door in his artificial doctrine of pre-existing harmony. But the deists had nothing to bind together the isolated selves: they viewed each individual as an all-knowing centre, adequate in its own self-sufficiency. Such was the result which followed from its own failure to understand the fact of man's social nature.

B. It must be pointed out further, that when once the fundamental assumptions of deism are accepted then naturalism and scepticism must inevitably result. Man by his own unaided reason can find out all the truth that he needs. God has apparently nothing to add; no new truths to disclose. The order of nature is thus a closed system in which there is no need for, and no possibility of, a rift. The veil is in no place rent, for God cannot reveal anything more of Himself than that which is already written into the laws of nature.

Tindal insists that God Himself is bound by this inflexible necessity. The will of God is always determined by the 'nature and reason of things'.[2] Therefore, 'Individual wisdom can have no commands, but what are founded on the unalterable reason of things.'[3] It is to be concluded, Tindal affirms, that 'God's will is so clearly manifested in the Book of Nature that he who runs can read it'.[4]

But the question arises, To what purpose would it be to read God's signature upon the universe when He stands beyond it in solitary isolation unknown and unknowable by any intimate acquaintance? The deists, in this respect, unlike Kant, did not even require God as a Dispenser of Happiness, as a Paymaster of Pleasure, renumerating those who obeyed the dictates of the categorical imperative. Tindal finds a natural connection between goodness and pleasure. Rewards and punishments, he contends, are the inseparable attendants of virtuous and vicious actions. God is consequently pushed aside as unnecessary. In this context a retort by Leyland can be appreciated, 'I do not see that he leaves

---

[1] *The Self in the Dramas of History*, p. 42.
[2] *Christianity as Old as Creation*, p. 65.
[3] Op. cit., p. 247.
[4] Op. cit., p. 24.

God anything at all to do in the matter.'[1] God has no finger in the pie; has nothing to do with rewards for virtue. The biblical assertion that we must all appear before the judgement seat of Christ to give an account of the deeds done in the body, is meaningless. As a result ethics have no divine standard. There is no ultimate reference. All is natural.

God is conceived to be a purely ornamental Being having no present or future significance for the world; but many people feel no sentiment for the purely ornamental. God may have started the world, but He no longer steers it. He moved it, but He does not now mind it. He is, as Carlyle says, 'An absentee God, sitting idle ever since the first Sabbath at the outside of the world and seeing it go.' A God so indifferent and inactive will soon not be believed in at all. Thus with a world rationally sufficient and a God completely indifferent, the logical result is naturalism and scepticism. As J. V. Langmead Casserley has observed, 'The deists saw that, although the physical science of their time required the idea of God as Creator, it could not tolerate the conception of any further divine interference with the course of the creation. Once the universe had begun to exist, all further explanations of what happens in it must be couched in scientific terms alone.'[2]

C. This leads to another important theoretical defect of which the deistic teachers were unaware. In a world of regularity and order the deists found the one sufficient reason for their idea of a Creator in the argument from Design. It was, indeed, logical enough to suppose, *a priori*, that the world could only continue without 'any further divine interference' if it followed an ordered plan. And the deists had no doubt here. They were optimistic about everything, for the world to them was flooded by an excess of light. They were content in their faith that the universe was brought into existence by a Happy Being, and it is, therefore, the best of all possible worlds. But what if God is no longer amused by it? That matters not, since all creation is good and beautiful and man reasonable and wise: then all is well. The evidences of design are so abundant, so the deists believed, that there need be no doubt about a Master Mechanic Who set it all agoing.

It was in this context that the deists proclaimed and maintained the authority and sufficiency of the teleological argument for the

---

[1] *Answer to Tindal*, p. 234.
[2] *The Christian in Philosophy*, p. 104.

existence of their transcendent Creator. The 'proof' was used of course with equal emphasis by their opponents. But there are two points to be made against the deist's gay use of the argument.

First, their optimism was not justified by all the facts. There is more in the world than the deists were ready to acknowledge. There is a sterner side of nature which must not be overlooked in the interests of a theory. The mood of deism was too gaily cavalier: 'all's well with the world'. But deism is not a true induction from the facts. Its major premise was a sweeping generalization which took no account of the negative instances. Those of deistic outlook should not have had to wait for John Stuart Mill's essay on nature to have been made aware of the evidences of dysteleology.[1] It is against the background of this emphasis of deism that the importance of Butler's *Analogy* is to be seen. Butler, by way of correcting the shallow optimism of the deists, may have gone to the other extreme, but he was certainly right to accentuate the gloomy aspect in contrast with the gaiety of deism. Against Tindal's assertion that nature is an open book in which anyone can read the facts of the Creator's existence, Butler showed that nature itself is mysterious and mystifying. Herein lies the supreme significance of the *Analogy*. It is important to remember that 'he is not arguing with atheists, but with Deists'.[2] The deists may reject vital doctrines of Christianity because they consider them to be unreasonable and mysterious, but if understandability and absence of mystery are the criteria, then, How can the deists be so sure that God created the world and set it off on its ordained path when there is so much evidence for the cruel, the unreasonable and the haphazard? Read in this context Butler's argument is certainly valid. If there is so much mystery in nature, is it not reasonable to suppose, on the principle of analogy, that there will be mystery also in God's special revelation? Divorced from its historical setting the *Analogy* is a weary and a dreary book. 'If we come to its perusal fresh from a course of reading in deistic literature; we should thankfully imbibe its teaching as a wholesome tonic after dipping into the honey-pots of optimism.'[3]

Then, secondly, by putting God out of touch with the world and beyond the experiences of men, it followed that the deists should

[1] Cf. 'In sober truth nearly all the things which men are hanged for or imprisoned are nature's everyday performances.' *Three Essays on Religion*, p. 28.
[2] C. D. Broad, *Religion, Philosophy and Psychical Research*, p. 20.
[3] A. B. Bruce, *Apologetics*, p. 126.

give exclusive place to the teleological argument for the existence
of God. They failed to appreciate that there were other points of
view. All 'transcendental theologies', indeed, seem committed to a
denial of the validity of the ontological proof. In this respect both
deist and orthodox alike followed Aquinas. The 'Angelic Doctor'
held that God is not the first to be known, but that we arrive at a
knowledge of Him by inference from the created world. E. L.
Mascall claims that this rejection of the ontological proof and
acceptance of the cosmological and teleological arguments as adequate is the 'traditional approach'.[1] His attempt to justify this
position in the 'Preface' cannot be considered convincing. To refer
to the Thomistic method as the 'traditional approach' is surely
straining the evidence. It was not, as a matter of fact, until the
time of Aquinas, for whom Aristotle was the supreme master, that
the idea of argument from nature to God found any significant
place. It has but to be remembered that the works of Aristotle had
only come to light again in the preceding century or two. The first
reaction to the rediscovered works of the Greek philosopher was so
much one of fear that the University of Paris solemnly condemned
them in 1215. It was not until we come to the time of Aquinas that
we find the heathen Greek baptized into the service of Christian
theology.

The Thomist, Gilson, rejecting the ontological argument, points
out that in Greek thought there is no trace of it. He explains the
fact like this, 'Thinkers like Plato and Aristotle, who do not identify God and being, could never dream of deducing God's existence from his idea; but when a Christian thinker like St Anselm
asks whether God exists he asks, in fact, whether Being exists, and
to deny God is to affirm that Being does not exist.'[2] His point,
however, proves something other than he intended. It shows that
the Greek approach of Aquinas is the essentially rationalistic
approach in distinction from the Anselmic. But as the Greek
approach of Aquinas was necessarily late it would be more just to
argue that the Anselmic is the specifically Christian 'traditional
approach'. Certainly Augustine, like Anselm, did not interpret
God through nature. For both, all experiences were to be understood in the light of the inner realization of God given in self-
conscious experience. All nature was to be understood through

[1] *He Who Is, A Study in Traditional Theism*, pp. 14–17.
[2] *Spirit of Mediaeval Philosophy* (E.T.), p. 59.

Him. 'How remarkable it is', exclaimed Pascal, 'that no biblical author makes use of nature to prove God!'[1] The traditional approach, then, seems to be, not through nature to God, but rather through God is nature interpreted and faith strengthened. However conclusive the Thomistic method has been considered in the past, and is still so to-day by such neo-Thomists as Maritain, Gilson, Box and Mascall, there are many not convinced that the conclusion is certain. There are those who maintain an opposite point of view.

Those, therefore, on the other side, whose religious philosophy gives greater emphasis to the immanence of God tend to make the ontological proof fundamental. Several writers would indeed maintain that all the so-called Theistic proofs begin from an already existing idea of Him. They contend that the proofs for the existence of God could never have been set on foot without prior belief in His existence, and the belief in His existence could never arise apart from God's own activity within. This means that some scholars can maintain that all cosmological arguments for the existence of God are based on the ontological, since there can be no belief in a transcendent Creator as such because that belief is itself evidence of His immanence.[2] Others press the point further and maintain that the ontological argument was not an attempt made by Anselm to prove the existence of God because it began with an already assured faith in Him. This is confirmed by the fact that Anselm's ontological argument occurs in his *Proslogion*, which is really a book of meditative prayer not a work on metaphysical philosophy.

Anselm himself, it is noted, affirmed that argument is belief in search of an understanding. The purpose of religious philosophy is not to originate a knowledge of God. Philosophy, indeed, in contrast with the exact sciences, does not lead to conclusions which lie in the realm of the completely unknown. Its purpose is rather to 'bring us to know in a different way things which we already knew in some other way'.[3]

The more writers on this side press the idea of the divine immanence the more they look within for the knowledge of God. Thus while all transcendent theologies make it a matter of

---

[1] Quoted in J. Baillie, *Interpretation of Religion*, p. 185.
[2] Cf. W. G. de Burgh, *Towards a Religious Philosophy*, ch. viii.
[3] R. G. Collingwood, *Philosophical Method*, p. 161.

inference, all immanentalist theologies make the knowledge of God a matter of intuition. Here again two points of view come into opposition.[1]

Our own conviction, however, believing as we do in the truth of what Archbishop Temple has described as the 'immanence of the Transcendence'[2] is, that this antithesis is false. The truth seems to be that in the act of religious knowledge there is a union of the two. There is, at the same time, an inference and an intuition. Rashdall refers to the exclamation of Helmholtz who had made some brilliant discovery: 'It was given me!' he said. But Rashdall's comment is a virtual contradiction of the statement, 'it was not true', he says, 'because it came to Helmholtz in this way, but because it was subsequently verified and proved.' This would seem, however, to make truth to depend upon verification — ultimately a pragmatist epistemology. Actually Helmholtz's words imply that it was more than an immediate inspiration. 'It was given me!' united with, 'I have got it!' There was both an intuition and an inference combining in the one act. In so far, therefore, as this conclusion is true, it means that the deist's complete repudiation of the intuitive and exaltation of the inferential method is not exact.

D. The deists made man a mere creature of reasoning and they failed to observe that, psychologically, religion is more deeply and broadly based. To identify revelation and reason is really to equate religion and philosophy. Herein lies one of the chief difficulties in all rationalistic theologies. Our interest in this place is not in a discussion of how the two may be said to be conterminous. Since both religion and philosophy are man's quest for ultimate reality it is evident that they must have elements in common.

It is, however, important to observe that religion and philosophy are not one and the same. 'The religious act or attitude,' says

---

[1] The same opposition has, of course, persisted. Cf., e.g. Hastings Rashdall, 'All religious truth, as I hold, depends logically upon inference,' again, 'I deny that the truth of God's existence can reasonably be accepted on the basis of an immediate judgement or intuition,' Hastings Rashdall, *Philosophy and Religion*, ch. II, cf., p. 106. See also, J. Caird, *The Introduction to the Philosophy of Religion*, ch. II. On the other side, cf., e.g. F. B. Jevons, 'All attempts to exhibit the existence of God as an inference from experience are foredoomed to failure.' *Religion and Evolution*, p. 134. Cf. also, 'The reality of the deity is not a *deduction* from religious experience, but the *content* of it — *that which is experienced*. If the immediate reality of the higher principle be taken away there could be nothing left of religious experience. It would no longer exist. But it does exist, and therefore that which is given and experienced in it exists also. *God is in us, therefore He is*.' Solovyof, *Justification of the Good* (E.T.), p. 164.

[2] *Nature, Man and God*, p. 277.

H. R. Mackintosh, 'is not merely a knowing act and attitude, otherwise it would be hard to distinguish it from science and philosophy.'[1] That the two are not to be equated should be obvious in spite of the rationalists' identification of them. There is a sense in which religion may be said to be, at the same time, narrower and wider than philosophy. One only needs to glance through the contents of any comprehensive text-book on Metaphysics to observe that there are many topics there dealt with which have no place in religion. Upon many subjects with which science has to concern itself, no Christian man would enter the claim that the interest is forbidden by religion. This does not mean that any doctrine of 'double truth' is permissible. Nor does it mean that religion is not concerned with the whole of life, but it does mean that there are provinces of philosophical enquiry and scientific investigation in which religion has no special concern.

On the other side of the paradox, it is equally true that religion is much wider than philosophy. If the two are to be identified then we would be committed to the fantastic position that the greater the philosopher the more truly religious he would be. This is obviously false. To be able to know is one thing, to be able to worship is another. A philosopher may seek to penetrate into the utmost secrets of the universe but the religious man must pray to the God of the universe. That which is the final problem for philosophy is the first assurance for the believer. Love, not learning, after all, is the primary truth about religion. The optimism which identifies knowledge with virtue has been so often proved false in the experiences of men that it is strange how it was raised by the rationalists to the final truth about human life.

The fact is that the religious kind of knowledge does not depend upon a man's metaphysical acumen. The peasant behind his plough may have a deeper religious understanding than the philosopher in his study. In the region of the spirit, the scientific and the academic are not the passport to greatness. As Schleiermacher long ago observed, if religion and philosophy were the selfsame thing then 'religion could be acquired by study — a thing not hitherto asserted'.[2] When one asks the question, To whom shall we go in our quest for an understanding of the deep things of the spirit? we are sure to be answered by the honest scientist and

---

[1] *The Christian Apprehension of God*, p. 36.
[2] *Reden*, tr. Oman, p. 102.

philosopher, who are only such, Come not to us for a knowledge of these things. We instinctively feel that one who is merely an adept in methodology is not the best man to meet the needs of an anxious enquirer. It was the washerwomen of Bedford who set John Bunyan on the way everlasting. This does not put a premium upon ignorance, but it is an assertion of the principle that it is the pure in heart who see God. It is to men of humble spirit that God discloses His secrets. On the final truths about God and man; life and death; sin and forgiveness; and the like issues of eternal significance, we rightly listen to the Man of Galilee rather than to the men of Greece. To Plato and Aristotle we may go if we would adventure into the secrets of metaphysical knowledge, but it is to Jesus Christ we must go if we would know of a Father and a Friend.

It is an error to take the thought-element in consciousness as the whole, since 'thought' and 'life' are not co-extensive. The human mind is not an active centre of energy which operates to trace out logical correlations or to observe uniform sequences. It is also a centre of value, or, perhaps more correctly, a subject of value. Religious knowledge cannot be limited to that which can be logically explained or expressed. Its deepest certainties lie outside the realm of the scientifically verifiable. 'Where God is present, He is active, and where He is active He needs no testimonial of character.'[1] God ever comes to the total life of man, not to the reason only, but to the whole psychical nature of the responding individual. And because this is so, God's revelation of Himself will not be irrational, on the one hand, nor can it be identified with reason on the other.

The deists would eliminate all that cannot be understood and yet they themselves begin from that which is an ultimate mystery, the inexplicable self. The paradox which dominates our spiritual life is, as Schweitzer has indicated, that if rational thought thinks itself out to a conclusion, it comes to something non-rational. As long as religion remains truly religion it must contain something which reason cannot fathom. It is true that a religion all mystery would be impossible for rational beings, but it is also true that a religion without mystery would be equally impossible for creatures who are more than intellect. Because religion is essentially a relation between a human self and a personal God there will be more in it

[1] H. Wheeler Robinson, *Redemption and Revelation*, p. 8.

than the reason will ever be able to comprehend. It is thus possible to accept the remark of Dean Mansel, 'Let Religion begin where it will it must begin with that which is above reason.'[1]

E. With a God completely indifferent and man inherently good and the world perfectly ordered, the question for the deist must arise, What need and what possibility are there for religion?

There is no need seeing that man has no urgent want to drive him out in search for an understanding and undertaking God. It is only when the soul cries out, 'O wretched man that I am! who shall deliver me from the body of this death?' (Rom. 7. 24), that there is the 'stuff' of religion. It is only when one is aware of the fact, that 'In me, that is, in my flesh dwelleth no good thing' (Rom. 7. 18), will one seek a Redeemer. Where there is no feeling of guilt there can be no need for God. Knowledge of sin is, after all, as Kierkegaard says, 'possible only in the presence of God.'[2]

On the other hand there is no possibility of religion in deism with its 'God' on the limits far withdrawn. 'The God of Deism', says Emil Brunner, 'is one who, after the creation of the world, withdrew to His own heritage, He is a God who has said farewell and gone away,'[3] this is the conception of God lashed by the ridicule of Goethe:

> 'What kind of God were this, who only from without
>   would move the world,
>   Letting the universe flow in circles round his finger?'

Certainly with a God of this kind revelation is impossible and prayer inadmissible.

The design of God, Tindal informs us, was to make men happy, and for this purpose the rules of rational religion were made known to all mankind. But, on the one hand, there is evidence enough that those who would live godly in the present world are not always happy; and, on the other hand, it may well be questioned if such a hedonist ideal is valid. Is it not more certainly the purpose of God to make men holy? The ultimate command of the Gospel is in fact: 'Be ye holy, for I am holy, saith the Lord.'

To such a statement, then, of revelation as infallible reason, a reaction was bound to set in. It was defective from every point of

---

[1] *The Limits of Human Thought*, p. 182.
[2] Quoted in E. Brunner, *Philosophy of Religion*, p. 78.
[3] E. Brunner, *Revelation and Reason*, p. 356.

view. 'Deism', says M. Reville, 'in sound philosophy is not tenable. It establishes a dualism, a veritable opposition between God and the world, which stand opposite to and limit each other . . . . A reaction in fact was inevitable. It was necessary that it should be at the same time philosophical and religious, and should come to the satisfaction of the needs that had been misunderstood or suppressed. In philosophy Deism could no longer hold up its head against the objections of reason. In religion, every one was weary of optimism and of empty declamations. Deism removed God so far from the world and from humanity that piety exhausted itself in the endeavour to rejoin Him in the icy heights of heaven, and ended by renouncing the attempt.'[1]

This discussion, it is worth while to point out, is not merely of historical interest. If deism, as such, quickly passed away, killed by the necessity for a religion to meet men's more fundamental needs, its main concepts found expression elsewhere. Its notion of God as remote and out of reach was erected into a more dignified philosophy by Kant. While its equation of religion and philosophy was given a more confident and a more plausible emphasis by Hegel. Today the same view is set forth with new vigour by the neo-Idealism of Benedetto Croce and Giovanni Gentile. These writers view religion as immature philosophy which is doomed to extinction when man reaches his intellectual stature. This excess of confidence in reason we have seen to be untenable. There is a knowledge wider and more satisfying than that which reason alone can discover.

[1] Quoted in J. Orr, *Christian View of God and the World*, p. 395.

CHAPTER IV

THE AUTHORITY OF THE SUBJECTIVE

I t is now necessary, so that we may have a full account of the types of revelation in our period, and a better understanding of the orthodox apologetic, to refer to a doctrine which may be more familiar to the general reader. Because of this acquaintance, no prolonged exposition need be attempted. Certain criticisms, however, which the doctrine demands will be made and certain contrasts which were implied will be investigated.

REVELATION AS INDWELLING LIGHT

(i) *An Understanding of the View*

It is not easy for us at this distance either to appreciate, on the one hand, the desires which gave birth to the spirit of 'enthusiasm', or, on the other hand, the repugnance with which it was regarded by the orthodox. In what has come to be called 'Enthusiasm', there was a reaction, and at times a violent one, from all ruling objective standards, whether Church or Scripture. To those who repudiated such outside curbs, revelation was regarded as something internal. It thus appeared excusable for each individual to do that which was right in his own eyes.

In some cases this doctrine developed as an avowed rejection of the Calvinist teaching of an elect number of saved souls for whom alone an atonement had been made. To stress the universal influence of Christ, emphasis was placed upon the Johannine declaration that, He was the light that lighteth every man that cometh into the world. For this reason, Henry Denne, for example, in a tract entitled, *The Draw-net of the Kingdom of Heaven*,[1] advocated the doctrine of the Indwelling Light. Denne is called by Thomas Edwards in his *Gangraena*, 'an antinomian and desperate Arminian,' who boldly asserts, 'that Jesus Christ has

---

[1] The full title of the work is, *Draw-net of the Kingdom of Heaven, or Christ Drawing all Men* (1646). Denne was a graduate of Cambridge who had received ordination into the Established Church. He later became a Baptist.

died for all men, Turks and Pagans' for 'Judas as well as Peter'.[1]

Numerous indeed were the companies of those who looked for the inner revelation of the light. Something of their variety can be found in a pamphlet which appeared in London in 1652, under the enchanting title, *The Pulpit Guarded by XVII Arguments*. The author, a Puritan Divine at Henley-in-Arden, volunteers the information; 'We have many sects now abroad, Ranter(s), Seekers, Shakers, Quakers and now Creepers.'[2] This list is by no means complete, for in another passage others are mentioned: and there are still to be added the Familists and Muggletonians and others of lesser account. But however these sects differed from each other, and whatever the precise relation between them, the general characteristic of all was that which goes under the description, given in opprobrium, Enthusiasm.

The doctrine of the indwelling light manifested itself in a particularly crude form among the Ranters, but in a more spiritual manner among the Quakers. The excesses of the Ranters were certainly abhorrent to the Friends, as their early literature abundantly testifies. A dark picture is given of the former in the *Ranters' Bible*, by one, Gilbert Roulston who, for a number of years, had been among them. They laid emphasis upon the sufficiency of the indwelling light, but were completely antinomian. That numbers of them were, what would be termed in these days neurotics, is beyond dispute. Ranterism was a 'Free Spirit' movement, which discarded all external standards. Unlike the Seekers, the Ranters did not allow to the Scriptures the position even of a 'secondary help'. They were thus their own sole authority, each finding, like Descartes, his sufficient assurance within his own subjectivity.

'The Seeker movement had undervalued objective religion and outward helps. The natural result was that those who pushed the ideas of the Seekers to their extreme limit and, throwing overboard all outward systems, acknowledged nothing Divine except the Spirit in themselves, had no fixed authority anywhere, no criterion of morals, no test of spiritual guidance, no ground and basis for goodness. Being "taught by the Spirit", they claimed that all

---

[1] Op. cit., p. 91. Edwards writes again: 'He professes all the Arminian Doctrines. That Christ died for all, and for Judas in particular and that he was confident: That he died for all, as well as for any,' p. 49. This page is out of place, following p. 76. In this the copy in Dr Williams' Library agrees with that in the British Museum.
[2] Op. cit., p. 15.

other teachings were of no use. They called the Scriptures "a tale", "a history, a dead letter," "a fleshly story, a cause of divisions and contradictions." They looked upon Christ as a "figure" or "type" of the TRUE DISPENSATION OF THE SPIRIT, upon which they claimed to have entered.'[1]

Arising out of their doctrine of the indwelling light in all men, the Ranters went on to assert a crude pantheism. 'There were probably varieties of Ranters theologically. Pantheism, or the essential identity of God with the universe, and His indwellings in every creature, angelic, human, brute or inorganic, seems to have been the belief of most of the Ranters that could manage to rise to metaphysics.'[2] God was in all and thus was all good and nothing to be refused. It was this conception which led the Ranters into the excesses of antinomianism which spread throughout the land both moral disease and religious fanaticism. So disturbing indeed was their influence that Parliament had to act to curb the tendencies which were making for 'the dissolution of human society'.[3]

It was perhaps such excesses which led Isaac Taylor, the recluse of Stamford Rivers, in the first half of the eighteenth century, to investigate the phenomenon. He published his conclusions in a book entitled, *The Natural History of Enthusiasm*. Possibly a statement by Locke concerning his *Essay on Enthusiasm* gave to Taylor his inspiration for the work. Locke had excused his own limited treatment of the subject by saying, 'To give an historical account of the various ravings men have embraced for religion under the name enthusiasm, would, I fear, be beside my purpose, and be enough to make a huge volume.' It was left to Taylor to supply this defect. The author certainly looked back to the past, for, he observes, his own age cannot be considered 'eminently or conspicuously an age of religious enthusiasm'.[4]

Some enthusiasm he traces to infirm constitutions,[5] other to an over-lively imagination, and, yet other to an exclusive preoccupation with prophetical interpretation,[6] and so forth. 'A chronic

---

[1] Rufus M. Jones, *Studies in Mystical Religion*, p. 469.

[2] D. Mason, *Life of Milton*, vol. 5, p. 18.

[3] 'Preamble to act of Parliament of blasphemous and execrable Opinions, Aug. 9th, 1650,' Scobell's *Collection of Acts and Ordinances*, pt. ii, p. 124.

[4] *Natural History of Enthusiasm* (2nd edition), p. 16.

[5] Cf., 'There was an element of fierce fanaticism in the movement, and among the Ranters there were some real lunatics.' R. M. Jones, *Studies in Mystical Religion*, p. 469 (Footnote).

[6] Cf., 'The adoption of an exclusive theory of exposition will not fail to be followed by an attempt to attach the special marks of prophecy to every passing

intellectual enthusiasm' he makes the source of heresy. In considering that unrestrained enthusiasm of which the earlier Ranters were such a tragic illustration, Taylor makes many cogent points. He who knows that he is really separated from God, not simply by means of distance which he can himself cross, but by a chasm which he cannot bridge, will not be tempted to give expression to the ravings of the enthusiasts. 'In a word,' he says, 'it may be confidently affirmed that no man becomes an enthusiast in religion, until he has forgotten that he is a transgressor — a transgressor reconciled to God by mediation.'[1] The great need of the enthusiast is for a profound awareness of his deficiencies. 'Genuine humility would shake the whole towering structure of this enthusiastic pietism.'[2] It is pride which inflates a person into enthusiasm. If, therefore, the sad error of the enthusiast lies in his thinking of himself more highly than he ought to think; the fundamental weakness is to be found in his 'outlawry from common sense and scriptural authority'.[3]

But it was in a form less violent and antinomian that the early Friends expressed their doctrine of the inner light. This milder manifestation was not however limited to the Quaker movement, since, as Dr Rufus Jones says in his Introduction to W. C. Braithwaite's, *Beginnings of Quakerism*, 'There were numerous persons, both outside and inside the Quaker group, who quite independently of George Fox, had the insight that religion, to be true and spiritual must be "well grounded in the witness of the Spirit".'[4] It is among the Friends, however, that we find societies organized to give expression and witness to the view. 'This doctrine of the inner light', it has been justly observed, 'was the only positive assertion that the Friends were prepared to make.'[5] But it is in the Quaker movement that it is seen at its best.

'The important fact is obvious enough, that here in the English Commonwealth there now appeared a group of persons — plain, simple, persons without technical learning — who succeeded in passing from knowledge about God, knowledge that consisted of demonstration from Scripture texts, "notional knowledge", they

event, and it is this attempt which sets enthusiasm in flame.' *The Natural History of Enthusiasm*, p. 115.
[1] *Natural History of Enthusiasm*, p. 49.
[2] Op. cit., p. 37.
[3] Op. cit., p. 79.
[4] *Beginnings of Quakerism*, Preface, p. xxviii.
[5] *Enthusiasm*, R. Knox, p. 156.

aptly called it, to inward, first-hand experience which was so vivid, so warm and intimate, so mightily transforming, that they one and all were convinced that they had found God in the present tense.'[1]

In the early pages of his *Journals*, George Fox tells how the understanding of the inner light came to him as a vivid and vital experience, an experience which put him, he believed, into marked contrast with the prevailing temper of his age. The period was one in which the idea of an immediate revelation was, for the most part, incomprehensible. Revelation was thought to be embodied in propositions to which an unquestioning assent had to be made; so ran the general view. Knowledge of God was thus second-hand, distant and dim. It was to the light within, George Fox asserts again and again, that he owed his understanding of God. He was led to see, he tells us, that the Light and Spirit had come before the Scripture, and, therefore, did not ultimately depend upon it. This light within, he proclaims, was given to all men. 'Now the Lord opened to me by his invisible power, that everyman was enlightened by the Divine Light of Christ; I saw it shine through all; and they that believed in it came out of condemnation to the light of life, and became children of it; but they that hated it, and believed not in it, were condemned by it, though they made a profession of Christ.'[2]

In the preface to the first edition of the *Journals* which appeared in 1694, three years after Fox's death William Penn lays it down as the Quaker's special contribution secured by their leader that, 'In his testimony on ministry he much laboured to open truth to the people's understandings, and to bottom them upon the principle, Christ Jesus the Light of the World, that by bringing them to something that was God in themselves, they might the better know and judge of Him and themselves.'[3]

Fox, according to his own story, had read the Scriptures, and listened to many preachers, but his spiritual condition was nothing bettered, but rather grew worse. He had to learn that God dealt with men directly and through the light within.[4] In the record of

---

[1] *Beginnings of Quakerism*, Preface, p. xxxvii.
[2] *Journal* (8th edition), p. 34.
[3] *Journal* (1st edition, 1694), Preface, p. xlvii.
[4] The following passage, taken without translation from Norman Penny's edition, 1911 (Cambridge University Press), illustrates Fox's position. 'I declared ye everlastinge truth of ye Lorde & ye worde of life (for severall houres) & yᵗ ye Lord & Christ Jesus was come to teach his people himselfe & to bringe yᵐ of all ye worlds ways & teachers to Christ there way to God: & layde open all

George Fox, then, we find him giving testimony to the universal indwelling light. 'In a day of shams,' writes William James with some warmth, 'it was a religion of veracity rooted in spiritual inwardness, and a return to something more like the original gospel truth than men had ever known in England.'[1]

It was twenty-five years before the eighteenth century dawned that Robert Barclay set forth this doctrine of the indwelling light in theological form. It is the mission of the Friends, he says, 'to preach Christ, and direct people to His pure Light in the heart.'[2] He finds, it is significant to observe, justification for his position in the writings of the Cambridge Platonist, John Smith, quoting from his *Discourses*, those passages in which a mere 'notional knowledge' of God is repudiated.[3] The tragedy of his day he sees in the rejection of the very doctrines for which he contends: 'nothing is less minded and more rejected by all sorts of Christians, *than immediate and divine revelation*; in so much that once to lay claim to it is matter of reproach.'[4] It is declared that the sons of God are led by the Spirit of God, yet anyone claiming to be so led is called 'an heretic' by the 'pretended orthodox'. It is this inner revealing of God which alone gives certain knowledge, for it is a direct manifestation of God within the heart; a very different thing this from 'soaring, airy head-knowledge'.

Passage after passage reiterates the thesis, 'that inner and immediate revelation is the only sure and certain way to the true saving knowledge of God.'[5] There is a knowledge of God claimed by some, but it is merely learnt off like the prattling of a parrot. The Socinians are rebuked for denying the inner operations of the Spirit and yet teaching that there is a light inherent in man. There is none however 'barbarous and wild' who has not 'found something in his heart reproving him for something evil which he has done'.[6] This 'something' is not to be equated with reason or conscience. It is a divine light, or, as he sometimes calls it, a 'seed' within the soul. The sum of what he has to teach is, he says, 'That

---

there teachers & sett uppe ye true teacher (Christ Jesus): & how they was judged by ye prophetts Christ & ye apostles & to bring y^m off ye temples made with hands y^t they y^mselves might know they was ye temples of God,' p. 42.

[1] W. James, *The Varieties of Religious Experience*, p. 7.
[2] R. Barclay, *Apology*, (10th edition, 1841), p. 169.
[3] Op. cit., p. 21.
[4] Op. cit., p. 17.
[5] Op. cit., p. 23.
[6] Op. cit., p. 126.

where the true inward knowledge of God is, through the revelation of his Spirit, there is all; neither is there an absolute necessity of any other.'[1] In every man, then, there is a light or seed of God; such did George Fox believe to be a true induction from his own experience, and such, too, was the view set forth by Barclay in theological form.

It was the conviction of the Quaker theologian that this doctrine of the indwelling light relieved men from 'the horrors of Calvinism'. But the escape was apparent only. In a manner which the Genevan theologian would have commended, Barclay stresses man's utter corruption and inability.[2] Even the light within is regarded as in no sense inherent in man *qua* man. It is to be likened to a candle in a lantern. But it is just here that 'the horrors of Calvinism' which Barclay had supposed himself to have escaped, is reintroduced by the back door, although Barclay, apparently, is unaware of the fact. All men have the indwelling light and by many it is rejected, with the consequence that the candle in the lantern goes black out, to leave the abandoned soul in the slough of eternal perdition.[3] Man can do nothing of himself to bring salvation within his reach. He must 'wait' the movement of the Spirit, and 'not resist' when it comes. But even these attitudes are not man's to achieve: they are the results of a supernaturally bestowed gift of faith. 'Faith', says Isaac Penington, one of the early Quakers, 'is not found in man's nature, so that it is a gift to be waited for and obtained from God.' Here we are back at a predestinarianism, no less strong, even if unconscious, as that of either Augustine or Calvin.

From this statement of the doctrine of revelation as indwelling light three deficiencies can be seen to follow. It falls, therefore, to consider

(ii) *The Weaknesses of the View*

A. First of all account must be taken of the total exclusion of reason. Barclay limits the activity of reason to 'things natural': it

---

[1] Op. cit., p. 24.

[2] Cf., *Proposition* iv, 'Concerning the Condition of Man in the Fall,' pp. 89–101. 'All Adam's posterity, or mankind, both Jews and Gentiles, as to the first Adam, or earthly man, is fallen, degenerated, and dead: deprived of the sensation of feeling of this inward testimony or seed of God; and is subject to the power, nature and seed of the serpent . . . , etc.'

[3] Cf., 'This divine and glorious life is in all men as a seed which of its own nature draws, invites, and inclines to God,' *Apology*, p. 129.

F

can have no place in 'things spiritual'. Indeed, in the realm of the spirit, reason is an obstacle, a stumbling-block, in the way of spiritual progress: 'the place where God dwells and manifests Himself was in men's hearts.'[1] Truth is consequently something experienced. It is significant that William James found the views of the Quakers congenial. His own *Pragmatism* is but the theoretic exposition of that which George Fox and his followers were here maintaining. Truth is based upon experience, it is, in fact, made by experience, and is estimated to be truth in so far as it does good to the soul. This is nothing other than the religious application of pragmatism; a principle valid enough in its way, but crippled by its complete subjectivity.

The early advocates of the doctrine of the indwelling light failed altogether to understand the place of reason in religious experience. The reason for this failure on their part may be twofold. The position they took up was one of reaction from the 'intellectualism' of the orthodox. But they were, as well, certainly hampered by their environment of ideas. It was the general notion that reason and reasoning were to be equated, and its only function was regarded as the setting forth of clear and distinct ideas. The Quakers had therefore no true psychology; no sufficient understanding of man's psychical make-up. Perhaps it is too much to expect that in the period in which they lived they should have grasped that 'there is no separate organ for the apprehension of divine truth, independent of the will, feeling and thought. Our knowledge of God comes to us in the interplay of those faculties'.[2] They did not see the full significance of the very chapter in John's Gospel to which they made such constant appeal: not only is Christ there revealed as the Light; He is the Logos also. It was this exclusion of reason which made inadequate their religious psychology. Although their misological attitude was limited to 'things spiritual' it is clear that it is just here that the real place of reason must be understood. Religion is essentially a relation, a relationship with God; it is, therefore, a relationship which involves the whole man in all the elements of his psychological nature. If it is not a contradiction in terms, it should be stated that there is no true religious epistemology which excludes from its account the activity of reason in the experience of religion.

[1] W. C. Braithwaite, *The Beginnings of Quakerism*, p. 34.
[2] W. Inge, *Personal Idealism and Mysticism*, p. 3.

B. Consequent upon this exclusion of reason and emphasis upon the indwelling light there followed an assertion of individual infallibility. When once all objective standards are swept aside and the subjective criterion is installed and crowned as all-sufficient, there seems little possibility of escape from the claim to personal infallibility. The early Quakers found themselves the object of such an accusation. The charge was not indeed without some real support, since some, at least, of the original Friends did not hesitate to make the claim. 'They believed', observes Braithwaite, 'that inspiration gave infallibility.'[1] That which others regarded as limited to the writers of the Scriptures they believed that they themselves possessed. 'In the light I met with infallibility,' says Penington, 'there the light of God's spirit is a certain infallible rule, and the eye that sees is a certain eye.' Justification for the view seemed clear enough. The indwelling light came from above, from God. Those who followed the light were 'the children of God', and it increased more and more until the perfect day. By coupling their experience of the indwelling light with their doctrine of Perfectionism there was the resultant notion of an almost complete identification with God. Thus George Fox can say 'he that hath the same spirit that raised up Jesus Christ is equal with God . . . which is a mystery . . . . According to the flesh I am the son of Abraham, According to the Spirit the Son of God, saith Christ'. Such an assertion was bound to lead to misunderstanding. He found it hard to explain himself and was, as a matter of fact, charged with blasphemy for making himself equal with God. That Fox was well satisfied with his own interpretation there can be no doubt, but his distinctions were not easily grasped by men of the world. As the quotation given above indicates, his point was that it was the spiritual man which is from above, that is one with God in Christ. Speaking in the saints, the Man from Heaven is the infallible one. But however much the position may be 'explained' and 'illustrated' it remains true that the early Friends, or some of them at least by actual claim, and all of them by the logic of their doctrine, did think of themselves as possessing infallibility. This was the natural conclusion to their teaching of revelation as indwelling light.

C. From the two points we have already made it was a further natural consequence that among the Friends there should be a

[1] *The Beginnings of Quakerism*, p. 109.

depreciation of the Scriptures. Fox stressed that the light came to him apart from the Scriptures. Barclay refers to those who agree that God is known only by an inward revelation but assert that such knowledge is mediated through the written word. He sees no possibility of, and no need for, such documentary mediation. Since all is ascribed to the action of the Spirit, the Scriptures are not to be given this intermediate position: 'the Spirit, and not the Scripture, is the foundation and ground of all truth and knowledge, and the primary rule of faith and manners.'[1] He uses a number of arguments designed to remove it from the exalted position given to it by the orthodox: arguments which were used later with such eloquent force by the deist, Tindal. Barclay would prove that God acts apart from the Scriptures since there are unlearned men who cannot read, and numbers of variant readings which put ordinary folk in doubt.

He will, however, allow to the Scriptures a 'second place'. Scripture would seem to be for Barclay as it is for Karl Barth a mere 'witness' to revelation as God chooses to make it. It is an attestation that God speaks and acts because it is a record that He has spoken and acted in the past.[2] Like Barth too, Barclay seems to teach that revelation is an act of God apart from the written word. Revelation is essentially and at all times *Dei loquentis persona*. It is God speaking, or, alternatively, Christ speaking.[3] In a manner, too, worthy of Brunner, Barclay likens the Scriptures to a 'looking-glass' and a 'window'.[4] Consonant also with his thesis, and like Brunner, he sees no conclusive reason to believe in a 'filled canon'.[5]

This doctrine of revelation which received its more spiritual significance and expression in the Quaker movement was, how-

---

[1] *Apology*, p. 67.
[2] Cf. K. Barth, *Church Dogmatics* (E.T., Professor G. T. Thomson), 1, i, pp. 57 f., 125 f., etc.
[3] Cf., *Church Dogmatics*, 1, i, p. 155 f.
[4] Cf., 'Just as the windowpanes are not there to be looked at, but to enable us to look through them at the view beyond, so we are not commanded to believe the Bible, but, through the window of the Bible, to see God's light,' E. Brunner, *Revelation and Reason*, pp. 181–2.
[5] *Apology*, p. 86. Cf., 'The dogma of the canon, like every other ecclesiastical decision of faith is not final and infallible, but it is possible and right continually to reexamine it, test it, and revise it.' Brunner acknowledges that the canonical decisions of the Early Church are not to be lightly set aside; and that there is a strong presumption that its decisions are likely to be accepted. He asserts however, that 'It would be easier, indeed, to envisage a reduction of the New Testament canon, such as Luther suggested'. *Revelation and Reason*, p. 132.

ever, in a very real way conditioned by the prevalent philosophical and religious Weltanschauung. It is this fact which distinguished it from a view which came afterwards into prominence, and which will be discussed later under the title, Revelation as Immediate Experience. The background of the doctrine here under review, Revelation as Indwelling Light, was the accepted dualism of the day, in which God and man, spiritual and natural, stood apart from each other. The Light or Seed within was, as we have seen, no part of man's nature. It was a foreign element. The line between human and divine was sharply drawn, and it was believed that never the twain could meet.[1]

Any suggestion that the light of God's spirit belonged to man's nature *per se* was obnoxious to the early Friends. It was a satanic temptation to be resisted. George Fox tells how he passed through such a period of darkness in which the devil had unleashed all his fury. But he came through to noonday and victory. On another occasion, in the Vale of Belvoir, a dark cloud overshadowed him and so completely obliterated was the world of spirit that, almost overwhelmed, he was tempted to say, 'All things came by Nature.' To speak thus was tantamount to declaring, 'There is no God.' It was only as he sat still and gave no heed to it, that at length hope arose within him, and the steadying assurance returned, 'There is a living God Who made all things.'[2]

It was the constant affirmation of William Penn, in his *Primitive Christianity Revived*, that the light within is, 'in man but not of man.' It is natural to men, he asserts, to have a supernatural light.[3]

'The light of which we speak', declares Barclay, 'is not only distinct, but of a different nature from the soul and its faculties.'[4] The relation of the divine to the human was conceived somewhat

---

[1] It would be interesting to draw out further parallels between the Quaker theologian and Barth. For Barth, God is conceived to be 'actus purus' (*Church Dogmatics*, 1, i, p. 44). Like Barclay he teaches that there is no continued and natural relation between God and man. Both begin from the idea of the divine transcendence. It would compromise the sovereignty of God if He were involved in the worldly process. It is incorrect, therefore, to speak of God as 'immanent' in the sense of a continuity between the divine and the human. More correct is it as W. F. Camfield interprets, to speak of the idea of 'immanence' as meaning that 'there is transcendence in the world'. (*Revelation and the Holy Spirit*, p. 157, cf., K. Barth, *Credo*, p. 34.) This means for Barth as it does for Barclay that there is no real identity between the word of Scripture and the Word of God (cf., *Church Dogmatics*, 1, i, pp. 310–11).
[2] *Journal*, p. 26.
[3] *Primitive Christianity Revived* (1606), 3, i, 2.
[4] *Apology*, props., 12, 14, 16.

after the fashion of a lighted candle within a darksome cave, or a lamp in a dismal dungeon. Those who preached the doctrine of a light within could not conceive of it as in any sense natural to the human spirit: to have done so would have been for them the denial of revelation and the expression of an undisguised Pelagianism. Thus while in their theology they repudiated any idea of a divine immanence, in their experience they allowed its reality. But it was just here, in the next era, those who emphasized the subjective element, in opposition to the sterile objectivity of the orthodox, found the starting-point of their view. Under the influence of a rising idealistic philosophy, the dualistic conception of the universe was giving way. Stress was put upon the divine immanence, and the clear-cut separation between natural and spiritual was abandoned. Neither nature nor man was considered to have existence apart from God. There was a natural unity between the divine and human; and it was urged that in the inmost depths of his being every individual was akin to God. The Spirit of God was immanent in the life of man, not as an alien element, but as a natural reality. It was, then, under the impact of an idealistic philosophy that later writers are to be found expounding their view of revelation within the immediacy of experience.

With the triumph of idealism, a point was to be reached when Sabatier could maintain: 'Supernatural gifts become natural; or rather, at this mystic height, the antithesis becomes meaningless and obliterated.'[1]

---

[1] A. Sabatier, *Religions of Authority and the Religion of the Spirit* (E.T.), p. 307.

CHAPTER V

THE THESIS OF THE ORTHODOX

Those who, in the period of our review, have come to be designated, *The Orthodox*, regarded both Dogmatism and Enthusiasm with unaffected horror. The orthodox apologists saw in deism an impossible exaggeration of reason, while the Methodist Movement was considered to be a new exhibition of enthusiasm. Thus, Bishop Butler, for example, in an interview with John Wesley dismissed the leader of Methodism as one such misguided fanatic. 'Mr Wesley,' said the bishop, 'I will deal plainly with you: I once thought you and Mr Whitfield well-meaning men, but I cannot think so now, for I have heard more of you — matters of fact, Sir. And Mr Whitfield says in his *Journal*, "There are promises still to be fulfilled in me." Sir, this pretending to extraordinary revelation and gifts of the Holy Ghost is a horrid thing, a very horrid thing.'[1]

Against these two branded enemies the orthodox felt it necessary to enter into battle. To undermine deism they had to exhibit the reality and utility of a revealed religion; to the enthusiast they had to prove its objectivity and authority.

Broadly the deists argued that the only revelation men were given or needed was the moral dicta written into the constitution of the universe, and discoverable by all rational beings. What the intelligence could not encompass cannot belong to the essence of religion. Opposing deism, the orthodox apologists sought to defend revealed religion by reason, and at the same time to indicate the defects of reason as an instrument.

The two fundamental assumptions of deism, namely, that reason was in no way inadequate, and that revelation was in no way limited were the focal points of the orthodox attack. Apart from the negative method of demolition, the two main positive arguments towards the establishing of a revealed religion, were, first, to show that reason itself could not go the whole way. Then, secondly,

[1] Quoted in Overton and Relton, *History of the English Church*, vol. 7, p. 93.

to show that the element of mystery was no objection to revealed religion since, 'as large a bill of complaints,'[1] can be brought against natural religion. This argument was pressed with polished vigour by Butler. The central problem of the discussion 'was to discover the valid, rational grounds for belief in Christianity, and to decide between rival claims of reason and revelation'.[2]

The general view taken by the orthodox was that revealed religion was a necessary adjunct to natural religion. They thus argued for

REVELATION AS COMMUNICATED EXTRAS

In two respects there was not much to choose between deism and its orthodox opponents. Firstly, neither side had any real insight into the meaning of history. The problems of theology were constructed in the abstract; they were unrelated to the development of the past. The defenders of revealed religion viewed history as divided into two separate periods, with revelation the special characteristic of the earlier. Since revelation was indicated in prophecy and attested by miracles, questions concerning both came necessarily into prominence.

Then, secondly, in the statement of their case both sides gave to reason the prior place. Already before the eighteenth century dawned, Tillotson, as we saw, gave expression to views which led directly to deism. At the same time he is to be found setting down the lines which the orthodox apologists were to follow. 'Natural religion', he says, 'is the foundation of revealed, and revelation is designed simply to establish its duties.'[3]

The battle with the deists had been joined and the method of attack made clear before the eighteenth century began. A year after the publication of Toland's *Christianity not Mysterious*, in 1696, came such replies as Browne's *Answer to Toland*, Prideaux's *Letter to the Deists*, and Leslie's *Short and Easy Method with the Deists*. Leslie's reply is neither short nor easy and it worked no magic in demolishing deism. Prideaux asked his opponents, 'whether the Christian religion be in truth really given by divine revelation from God our Creator; or else a human invention contrived by the first propagators of it to impose a cheat upon man-

---

[1] William Law, *The Case of Reason*, p. 66.
[2] V. Storr, *The Development of English Theology in the Nineteenth Century*, p. 46.
[3] *Works*, (Edition, 1857), vol. 2, p. 333.

kind?'[1] He concludes that there is only one answer, for Christianity bears all the marks of its supernatural origin.

(i) *The Basis of Revealed Religion*

The fundamental importance and the prior position of natural religion is axiomatic to the apologists. Thus Bishop Butler can say, 'Natural religion is the foundation and principal part of Christianity.'[2] Ably as Butler answered the deists, he worked from the same premise as they. His position is that Christianity is essentially a republication of natural religion, with the exception that revealed religion adds some essentials which natural religion lacked. It is by the medium of natural religion, Butler argued, that the significance of the divine Fatherhood is discovered. The further relationship to the Son and the Spirit is brought about by revealed. Reason constitutes the prior relation, revelation indicates the second. 'The essence of Natural Religion may be said to consist in religious regard to God, the Father; and the essence of revealed Religion, as distinguished from Natural, to consist in religious regard for the Son and the Spirit.'[3]

In the Boyle lectures of 1705, Dr Samuel Clarke likewise based the extras of revealed religion upon the assurances and obligations made certain by natural religion. H. Stebbing in his *Defence of Dr Clarke* writes of the Gospel as 'an Instrument to restore Natural Religion'.[4] To believe it to be anything other than this would be to misunderstand the significance of both. Leyland, who became Butler's successor in the bishopric of Bristol, believed that reason itself could discover with certainty the facts of God's existence and attributes. He maintained that God's moral attributes are also fully comprehensible to the human understanding. Equally known to the single individual, without any special revelation, is his duty towards God and man. Even the meanest of men have sufficient knowledge of the general points of morality.

Sykes insists that there is an unchangeable law of action to which all reasonable beings are necessarily committed. The law of human action is the eternal law of truth to which even God Himself must conform, for 'the will of God itself is governed and

---

[1] *Letter to the Deists*, p. 5.
[2] *The Analogy* (New edition), p. 195.
[3] Op. cit., p. 202.
[4] *A Defence of Dr Clarke's, Evidences of Natural and Revealed Religion*, p. 5.

directed by Truth'.[1] To conform to this law, which reason can discover, is the whole duty of man. Indeed man's actual conformation to this law is itself religion. Sykes seems to make little, if any, distinction between religion and morality. 'Nor ought Religion', he writes, 'to be distinguished from Morality, as if it had no Relation or Concern with it.'[2] It is known by all people in every age that virtue should be practised. 'The Gentiles had not their moral knowledge from Revelation.'[3] Yet they still knew God and His attributes; their social relation and their duties; the truth of a future state and the reality of punishments and rewards. 'And if it appears that they had right Notions concerning their Duties, and had right Principles sufficient to lead them to right Action, it will follow, that the Light of Reason is not that uncertain, weak insufficient, inconsistent thing, that is by some pretended; nor ought it to be treated as something carnal and dim.'[4] Sykes sets out a long catalogue of items which the moral philosophers of heathendom designated either good or bad. It was the light of reason which was for them the sufficient guide. He goes so far as to contend that the gospel has nothing to add to the eternal rules of truth. 'Jesus Christ never particularly or directly intimated any Design to vary from the Law of Nature; Nay, by his preaching upon the Doctrine of Repentance, he called Men back to that Law, as what they had violated by Sin.'[5] Revelation is therefore but a reinforcing argument providing new motives for the fulfilment of natural duties.

Sykes, it must be allowed, goes further in his approximation to deism than most of those who were its opponents. Nevertheless it was the fundamental assumption of all the orthodox apologists that natural religion is no meagre affair. It has provided men with a large quota of religious necessities.

In proclaiming that natural religion is the basis of revealed the apologists of the eighteenth century were merely reiterating the traditional Thomistic doctrine. It is well known that Aquinas in the thirteenth century, by the use of the Aristotelian logic, built up his natural theology in the confidence that reason could go a long way along the road to a knowledge of God. Revelation comes in then to fill up that which is behind in the searchings of reason.

[1] *The Principles and Connection of Natural and Revealed Religion, etc.*, p. 19.
[2] Op. cit., p. 94.
[3] Op. cit., p. 434.
[4] Op. cit., p. 385.
[5] Ibid.

For Aquinas there is no ontological argument possible, for that would start from a prior recognition of God's existence. The mind, to begin with, has no innate ideas; knowledge is built up, little by little, on the basis of sense experience. A divine intuition is for Aquinas in this life impossible. 'In those things which we hold about God there is truth in two ways. For certain things that are true about God wholly surpass the capability of human reason; for instance, that God is three in one: while there are certain things to which even natural reason can attain; for instance, that God is, that God is one, and other like things, which even the philosophers proved demonstratively of God, being guided by the light of natural reason.'[1]

The eighteenth-century apologists, then, began with the acceptance of this Thomistic dichotomy of natural and revealed religion, in which division of labour, each part contributes its own separate elements. They wholeheartedly believed that reason was sufficient of itself to discover certain fundamental truths to which other knowledge is added as a divinely disclosed extra, a *donum super-additum*. Revealed religion was like a second volume designed to extend the knowledge already given in the first. As volume one was the foundation and principal part of religion attention was naturally focused upon it. Were not the main facts of religion, after all, matters of general concern? And thus they must be capable of advocacy and proof by plain common sense. Common sense was indeed the watchword of the age. 'The defect of the eighteenth century', observes Mark Pattison 'was not in having too much good sense, but in having nothing besides.'[2] It was as a result of this that natural and revealed religion were somehow brought into opposition. 'Revelation may serve, perhaps, to introduce the conclusions of natural religion to people who are too simple and uneducated to excogitate them for themselves, although, even so it must function within the limits of reason, but revelation confronts the mind with no new facts with which the philosopher must wrestle and by which his thought may be fertilized and inspired. There are no mysteries. This post-Cartesian rationalism moved in a world in which all, even in religion, is rather insipidly clear and distinct.'[3]

It was, as has been noted, Butler's interesting contention that

[1] *Contra Gentiles*, 1, 3.
[2] *Essays and Reviews*, p. 297.
[3] J. V. Langmead Casserley, *Retreat from Christianity*, pp. 43, 44.

'the relation we stand to God the Father is known by reason, the relation we stand to Christ by revelation only'. The question, however, arises, What connotation has the term 'Father' for Butler? Is it used as a synonym for Creator? This would seem to be the case. But there are many who would be ready to repudiate the suggestion that natural religion can give a certain idea of a creator. Kant later argued that the only conclusion possible from the data provided by the observation of physical phenomena is that of a 'Cause' and an 'Artificer'. Certainly Butler's view that natural religion brings us into religious regard to God the Father is too sweeping. It may be questioned whether experience confirms or the evangelical records countenance the doctrine that such a knowledge of God as Butler suggests comes through the activity of human reason. The finest ratiocination does not lead men into a filial relationship. It is, we believe, the central message of the New Testament that it is in the Sonship of Christ that the Fatherhood of God is known. It is in and through Jesus Christ that we have the right to say, Abba, Father.

It is no mere accident that the apostle Paul gives the words of his benediction in 2 Corinthians xiii. 14 in the order he does. By putting the grace of the Lord Jesus Christ before the love of God, Paul is being true to the facts of experience. It is by the grace of Christ that the love of God is known. 'The order of the clauses in the great Trinitarian benediction,' observes Professor James Stewart, 'where "the grace of the Lord Jesus Christ" stands first, followed by "the love of God", may be taken as a transcript of Paul's own experience: it was through this meeting with Christ, a Christ Who was all grace, that he entered on the knowledge of love divine.'[1] Dr James Moffatt in a comment on the same passage says, 'Grace is put first, since it is through this manifestation that the divine love is realized.'[2] Butler's neat arrangement of natural and revealed religion and his clear-cut attribution of separate relationships arising from each have, we believe, little justification.

The whole notion that revealed religion is to be conceived as a number of divinely communicated extras to natural religion calls for some general criticisms.

A. Influenced as they were by the scholastic tradition and Cartesian rationalism the 'evidence' writers appear to have had too

---

[1] *A Man in Christ*, p. 140.
[2] *Grace in the New Testament*, p. 151.

optimistic a view of man's natural ability. Whatever interpretation
is to be put upon the idea of the *Imago Dei*, it is impossible to give
to reason the credit the apologists were wont.[1] Man does not see
through the unclouded glass of an impartial reason. There is this
truth in the Freudian thesis that all reason is fundamentally
rationalization, that it is natural for man to seek the things which
self-interest dictates. No single individual is completely exempt
from that irrationality which has its source in man's selfish desires.
There is a sense in which every man is 'eccentric', is 'off the centre'.
Refusing to have God in their knowledge, men were given over to a
'reprobate mind' (Rom. 1. 28). Man whose original position was
to be relationship-in-love is now, in some sense, existence-in-
hostility. In this respect we think Brunner's words are correct.
Maintaining that man is a being capable of responsive love to a
holy and divine Father, he declares that he 'has set himself in
opposition to his origin'.[2] In the light of all the facts we are convinced that the notion of the apologists that there is a large quota
of knowledge of God to be gained by man's native rationality was
too extravagant.

B. By the orthodox apologists the notion of religious knowledge
was too metaphysically conceived. It was as a result of their conception of man's reasoning abilities that the anti-deists were able
to regard natural religion as the result of man's unaided intelligence. The Cartesian doctrine of man as a rational being whose
reason could bring out clear and distinct ideas lay behind their
polemic. They accepted the definition of man as a rational animal;
and they followed Aristotle in the place he gave to reason, and
reason 'meant for Aristotle and for all Western thought since his
day, the logical and analytical faculties of the mind'.[3] God, it was
believed, could be confined in man's neat syllogism. The apologists never seemed to understand that man is not all mind; they
never seemed to grasp that there are more ways of knowing than

[1] Irenaeus' doctrine that the 'Fall', which meant for man the loss of a super-
added gift of righteousness with his essential rationality left undimmed is, to
us, unacceptable; so, too, is the opposite view that the 'image' was completely
defaced and effaced. To maintain that the 'image' is totally destroyed is to put
man so out of touch with God that he could not ever be aware of the separation.
To say that the Imago Dei is altogether destroyed involves a contradiction since
a recognition of God is implied in the statement.

[2] *Man in Revolt*, p. 114. Cf., 'Man is a sinner, i.e. his actual existence is
diametrically opposed to his origin.' E. Brunner, *The Christian Understanding of
Man*, Essay, p. 161.

[3] *The Self and the Dramas of History*, Reinhold Niebuhr, p. 15.

the 'scientific'. It is the perpetual fallacy of rationalism to assume that, 'it is, *prima facie*, of the nature of a thinking being to frame true and adequate thoughts.'[1]

To raise here the question of the character and the channel of religious knowledge would be to go beyond our purpose. It is, however, relevant to point out that because they did not understand the fact that religious knowledge is conditioned in a religious way that the work of the opponents of deism was for the most part ineffective. Spiritual things are not merely observed *ab extra*. There is a sympathetic union which gives a deeper assurance. Spiritual things are spiritually discerned. We cannot refer to God as *das Ding*. God is personal and we can therefore know Him only by the direct communion of sympathetic intercourse. It is this personal intercommunion which is the fundamental certainty in religion. Where this is, the most flawless 'proof' of the sceptic cannot disturb, and where it is not, the most carefully marshalled 'evidences' are no substitute for it.

If this is called 'mysticism', then mysticism we must have, for man is more than a creature of reason. The alternative to this is scepticism. If religious knowledge depends upon reason alone, then the result must be agnosticism since man by reason cannot find out God. 'Certainly the sense of awe, derived by the religious soul from its vivid apprehensions of the greatness of Reality, a Reality experienced as so much deeper than the soul can ever express, is specifically different from any sense of uncertainty as to the existence and the super-human nature of Reality underlying this apprehension.'[2] This, indeed, is, as von Hügel goes on to say, 'healthy mysticism'.

C. The apologists do not seem to have been able to find a satisfactory account of the significance of natural religion. The paradoxical fact is that, on the one hand, it was given far too exalted a position, and, on the other hand, it was not given a place important enough.

Anyone acquainted with the works of Clarke, Stebbing, Conybeare, Butler and Paley will agree that they made natural religion fundamental. So evident is this that Collins could make the scathing retort that no one disbelieved in the existence of God until

---

[1] Quoted from Spinoza by B. Bosanquet in *The Meeting of Extremes in Contemporary Philosophy*, p. 82.
[2] F. von Hügel, *Essays and Addresses on the Philosophy of Religion*, p. 21.

Clarke set out to prove it in his Boyle Lectures. Paley raises the question concerning the usefulness of his *Natural Theology*. He allows that most of those who will read his book will have no uncertainty regarding the existence of the Divine Being. Nevertheless the argument, he thinks, will not even then be in vain, for it will give stability to those whose faith is challenged, and it will give support to those who have believed on authority. Paley, however, goes further and asserts that the supreme value of proving the existence and character of God is, not only that human speculation may be satisfied, but that the foundation is laid for a fuller disclosure of God which the knowledge gained by natural religion assures. He writes; 'we may well leave to Revelation the disclosure of many particulars, which our researches cannot reach, respecting either the nature of that Being as the original cause of all things, or the character and designs as a moral governor, and not only so, but the more fuller confirmation of these particulars, of which, though they lie beyond our reasonings and our possibilities, the certainty is by no means equal to the importance.'[1]

Paley here refers to 'many particulars' which it is the province of revealed religion to add to the discoveries of human reason. Others were not so generous in their estimation of the extras so disclosed. John Foster, for example, is content with a small sum of additions. Christianity, he informs us, has 'two or three plain and useful positive duties',[2] which are given to supplement those already found by the light of reason. The more important place was thus given to natural religion, and, as a result, in 'the eighteenth century even what passes for orthodox religious thought was closer to and more sympathetic towards deism than "enthusiasm" '.[3]

Natural religion held such a large place in the thinking of these writers that we are left with the impression that it was only a matter of time before sufficient knowledge would have been gained. However, as things were, revealed religion has added its limited particulars. So large an amount is supplied by natural religion that it appears to be well nigh enough.

On the other side, however, it was this very magnifying of natural religion which resulted in the minimizing of it. Natural religion was not really important enough, restricted as it was to

[1] 'Natural Theology', *Works*, vol. 4, p. 424.
[2] *The Usefulness, Truth and Excellency of the Christian Religion*, p. 302.
[3] J. V. Langmead Casserley, *Retreat from Christianity*, p. 45.

those very realities which were not of primary value. It is but a small thing to be convinced of the existence of a mere Designer or Conserver of values. But it is not a First Cause the human heart needs but a Father's heart, 'a Friend behind phenomena.'

'It is common to hear proofs offered in support of the claim there is "a God",' observes W. N. Clarke, 'but to say, "I believe in a God," may mean much or little. "A God" may be simply a creator, or a first cause, concerning whose character or relation to man little or nothing is asserted. Only unsatisfactory proof of the existence of God is possible while the idea of God is undefined and the name ambiguous. To prove that there is a God, is far less than to prove that God as now conceived is a living Being; and the question in Christian Theology is the same as that which is vital for all mankind, whether the good God is real.'[1] It is the deep things of God's being — things which are of eternal significance for man — which the apologists, for the most part, left outside their reckoning. By accepting the clear-cut division between natural and revealed religion the orthodox failed to apply their own presuppositions. They ought to have carried through their fundamental principles and maintained the exclusive supremacy of reason. Instead they began with the existing dichotomy and confined themselves to those truths believed to be proper subjects for reason's investigation. Their purpose doubtless was to leave the other beliefs aside as irrational and to eliminate them from the possibility of intellectual enquiry. As a consequence, natural religion was rigidly confined, and the very themes of deepest significance to man were excluded from review. 'Thus it could come about that David Hume should compose his Dialogue on Natural Religion, so cogent in argumentation, so urbane, so devastatingly polite, at a moment when John Wesley was altering the characters of thousands and the course of English History by preaching salvation through the Precious Blood — a theme which one suspects that Hume and his friends would have thought ill-suited for refined conversation. If Natural Theology is restricted, or restricts itself, to the study of what has never been of a supposed revelation, then it is concerned with what is very unimportant alike to its own students and to all mankind.'[2] The paradox, then, revealing itself in the literature of those whose concern it was to keep faith alive in a period of indifference

---

[1] *Outlines of Christian Theology* (2nd edition), p. 103.
[2] W. Temple, *Nature, Man and God*, p. 9.

and attack is that natural religion was accorded a place in excess of its importance, and yet, because it was limited to what was least significant, it was not given a place important enough.

The trouble arose, of course, from the stress laid upon the divine transcendence by both the deists and their opponents. The latter were unable to see that the sharp division between natural and revealed religion was ultimately unsound. Instead of looking upon natural and revealed religion as two-distinct volumes (although the first was regarded as a tome and the second as a pamphlet), with man the author of the former and God of the latter, they ought to have observed as Augustine had done earlier, that God was in a real sense the author of both. This does not mean that revelation is all of the same sort, but it does mean that in a significant way all knowledge of God is revealed. 'All religious knowledge of God, wherever existing, comes by revelation; otherwise we should be committed to the incredible position that man can know God without His willingness to be known.'[1]

It is incorrect, therefore, to speak as the apologists did, of a natural religion resulting from man's intellectual discovery and a revealed religion resulting from God's self-disclosure, as if the two were somehow unrelated. The notion that revelation is a mere addition to the discoveries of reason does not fit the facts. It is more in accord with the facts to conceive of special revelation as illuminating and vindicating the truths given in general.

It was the conviction of Augustine, as Professor B. B. Warfield has shown, that 'all knowledge rests ultimately on revelation'.[2] Augustine's problem was 'not how to supplant a strictly natural knowledge by a strictly supernatural knowledge'. His concern was with the restoration of those capacities whereby man could regain that knowledge described as natural. Man *qua* man cannot profit by general revelation: God must come creatively to bring about this result. 'The intervention of God', according to Augustine, 'by a special revelation works, therefore, harmoniously into a general scheme of the production of knowledge of God through general revelation.' This harmonious union of natural and revealed religion the anti-deists failed to achieve.

The Old Testament is the historical account of the dynamic belief that God is known only as He makes Himself known. It is

---

[1] H. R. Mackintosh, *The Christian Apprehension of God*, p. 65.
[2] *Studies in Tertullian and Augustine*, p. 222 f.

G

the assurance of its religious men that God must remain forever in unknown isolation unless and until He reveals Himself. 'If men know God, it is because He has made Himself known to man. The idea of men reaching to a knowledge or fellowship of God through their effort is foreign to the Old Testament.'[1] The very fact that man has 'The Instinct for Transcendence',[2] means that eternity is set in the human heart. However foolishly men may have expressed their fundamental longings they are testimony to his nostalgia. He is aware of 'the Beyond that is within', and he is sure of what Dr Matthews calls 'the Beyond that is akin'.[3] It is this very fact that makes man a religious being. 'He carries within himself a supernatural reference, and he cannot rescind it; or if excision there be, a scar is left, and the scar is testimony.'[4]

Revelation is a disclosure of God to man, whether it be termed general or special. God is the source of it; man is the object of it. It is from God, it is for man.

This means that there will be a revelation of God in nature because it is man's environment. Man is in God's world, and it cannot be doubted that He has written His signature upon His vast works for all men to read. He has never left Himself without witness; 'on each of His works', says Calvin, 'His glory is engraven in characters so bright, so distinct, and so illustrious, that none, however dull and illiterate can plead ignorance as their excuse.'[5] But while none can plead ignorance, all must confess blindness. 'It is true', observes Paul Tillich, 'that the history of culture is a history of permanent demoniac distortions of revelation and idolatrous confessions of God and man.'[6] God's signature and hallmark were set upon the spacious firmament, but man has sought to erase them, to carve his own instead. But they are there still for all to read; and they can be read still by those who stand within the full light, evidences of God's eternal power and divinity.

It can be asserted further that there must be a revelation of God in history because it is man's story. The apologists, no less than their opponents, had no sense of the historical; they had no idea of the meaning of history. Yet history in general is a revelation of the

---

[1] *Hastings Bible Dictionary*, vol. 2, p. 197.
[2] Evelyn Underhill, *The Mystic Way*, ch. 1, sect. 1.
[3] *God in Christian Thought and Experience*, p. 10.
[4] E. Lewis, *The Philosophy of the Christian Revelation*, p. 28.
[5] *The Institutes of the Christian Religion* (Beveridge's translation), vol. 1, p. 51.
[6] *The Protestant Era*, Preface, p. xliv.

divine purpose. In history God is active, and it is this 'actuality'[1] of God in history which constitutes it as revelational, it unfolds the deeds of God. We cannot agree with H. A. L. Fisher that history is without 'a plot, a rhythm, a pre-determined pattern'.[2] History is no accident, its web is woven on the loom of a divine purpose.

But the key to history is not found within history itself. Nor yet can history be interpreted through nature. This is the fallacy of the Marxian dialectic which conceives of history as due to the human machine's need of fuel. 'The truth is', says Alan Richardson, 'that the meaning of history will not be found within.'[3] It thus becomes impossible 'to interpret history at all without a principle of inter-pretation which history as such does not yield'.[4]

This understanding of history as somehow revelational is itself derived from revelation. It was the prophets of Israel who first made the bold announcement that Jehovah (Yahweh) was Lord of History. This means that the appreciation of all history as a medium of revelation was brought to light through special revela-tion. The prophets saw God active within the history of their people. This was indeed the stand-point from which they surveyed their national events. They saw God as having a personal interest in affairs, 'The Jews were the first to introduce the principles of the historical and a keen feeling for historical destiny into the life of mankind.'[5] It was indeed out of this understanding of the historical as the sphere of the divine activity that the God of history was seen to be the God of nature. Nature was consequently viewed reli-giously in the context of the 'divine history'. For the people of Israel there was really no clear-cut division between 'history' and 'nature'. 'In emphasizing "history" as the primary field of God's revelation we must not imply that "nature" is excluded. It is excluded as the primary field but included within "history" as part of the Living God's revelation to his creatures.'[6] The fact is, as Dr H. Wheeler Robinson has pointed out the Hebrew people lacked a word for 'nature'. The reason is, of course, that they allowed no 'middle neutralities'; so that when modern man talks of 'nature' the Hebrew would have spoken of 'God'.

[1] H. Wheeler Robinson, *Redemption and Revelation*, chs. iv, vi.
[2] *The History of Europe*, (1935, Miffin), p. vii.
[3] *Christian Apologetics*, p. 99.
[4] Reinhold Niebuhr, *Nature and Destiny of Man*, vol. i, p. 151.
[5] N. Berdyaev, *The Meaning of History*, p. 86.
[6] W. J. Wolf, *Man's Knowledge of God* (The Christian Faith Series), p. 73.

But while all history was seen to be the workshop of God, in the light of God's dealing with the chosen people of Israel, this 'special' history, in its turn, is seen to be more vividly and dramatically God's workmanship in the historical Person of Christ. It is 'only through Jesus Christ that history can be defined as world history'.[1] God's supreme revelation has taken place in time. The gospel story is dated: it is grounded in history. Here is special history, significant history, saving history. Thus is Christianity not a fleeting theosophy, but a final theophany; it is not a philosophical concept, but a historical culmination. Here the process found fulfilment — the progressive revelation through the Old Testament story is fulfilled and filled full, ἐφάπαξ, 'once and for all,' in God's ultimate and best disclosure, His own Son — a historic Person. It is in the light of the special historic revelation in Christ that the whole drama of history is seen to be the activity of God.

This means that in the final disclosure, God has revealed Himself in Personality because it is man's essence. In man, made in the image of God, there must be some revelation of Him. Man still contains within him, as Bacon says, 'the sparkle of his first purity.' 'What shall we say,' exclaims Calvin, 'but that man bears within him a stamp of immortality which can never be effaced?'[2] Man's conscience, sometimes excusing and sometimes accusing, is an inward witness to God. Although 'man is a god in ruins' as Emerson remarks, he is still, out of the wreckage, aware of a glory that was meant to be his. But once again it is in the Personality of God made Man that human personality itself is understood.

As personality is the essential thing in man it is just here that God has disclosed Himself in His clearest and final form — in a Face like my face. It is for this reason that the Christian points to the living Personality of Christ as the final Exegete of God. Here is God speaking in word and deed. 'Incarnation is the highest possible form of divine revelation to us since human personality is the highest created form of existence known to us.'[3] The fullness of time had come in the fifteenth year of Tiberius Caesar, when Pontius Pilate was governor of Judaea. Then God at last spoke in One Who is Son of God: then was the Life manifested. The Truth of God was embodied in a life. God had appeared on the arena of

---

[1] E. Brunner, *Revelation and Reason*, p. 405.
[2] *Institutes of the Christian Religion*, vol. 1, p. 54.
[3] W. Y. Mullins, *Freedom and Authority in Religion*, p. 315.

human experience. The Word was made flesh. The literature of Heaven was translated into the language of earth. Hitherto, in history, in conscience, God had revealed His hand. Now in Christ He has laid bare His heart in a final unfolding of Himself for which He had been preparing through the selection of Israel.

Since this is, we are persuaded, the true understanding of God's unveiling of Himself, it means that special revelation is no mere appendage to general. The position is rather that special revelation is 'the means by which the truths given in general revelation can be adequately apprehended and known to us'.[1] It was such facts as these that the anti-deists failed to appreciate: and by failing to appreciate them they made their doctrine of revealed religion trivial and unconvincing.

(ii) *The Need for Revealed Religion*

In order to make secure their polemic against the deists, it was necessary for the apologists to indicate the value of a revealed religion. It is here that something of a contradiction is to be found. The reason which has been earlier so highly estimated is now to be shown, by some to be inadequate, and by others to be distorted.

Clarke contended that an understanding of early philosophy and an observation of the human heart would indicate that a revelation was 'plainly wanting'.[2] The early philosophers show the need for the extras which are given by revealed religion. They had their certainties regarding morality, immortality, and so forth, but their greatest and best were 'never able to frame to themselves any complete, regular and consistent system or scheme of things: but the truths which they sought were single and scattered, accidental, as it were, and hit upon by chance, rather than by any knowledge of the whole true state of things; and consequently less universally convictive'.[3] The ultimate end the chiefest philosophers of ancient days could not see, while the multitudinous differences between them gave them no sure resting-place. The duties of life of which they were certain they had no authority to enforce. They could approve the best, they could not achieve it. They were aware of a malady which afflicted mankind but they had no idea from whence it came. They were 'entirely ignorant of some Doctrines absolutely

---

[1] A. Richardson, *Christian Apologetics*, p. 134.
[2] *Discourse concerning, etc.*, p. 306.
[3] Op. cit., p. 301.

necessary to bring about this great End of the Reformation and Recovery of Mankind'.[1] Philosophy was for the Greek, as the law was for the Jew, their schoolmaster to bring them to Christ. The rest of men, he sees involved in 'nothing but Words and Subtility, and Strife, and Empty Contention'.[2] So indolent the nature, so violent the passions that the majority of men show little eagerness to discover and little desire to understand. Only a few select souls have been able to penetrate far into the divine secret of the universe. The rest of men 'have great need of particular Teaching and much Instruction, not without some weight of Authority as well as Reason and Persuasion'.[3]

In the first of his eight sermons, published under the title, *The Use and Necessity of Divine Revelation*, Dr John Rogers, Canon of Wells, argues that revelation is essential to fix a rule of morality. He asserts that God constantly gave particular revelations until Christ appeared. He expresses amazement that there should be those, at so late a date, who, having witnessed the progress of Christianity, can believe that God left men 'without any other Rule than the Collections of Natural Revelation'.[4] God Who has given ample evidence of His existence and His concern for men's happiness, has in revealed religion, not only clearly exhibited the duties requisite for the fulfilment of that happiness but has also supplied therein a motive.

Those who hold the sufficiency of reason must suppose it equal in all men. Experience does not confirm this; and allowance must be made for the passions and lusts which discount its effectiveness. Philosophy cannot reform the libertine — ' 'tis vain to expect that the generality of man will ever be governed by sober and dispassionate Reason.'[5] Hobbes' social contract theory is not adequate for the regulating of man's selfish motives. Some guiding authority there must be, but no human one is without impossible difficulties. 'If, therefore, human laws are the ultimate Rule and Standard of moral Good and Evil, if nothing is Good but what they direct, and nothing Evil but what they forbid, Men are left in these cases without Rule, without any Motive or Obligation to these Duties, or any Restraint from acting contrary to them.'[6] If, however,

---

[1] *Discourse concerning, etc.*, p. 290.
[2] Op. cit., p. 289.   [3] Op. cit., p. 280.
[4] *The Use and Necessity of Divine Revelation*, p. 4.
[5] Op. cit., p. 11.
[6] Op. cit., p. 19.

revelation is accepted, then is the way of life made clear, and the motive for living disclosed. The Gospel provides 'A Rule worthy of that Wisdom of the Author, fitted for the Direction of every Regulation, Office and Condition of Life, and equally conducive to the Happiness of All'.[1]

In his *Answer to Tindal*, Leyland catalogues a formidable and frightful list of evil deeds for which man's stupidity and ignorance are responsible. He considers that in this way the competence of reason is in some way undermined. Without a divine revelation, he then remarks, there would be no way of bringing such deeds under condemnation. Revelation acts, as the law did for Paul; it makes sin stand out as sinful. If Paul could say, I had not known sin except the law saith, 'Thou shalt not,' it would appear that for law, Leyland can substitute revealed religion.

In his Boyle Lectures, Dr Samuel Clarke had asserted that reason was a God-given guide which cannot be at fault. Its deficiencies arise from 'man abusing his reason'. This is the position that Stebbing defends against the attacks of Tindal. Stebbing contends that the more reason is abused by man the less is he able to follow its light without the aid of some outside help. 'The End of the Gospel Revelation', he concludes, 'was to repair the Breaches of that very Law which subsisted antecedently to this state of sin and corruption.'[2] Somehow the gospel is subordinate to the original law of nature. It is Tindal's error to suppose that 'because the Law of Nature is the Supreme Law, therefore, it must be the Sole Law, whereas it is very clear, that although the Supreme Law will admit of no Law in opposition to it; yet in subordination to it, it will admit of many'.[3] Revelation indicates more precisely that which has a manifest tendency to promote God's honour, and man's good. By it alone can 'the particular Method of external Worship be determined'.[4] Man's state makes the need of a revelation imperative. The question of how man 'fell' into a condition in which the usefulness of reason should be in some measure nullified is admittedly a difficult one, but 'Natural Religion sees the Evil, but has no Remedy for it; Revelation sees it; and has provided the cure'.[5]

Conybeare, whose *Defence of Revealed Religion* is referred to by Warburton as one of the best reasoned books in existence, sees

[1] Op. cit., p. 37.
[2] *A Defence of Dr Clarke's, Natural and Revealed Religion*, p. 26.
[3] Op. cit., p. 32.   [4] Op. cit., p. 58.   [5] Op. cit., p. 65.

revealed religion as a short-cut method of attaining knowledge. It is
a quick way into the land of promise which avoids the dreariness
of the desert and the weariness of the wilderness. Knowledge is
built up by the slow and painful process of adding, here a little,
there a little. A complete synoptic view, if it were possible to gather
together all the pieces, is beyond the ability of any single human
reason. God has, however, delivered man from this tedious process
in the sphere of religion. At one stroke final moral realities are
made known. Revelation has put man in possession of first principles which otherwise must be long withheld. God has placed,
Conybeare tells us, a 'telescope'[1] in man's hands; it is possible to
see the first principles of duty and religion.

Newton set before men the basic facts of geometry, they
stand forth clearly revealed. A teacher may still be required to
draw out the implications and to press home the applications of
these fundamental facts. So it is in morality: God has unveiled the
ultimate moral necessities of life all at once. While reason can discover some general points of morality, there are special propositions which only a direct revelation can disclose. Like other of the
anti-deistic writers, he conceives of revealed religion as giving the
'how' to that worship which natural religion shows to be required.
God, he argues, has a perfect right to demand a certain method of
worship, and in making His demand He is relieved of all partiality.
Earthly authorities make their demands and are not charged with
injustice as a result, 'surely God hath an equal right to do the same,
and if it be upon several accounts fit and proper that such matters
should be determined, I cannot see why God should not as reasonably determine them as man; especially as the Divine authority is
much more indisputable, and as such must . . . have an infinitely
greater weight.'[2]

A. Sykes thinks of revealed religion as supplying 'us with a new
Fund of Arguments'[3] for the fulfilment of the moral law. Revealed
religion urges the doing of right 'from the Consideration of God'.[4]
Yet religion is not to be defined as 'Man's duty to God'. It is
rather the doing of duty in whatever state a man finds himself
'from the Principle of believing there is a God'.[5] Revelation is but

---

[1] *A Defence of Revealed Religion*, p. 202.
[2] Op. cit., p. 204.
[3] *Principles and Connection of Natural and Revealed Religion*, p. 94.
[4] Ibid.
[5] Ibid.

an additional urge to the fulfilment of the good. If some follow virtue from the belief in God assured in nature then, 'If a Revelation were to supply us still with more and different Arguments to practise what is right, it would not but be of singular advantage.'[1]

It was this statement of the case which called out against Sykes the criticism of Warburton who charges him with supposing 'Obligation without Law, a revelation of Natural Religion without a Deity'.[2] Sykes makes a gallant effort to rebut the charge and to justify his position that there is an eternal law of things to which even God Himself must conform. God, he insists, is necessarily good. He will ask his opponent, Is this not so? He will go on pressing the question; 'I shall continue "teazing" him, till I force him to prove that God is necessarily good.'[3] Sykes assumes that if this is allowed then his own case is proved.

In a chapter entitled, 'The Advantages of Revealed Religion,' Sykes raises the question concerning the usefulness of a particular disclosure of God in view of the undoubted sufficiency of reason. It is not right, he thinks, to decry revelation. On the other hand it is folly to seek to undermine reason in order to enhance the benefits of revelation. Revelation does not fix a rule of morality for such was known prior to its coming. Neither does it assure religion, for religion consists in doing our duties from a sense of God's being, and this the natural light of the understanding gives. To answer the question, then, Sykes specifies the advantages of revelation to be that, 'It contains Motives and Reasons for the practice of what is right, more and different from, what Natural Reason without its help can suggest.'[4] These motives and reasons are to be found in the several particulars peculiar to the New Testament, as, for example, the final triumph of God's kingdom through Christ, the doctrine of the Trinity, the positive institutions of Baptism and the Lord's Supper.

In order to indicate the necessity for a revealed religion, Butler bids his readers contrast the state of religion where it is enjoyed with that where it has not come. The greatest of the ancients, the bright lights of antiquity, reveal how urgent was the need for the

---

[1] Op. cit., p. 101.
[2] *The True Foundation of Natural and Revealed Religion Asserted, Being a Reply to the Supplement of a Treatise entitled, The Nature, Obligation, etc., of the Christian Sacraments*, p. 5.
[3] Op. cit., p. 24.
[4] *The Principles and Connection, etc.*, p. 244.

republication of the obligations arising out of natural religion and the giving to them a new authority. Butler draws a contrast between moral and positive commands. The former are superior because they are the ends to which the positive precepts are directed. Between the two there can be no ultimate opposition. Yet the positive commands are as binding as the moral the moment they are seen to be the word of Him with Whom we have to do. Thus, while positive duties are, 'those the reasons of which we do not see'[1] and are 'external commands', they demand unhesitating obedience when they are recognized to be God's.

To see, then, revealed religion as the anti-deists did, as a reinforcement of natural religion, or as a source of inspiration for morality, or as a standard by which deviations from natural morality is to be judged, is not a very convincing account of the usefulness of a revealed religion. The statement of these particulars is itself sufficient to exhibit the defectiveness of the whole polemic. There is nothing here to grip. Revealed religion merely adds a number of extra 'positive commands' to which obedience must be given. The Person of Christ becomes almost lost in the precepts for conduct. The Sermon on the Mount is of more significance than the Sacrifice on the Hill. Jesus is regarded as the publisher of extra moral dicta. The whole attitude results in giving a false view of the Person and place of Jesus Christ.

The anti-deistic literature, from Browne to Butler, is vitiated by the untenable notion that Jesus set out a number of additional propositions to which assent was to be given. Bishop Browne misconceives the real essence of the Gospel when he writes of faith 'as an Assent to a revealed and express Proposition upon the Testimony of God; and till something be so revealed by him there could be no assent by us to any such Proposition; we cannot believe in his express Word before he spake to us by the Prophets and His Son. And now that all these things concerning himself and us are delivered to Mankind, Men still have it in their own natural Election whether they will either Consider them, or give Assent to them; but we are told that he that Believeth them shall be Saved, and he that Believeth not shall be Damned.'[2]

This notion makes the Christian gospel regulative but not redemptive. Jesus appears as a lecturer in ethics Who propounds a

---

[1] *Analogy*, p. 206.
[2] *The Procedure, Extent and Limits of the Human Understanding*, p. 335.

system which all must acknowledge as being in accord with the reason of things. It regards the words of Jesus as single pieces of an artistic mosaic instead of diamond rays flashing from a divine personality. It makes faith mere assent to certain formal propositions instead of warm and living trust in a present Saviour. The doctrine of these apologists may be Scholastic, but it is not Scriptural: it may claim to be Thomistic, but it cannot claim to be Pauline.

What the period needed, and, alas, what the period lacked, was a man like P. T. Forsyth to write with conviction and appeal upon the Person and Place of Jesus Christ. In Christ God did not simply countersign the best intuitions of the heart or the highest productions of the reason. It is only in faith that the final significance of Christ is understood, not a believing *as* Christ, nor yet a believing *with* Him, but a believing IN Him. 'The deity of Christ cannot be proved, to either the lower or the higher rationalism, either to the deistic or the idealistic, the Wolffian or the Hegelian.'[1] The question must face us as the most urgent, the most critical and the most far-reaching: Did Jesus connect His saving mission with His Person or with His precepts? With His ideas or with His work? 'Is saving faith a Rationalism, i.e. a faith in universal ideas, intuitions, or processes, which have no exclusive relation to a fixed point in history?'[2] Are we to start with the World or with the Word. 'Are we to demand that Christ shall submit to the standard of certain principles or ideals which we bring to him from our human nature at its heart's highest and its thought's best? Or as our new creator is he his own standard, and not only so but both judge, king, and redeemer of human nature, and the fountain of new life, autonomous in Him, and for all the rest derived? Is he the prophet and champion of man's magnificent resources, or is he the redeemer of man's spiritual poverty and moral wreck? Did he come to transfigure before men the great religious and ethical ideas, or to infuse into men new power, in the thorough, final, and godlike sense of endowing them with a new and ransomed life? Did he refurbish Humanity, or redeem it? Did he release its best powers, or bestow them? This is the last issue, however we may blunt its edge, or soften its exigency in particular cases. It is between a rational Christianity and a redemptive. And it is not to be obscured by

[1] *The Person and Place of Jesus Christ*, p. 94.
[2] Op. cit., p. 95.

extenuations which plead that the function of ideas is redemptive, or that redemption is the profoundest rationality in the world, the "passion which is highest reason in the soul divine". That was the line that nearly lost Christianity to the pagan public in the old apologists, whose great object was to make their religion stand well with the Universities and the State — a perilous attempt for Christianity.'[1]

(iii) *The Proofs of Revealed Religion*

It was the business of the orthodox, not only to show why a revelation was 'plainly wanting', but also to adduce evidence that it was actually given. Having set forth the advantages that would result from a revealed religion, it was asserted that this divine revelation was given in the truths of the gospel. But a revelation supernaturally given must be supernaturally guaranteed. There must be infallible signs to attest its divine origin: there must be adequate and authentic 'external evidences' which will assure that it is not unreasonable to accept the truths disclosed by revealed religion.

Dr Clarke thus asserts that revealed religion 'to the judgement of Right and Sober Reason, appears of itself highly credible and probable'.[2] He goes on to declare that Christianity 'as taught by the Holy Scripture, has all the Marks and Proofs of it being actually and truly a Divine Revelation'.[3] There are truths which reason itself cannot discover and these have been made known by a particular revelation of God, and as these revealed truths were demonstrated by divine testimonies it was no longer unreasonable to accept them. By these external signs their authenticity was assured. The special authenticating proofs by which revealed religion was established are miracles and prophecies. In the polemic of the period, therefore, we find long and laboured sections devoted to the argument from miracle and the argument from prophecy.

The case is put in an almost naïve manner by Stebbing. He premises that man's happiness depends upon his doing good according to nature. To forbear to do good is 'contrary to Reason, and if it is contrary to Reason it is contrary to our own happiness'.[4]

---

[1] *The Person and Place of Jesus Christ*, pp. 95, 96.
[2] *A Discourse concerning, etc.*, p. 157.
[3] Op. cit., p. 155.
[4] *An Enquiry into the Evidences of the Christian Religion*, p. 38.

It is agreeable to the nature of God to disclose to man those particulars requisite for his happiness. But the question must be asked, Has this revelation been made? A divine doctrine, Stebbing says, is not only 'suitable to the Divine nature',[1] but it is also in harmony with the knowledge of God assured by natural religion. A fuller certainty is, however, required, for, 'if God has given us a revelation, he has given us full Evidence that it is his Revelation.'[2] The first of these sure proofs is miracles. To this is to be added one other crowning and conclusive proof, for 'we have another key given to us to detect the Imposture, if it be one; a key put into our hands even by the Founder of this Religion himself; and that is, a Pretence in him to fulfill Prophecies'.[3]

Sykes refused to make an exact equation between the Scripture and revealed religion. The Bible, he maintains, contains, besides general facts of history and social life, a large number of moral maxims which the light of reason discovered. He leaves us with a small residue of revealed items. He then asks, 'how are we to distinguish Matters of Reason from those of Revelation, or how are we to know which facts are wrote [sic] from human Testimony, and which are wrote [sic] by the Inspiration of God.'[4] Sykes considers that inspiration and revelation are one and the same reality; he therefore asserts that there must be sure and certain evidences both in the man himself and in the matter of his claim.

With regard to the first, if the truth is discoverable by reason then the claim to a particular revelation can be set at nought. But inspiration itself is an occasional matter. The man inspired is not always so, consequently there must be some way to distinguish between what is spoken under the urge of God and what otherwise. God, when He makes a prophet does not make a puppet. On the other hand, nothing is to be regarded as revealed which contradicts the natural reason. It is only the credible which has consequence for us.

There are, however, some truths assured by prophecy. If matters are before announced as of extraordinary nature and later history records their fulfilment, then there is a powerful evidence of their truth. Sykes meets the deistic argument against prophecy and its evidential value. The deists urged that those passages which the orthodox adduced as prior disclosures of events yet to be, are

---

[1] Op. cit., p. 47. [2] Op. cit., p. 50. [3] Op. cit., p. 73.
[4] *The Principles and Connection of Natural and Revealed Religion*, p. 114.

really later interpolations, deliberate fabrications or *post factum* accounts. All these assertions Sykes meets with real ability.

He notes, for example, the objection to the Book of Daniel on the hypothesis that he wrote, or rather that the book was written, after Antiochus Epiphanes' reign. The argument, he observes, is taken from Porphyry, the heathen critic of early Christianity. This source must be held to destroy its strength.

He meets, too, the notion that certain prophecies are merely 'Theological or Poetical method of conveying Religion to Mankind'.[1] Prophecy is not to be regarded as 'an art or science', as some would maintain on the basis of those passages which refer to 'the schools of the prophets'. Prophecy, Sykes teaches, is due to God's will and design Who inspired men as He saw fit. With the gift of prophecy there goes also the confirming evidence of the ability to perform miracles.

The positive evidences for Christianity, Butler likewise considered to be miracles and prophecies. They are, indeed, the 'two direct and fundamental proofs'.[2] For the first Christians miracles and the dynamic influence of the gospel message on its first professors provided strong evidence, whereas 'we or future ages', from conformity between prophetic history, and the state of the world, and of Christianity, 'may possibly have proof of it, which they could not have.'[3]

Such then were the proofs adduced for the reality of a revealed religion by the anti-deistic apologists. What was said by Clarke, Stebbing and Butler was reiterated by the others. Reason assured natural miracles and prophecy authenticated revealed religion. For the deists natural religion was alone sufficient, consequently miracles were unnecessary. With them there was begun the first all-out attack upon the miraculous. Yet their assault was based upon some very definite philosophical presuppositions. Miracles are swept aside because reason was considered to be adequate. There was no serious attempt made to discuss their historical evidence. The deistic rejection of the miraculous rested upon *a priori* considerations. 'The disavowal of the miracles by those who generally styled themselves Christians occurred first as the consequence of a view of our knowledge of God which set aside the

[1] *The Connection of Natural and Revealed Religion*, p. 164.
[2] *Analogy*, p. 275.
[3] Op. cit., p. 260.

classical Christian conception of a supernatural revelation and was itself derived from the rationalism of the new philosophy of Descartes and his successors.'[1]

(a) The Anti-deists and the Argument from Miracles

The apologists of the eighteenth century, in their use of the argument from miracles, continued the traditional statement. The special miracles of the Gospels were the divine attestation that the gospel itself was 'from above'. The miracles, it was believed, could be adduced as evidence that the authority of revealed religion was itself reasonable. The items which reason could not prove have been vouched for by miracles. What was thus confirmed by a special intervention of God was to have unqualified assent.

The general attitude was that it was only a revelation which had the higher evidence of the miraculous action of God could claim authority over the conscience of men. Thus while the deists would say that no reasonable person can reject the religion of reason, therefore no reasonable person can believe the miracles because, not only does the reason provide all that is necessary, but also because the miracles are not 'reasonable'; the orthodox replied that no reasonable person can refuse assent to a religion which has been so signally approved by God's special intervention.

This last term recalls us to the fact that the anti-deists by explaining miracles as a divine intervention were in line with the traditional doctrine which is accustomed to put the miracles among the external evidences for the truth of Christianity.

It is not until the time of Augustine that we find any attempt made to treat of miracles in a scientific manner. Prior to his day they were not strange phenomena. Origen, for example, asserts that the miracles wrought by Christ were still being performed in his day.[2] At the same time the reality of heathen miracles was allowed and Origen admits that in and by themselves the ability to work miracles and to utter prophecies is no infallible sign of divinity. The real tests are: Is the worker of miracles himself morally pure? and, Is the race of men made the better by their performance? So long as demoniac wonders were regarded as possible the 'argument from miracles' could not be pressed. By Augustine's day miracles seemed to have ceased, as he looks back

[1] A. Richardson, *Christian Apologetics*, p. 158.
[2] *Contra Celsus*, 1, 2, 26, cf., also, 3, 24, 26.

upon a period, now remote, when these strange happenings took place.

Augustine taught that miracles were not contrary to nature.[1] They were happenings which could not be fully explained because all the workings of the natural order were beyond the human understanding. They were not therefore irrational. He believed that some miracles could be interpreted on the hypothesis of the speeding up of natural processes. In the story of Moses' rod turned into a serpent there is an instance of this acceleration of the ordinary course of things. It was believed that in decaying wood serpents might quite naturally originate, and on this occasion the gradual process was, by divine action, made instantaneous.

Augustine goes into the subject of the nature of miracles with penetrating details, and his teaching was to shape the thinking of succeeding centuries. There are miracles, on the one hand, which are the outcome of inherent causes, or *semina occulta*, introduced by God at the first creation. There are those, on the other hand, which are mysterious happenings resulting from God's occasional intrusion into the natural order. Thus, briefly put, Augustine attributed miracles to the workings of either some inherent seed or an outside Sovereign. It was out of this distinction that two historic views developed. Some came to regard miracles as an extra work of God outside the usual activity of nature. This was the doctrine elaborated by the Scholastics and the anti-deistic writers of the eighteenth century. Others denied the need for any such extra divine works. They asserted that enough was introduced by God 'in the beginning'. All the events of the world result from *semina* inherent from the first creation. A deistic system, with a denial of the miracles in the strict sense, was the natural conclusion to this line of thought.

For the orthodox, then, that was to be designated a miracle which was the result of the transcendent God breaking into the natural order. Thus Stebbing defines a miracle as 'an Intrusion of the Divine Being to change the Laws of Nature'.[2] The miracle is an abrupt act.

Beginning with this conception of a miracle as 'a violation of the Laws of Nature',[3] Hume set out to upset the whole orthodox

[1] *De Civ. Dei*, bk. xxi, ch. viii, cf., as well, *Contra Faust. Manich.*, xxvi, 3.
[2] *Enquiry into the Evidences of Christianity*, p. 53.
[3] *Essays* (Edition, 1788), 2, p. 19.

apologetic. The task was not, indeed, difficult for, as Johannes Wendland has observed, 'A wrong idea of miracle is the necessary result of conceiving of God's relation to the world as exclusively transcendent; for then His action must come breaking in upon the phenomenal order in miracles which are isolated and abrupt. This is the point of view which leads inevitably to the idea of "violation of the laws of nature", "abrogation of the natural order," "breach of the causal nexus." And the polemic against the miraculous justly makes positions of this kind an object of attack.'[1]

The apologists, like Aquinas, restricted miracles to events within the sphere of sense. For the Thomists such realities as, for example, the Incarnation and God's redeeming action in human lives, are not miracles, since they are not a departure from the natural order. By thus restricting miracles within the area of the sensory the 'argument from miracles' advanced by the anti-deists was without spiritual appeal.

Luther gave to these external evidences a place of little value. For him, the supreme miracle was Christ Himself, His words and His works are divine wonders. He points out that, although the world demands outward signs, it refuses to receive them, whereas, miracles of greater and more striking worth are all the time taking place in the moral experiences of men.

An examination of the New Testament will reveal, we think, that there the miracles are mainly subservient to the saving work of Christ. It is in the light of His redeeming activity that they are to be understood. They are not presented as isolated events, and their unusualness, as such, is not generally adduced as proof of a Divine activity. 'Christ and His works are all of a piece, and he who has apprehended Christ, or rather been apprehended by Him, will not seek to reduce the self-manifestation of the Saviour to the measure of humanity. To prove the miracles one by one is as impossible as to disprove them in the same way, but they unite with the Person and the words of Jesus into one divine whole through which God reveals His very heart to men.'[2]

The miracles of the New Testament are outflashings of Christ's divine Person. They are no mere wonders. The whole of Christianity rests upon a supernatural basis and the gospel story unveils a supernatural Person, not only when, what are called miracles are

[1] *Miracles and Christianity* (tr. H. R. Mackintosh), p. 3.
[2] James Denney, *Studies in Theology*, p. 208.

being wrought. The anti-deists failed to observe that the 'question is not about isolated "miracles", but about the whole conception of Christianity — what it is, and whether the supernatural does not enter into the very essence of it? ... Is there a supernatural Being — God? Is there a supernatural government of the world? Is there a supernatural relation of God to man, so that God and man may have communion with one another? Is there a supernatural Revelation? Has that Revelation culminated in a supernatural Person — Christ? Is there a supernatural work in the souls of men? Is there a supernatural Redemption? Is there a supernatural hereafter? It is these larger questions that have to be settled first, and then the question of particular miracles will fall into its proper place.'[1]

(b) The Place of Analogy

Since they began with the world rather than from the Word to arrive at a knowledge of God, it was inevitable that the apologists should give a supreme place to the argument from analogy. This position, fundamental to the anti-deists as a whole, is set forth in the clearest manner by Bishop Browne. He states quite emphatically that analogy is the only method for the attainment of divine knowledge. Whilst the real nature of the Christian mysteries cannot be understood, Browne asserts that 'all can both Know and Believe them under Analogical Representations and Conceptions'.[2] The purpose of his book, he says, is 'to trace the whole Extent and Limits of the Human Understanding; to trace out its several steps and degrees of its Procedure from the first and simple Perception of sensible Objects, thro' the several Operations of the Pure Intellect upon them, till it grows up to its full Proportion of Nature; And to shew how all Conceptions of things Supernatural are then grafted on it by Analogy; and how from thence it extends itself immensely into all the Branches of Divine and Human Knowledge.'[3]

The knowledge of God, like any other knowledge, Browne insists, is derived from the senses and the reason. The senses are the 'groundwork' of both. Rejecting the notion of innate ideas, and consequently the possibility of any ontological argument for the

---

[1] J. Orr, *The Christian View of God and the World*, pp. 10, 11.
[2] *The Procedure, Extent and Limits of the Human Understanding*, p. 30.
[3] Op. cit., p. 33.

existence of God, Browne asserts the empiricist's dictum, *nihil est in intellectu quod non prius fuit in sensu*; 'Nothing is more true to the fact,' he declares, 'than that we have no Ideas but of sensible Objects; upon these it is that the Mind begins to assert its Operations.'[1] Knowledge of God is not derived, therefore, from 'any Ideas we have of Him, or from any direct Intuition of the Intellect; but from Observations and Reasoning of the Mind upon Ideas of Sensation'.[2]

God is known in the 'mirror' of creation and of our own selves. Reference is made to the apostle's words, 'we see through a glass darkly,' in contrast with the face to face knowledge of the future life. The glass does not exhibit the reality and substance of the thing represented, and yet it is right to maintain that we see the thing, the face, the man. 'Thus we say we see a Man in a Glass, when we see no such thing: for the Appearance hath nothing of the real nature of the Man in it.'[3] But analogy is not to be confused with metaphor, although it must be insisted that analogy is 'absolutely necessary' for our knowledge of God.[4] Thus while knowledge of God is the 'mirror type' and is analogical it is not merely metaphorical. Metaphor is 'never used but to express something already known and conceived by the Light of Nature, or revealed by God with more Exactness through the Mediation of Analogy'.[5] It is the reason's operations upon the things of the senses which gives the certainty of God's existence and attributes.

There are, however, truths about God, like that of the Trinity in Unity, which 'could not have been the Invention of Man because it is itself altogether incomprehensible'.[6]

By giving analogy the supreme place Browne was merely carrying on the mediaeval tradition, in which Aquinas stands forth as the greatest of its teachers. It is Browne's contention that the 'incomprehensible things' are themselves revealed under analogy of such relations as are familiar to us, like that of Father, Son and Spirit. Only in this way, it is maintained, could an understanding of God be gained.

Hubert S. Box justifying the Thomistic teaching states that 'few philosophers other than scholastics have realized the necessity in metaphysics of analogical prediction. Because they have not

---

[1] Op. cit., p. 64.   [2] Op. cit., p. 81.
[3] Op. cit., p. 116.   [4] Op. cit., p. 134.
[5] Op. cit., p. 134.   [6] Op. cit., p. 302.

grasped the analogical character of things, many thinkers are afraid of interpretating the Being of God in terms of human experience'.[1] Box, as a neo-Thomist, accepts the doctrine of Aquinas and denies that a knowledge of God comes in any other way except by the 'negative-positive' principle.

It is not our purpose to enter into a detailed investigation of the place of analogy in religion. The use of the principle in this realm raises fundamental and complex questions. So difficult is the problem that E. L. Mascall in his book, *He Who Is*, which is a study of the 'Five Ways' of Aquinas, makes this the excuse for avoiding a discussion of the method.[2] On the other hand, F. C. Copleston, S.J., in his exposition of the philosophy of Aquinas devotes a section of his book to the Angelic Doctor's use of analogy, but his exposition is far from clear.[3]

It is cogent, however, to point out that the eighteenth-century evidence writers who, in their understanding of the origin of religious knowledge, followed Aquinas closely and asserted the doctrine that our ideas of God are built up by way of the senses, could not conceive of any other position as possible. Obviously, where all ontological knowledge is denied, the conclusion follows. But it should be noted that Berkeley, to whom ontological knowledge of God was acceptable, rejects this application of analogy.

Those who developed, as a reaction from the objective view of the apologists, an understanding of revelation as given immediately within experience, also repudiated analogy as the method by which a knowledge of God is gained. A God inferred and invested with attributes on the principle of the extension of human qualities or the negation of these qualities, was considered to be too distant. Whereas, if God can be known 'face to face', then, it was argued, He reveals Himself immediately and directly to the trusting soul for Who He is.

In our own day there is a vigorous repudiation of the method of analogy as used by the Thomists. Professor James Baillie, for example, maintains that the idea of God as perfect is not the result of comparing the less perfect with the more, because the standard

---

[1] *God and the Modern Mind*, p. 247.

[2] Mascall, it is true, in a sequel to, *He Who Is*, entitled *Existence and Analogy*, has attempted to make up for the deficiency of his earlier work. The viewpoint is essentially Thomistic and consequently the supremacy of the *analogia entis* is asserted.

[3] F. C. Copleston, *Aquinas*, pp. 67-8, 129-36.

of perfection must be already apprehended before the comparison itself is instituted. A cannot be compared with B unless both A and B are somehow already known. Professor Norman Kemp Smith takes a similar position. He contends that God cannot really be known by analogy. He argues that, without antecedent or independent knowledge of God, it would not be possible to arrive at any knowledge of Him by the principle of analogy. He assures us that if we start with the creaturely as exhibited in man and nature, and, on the pattern of what is found in the creaturely, we endeavour to construe to ourselves concepts of the divine, we are foredoomed to failure.

Those who are not convinced by these arguments can with some justification, stress Aquinas' 'analogy of Being'. It certainly does seem possible, in some way, to argue from the known to the unknown, from, for example, the idea of man to that of super-man.

An opposition to the Thomists, latent, at least, in Calvin, has been taken up in recent times by the Barthians. Whereas the earlier rejection of the principle of analogy derived from an insistence upon the divine immanence, Barth's arises from an accentuation of the divine transcendence. Brunner credits Barth with being the first theologian who has seen in the application of the principle of analogy the main difference between the Roman and the Reformed theologies. For Barth God is the 'Wholly Other'. He is *'actus purus'*.[1] Man, on the other hand, has lost all 'point of contact' with the divine: the Imago Dei is entirely effaced. He is without a trace of his divine original. Thus, if man would know God, it can only result from an inbreaking of God from without, an 'invasion' from above. This is the understanding of revelation of which, for Barth, the Bible is a 'witness'.[2] The Bible is the human testimony to the fact that God has spoken directly to men in the past, and that He will do so again.[3]

Clearly with such a doctrine there can be no place for analogy. No human being can gain any knowledge of God by the exercise of

[1] *Church Dogmatics*, 1, i, p. 44.

[2] Cf., *Church Dogmatics*, 1, ii (E.T., 1956), p. 457 ff.

[3] Cf., *Church Dogmatics*, 1, i (E.T., 1936), p. 125 ff. It is right, however, to point out that Barth, later in his *Dogmatics*, writes: 'Apprehension of the Word of God could not take place, where there is not in and along with this event something in common between God who speaks and man who hears, an analogy a similarity, for all the dissimilarity involved in the difference between God and man, a "point of contact" — now we may use this concept too — between God and man'. Op. cit., 1, i, p. 373. In this quotation the important words are 'in and along with the event', for they explain his view. Prior to the apprehension of the

a reason which is altogether distorted by sin. Any notions which men can construe will not be of the true and living God; they will be of 'no God', the very negation of the real. Thus for Barth the analogical method leads logically to a *theologia naturalis*, and therefore is anathema.[1]

It will be seen, then, that both the subjectivists, because of their emphasis upon the divine immanence, and the Barthians, because of their emphasis upon the divine transcendence, repudiated the method of analogy. On our view the exclusive application of the principle, on the one side, and the total rejection of it, on the other, are untenable. The use of the method is certainly beset with real difficulties especially when the resemblance 'is interesting or emotionally satisfying'.[2] Miss Stebbing contends that 'the greater our ignorance of the subject-matter, the more likely are we to be misled by a weak analogy',[3] and she quotes Dr J. M. Keynes' remark that 'the common sense of the race has been impressed by weak analogies'.[4] Such statements are, of course, no sufficient reason to repudiate the analogical method as such. They do serve, however, to show that it must be used with caution and understanding.

The fact that man is made in the image of God, and that however affected he may be by sin, some relation to God still persists, is adequate justification for the use of the method of analogy. 'We must think of the divine on the analogy of all that is richest and most human, not only in our actual character, but in the better we

---

'word', the 'point of contact' does not exist. It is in 'faith' that it comes to be. It is then and there restored. 'The reconciliation of man with God in Christ includes in itself or else begins with a fresh establishment of the lost "point of contact". This point of contact is, therefore, not real outside faith but only in faith. In faith a man is created by the Word of God for the Word of God, existing in the Word of God, not in himself, not in virtue of his humanity and personality, nor from the standpoint of creation, for what is possible from the standpoint of creation from man to God has actually been lost through the Fall,' *Church Dogmatics*, 1, i, p. 273. The whole section of the *Dogmatics*, entitled, 'The Word of God and Faith,' p. 260 ff., is intended to make this teaching clear. But it is still not clear how man, who has lost all natural *capax verbi divini*, now receives it in the act of faith. One is left wondering whose is the 'point of contact', Is it God's or man's?

[1] Barth, although he rejects the *analogia entis*, allows that there still exists the ἀναλογία τῆς πιστεως. 'We thus', he writes, 'do not oppose the Catholic doctrine of the *analogia entis* by a denial of the concept of analogy. But we say that the analogy in question is not an *analogia entis*, but according to Rom. 12. 6, ἀναλογία τῆς πιστεως.' *Church Dogmatics*, 1, i, p. 279.

[2] I. M. Stebbing, *A Modern Introduction to Logic*, p. 254.

[3] Op. cit., ibid.

[4] Op. cit., ibid.

aspire to be.'[1] Analogy certainly can be used to confirm and clarify our religious knowledge. It 'plays a part in suggesting ideas and in aiding our thought'.[2] So much, at least, may be granted. This means that the rejection of the principle, from either an idealist or a Barthian standpoint, is invalid. On the other hand, against the apologists, we feel bound to contend, that they were too optimistic and too dogmatic in their use of the method. They did not see, and they could not grant, that any other idea was possible.

There were two particular arguments used by the deists which their opponents had to answer. It was the contention of the former that there could be no revealed religion beyond that already provided for all in the dictates of natural religion. They argued, firstly, that there could be no disclosure of God limited in extent and action to a select section of humanity. They felt that the claim to a revealed religion which involved only a particular people would impugn the justice of God. Then, secondly, they rejected anything as revealed which had to be described as mysterious. Mystery was, for them, *per se*, proof that the claim could not be upheld. Only the understandable could be the revealed.

(c) Revealed Religion as Limited

Stebbing rejects the validity of the argument against a revealed religion on the grounds of its want of universality. He asks his opponent, 'If of two men you relieve one, Can it be said that one is not relieved?'[3] Revelation is, after all as Clarke has contended, an act of God's mercy, it is not a matter of justice. The necessities of men are not the sole reason for God's actions. Nor is the happiness of men the only consideration. If it were so, it might be argued that nature would have provided it, and omnipotence bestowed it. Conybeare urges as a justification for the limitation of revealed religion the absolute freedom of God. It is with Him 'to bestow or not bestow a revelation as he pleases', since He is 'the most proper judge when and to whom to grant it'.[4]

Foster attacks the deistic thesis, pointing out that reason itself is restricted. Some races are little more than brutes. It is said that God ought to give to all what he has given to some. The assertion, he agrees, is plausible, but we have to accept, not what we think

---

[1] A. E. Taylor, *The Faith of a Moralist*, vol. 1, p. 62.
[2] G. Galloway, *The Philosophy of Religion*, p. 342.
[3] *Defence of Dr Clarke*, p. 80.
[4] *Defence of Revealed Religion*, p. 419.

God should have done, but what, as a matter of fact, He has done. It appears reasonable to argue that God should have made all men good logicians, yet He has made some 'downright idiots'.[1]

Butler notes the 'great weight' attached by the deists to the restricted nature of revealed religion. Butler replies to the deists by stressing the two main points of the Analogy. First, he observes, nature itself provides instances of the same restriction. Evidently the Author of nature 'bestows that upon some which he does not upon others, who seem equally to stand in need of it'.[2] As we cannot understand this in the natural sphere still less can we do so in the spiritual. Then, secondly, Butler would have us constantly to recognize our ignorance. Religion, he says, has not come to satisfy the curious mind, but 'only to regulate' the lives of men, and to 'teach them their duty'.[3] The judge of all the earth, we are to believe, will do right. For those who act in accord to the moral principles known to all men, God will make merciful allowance. And even if the deists were right in arguing that a revelation must be universal, there would still be disadvantages rising from man's capacities, length of days, education, external circumstances, and so forth.

According to Alan Richardson this conception of a limited revelation has special difficulties for the 'modern mind'.[4] It is therefore of interest to observe that it was a problem the anti-deistic writers had to face. They had insisted that God revealed Himself at a set period and to a selected people. We have seen how some of the apologists met the charge that this was arbitrary and irrational. Cogent as were some of the points made in their replies, their position would have been more secure if they had seen the significance of the message proclaimed by the Hebrew prophets. It was they who announced Jehovah as Lord of history. There was no favouritism in God's selection of Israel. The records of this people are not devoid of all that would glorify them. Indeed their sins are chronicled with a starkness and a vividness which startles. And upon the children of Israel the judgements of God are meted out with an unsparing severity. It was the prophets who were the true interpreters of Israel's history as significant.

'Taught by the prophets the Hebrew people of the Old Testa-

---

[1] *The Usefulness, Truth and Excellency of the Christian Religion*, p. 67.
[2] *Analogy*, p. 259.
[3] Op. cit., p. 361.
[4] *Christian Apologetics*, p. 139.

ment times, when they were true to themselves, were unique amongst the nations of the world in regarding themselves as bound in a Covenant-relationship to the God Who was discerned as the Lord of history and they thus recognized themselves to be committed to the realization of the will and purpose of God in their national life. In the great crises of Israel's history there arose a succession of prophets who interpreted to those who would listen what God was doing in the various upheavals and reconstructions of their life as a nation. It is an indisputable fact that such a prophetic interpretation of history arose in Israel and nowhere else. God indeed worked through Egypt, Babylon, Greece and Rome; but these nations and empires produced no prophets of the biblical type to interpret what God was doing; they remained blind to the operations of the Lord of history, and hence no special revelation came forth from them. The events of history as such do not themselves constitute a revelation; it is the prophetic interpretation of the historical events which is the vehicle of special revelation in the sense which the biblical and Christian tradition understands that conception. Where there are no prophets there can be no special revelation. And if the phenomenon of prophecy is found nowhere except in the Jewish-Christian tradition, then we must cease to complain about "the scandal of particularity" and resolve to accept the facts as facts, refusing to explain them away in obedience to a quite unscientific predilection for a general theory which was conceived before the facts were examined. If we ask why this special revelation and special type of knowledge of God active in history should have arisen in Israel only, or why other nations did not give birth to prophets of the biblical type, we are in the presence of mystery; we do not know the answer to this question, which must inevitably remain concealed within the secret counsels of God: this is the mystery of "election", which is not, after all, an invention of theologians but an admission that there are facts which we cannot explain but must not try to explain them away. That we cannot explain why God chose the Jewish people to be the special instrument of His purpose in history is no reason for denying the plentiful evidence that He did choose them.'[1]

(d) Revealed Religion as Mysterious

Once it is realised that reason does not hold the infallible position

[1] A. Richardson, *Christian Apologetics*, pp. 140, 141.

that the deists accorded to it, it naturally follows that there are
some areas of knowledge beyond its scope. It was in this way
that their opponents forced their point that it was no discredit
to revealed religion to insist that all its items could not be reduced
to clear and distinct ideas.

John Foster declared that the true attitude for men to adopt
before God is an attitude of reverent agnosticism, and to confess
that He may have reasons we know not of. It is unreasonable to
reject the propositions of revealed religion because it sets forth in
its agenda items which are beyond the researches of the understanding. God can give positive rules without clear reasons for
them: the right is His, and His divinity is revealed in the exercise
of it. God has rights beyond those which we credit to Him.

Rogers gives expression to the view, in opposition to the deists,
which was later elaborated so eloquently by Bishop Butler. In
nature, Rogers points out, there are things which we cannot
understand. Of things remote we can but know one side, while
things near are only known by appearance. There is a point beyond
which we cannot go; 'Our Prospect is terminated by a narrow
Horizon.'[1] 'The gradual Advancement of Human Reason in what
it does know, the Boundaries that stop its Progress and confine its
Perceptions, oblige us to conclude, that there must be many Truths
beyond our Discovery or Comprehension.'[2] There must be, therefore, more in the attributes of God than the reason can discover,
and, possibly others besides which it can never find out. Many of
the propositions of revealed religion must consequently be unintelligible. There is no reason to reject them for they are guaranteed by the veracity of God. The positive ordinances of Christianity are not to be set aside because God 'may annex his Graces
to what Ordinances he thinks fit'.[3]

It is, however, to Butler we must turn for the most telling use of
the argument. Butler assures us that reason alone can judge of the
credibility and consistency of revelation. But he goes on to maintain that if it be allowed that a revelation has been given then 'it is
highly credible beforehand, we should be incompetent judges of it
to a great degree'.[4] Of the scheme of nature we are not fully aware,
and in the natural sphere there is much too deep to be fathomed,

---

[1] *The Use and Necessity of Divine Revelation*, p. 80.
[2] Ibid.
[3] Op. cit., p. 100.
[4] *Analogy*, p. 219.

too high to be understood. Thus, argues Butler, 'our being in-competent judges of one, must render it credible that we may be incompetent judges also in the other.'[1] In an apt illustration Butler clinches the matter. When a citizen of a kingdom reveals him-self an incompetent judge of how the laws should be carried on, there is no reason to think that he will be a fit one when extra-ordinary measures are needful. If we show our ability to be in-sufficient when natural instruction is concerned, it is unlikely that we can have any assurance of certainty in the supernatural realm. This being so we cannot lay it down *a priori*, the method, the measure or the meaning of revelation. This insistence on the inability of reason is stressed in a powerful sermon 'Upon the Ignorance of Man'. This is the last of Butler's sermons — fifteen in all — preached at the Rolls Chapel and published in 1726.

The text for the sermon is Eccles. viii. 16, 17, and the passage, attributed to Solomon, is made to express the king's 'great ignorance of the works of God, and the method of his providence in the government of the world'.[2] The limits of the human under-standing are clear. The world without and the world within are beyond our utmost reach. In the 'scheme of Providence, the ways and works of God are too vast, of too large extent, for our capacities'.[3] A veil has been drawn over God's power, wisdom and goodness. But this very ignorance is an occasion for faith, and those who obey the gospel, 'upon less sensible evidence than Thomas, earn the Saviour's commendation, "Blessed are they that have not seen, and yet have believed." '[4] Happiness does not consist in being well instructed. Virtue is the real source of man's true life; thus the lesson is, to depart from evil and to fear God. This realization of ignorance he finds to be 'the proper answer to many things which are called objections against religion'.[5]

Mystery is to be expected in religion as well as in nature, and it is the essence of folly to reject the evidence we have because it is not what we desired. It is unreasonable to scorn lesser lights to guide the way because the sun is not shining in its strength. If a man had to take a journey by night he would be thankful for any light to illuminate the darkness until the daybreak and the shadows flee away.

[1] Op. cit., p. 502.
[2] *Sermons printed with Analogy* (new edition, 1882), p. 531.
[3] Ibid., p. 533.   [4] Ibid., p. 535.   [5] Ibid., p. 537.

In the second part of the Analogy it is premised that 'Christianity is a scheme quite beyond our comprehension'.[1] Butler summarizes the main articles of the gospel and urges that Scripture itself indicates the incomprehensible nature of its revelation when it speaks in 2 Timothy iii. 16, of 'the great mystery of godliness'. When the separate particulars of the message are examined we 'immediately run up into something which shows our ignorance in it'.[2] The laws of God's general activities are but imperfectly known to us, and the laws which govern His extraordinary ways are entirely unknown to us. The whole scheme of divine revelation is disclosed only in part. In temporal affairs men must act on evidence which must necessarily be inconclusive. After all 'probability is the guide of life'.

There is much in this anti-deistic insistence upon mystery in revelation which cannot be denied. It is, however, not easy to approve of Butler's method. The question arises, Is the best way of meeting a problem to raise a crop of new ones in a related topic? Are we likely to accept revelation because we are told that we cannot explain nature? Yet it would appear that the method was the only one possible for the apologists beginning as they did with the notion of an exclusively metaphysical epistemology.

A survey of the foregoing pages will leave little room for doubt that the anti-deistic apologists somehow missed the mark. Not only were they too close to their deistic opponents for mortal combat, but they failed to get into contact with the deeper needs of the human soul for a religion more personal and more soul-satisfying. While the God of deism was heedlessly remote, behind the universe; the orthodox deity was helplessly confined within a logical system. The one was indifferent, the other was imprisoned. Consequently neither the one nor the other sufficed for the soul, sin-sick.

Deism was, therefore, not destroyed by the burning sarcasm of a Conybeare nor the brilliant argument of a Butler. It was to the preaching of Whitfield and Wesley that the heart of the people responded.

There is one name among the host of those who entered the list against deism whom we have left for special consideration because of his penetrating understanding of the deistic doctrine.

---

[1] *Analogy*, p. 233.
[2] Op. cit., p. 235.

(e) William Law's attack on Deism

In William Law's book, *The Case of Reason, or Natural Religion Fairly and Fully Stated*, there is a new depth of argument. The subtitle tells us it is directed against Tindal's *Christianity as Old as Creation*. Law comes to the attack with a forcefulness and originality which were lacking in the other writers on the same side as he. They, for the most part, gave the impression of half-accepting and half-protesting. Law does not repeat second-hand arguments and ineffective shibboleths. He attacks the central territory of his enemy. He directs his arrows to the heart. He comes, not to skirmish, but to slay. And it is beyond doubt that Law wins a decisive victory and remains a conqueror on the battlefield.

Tindal argued that God must act according to the fitness of things, if He did otherwise He would be arbitrary. Law replies that if the premise is accepted, the conclusion does not follow. The 'whole argument', contends Law, 'proves directly the contrary to that which the author intended to prove by it.'[1] The fitness to which God's acts must conform cannot be anything in nature, it must be grounded in His own being. To act in this manner means that many of His works must be incomprehensible. He would act arbitrarily if He did anything contrary to His nature. The reason of things cannot tell us why He created man as He has, or rules them as He does. No necessary fitness can be observed in many of God's ways. 'And don't you say', Law asks his opponent, 'that God has made you for your own sake, ought you not therefore to know the reasonableness and fitness of things?'[2] The fact is that there is much we cannot examine or explain. We must believe where we cannot prove. If reason and fitness are considered necessary to salvation they must likewise be considered so for nature. 'For it is just as wise and reasonable to allow of no mysteries or secrets in Creation and Providence.'[3] What is fit for God as Creator is as much above our power to understand as it is for us to govern the universe.

Law meets Tindal's objections to the atonement and shows the folly of rationalizing this central doctrine. 'He who rejects the atonement for sins made by the Son of God, as needless, because he cannot prove it to be necessary, is as extravagant, as he who would deny that God created him, by his only Son, because he did

---

[1] *The Case of Reason*, p. 62.
[2] Op. cit., p. 64.   [3] Op. cit., p. 66.

not remember it.'[1] And our memory is as proper a faculty in the one instance, as reason is in the other.

Tindal errs in making God the slave of some outside fitness to which He must conform. There is no such prior pattern. God's attributes cannot be founded on anything outside Himself. God is Himself the ultimate cause of all; the final fitness, and 'we have not found out God, till we have found out a Being that has no cause'.[2] 'To ask, therefore, whether there is not something right and wrong, antecedent to the will of God, to render his will capable of being right, is as absurd as to ask for some antecedent cause of his existence, that he may be proved to exist necessarily.'[3] 'Dare any one say that God's laws are not founded on the eternal reason of things?'[4] exclaims Tindal. Law dares to say it. God's existence is not founded on the eternal existence of things; to say that God's laws depend upon eternal reason is like saying that His power is founded on the eternal capacities of things. 'And as to the existence of God, because it contains all perfections, cannot, for that reason have any external cause; so the will of God, because it is all perfection, cannot, for that reason, have any external rule or direction.'[5] God's goodness *is* arbitrary, and His arbitrariness is His goodness.

Tindal lays it down that God must act according to the relation in which He stands towards His creatures. This relation, he asserts, is also based on the fitness of things. In other words, as Law shows, it is based upon God as He is in Himself, the omniscient Creator, the governor of all and so forth. These are items of the divine nature beyond our comprehension far. If then 'the relation itself is incomprehensible, then those actions that have their fitness in it, must surely be incomprehensible'.[6] This argument is forcefully pressed, and it is shown that none can tell the degree of reason which rational beings possess, or how much new and revealed knowledge God may see fit to add. Tindal thinks that if God designed good for His creatures He would not have deferred the communications of those requirements which make for their good 'till the time of Tiberius'. Law answers, but if God acts according to His relation with His creatures, then it must be concluded that this relation, directed by His foreknowledge, means that He was not acting other than for the good of men by giving

---

[1] Op. cit., p. 74.   [2] Op. cit., p. 86.   [3] Op. cit., p. 88.
[4] *Christianity as Old as Creation*, p. 385.
[5] *The Case of Reason*, p. 90.
[6] Op. cit., p. 93.

such a revelation, at such a time, and to such persons. His deferring it 'till the time of Tiberius' is, in fact, a supreme evidence of God's concern for His human family. God's foreknowledge took account of 'the actions and state of free agents, and of the effects of his revelation'.[1] His revelation was given at a time when its results would be greatest.

Since God's acts are grounded in the fitness of His own Being, then it was the fittest occasion for Him, Who is supremely good, to do good to all. From the state of the relation which exists between God and man, the reasons for the time, matter and manner of the divine revelation are beyond human discovery. It must be concluded that God's revealed truths are in fact mysterious and incomprehensible.

Law is ready to meet the question, How then can they be received as divine? He points out, as Butler did later, that the creation is accepted as the work of God although it abounds in mystery. 'And the relation itself is therefore, mysterious, because creation and providence cannot be delivered from mysteries.'[2] Instead of this leading to atheism it should lead to adoration.

Law appeals to miracles and prophecies on which, he declares, Christianity is founded, as a sufficient proof that it is a divine revelation. He does not accept the position of the other anti-deistic writers that a miracle cannot ever attest anything contrary to reason. Tindal asserted that since evil spirits are supposed to be able to work miracles then no value can be attached to them as proofs. Law retorts: 'if the creation must of necessity be allowed to be the work of God, notwithstanding any unknown degree of power in evil spirits; if we can as certainly ascribe it to God, as if we really knew there were no such spirits; then in some cases, miracles may be a full proof of the operation, or the inter-position of God, as if we really knew there were no such spirits in being.'[3] If God is to be accepted as the Creator, then it follows of necessity that He still presides over the universe. Providence attests His actions in things ordinary, and if God works in things ordinary then there is no reason to deny extraordinary activity to Him. But if the incomprehensible is attributed to evil spirits, then there is no reason why the ordinary should be attributed to God.

Law believes that miracles are absolute proof. 'It seems therefore

[1] Op. cit., p. 95.   [2] Op. cit., p. 103.
[3] Op. cit., p. 108.

to be needless, and too great a concession, which some learned divines make in this matter, when they grant that we must first examine the doctrines revealed by miracles, and see whether they contain anything in them absurd, or unworthy of God before we receive His miracles as divine.'[1] There is no appeal from the evidence of miracles. To judge a doctrine by reason, and then the miracles by the doctrines is to begin at the wrong end. The doctrines are revealed 'because of our ignorance of the nature and reasonableness of them', and the miracles are wrought with the purpose of preventing us from acquiescing in our judgement of the worth and value of the doctrines.

In another chapter Law turns the tables on his opponent. Freethinkers make a great show of reason, they assume the position of champions, pretending to vindicate the right of all men to judge according to its dictates. Law replies with the observation that this is trite, for reason is the only way rational creatures can determine anything either theoretical or practical. 'It is not a matter of duty for men to use their reason, but of necessity.'[2]

The human reason, however, far from being, the be all and end all, is precisely that which renders men fit recipients for the revelation of God. It is as natural for men to use their reason as it is to see with their eyes. The unbeliever is opposed, not because he reasons, but because he reasons falsely. The question, then, is 'not whether reason is to be followed, but when it is best followed? not whether it is to be our guide, but how it may be our safest guide?'[3] And it is our best guide when it admits its imperfection and follows the light of heaven. It cannot ever be a true guide since, in his last chapter, Law sets out to show, 'that all the disorders of our passions, the corruptions of our hearts, all the reveries of the imagination, all the contradictions and absurdities that are to be found in human life, and human opinions, are strictly and precisely the mutability, the disorders, corruption and absurdities of the human reason.'[4]

---

[1] *The Case of Reason*, p. 109.   [2] Op. cit., p. 115.
[3] Op. cit., p. 116.   [4] Op. cit., p. 128.

CHAPTER VI

THE CHANGE OF AN EMPHASIS

The passing of deism gave the orthodox apologists opportunity to turn their attention to the Methodist movement, which was regarded as a recrudescence of 'enthusiasm'. There was an understandable anxiety among many convinced Churchmen lest the activities of Whitfield and Wesley should upset the ordered structure of the Established Church. It was feared that a schism, like that of early Montanism, would weaken the authority of this ordained institution, and give occasion for the rise of all sorts of irregularities, each claiming the sanction of an immediate revelation. It was out of this anxiety and fear that there appeared a flood of books and pamphlets all aimed at curbing the Methodist excess. Such works as Green, *On Enthusiasm*, and Bishop Gibson, *Against Enthusiasm*, had this avowed design.

The best known of these anti-enthusiast volumes — a work which John Wesley himself felt compelled to answer — was Bishop Lavington's *The Enthusiasm of the Methodists and Papists Compared*. The Bishop had written of Wesley as pretending to special and immediate revelations, and he likens enthusiasm to 'a kind of drunkenness'.[1] This charge, with a long list of others, Wesley denies, maintaining that, 'the Mystic Divinity was never a Methodists' doctrine.'[2]

But interest in the enthusiasm of the Methodists was soon turned, to what was regarded as another expression of the same spirit in a different realm. The beginning of the nineteenth century marked the commencement of a new state and stage in scientific activity. Not only had Dalton, in 1803, announced his atomic theory and Sir Charles Bell turned attention to the study of the brain to indicate the difference between the sensory and the motor nerve mechanism, but Lamarck had stood forth as the precursor of the scientific doctrine of evolution. The early years of the century

[1] Op. cit., p. 75.
[2] *Works* (1809), vol. 13, p. 55.

saw an increasing use made of the mathematical method in physics. There was everywhere a growing unrest with anything that savoured of the mysterious. The claim was being made that no province of the universe could be shut off from scientific investigation. Theologians were ordered to abandon their territory. Theological and metaphysical assumptions were not to be allowed to erect a 'No Thoroughfare' notice anywhere. Theologians were refused the right to say to the scientist, Thus far shalt thou go and no farther. The time had come, it was being announced, when science must free itself from the dictates of metaphysics.

Thus it was, with the stabilization of Methodism the orthodox turned their attention from the religious enthusiasm to the scientific. Yet the scientific world of the early nineteenth century differed only from the earlier deistic one in the fact that the God of deism was eliminated. The remote God of deism was now removed, and the throne of the universe was left unoccupied.

In this scientific climate there arose a fervent unbelief, eager to accost and attack the protagonists of revealed religion, ready to undermine the bulwarks of the faith. The Report of the Society for Promoting Christian Knowledge for 1832 gives the information that, in London, productions claiming to be directed towards the diffusion of science, but hostile to revealed religion, were disseminated to the amount of three hundred thousand a week. Their zeal on behalf of unbelief was regarded as another manifestation of the enthusiastic spirit. Here was 'an unauthorized outstripping of all rightful bounds of reason'. If the religious enthusiasm was responsible for incredulity, this new scientific enthusiasm gave vent to infidelity. Dr Bidlake in the Bampton Lectures of 1811, traces the fanaticism which springs from religious enthusiasm, and the unbelief in a divine revelation, which in the name of science, conceives of the world as a closed system, to the same root. 'Having therefore endeavoured', he writes, 'to show the regular consistency of all schemes of providence, and the demonstrative probability of the truth of the Christian religion; we must show the unhappy tendency of pretentions which would destroy all consistence, and render religion contrary to what God has designed it to be; making it, instead of a system of practical piety and goodness, a visionary illusion. It is highly probable that these opinions originate from the same strong and restless passions of the mind which influence other men to

deviate into the extreme of infidelity. These extremes of error
spring from the same evil root. The same principle of ambition is
observable in both. If the infidel is gratified by assuming the
solemnity of doubt, of suspicion, of scorn, and in thus defying the
armies of the living God; the pride of the enthusiast is equally
flattered by the idea of his being the chosen favourite of Heaven.'[1]

Both the fanatic and the infidel must be made to see that God's
revelation is complete and final. While the latter treats Christianity
with a cold indifference, the former 'ask for no evidence'. They
'trust only to certain inward and equivocal feelings'.[2] The infidel
is disposed to believe nothing and to revile everything. The enthusiast acts under the sway of some internal and imaginary impulse. He impudently aspires to familiarity with the Sovereign of
the Universe. But asks Bidlake, 'of what avail are ordinances, if
men can be saved by instantaneous conversion?'[3] He thinks that
the enthusiasts' sense of guilt is the offspring of mental gloom;
while the assertion of the inner feeling of grace received is rejected
because it is built upon the notion that 'good and religious conduct
will not render him worthy of acceptance with God'.[4] Faith,
according to Bidlake, is 'the assent the reason gives to the word of
God'.[5] It is built upon the impartial weighing of evidence, and it is
only the man of integrity who will give unprejudiced attention to
the proofs. Indeed the evidence of his integrity is seen in the fact
that he gives his 'Amen' to the doctrines as divine. The enthusiast,
therefore, puts immediate inspiration in the place of patient
instruction. The infidel, on the other hand, puts arrogant declama-
tion in the place of reverent devotion.

Against the latter, Bidlake will show 'that the evidences of revealed religion are capable of a very high demonstration; that the
scheme of divine revelation is grand, comprehensive, consistent
and harmonious in its general design; agreeable to the attributes of
the Deity, and to the analogies of his economy in the natural and
moral world'.[6] He attributes the motives of unbelief in a 'superintending Providence' to apathy, impiety and pride. The desire for
novelty is also a potent force. The bravery of the soldier in the

[1] *The Truth and Consistency of the Divine Revelation; with some Remarks on the
contrary extremes of Infidelity and Enthusiasm* (2nd edition), pp. 154, 155.
[2] Op. cit., p. 153.
[3] Op. cit., p. 154.
[4] Op. cit., p. 169.
[5] Op. cit., p. 197.
[6] Op. cit., p. 6.

ranks can go unobserved, but he who meets the enemy single-
handed is brought to the notice of every eye. Thus 'to tread in the
accustomed path is to be lost in a crowd, men hope from every
deviation to acquire a degree of pre-eminence or at least to attract
attention'.[1]

In order to confound the infidel, Bidlake sets out to prove the
reality of a particular providence. He uses the cosmological argument to secure his evidence for a 'superintending First Cause'.
Reference to second causes is not sufficient to account for the
continual adaptation of nature to an over-arching purpose. The
Mosaic account of creation, the Fall, and the Deluge bears the
marks of a divine disclosure, a fact made obvious when the account
is contrasted with the mythologies and polytheism of other
peoples. 'If then no conception of natural religion were so clear, no
declarations so express, as are evident in the Jewish revelation, is it
not to be concluded that the Scriptures must have derived their
origin from a source superior to human?'[2]

There is much greater evidence for the New Testament, whose
universal appeal, superior morality and central Figure give it a
quality and an authenticity which none can gainsay. In the light of
these overwhelming proofs, the infidel, like the enthusiast, is
charged with blindly rejecting the reality and the authority of
revelation as a body of revealed doctrines. The infidel would have
us 'reject the promises of revealed religion, which alone afford
rational hope and firm conviction'.[3]

REVELATION AS A BODY OF REVEALED DOCTRINES

Two enemies, then, the apologists at the close of the eighteenth
and the beginning of the nineteenth centuries, felt themselves
bound to combat. There were the enthusiasts who had to be restricted to the Scriptures as the full and final revelation, and there
were the infidels who had to be convinced of the Scriptures as a real
revelation. This fact can be illustrated by a comparison of two
series of Bampton Lectures which appeared in the first half of the
nineteenth century. In 1802, G. F. Nott took as his subject, *Religious Enthusiasm*, while in 1833, F. Nolan discoursed on *The
Analogy of Revelation and Science*.

For Nott the tragedy of religious enthusiasm was that it upset

[1] Op. cit., p. 10.   [2] Op. cit., p. 92.
[3] Op. cit., p. 32.

the communicated body of revealed truths. Where there is a desire for 'immediate revelation, rather than the study of Scripture, it will be easy to trace the progress of enthusiasm'.[1] For Nolan the tragedy of 'Scientific' infidelity was its rejection of revelation. 'In the increasing ardour', he writes, 'with which scientific enquiry is now pursued, when every facility is not merely afforded to individual exertion, but means are used to draw out the general strength of combined operations; some anxiety, if not apprehension, may be felt, as to the direction in which this growing power may be ultimately turned. When the interests of Philosophy are exclusively advanced; there can be no room to attend to the unobtrusive claims of Religion. Experience has unfortunately proved, that as the one advances its pretentions, the other is found to decline in its reputation.'[2]

The works of Nott and Nolan are important, then, first, because they indicate the awareness by the orthodox of their opponents. In their view the religious enthusiast was guilty of the sin of undermining, while the scientific infidel was guilty of the sin of unbelief. Against both, the apologists sought to defend Christianity as a body of 'revealed truths from which it is impossible to deviate without incurring guilt'.[3] To the first, therefore, had to be proved the finality of the Scriptures as a system of doctrine, to the second the actuality of revelation within the communicated word.

(i) *The New Enemies*
(a) *Religious Enthusiasm*

G. F. Nott began his series of Lectures with an investigation of the meaning of the word 'enthusiasm'. It denotes, he concludes, 'that self-sufficient spirit, which placing the conceit of human fancy on a level with real inspiration has ever proved by its results, that it is not of God.'[4] He unhesitatingly attributes such enthusiasm to the ultimate agency of the devil. He will be content to assert, however, that in men like Whitfield and Wesley it is due to a vehement action of the imagination. 'The first conceit of divine illumination in the mind of the Enthusiast is owing to the inordinate action of imagination, which, when vehemently excited, is known to represent ideal objects so vividly to the apprehension,

[1] G. F. Nott, *Religious Enthusiasm*, p. 48.
[2] *The Analogy of Religion and Science*, p. 33.
[3] *Religious Enthusiasm*, p. 324.
[4] Op. cit., p. 6.

that they are mistaken for material ones.'[1] The tragedy is that the enthusiast, while claiming to justify himself from Scripture, in reality denies its finality and authority. 'All pretence to rapturous communications of divine knowledge is enthusiastic delusion.'[2]

Enthusiasm is stimulated by pride, vanity and ambition. There is a curiosity which drives some to be wise beyond what is written; there is an unsanctified ambition for spiritual pre-eminence. Some have a consuming desire for immediate revelations, and seeing that no such private communications are possible, they are soon created by the obliging imagination and believed in as undoubted realities. 'If they did not think themselves inspired,' says H. More, 'they were not enthusiasts.'[3]

The most awful result of this fevered spirit is that it openly violates the unity of the Church. And the Church for Nott is a visible institution by law established. The providence of God has 'preserved among us the Established order entire'.[4] To be the occasion for schism is to be guilty of the darkest sin.

Having set forth the causes and the characteristics of enthusiasm, Nott goes on to apply his conclusions to Whitfield and Wesley. They are both to be designated 'enthusiasts' because they have pretended to special revelations, and by their conduct have separated from the established Church. They 'believe themselves, like the Prophets and Apostles of old, to have received a particular communication of divine authority'.[5] They believe themselves to be specially raised up of God to deliver the people, they fancy that God intervened on their behalf by miraculous interpositions, they arrogate to themselves words which should only be attributed to Christ and His apostles, they preach false doctrine. Concerning the last charge Nott singles out three 'errors' which are specially repugnant: (1) The assurance of salvation and forgiveness by the immediate activity of the Holy Ghost, (2) Perfectionism, (3) regeneration as a conscious act taking place in the heart, sometimes with an agony issuing in joyous peace. With these and other arguments Nott concludes, 'that the Authors of the Sect were, in the strict sense of the word, Enthusiasts.'[6]

Being thus deluded they must have been overcome by the passions of pride, vanity, and ambition. The works of Whitfield and

---

[1] *Religious Enthusiasm*, p. 37.   [2] Op. cit., p. 31.
[3] *Divine Dialogues*, p. 469.   [4] *Religious Enthusiasm*, p. 85.
[5] *Religious Enthusiasm*, p. 216.   [6] Op. cit., p. 251.

Wesley are made to yield the necessary proof, and, of course, use is made of Lavington to assure the correctness of the conclusion. Can there be any doubt that they grasped at public fame? If there should be any then Nott will remove it. Any admission of unworthiness, any claim to a divine guidance, any reference to extraordinary manifestations of the Spirit, and the like, are all laboriously marshalled and skillfully used to draw the same conclusion. Can their doctrines be true? it may be asked. How can they be? The test of true doctrines is that 'they are perfect at the very time of their delivery'.[1] But the leaders of this Sect have admitted to altering their views. They stand, therefore, self-condemned. 'For though the founders of this Sect asserted, that they were filled in a peculiar manner with the Holy Ghost; and that they were instructed of God, what they were to teach to mankind; they nevertheless contradicted not only themselves, and one another, but even the very Scriptures.'[2]

The result of such enthusiasm was inevitable. By following the dictates of their own inclinations they have repudiated the authority of the Church: 'if men believe that the Almighty communicates his will to them by impressing forcibly upon their hearts what in every situation he would do, they would naturally suspect that every strong impulse, or inclination which they feel may be a divine suggestion.'[3] They have lost sight of the fact that the complete system of religion has been communicated entire. They would add thereto the fancies of their own fevered minds and their own fictitious messages. 'How can it be a mark of a superior mind, to be indifferent as to the deviations which are made from the one unalterable standard of Revealed Truth.'[4] Religion of *this* enthusiastic origination is not from above.

When once enthusiasm is allowed to continue its disrupting influence it will be content, not merely to tear asunder the unity of the Church, but with nothing less than the break up of social solidarity, by dissolving the ties of natural affection and the harmonies of public business and private families. It will even extend its baneful influence further, and, by exciting public dissentions, lawful government itself will become impossible. To such a conclusion then, must enthusiasm lead; to such an awful end are carried those who seek personal revelations from God.

[1] Op. cit., p. 302.
[2] Op. cit., p. 305.
[3] Op. cit., p. 329.
[4] Op. cit., p. 380.

(b) Scientific Scepticism

Nott considered himself to be defending the fully-revealed scheme of doctrine from the attacks of the religious enthusiasts. But it was for Nolan to maintain the same position, some thirty years later, against the prevalent scepticism of his day. The task, he feels, to be of special urgency, and it is not to be 'looked upon as uncalled for at a time, when the interests of Revelation are not merely overlooked, but the subject deemed incompatible with the cultivation of Science'.[1] It is the purpose of Nolan to show that there is no disharmony between Revelation and Science. He therefore takes up the Biblical account of the Creation, the Fall, the separation of the races, and related topics, and maintains that nothing that a true science can discover has rendered these impossible. 'The sacred legislator, it is admitted, addresses us in a religious, not in a philosophical character; but in demanding our assent to communications, as delivered by inspiration, we have some right to expect, that as far as they extend, they should maintain their pretensions to infallibility.'[2]

Moses, he asserts, was no illiterate primitive, for 'he must have been sufficiently versed in the principle of science, to have accommodated his descriptions to the views entertained of it by the moderns'.[3] In these intricate lectures reference is made to ancient cosmologies, and recent advances in geological, physiological, zoological and geographical knowledge. It is concluded that 'the disclosures of Revelation, are consonant to the decisions of Science'.[4] Nothing has been discovered that renders a belief in a Deluge impossible. The longevity of the patriarchs is considered to be sufficiently explained on the hypothesis that an Egyptian scheme of chronology was used, in which, instead of a year of twelve months, seasons of three are computed. This means that the age of any one recorded individual is already reduced to one-fourth of that period. Methuselah's real age is consequently 242 years. When allowance is made for the relative purity and simplicity of their lives and the unhurried nature of their existence in a leisurely environment this number of years is not difficult to accept.[5]

[1] *The Analogy of Religion and Science*, p. 356.
[2] Op. cit., pp. 44, 45.
[3] Op. cit., p. 48.
[4] Op. cit., p. 314.
[5] In a footnote, Nolan quotes from the parish register of St Leonards, Shoreditch, London; Thomas Carn, died Jan. 28th, 1588, aged 207 years.

He is certain also that naturalists are agreed that the whole human race was developed from one human family. In Lecture 5 he states that, 'Whatever, therefore, be the test by which the scheme of Revelation is tried; whether it be estimated by the attributes of the Deity or the constitution of nature; by the immutable principle of good and evil, or the decisions of ethical and physiological science; under every trial it bears testimony to the goodness and benevolence of its Author, not less striking than the works of nature supply of his power and wisdom.'[1]

Christianity is clearly a body of revealed truths: and the authors of the sacred books 'deliver a communication from Him who can as little err himself as conspire in deceiving others'.[2] It is when the ablest systems which men have devised to solve the riddle of the universe are found to leave the reader as perplexed as before, that one turns to the Scriptures with the assurance of their divine origin. Problems which throughout the ages have agitated enquiring minds, like the origin of sin and the diversity of languages, are here solved. With a simplicity which is at the same time profound, its divine system of truth satisfies the most eager mind, and it is, at the same time in harmony with the best results of human knowledge. Nolan concludes his discussion with the hope that his endeavours will 'restore Revealed Religion to that importance which natural (religion) has engrossed'.[3]

(ii) *Contrast with the Earlier Polemic*

This last observation of Nolan provides us with the contrast between the earlier polemic against the deists and the present one against the 'enthusiasm' of the Methodists and the unbelief of infidels. Here there is little discussion of natural religion. Religion as revealed is the important thing, and this is no longer regarded as adding a few positive commands to natural religion. The whole concern is now with the reality and finality of that which God has specifically disclosed in a system of communicated truths. In George Chandler's brilliant work the point is made that true religion is from first to last revealed: 'knowledge of divine things was communicated, not by metaphysical arguments, not by subtle disquisitions on the nature and attributes of God, processes which our

[1] Op. cit., p. 192.
[2] Op. cit., p. 222.
[3] Op. cit., p. 357.

own experiences tell us are in the least degree suited to convey
information on the subject to the immature mind, but demonstratively and palpably.'[1] What is called general revelation was
communicated in common to the whole race of men. Religion was
necessary to man, but it was something he was unlikely to discover, yet he was 'fully capable of receiving it, when imparted'.[2]
God gave to the whole race knowledge of Himself as Creator and
Judge, and the necessity of every man to live before Him in
righteousness.

In addition He has given a particular revelation 'taking its rise
from the Fall'. In increasing measure and at definite stages of man's
development, as he was able to receive it, 'God established a direct
communication first, with a particular individual; next, with the
immediate descendants of that individual; and then, as those descendants multiplied into a people, with the people derived from
the original ancestor.'[3]

With Abraham a new epoch was begun. Then again with Moses
'a highly interesting era commences' in which, for the first time,
the divine words were preserved in written records. In between
the periods when God made some new communication, there arose
the 'testimony of prophecy' which acted 'at the time, to animate
the passing generation with hope for the future; afterwards, to
afford a retrospective argument for the truth of His words'.[4] At
length, in the fulness of time, He appeared Who was the subject of
all prophecy, and in His light, the race, which had reached the
'adult state of human reason',[5] saw clearly those truths which were
but dimly apprehended in earlier days. From henceforth Christianity is confirmed, no longer by the continued exhibition of
miraculous agencies, for man has learned to put away childish
things: no longer is its truth impressed upon the mind by the
strength of irresistible demonstration; but, since man has become
able to weigh moral evidence, it requires to be investigated and
examined. The divine word was embodied in a writing to become
the building agency of the Church's life and the binding authority
of the Church's doctrine.

[1] *The Scheme of Divine Revelation considered Principally in its Connection with
the Progress and Improvement of Human Society*, p. 49.
[2] Op. cit., p. 6.
[3] Op. cit., p. 81.
[4] Op. cit., p. 96.
[5] Op. cit., p. 185.

With the passing years men invented ideas which they first set side by side with the Word, and then, inevitably, these human notions usurped the ruling place, claiming an allegiance which was never intended, thereby corrupting the pure faith. At length in the providence of God, at the Reformation, the authentic message was recovered, and the extraneous ideas swept away. It is the glory of the Reformation, that among other blessings of lasting worth, 'above all, it has established the grand, the fundamental doctrine of the supremacy of the scripture. It has pronounced the scripture to be the guide of life, the rule of faith, the test of truth. It has declared that no earthly power has authority in religious matters, unless that authority be given by the word of God.'[1]

The Principle of Selection

The nineteenth century had not far advanced before the Methodist movement showed that it would not fulfil the prediction that it would destroy the whole framework of Christianity. Its continued existence however was considered by some Churchmen to be a weakening of the revealed order. Although its enthusiasm might, in some measure, have 'cooled off', it was still regarded as an enemy, because its fundamental doctrine of immediate revelation was as opposed as ever to that of revelation as a body of revealed doctrines. At the same time, as we shall see later, there were within the Established Church itself, men who vehemently repudiated this view of revelation, and, by advocating a doctrine of revelation within the immediacy of experience, they found in the Methodist movement a natural ally.

It is for this reason that F. D. Maurice, for example, saw a significance in the Methodist teaching which was more akin to his own position than the cold assent to infallible truths which the orthodox appeared to demand. It was as a result of this that Maurice was plunged into the violent controversy with Dean Mansel, on the subject of revelation, which closes the period of our review.

But with the waning concern for the Methodist enthusiasm there went a growing awareness of the infidel challenge. The new world science had presented seemed to crowd out the possibility of revelation; or, at any rate, what was regarded as the 'assured results' of its discoveries, had rendered its claims and conceptions impossible. Scepticism was thought to be justified by science. Sir

[1] *The Scheme of Divine Revelation, etc.,* p. 231.

Oracle had spoken and no dog was supposed to bark. Of the growth and influence of infidelity many believing men were aware. In the introduction to a remarkable work, entitled *An Essay on the Nature and Immutability of Truth in Opposition to Sophistry and Scepticism*, Dr John Beattie, Professor of Moral Philosophy and Logic in the University of Aberdeen, noted that 'Scepticism is now the profession of every fashionable inquiry into human nature; a scepticism which is not confined to points of mere speculation, but has been extended to the practical truths of the highest importance, even to the principles of morality and religion'.[1] The same understanding of the times is given in the General Appendix of Watson's *Apology for the Bible*. 'The present', we there read, 'has been called — the age of philosophy — the age of reason: if by reason and philosophy, irreligion is understood, it undoubtedly merits the appellation; for there was never any age since the death of Christ, never since the commencement of the history of the world, in which atheism and infidelity have been more generally professed.'[2] The Bishop of London, Dr Porteus, in 1816, felt compelled to issue *A Summary of the Principle Evidences for the Truth and Divine Origin of the Christian Religion*, because it was a time, when, he says, 'new compendiums of infidelity and new libels of Christianity are dispersed continually, with indefatigable industry, through every part of the kingdom, and every class of the community.'[3]

The influence of Paine and Gibbon was apparent in all strata of society. By many, both these opponents of a divine revelation were hailed as the high-priests of a new worship of nature and as the apostles of a triumphant infidelity. In the preface of Simpson's *Plea for Religion and the Sacred Writings* — a work directed especially against the daring unbelief of the author of *The Age of Reason* — there is the observation: 'It will be allowed by every dispassionate observer, that if ERRONEOUS AND NOXIOUS TENETS were ever diffused among men in every age, they are eminently so in the present.'[4]

But the orthodox had men of no meagre ability who were eager to meet the infidel challenge. A host came to their help against the

[1] *The Evidence of the Christian Religion*, (*A collection of Works, Tracts, and Essays on the Subject, 1812*), vol. 3, p. 3.
[2] *Apology for the Bible*, p. 560.
[3] *A Summary of the Principle Evidences, etc.*, Preface, p. iv.
[4] *Plea for Religion and the Sacred Writings*, Preface, p. iii. Cf., also Publisher's Appendix, p. 401.

might of the enemy. The evidence of their work can still be seen in a large, if little read, literature. Something of the extent of their labours is indicated by Jortin, 'Fabricus has reckoned up', he tells us, 'some hundreds and doubtless several treatises might be added which have escaped his diligence,'[1] all assuring the reality of a revealed religion.

A large number of volumes were added between the time that Jortin wrote and the end of the period with which we have to do. So large is the list that some principle of selection is needed, for these many volumes cover the same ground as an examination of their contents will reveal.

The following principle of selection is adopted. A number of the most important of the Bampton lectures on our subject and a number of the most cogent works from general literature have been singled out to illustrate the way the newer apologists sought to confound the infidel and incidentally to check the enthusiast.

Two titles, one from these Bampton lectures and the other from this general literature, will indicate the nature of the reply. In 1847, W. A. Shirley, Bishop of Soder and Man, was responsible for the lectures which were published under the title, *The Supremacy of the Scripture*.[2] Earlier Jacob Bryant, in a vigorous volume, entitled, *A Treatise upon the Authenticity of the Scriptures*, drew attention to what he referred to as the 'divine volume'. The very titles of these two books will make it clear that for these later apologists revelation was identified with its record. God's special disclosure was equated with the Scriptures. Consequently a defence of revelation and a defence of the Bible were the same thing.

(iii) *The Bampton Lectures and the Biblical Revelation*

The following five series of Lectures,[3] delivered over a period of half a century will help towards an understanding of the outlook

[1] *Discourse Concerning the Truth of the Christian Revelation* (2nd edition, 1747), Preface, p. iv.

[2] Only four of the eight lectures given by Shirley were published. As a matter of fact, only two of the four were delivered owing to the illness and the subsequent death of the lecturer.

[3] The five chosen are as follows: (1) James Williamson (Prebendary of Lincoln), *The Truth, Inspiration, Authority, and end of the Scriptures, Considered and Defended*, 1793; (2) E. Nares, *A View of the Evidences of Christianity at the Close of the Pretended Age of Reason*, 1805; (3) John Miller, *The Divine Authority of the Holy Scriptures Asserted, from Adaptation to the Real State of Human Nature* (2nd edition, 1817); (4) T. W. Lancaster, *Popular Evidences of Christianity Stated and Examined*, 1831; (5) W. A. Shirley, *The Supremacy of the Holy Scriptures*, 1847.

which prevailed in the first half of the nineteenth century. By identifying special revelation with the Scriptures it was immaterial as to whether the works of the era were entitled, *Evidences of Christianity*, or, *The Truth of the Bible*. The two stood or fell together. And as the Old and the New Testaments belonged together any error in the former would necessarily undermine the validity of the latter. If the foundations were insecure the superstructure could not stand.

(a) Revelation and the Scriptures

Those who discoursed on the subject in the late eighteenth and early nineteenth centuries saw it as their task to prove that the 'Scriptures are authentic', and with that established it must follow that 'Christianity is true'.[1]

James Williamson does not think of this as a 'blind and implicit acquiescence' in the Scriptures, because each man is 'at full liberty to examine with candour the grounds and evidences of Christianity'.[2] He proceeds then to draw together the proofs for the truth and authenticity of the Bible. A written revelation is a more secure method, he argues, than oral tradition, for the conveying of the pure doctrines of Christianity to distant generations. So strong are the evidences that we cannot refuse our assent to the whole of the divine revelation. The Jewish belief in their Scriptures as of 'heavenly origin' was confirmed by our Lord. 'The doctrines of Christianity, the predictions of the prophets, and the precepts of the law, which we are informed was our schoolmaster to bring us to Christ (Gal. iii. 24), cannot be denied to be of divine original by any, who does not wish to disbelieve all inspiration.'[3] None dare say that the 'holy penmen' mixed falsehood with truth.

T. W. Lancaster states that it is his purpose to deal with 'the proofs of revealed religion, as may suffice for the reasonable conviction of all men'.[4] It is only a small number of persons who can discover and estimate the whole body of external evidences adduced as proof of Christianity; and Lancaster refuses to believe that the faith of the many has to be built on the credit of the few. He asserts, therefore, with Athanasius that, 'The Christian faith

---

[1] W. T. Lancaster, *Popular Evidences of Christianity, etc.*, p. 155.
[2] *The Truth, etc., of the Scriptures*, p. 102.
[3] Op. cit., p. 61.
[4] *Popular Evidences of Christianity Stated and Examined*, p. 3.

carries within itself the discovery of its own authority, and the holy
scriptures which God has inspired, are all-sufficient in themselves
for the evidence of their own truth.'[1] No direct revelation has, or
need, come to us. All that God has disclosed is found within the
divine book.

This leads Lancaster to raise the question, Are these Scriptures
really deserving of such high credit? The New Testament, he
insists, must be authentic because it is not likely that the early
believers were hoodwinked by forgeries. The Scriptures 'profess
to deliver a doctrine on which the salvation of mankind depends,
and which, on pain of eternal ruin, demands the obedience of all
men. Such books would surely never get into currency, unless
those who first received them were satisfied that they were written
by persons duly authorized'.[2]

No one can think of an imposture beguiling all the people with a
forged law as if it were an authentic act of Parliament. More
especially would this be impossible if that 'law' demanded considerable sacrifices and required painful duties. Lancaster does not
think that the usual way of proving that certain books were received as canonical to be the best. The usual method runs something like this: citations from the books now accepted are found in
some early Christian writer or other, and it is then concluded that
their authority is established. But, according to Lancaster, this
does not follow, since the authority of the writings from which
quotation is drawn must be first made certain. No such circuitous
method is necessary.

If a question were raised concerning a person's title to an estate,
who would be prepared to believe that there was a flaw in the grant
five centuries back? 'Who does not see, that a title of this nature
might be presumed to be good; that it would not have been admitted from the first, if its legality had not been fully proved; and
that the evidence MUST, in the nature of things, have now perished,
which formed its original basis? Why then desire to try over again,
at this time, a question, the true grounds of which have been un-
avoidably swept away from human knowledge? Yet it is by such a
process that we try the authenticity of the canon of Scripture: this
is what the enemies of revelation demand; and it is a demand in
which the advocates for revelation are too ready most judiciously

[1] *Popular Evidences, etc.*, p. 32.
[2] Op. cit., p. 62.

to acquiesce.'[1] But the question is already settled. Only those who were contemporary with the need to make the decision could do so. And they did. They were the only people, in the nature of the case, who could be vigilant against impostures. They were called upon to attest by pain and martyrdom the faith which they held, it was not likely, therefore, that in these circumstances, they would have accepted the fictitious.

It was, indeed, because they were so watchful that some books only gained recognition after long trial. This fact is itself testimony that not everything coming forth in the name of Christ was grasped at, and that the acceptance of any book is proof sufficient of its authenticity.

This genuineness has the moral attestation of every believing man. There is within man an intuitive faculty which under the influence of the divine Spirit can authenticate the revelation. God has given to the natural man senses to discern. This being so, 'it is only reasonable to think, that God, in offering a revelation to his accountable creatures, should both IMPRESS UPON THAT REVELATION the distinctive characters of his own wisdom and goodness; and also IMPART TO MAN an adequate and adapted faculty of perceiving and discriminating these characters.'[2] If bodily organs are given, can spiritual ones be denied? Those whose spiritual eyes are open will see God's own image and superscription on the Christian revelation. In the Bible he reads, he will discover a wisdom, a virtue and a doctrine not of this world.

But Lancaster goes on to insist that this inner persuasion does not lead to fanaticism (enthusiasm), which is a 'natural disposition of the mind, in which the imagination is strong, but the reason weak'.[3] A recognition of the Church as a divinely sanctioned institution, with a lawfully appointed order of bishops, 'whose authority, by legitimate succession, is derived from them to whom Christ first gave it,'[4] will curb fanatical excess. All uncredited pretentions to divine authority, all unauthorized administrations in the name of the Gospel, are invalid, and consequently 'wholly unavailing to the purpose of giving a title to God's covenanted mercies'.[5] Every claim to a 'special revelation' based upon an 'alleged inward light' is therefore to be set aside. Thus certain

---

[1] *Popular Evidences, etc.*, p. 78.   [2] Op. cit., p. 181.
[3] Op. cit., p. 219.   [4] Op. cit., p. 311.
[5] Op. cit., p. 326.

assertions of the Calvinists, and the Methodists are to be refused; as are those of the Arians, the Socinians and the Deists. While the 'Gnostick, in the primeval heresy', and the 'Evangelical, in these times', discover 'a fond allegiance to the same pretentions'.[1]

Shirley in his lectures rejects 'implicit faith' in any Church tradition. The essence of saving faith is a practical trust in God's revealed word. The Bible is, in itself, no 'dead letter' to be awakened to significance and relevancy by our own reason; such a view is 'essentially rationalistic'.[2] The purpose of his discourses is 'to maintain the SUPREME AUTHORITY OF HOLY WRIT against the claims of tradition and authority on the one hand, and presumptuous and rationalistic speculations on the other'.[3] John Miller sought to assure The Divine Authority of the Holy Scriptures, by arguing that its own internal evidence and authority are inescapable. Many persons matured in homes where the Bible is reverenced as the authentic revelation from God submit to it as an infallible guide. This devout reception of the Bible, as the Word of God, for the reason that it is presented as such from the first, is not to be swept aside as mere implicit faith. That such faith is real cannot be denied. After all, while it is a blessing to be able to enquire, not all have the ability to do so. But while all cannot enquire, all can experience the truth of the sacred volume, and it is, 'that which attests the divine authority of the holy Scripture to our own hearts.'[4] It is, indeed, the purpose of the discourses to stress the 'internal excellence and character of holy Writ itself'.[5] External proofs are not, of course, without value. They are, however, introductory; they are 'as it were, the title deeds of our inheritance'.[6] The Bible is, then, itself, 'the statute-book of an everlasting kingdom.'[7] First there is that which is 'natural', and such was the old Mosaic dispensation. Its concern was with the present and the palpable. Then there is the 'spiritual', the 'Evangelical', wherein man is addressed as a spiritual and immortal being. Yet the same divine Spirit is the author of both, and thus the substance of the divine plan was in each age the same. Their difference lies in the manner of their appeal. The Old appealed to the immediate and the external. Temporal blessings were its reward for good conduct.

---

[1] Op. cit., p. 327.
[2] *The Supremacy of the Holy Scriptures*, p. 5.
[3] Op. cit., p. 8.
[4] *The Divine Authority of the Holy Scripture, etc.*, p. 15.
[5] Op. cit., p. 23.   [6] Op. cit., p. 18.   [7] Op. cit., p. 29.

K

The promised rest was expected by most to find its fulfilment in the present life. Because the appeal of the Old was to the sensuous, it followed that the 'apostasy of the Jews became IDOLATRY'.[1] The new order, bringing life and immortality to light, addressed itself to the spirit of man, to that which does not belong to time and which is not satisfied with the temporal. The present dispensation eclipses the ancient by reason of its spiritual pre-eminence. The rejection of revelation is the modern apostasy, it is 'the SPIRITUAL and INTELLECTUAL REJECTION of the Deity'.[2]

Because, therefore, the new is addressed to man as a morally responsible being 'we must receive it in that INNER MAN, to which it is so pointedly offered'.[3] The doctrine which has received such eloquent emphasis by Emil Brunner, trembles on the lips of the Lecturer. Miller sees man as a being of 'capacity' and 'destiny'.[4] Man *qua* man is a 'responsible' being.[5] Man is capable of making 'response'.[6] He is a creature 'addressed' by God,[7] to Whom he must make the response of faith.

Miller finds reason for 'the believer implicitly confiding in Scripture' in the consideration that what was said of Christ, can be said of it; it 'knew what was in man'.[8] Although a book of 'small substance' it is sufficient for every phase of man's existence and every contingency of man's experience. 'Were the BIBLE not divine, it would have failed by excess of precept. It would have attempted too much.'[9] Yet in a volume so limited, it presents man with a picture of himself that he could not have wished, with a remedy which he could not have devised and with a destiny which he could not originate. Here is a book of which each can say, it told me all things that ever I did. Is not this of God?

In every age Scripture was adapted to human needs. In the old

---

[1] *The Divine Authority of the Holy Scripture, etc.*, p. 44.
[2] Ibid.   [3] Op. cit., p. 49.   [4] Op. cit., p. 52.
[5] Cf., 'The kernel of man's being is responsibility and responsibility is the essence of humanity.' E. Brunner, *Scandal of Christianity*, p. 59. 'It is not that man receives responsibility as a quality to be added to his human existence; but responsibility is the same thing as human nature.' *The Christian Understanding of Man* (Church Community and State), vol. 2, p. 157; also, *Man in Revolt*, p. 102.
[6] Brunner argues that 'responsibility' implies 'respondability', i.e. 'the ability to respond'.
[7] Cf., 'Man's distinctive quality consists in the fact that God turns to him and addresses him. In this "address" God gives man his distinctive quality.' *The Christian Understanding of Man*, p. 156. Cf., God created man 'as one who can hear His call and answer it'. *Man in Revolt*, p. 75.
[8] *The Divine Authority of Holy Scripture, etc.*, p. 75.
[9] Op. cit., p. 78.

dispensation God taught man more by fear than by love. The supreme note was one of terror rather than of tenderness. When Christ came 'grace' and 'love' were the major themes. After Him there were the Apostles who spoke 'neither the denunciatory tone of the Prophets, nor yet the peculiar, unequivocal authority of their divine Master'.[1] They entreated and exhorted against the background of the grace and love which they had experienced in Him. Not only was the whole scheme admirably adapted to God's progressive unfolding of Himself, but the same scheme comes down to the experience of every individual. There is the denunciation of sin which reveals it for what it is. There are the conduct and the character of Christ, which come as power and pattern. There is the life which we are exhorted to follow in the 'apostolical writings'. Thus is the whole plan of revelation meant for ourselves. The law and the prophets speak to us: the gospel records have us in view: the letters which follow are for our lives. 'All are fresh, as applicable to the exigencies of our existing nature, as if they were fruits gathered into the storehouse of truth only yesterday.'[2] All vital truth is, therefore, to be sought in the Scripture alone, and 'the law of life proposed to us in the holy Scripture', is 'sufficient (a law) for the wants and wishes of every individual person called into obedience to it'.[3] For Miller, then, the process of the Scripture is the process of experience: first law, then love and finally learning. And it is this very fact which assures the book to be divine.

(b) The Mosaic Record as History

The special subjects central in the 'scientific' attack upon the Bible as the revelation of God, were the Mosaic account of the Creation and the Fall. It was to these themes, therefore, that the defenders of revelation had to give special attention. Each part of the Genesis story was regarded as historical and factual. The 'scepticism' of the day demanded a freer treatment of the Mosaic cosmology. In the Introductory Preface to Dr Geddes' version of the Pentateuch a plea is put forth for regarding the stories as nonhistorical. He asks his readers to 'weigh his arguments in the scale of reason, devoid of theological prepossessions'. The 'rude and

[1] Op. cit., p. 151.
[2] Op. cit., p. 170.
[3] Op. cit., p. 203.

unpolished' account, made up of 'popular traditions and old songs',[1] is not to be read as history. They are mythological representations; they are the means whereby a certain truth was conveyed to those in an earlier and non-scientific age.

But the stigmatization of the stories as 'myths' had in the early days, an origin outside the Church. Its source was the scientific scepticism of the day. It was a way of escape from 'literalism', and a method of 'explanation' whereby the Genesis stories could be fitted into the framework of the assumed finality of the scientific 'world-picture'. Thus would all Christians, but the most obdurate literalists, be satisfied. The apologists of the period certainly felt themselves under pressure from their sceptical opponents, in the urge to abandon their notion of Genesis as historical.

'It has been one of the concessions most peremptorily demanded of us of late', says Nares, 'that we should agree to acknowledge it (i.e. the account of the Fall) to be no better than a mythological representation of things, a description merely imagined to account for known phenomena.'[2] Nares, in common with those who were defending the Biblical revelation, could not agree to the demand. He contends, rather, for the historical reading of the stories. The Fall, he insists, was a real fact, and basic to the subsequent unfolding history of man's redemption. 'If we will not be informed of these matters historically,' he writes, 'and I may add, in regard to the creation at least supernaturally, we must be content to be ignorant.'[3] The historical, he feels, cannot be allegorized nor could the mythological be historicized: 'for it is certainly not a fanciful representation of the creation of man, and the origin of evil, that we want; but the exact and positive history of those events, as the first and indisputable foundations of religious and moral responsibility.'[4] Nares rejects the idea that the stories are 'representations of present appearances'. 'They are facts and events, certainly not capable of being explained by allegory; and a figurative representation of such things is altogether useless.'[5]

In no less vigorous language, James Williamson, the Prebendary of Lincoln, rejects all mythological interpretations of the Genesis records. The account, he asserts, bears the evidence of history.

---

[1] *Introductory Preface to the Pentateuch*, p. iii.
[2] *A View of the Evidences of Christianity, etc.*, pp. 110, 111.
[3] Op. cit., p. 121.
[4] Op. cit., p. 117.
[5] Op. cit., p. 155.

The stories 'cannot be perverted into allegory and hieroglyphic'. He regards it as of 'no small importance whether we believe or deny the truth of this history; since it is closely connected with Jewish and Christian doctrines'.[1, 2]

(c) Scripture and Tradition

W. A. Shirley raises the question of the oral tradition behind the Gospel records and he can be said to anticipate the work of the more recent Form Criticism. The Son of God proclaimed the Father's love 'by oral teaching, and did not during his personal ministration dictate any written document'.[3] The 'salvation spoken by the Lord' . . . 'was verbally handed on, and confirmed to the

[1] *The Truth, Inspiration, etc., of the Scriptures*, p. 72.

[2] This part of the discussion will be of interest in view of the modern concern with 'demythologizing', which has come into such vogue with the publication of Bultmann's essay, '*Neues Testament und Mythologie*, which initiated the lively Entmythologisierungs controversy.' Ian Henderson, *Listener*, March 15th, 1951. The defenders of Biblical revelation in the early nineteenth century could not have foreseen that the principle which they felt bound to reject would one day be extended, within the Church, to the New Testament itself. For Bultmann the whole New Testament is 'legend-tinted'. For the 'scientific sceptics' of the earlier period the Genesis stories certainly were. They were, therefore, not to be taken literally if they were to come to any sort of terms with science. Does not a certain scepticism actuate Bultmann? When his *Theology of the New Testament* (vol. 1) was published in English, the question appeared in the *Expository Times* (vol. LXIV, No. 4, Jan. 1953), 'Should we find in this book less of the thorough-going scepticism which marred his *History of the Synoptic Tradition* and his *Jesus* written more than twenty years ago? Had the most radical New Testament scholar since Strauss mellowed somewhat with the years? We are sorry to say that we cannot report any recantations. The passage of twenty years has not altered Bultmann's scepticism about the Gospels as historical documents. Scepticism, to be sure, has its value, if only it drives us to re-examine the historical foundations on which our faith is based . . . . But there is a scepticism which by its sheer extremeness overreaches itself and alienates the sympathy of reasonable men. And this kind of scepticism, alas, spoils Bultmann's book at the very beginning.' Bultmann feels the need for 'demythologizing' to be a scientific necessity. 'When I demythologize the Bible,' he explains in a broadcast address, 'I reckon with the fact that the thinking of modern times has ceased to be mythological and is determined by science.' (*Listener*, Feb. 5th, 1953). He insists that he is seeking an 'explanation', but we feel, as did the earlier apologists against the scientific scepticism, that he is 'explaining away'. Bultmann seems too sensitive to the 'scientific' atmosphere, and almost assumes that 'modern science' is the final truth. The present writer regards his efforts to demythologize to be both impossible and unnecessary. It is impossible, because in whatever language he restates the Gospel, be it ever so 'scientific' is it thereby any the less 'mythological'? The world pictured by the scientist is no more 'real' than that of religion. Is there anything less 'mythological' in such notions as 'matter', 'atoms', 'protons' and the like? On the other hand we feel that there is too much talk about 'explaining' the Gospel for the sake of that fiction the Modern Man. The need is for proclamation not for explanation. 'Instead of demythologizing the Bible, every sound spiritual energy in contemporary society urges us to re-mythologize man.' U. E. Simon, 'The Unconscious Use of Myth,' *Listener*, Feb. 26th, 1953.

[3] *The Supremacy of the Holy Scriptures*, p. 13.

faithful by those who heard him.'[1] The question is not then between an oral and a written form, since in the later written documents we have a faithful record of the teaching already made known in oral tradition.

The written records become therefore the exclusive authority, since, the floating testimony of tradition is no longer a sure basis for doctrine. Therefore, 'when once we drift from the sure anchorage of God's written word, there is no saying into what ocean of superstitious reveries, mystical hallucinations, rationalistic speculations, and even of unlimited and bottomless scepticism, we may not be carried, before we are aware, and even while we deem ourselves most secure in the guidance of primitive orthodox and catholic consent.'[2]

God might have continued to convey His mind by an 'unwritten tradition', but the existence of the Bible is itself proof that He preferred it otherwise. The Roman Church claims to be in possession of a binding tradition to be given the same assent and un-enquiring submission — *pari pietatis effectu* — as the written word; but such a claim cannot be granted, therefore such assent and submission are inadmissible. There is evidence enough in the Bible itself of the insecurity of tradition. Just as the five books of Moses, 'written by one to whom God had been so nigh, descended to us with a sanction to which no merely human document, written or unwritten can lay claim, and this divine record at once supersedes all reference to oral traditions which had gone before, and which are in fact embodied in its sacred and mysterious contents,'[3] so is it with the rest of the Old and New Testaments. The attitude of our Lord Himself to the traditions of the elders of Israel is decisive. That He recognized the Old Testament 'as the oracles of God, the authentic exponent of the Father's will, and the supreme guide of man in all that he was to achieve, and do, and hope for',[4] is, he thinks, beyond question. The elders had set up beside the written word an infallible tradition, and, as a result, 'made the word of God of none effect by their tradition.' In a way parallel the Roman Church has added traditions for which an equal reverence is demanded: thereby 'teaching for doctrines the commandments of men'.

Yet Christ did accept the restrictions of certain ecclesiastical

[1] Op. cit., p. 14.   [2] Op. cit., p. 30.
[3] Op. cit., p. 41.   [4] Op. cit., p. 48.

ordinances as of confessedly human institution. He thus set an example of good order in the Church to which all wise-hearted and humble people will submit; but with the realization that these are not 'a matter of divine command, and therefore essential to the very being of the Church'.[1]

The significance of this Shirley deems important. It is the essential and authentic word which is the rule and guide. He points out that in the great controversies within the Church, appeal was not made to oral tradition, to any special revelations, or to any mysteries reserved for the favoured elect. There is 'no reference to any authorized interpretation of Scripture, none to any authority in matters of faith, and still less to any one visible centre of Christian union, other than the living Head, even Jesus, and the one faith in Him'.[2] Shirley goes through the Apostolic Fathers and shews that since they did not appeal to any authoritative traditions the first link in the chain is missing. Some have argued that because the inspired interpreters of Scripture are no more, there must be some authority to fix the sense. The idea, however, not only 'discredits the promised aid of God's Holy Spirit to every devout and humble enquirer',[3] but has led to a 'crop of errors, as, for example, the notion of an infallible line of teachers and the practical infallibility of the universal Church'. The Fathers appealed to Scripture directly and not to any oral tradition. They gave their own understanding of the sacred words and they were not bound by any authoritative tradition, or interpretation. It was the Gnostics who were, perhaps, the first to seek for a seat of infallibility and they fancied they found it in a select body of intellectual speculators. But against their pretended secret knowledge and higher understanding the Fathers took their stand upon the Scriptures alone.

The Montanists, on the other hand, sought infallibility in an immediate revelation and thus went beyond what was written. 'The Gnostic obtaining authoritative interpretation, by a rationalistic tradition, and the Montanist obtaining an infallible guide by direct inspiration, but both explaining away, or superseding the written word, and leaving the Church practically to human guidance.'[4]

Shirley calls on those who would preach and teach the Christian

[1] Op. cit., p. 48.   [2] Op. cit., p. 64.
[3] Ibid.   [4] Op. cit., p. 128.

message to shut themselves up to the written word, and to treat the whole Bible as 'the very voice of God Himself'.[1] The Bible is the 'very book of God'.[2] It is still true that some wrest the Scriptures to their own destruction 'even as their table and the common daily mercies are a snare to many'. But this does not mean that the 'one standard of truth' should therefore be withheld. Rather is it to be widely circulated and continually preached. 'We can trust God with the effect of his own book on the souls of men'.[3]

(iv) General Literature and the Biblical Revelation

Turning to the general apologetic literature in the defence of the Scriptural revelation it will be found that, while there is not the same understanding of the issues involved, not the same hints at developments yet to take place, there is, broadly, the same appreciation of revelation as a body of communicated truths embodied in the Scriptures. Out of the large literature open for review five volumes have been selected as representative of the rest.[4]

Jortin's date puts him more akin to the earlier apologetic. He asserts that the 'Christian revelation is founded upon natural religion'.[5] He does not however enter upon any discussion of the latter. His concern is with revealed religion. He regards Christianity mainly as a body of doctrines and moral precepts. 'The Gospel', he tells us, 'promised eternal happiness to those who lead religious lives, and to impenitent sinners denounced the most dreadful punishments.'[6] The sacred books are amply attested by external evidences. The fact that the New Testament volumes were written by apostles and friends of apostles guarantees their integrity and supremacy. The writers did not invent discourses and attribute them to Christ. 'If they had followed this method, they would probably have made his discourses, exhorting to virtue and dissuading to vice, in general terms; it would not have entered into their thoughts to have crowded together so many allusions to

---

[1] Op. cit., p. 78.   [2] Op. cit., p. 66.   [3] Op. cit., p. 67.
[4] The five chosen are: (1) Jortin, *Discourse Concerning the Truth of the Christian Revelation* (2nd edition, 1747); (2) R. Watson (Bishop of Landaff), *Apology for the Bible*, 1796; (3) Edward Maltby, *Illustrations of the Truth of the Christian Revelation*, 1801 (2nd edition, 1803); (4) Jacob Bryant, Esq., *Treatise upon the Authenticity of the Scriptures, and the Truth of the Christian Revelation* (3rd edition, 1810); (5) Beilby Porteus (Bishop of London), *A Summary of the Principal Evidences for the Truth and Divine Origin of the Christian Religion*, 1810.
[5] *Discourse Concerning, etc.*, p. 73.
[6] Op. cit., p. 26.

time and place, and to other little occurrences, which nothing, besides the presence of the object, would suggest.'[1]

The gospel has taught truths we should not otherwise know. It declares that God is good, and we can therefore be assured that where there is a genuine effort to follow after righteousness He will reward with the remittance of punishment. Amendment of life is necessary to the attainment of truth. Most of those who came to accept Christianity were, he thinks, earnest seekers after the good. If it be urged that several 'had led bad lives before' it is to be remembered that 'there are degrees of wickedness, and there is no reason to suppose that these sinners were for the most part of the worse sort'.[2] Jortin seems to think that there is need to live well before the truth of Christianity can come to us. We are to understand 'that the practice of Morality leads to the practice of Christianity, and that, since conversion is brought about by stages, and revealed religion is founded on natural religion, he who is moved to embrace the Gospel must first be sensible of the difference between good and evil, truth and falsehood, virtue and vice, must love the one and abhor the other, must repent of his former transgressions and receive the sacred knowledge, which is offered to him, with gratitude and a firm resolution of performing his duty'.[3]

A reading of Bishop Watson's ten letters, in which he attacks the second half of Paine's *Age of Reason* makes it a matter of amazement that the Rationalist Press still persists in publishing the sceptical work.

Paine impugnes the morality of the Bible, and yet he professes to accept natural religion. But the 'morality' of the natural order can also be called in question. So Watson asks, 'Why do you not spurn as spurious, the book of nature in which the fact is certainly written, and from the perusal of which you infer the moral justice of God.'[4] Paine makes an attack on the several books of the Bible. He uses all the arguments, but without the inhibition and reserve, of the later liberal critics. The first five books of the sacred record are dismissed as 'spurious, and (that) Moses is not the author of them; and still further, (that) they were not written in the time of Moses, nor till several hundred years afterwards.'[5] Paine actually

---

[1] *Discourse concerning, etc.*, pp. 220, 221.   [2] Op. cit., p. 6.
[3] Ibid.
[4] *Apology for the Bible* (published with Simpson's *Plea for Religion and the Sacred Writings*, 1812), p. 423.
[5] Op. cit., p. 432.

assigns them to 'stupid pretenders to (Mosaic) authorship' at the time of Ezra. Watson repudiates the notion and meets the arguments one by one. The books of Joshua and Samuel are referred to a late anonymous writer: Paine, in fact, makes much of their anonymity. Watson replies that their authority is not lessened because of this. 'Doomsday Book is anonymous' and 'yet our courts of law do not hold it without authority'.[1]

Chronicles is put by Paine after the reign of Zedekiah and as there are verses found in Genesis similar to verses in Chronicles, he argues that therefore Genesis must be later still. Watson retorts; because there are 'a few verses in the book of Genesis which could not have been written by Moses; therefore, no part of Genesis could have been written by Moses; a child will deny your, therefore'.[2] On Isaiah, Paine is specially severe. He has an idea of what has later come to be referred to as 'deutro-Isaiah'. Parts of the last chapters must belong to the age of Cyrus since, of course, prophecy is not possible. The book of Jeremiah is disordered and is therefore to be distrusted. Daniel belongs to the Maccabean period. Watson recalls, in reply, a story of a 'learned Rabbi' who, presiding at a disputation with Christians, exclaimed, 'Let us shut our Bibles; for if we proceed in examination of this prophecy (viz. that of the Seventy Weeks), it will make us all become Christians.'[3]

Paine extends his critical work to the New Testament. The Virgin Birth, the genealogies, the massacre of the innocents, the words over the cross, the time of the Crucifixion among other items are all held to contain evidence of imposture. The phrase in Matthew 'unto this day' is made to prove 'that the book must have been manufactured after the lapse of some generations at least'. Paine will not believe in revealed religion because there is so much which cannot be revealed. 'What is there you can account for?' asks Watson. The germination of a blade of grass and the fall of a forest leaf are beyond comprehension. Thus Paine is asked, 'will you refuse to eat of the fruits of the earth because God has not given you wisdom equal to his own? Will you refuse to lay hold on immortality, because he has not given you, because he, probably, could not give to such a being as man, a full manifestation of the end for which he designs him, nor the means requisite for the attainment of that end.'[4] Watson then draws together natural and

----

[1] Op. cit., p. 450.   [2] Op. cit., p. 465.
[3] Op. cit., p. 490.   [4] Op. cit., p. 552.

revealed religion and states: 'For my own part, I can see no reason why either revealed or natural religion should be abandoned on account of the difficulties which attend either of them. I look up to the incomprehensible maker of heaven and earth with unspeakable admiration and self-annihilation, and am a deist, — I contemplate, with the utmost gratitude and humility of mind his unsearchable wisdom and goodness in the redemption of the world from eternal death, through the intervention of his Son, Jesus Christ, and am a christian.'[1]

Maltby's book is of considerable importance. For him the internal evidences for the genuineness and authenticity of the biblical record are conclusive. The language of the New Testament books is 'of a manner of thinking and expression very consonant with the opinions and practices of the inhabitants of Judaea'[2] at the time they were written. The vividness of the detail marks them out as the work of an eyewitness. They are free from party spirit. There is no attempt to panegyrize the central Figure or to palliate the failings of those who surrounded Him. In the several writings the same Personality is unveiled. The existence of the numerous apocryphal books is evidence that there were genuine ones. When once the canonical Scriptures are compared with these apocryphal works the reality of the counterfeit is not difficult to detect. The apocryphal works are evidently written with a purpose, and tend, like the so-called 'Epistle of Mary the Virgin to the Inhabitants of Messina and Florence', to justify some strange doctrine or other, as this fabrication does Mariolatry, and the worship of relics. The disgusting pomposity of some of this literature is in marked contrast with the natural simplicity and unadorned and unornamented style of the accepted books. The vulgar efforts to satisfy natural curiosity concerning our Lord's early years, seen in other apocryphal writings, just reveals how totally out of harmony they are with the real truth: 'the apocryphal writers have shewn themselves so little expert in their trade of fiction, that they have described this exalted character in a manner suited only to a vain and petulant boy, exerting his miraculous powers for silly ostentation, or the worse purpose of gratifying some malignant passion.'[3] Jesus resolutely refused to fit Himself into the Jewish pattern of the

---

[1] Op. cit., p. 554.
[2] *Illustrations of the Truth of the Christian Religion*, p. 4.
[3] Op. cit., p. 61.

Messiah. But this is what an impostor would have done. His final claim to be the Holy One of God, if it were not true, was to add the outrage of insult to the bitterness of disappointment. He made Himself equal with God. His 'scheme' of doctrine is such that no impostor could have adopted it nor any enthusiast conceived it. Christianity could not have survived if it were not true since it cuts across all that men hold dear. It was published to the world without regard to men's cherished notions, and it has triumphed; 'it is to the last degree improbable, if not morally impossible, that Christianity should have originated in mistake or artifice.'[1] The disciples found Christ's doctrine 'a hard saying'; it was only the gradual acceptance of His message as true led them to abandon their Jewish rituals and to accept the Gentiles as fellow-heirs of the promises made to Israel.

Maltby, it may be observed, meets the argument of Bolingbroke and Chubb who drew a distinction (which some deem modern) between the Jesus of history and the Christ of Paul.

Bolingbroke conceived of Jesus as a religious Jew seeking to revitalize Judaism and One whose interest was with the Jew only. To Paul belongs the doubtful honour of 'universalizing' His message and expunging from it the Jewish elements. Maltby shows how Jesus, although He did send His disciples, in the first place, to 'the lost sheep of the house of Israel', yet by precept, practice and parable He looked beyond the bounds of Israel to the Gentile world. In His final commission He expressly states that His gospel is for 'every creature'. At the same time Paul always made it his business to address himself first to his own people. 'And this same Apostle, who has been so unjustly accused of setting up his own gospel in opposition to Jesus Christ, though he strenuously contends that there is no distinction between the Jew and the Greek, yet, whenever a priority can be maintained pleads in favour of the Jews: "to the Jew first, and also to the Greek." '[2]

A host of opponents of Christianity attest the purity of Christ's character, and if His virtue be attested, How can His doctrine be denied? As a man of acknowledged truthfulness Jesus could not have taught that which was false. He certainly shared the Jewish belief that the Mosaic law was divine. It is therefore relevant to ask, Is it credible that being 'himself a believer in the law of

---

[1] *Illustrations of the Truth of the Christian Religion*, p. 85.
[2] Op. cit., p. 198.

Moses, he nevertheless attempted to supersede it by a system originating in fallible speculation and supported by groundless assertion'?[1] To suppose such a thing would be to deny that He was a man of virtue and make Him a schemer for the overthrow of the religion He Himself believed to be the revealed will of God. He who thus claimed to be 'of God', is thereby found undermining God's laws: 'this surely is to suppose him guilty of gross deceit. He frequently asserted its authority in such a way as to give the impression that He believed it to be a divine legislation. He solemnly asserted that He bore witness to the Truth and yet, How can it be held that He is virtuous still, if, while proclaiming the authority of Moses, He did not believe it were so?' Is it possible that such a character as this would have engaged in such a complicated scheme of cunning, hypocrisy and impiety?[2] There is no doubt that the Jewish was the best form of religious and civil polity then existing in the world. 'If Jesus overturned this merely to establish a code of his own fabrication, he cannot escape the charge of impiety. If we add too the fixed conviction of the Jews that their national prosperity and happiness depended upon their adherence to the commands of Jehovah, as delivered by Moses, there appears a degree of rashness and cruelty in thus destroying the palladium of the Jewish state, from which, on the infidel hypothesis, the character of Jesus cannot be exempted. Nor can it be regarded as more excusable in the means adopted, than in the ends pursued, if the religion he established had no warrant for its excellence or permanence than the sagacity of his own views or the comprehension of the intellect. The holy and venerable name of the Lord of heaven and earth was the cloak, upon this supposition, as the assumed cover of his fictions: and the intimate union and connection by which he professed to stand related to the Deity could only be an additional and unnecessary outrage against the divine majesty. To destroy the institution of this august and incomprehensible Being, under pretence of showing him greater reverence; to do away the peculiar rites with which he had signified his command that his people should honour him, under the fictitious assumption of authority from that very Being; especially when we consider the profound and unparalleled reverence entertained by all the Jews for that holy name and those sacred institutions; would have been a procedure at once so unaccountable and so

[1] Op. cit., p. 229.   [2] Op. cit., p. 231.

desperate, that it would scarcely be imputed to any man, however audacious and however resolute in the prosecution of his purposes:— far less could it be imputed to the meek and unassuming, the spotless and irreproachable Jesus.'[1]

Jacob Bryant makes the point that rational religion has never been able to uplift a people. The most successful missionary method is to go straight to the wounds of Christ. The experience of the Moravian missionary Grantz is quoted to show that rational arguments for the existence of God and for His attributes, as the basis upon which to enforce resulting moral obligations, have been proved futile. He goes on to argue that the Old Testament prophecies concerning the Messiah, into which Christ so wonderfully fitted, cannot be the *post factum* work of biased Christian writers who sought biblical proof for their beliefs. The sacred books were, after all, in Jewish hands, and they were 'particularly scrupulous about the conservation of the sacred volumes so that they would not suffer a single word to be added or omitted'.[2]

The New Testament records are no less authentic and trustworthy. 'No histories have been transmitted with such incontestable marks of truth as the Evangelical writings.'[3] They bear the very stamp of divinity; the hall-mark of heaven. 'We have been told a great deal', observes Bryant, 'about nature, and the light of nature; and Christianity has been pronounced AS OLD AS CREATION. By this was meant, that all the essential truths, which were taught in the Gospel, were antecedently known by this light; and the Christian system, in consequence of it, was neither new, nor necessary.'[4] But how contrary to the facts is such a contention. The whole world groaned for some divine doctrine, for some infallible instruction, and God in mercy met the cry of the human heart. Thus the 'grand system' of inspired Scripture has been delivered to us. And if some difficulties remain for us after careful and prayerful study then 'it is our duty to acquiesce, and trust the word of God, which cannot deceive'.[5]

Bishop Porteus likewise maintains that the New Testament is a 'faithful history of Christ and his religion'.[6] He gathers together, for the help of those recently confirmed, all the lines of evidence into one grand summary. Indeed, in a masterpiece of compression,

---

[1] *Illustrations of the Truth of the Christian Religion*, p. 244.
[2] *A Treatise upon the Authenticity of the Scriptures, etc.*, p. 77.
[3] Op. cit., p. 117.   [4] Op. cit., p. 163.   [5] Op. cit., p. 180.
[6] *A Summary of the Principal Evidences*, p. 7.

he has presented all the arguments of the Bampton Lectures and the general literature as a sort of grand finale: 'when we consider', he writes, 'the deplorable ignorance and inconceivable depravity of the heathen world before the birth of Christ, which rendered a divine interposition necessary, and therefore highly probable; the appearance of Christ upon the earth, at the very time when his presence was most wanted, and when there was a general expectation throughout the East that some great and extraordinary personage was to come into the world; the transcendent excellence of our Lord's character; the calmness, the composure, the dignity, the integrity, the spotless sanctity of his manners, so utterly inconsistent with any idea of enthusiasm and imposture; the sublimity and importance of his doctrines; the consumate wisdom and perfect purity of his moral precepts, far exceeding the natural powers of man born in the humblest situation, in a remote and obscure corner of the world, without learning, education, language, or works; the rapid and astonishing propagation of his religion, in a very short space of time, through almost every region of the East, by the sole effort of himself and a few illiterate fishermen, in direct opposition to all the power, the authority, the learning, the philosophy, the reigning vices, prejudices, and superstitions of the world; the complete and marked opposition, in every essential point, between the character and revelation of Christ, and the character and revelation of Mahomet, exactly such as might be expected between truth and falsehood; the intimate description of all the most material circumstances of his birth, life, sufferings and death, and resurrection, given by the ancient prophets many hundred years before he was born, and exactly fulfilled in him, and him only, pointing him out as the messenger of the Jews and the Redeemer of mankind; the various prophecies declared by Christ himself, were all punctually accomplished, more especially the destruction of Jerusalem by the Romans; and many astonishing miracles wrought by Jesus, in the open face of day before thousands of spectators, the reality of which is proved by multitudes of the most exceptional witnesses, who sealed their testimony with their blood, and was even acknowledged by the earliest and most inveterate enemies of the Gospel; and, lastly, the most astonishing and well-authenticated miracles of our Lord's resurrection, which was the seal and confirmation of his own divine origin, and that of his religion: — when all these various witnesses are brought together, and impartially weighed, it seems hardly within the power of a fair and ingenious mind to resist the impression of their united force. If such a combination of evidence is not sufficient to satisfy an honest inquirer into truth, it is utterly impossible THAT ANY EVENT, WHICH PASSED in former times, and which we did not see with our own eyes, can be proved to have happened by any degree of testimony whatever. It may be safely affirmed that no incident can be produced by any one fact or event, said to have taken place in past ages, and established by such evidence as that on which the Christian revelation rests, that afterwards turned out to be false. We challenge the enemies of our faith to bring forward, if they can, any such instance. If they cannot (and we know it to be impossible), we have a right to say that a religion supported by such an extraordinary accumulation of evidences, must be true, and that all men, who pretend to be judged by argument and by proof, are bound, by the most sacred obligations to receive the religion of Christ, as a real revelation from God.'[1]

[1] *A Summary of the Principal Evidences, etc.*, pp. 40, 41.

CHAPTER VII

THE FOCUS ON THE INWARD

The orthodox apologists, as has been shewn, in the defence of their position against the exaggerations of the deists conceived of revelation as a limited number of moral dicta, extra to those already known by natural religion, and against the excesses of the enthusiasts they regarded it as a body of communicated truths demanding an unquestioning assent. The result of such views of revealed religion was to make the preaching of the period lacking in life and warmth. It was coldly apologetic and fiercely polemical. Religion was a matter of debate, the attainment of right notions. Thus in the pulpit, as Dr Johnson informs us, 'the apostles were tried once a week on the charge of committing forgery.' It was all wonderfully impressive, but weakly ineffective; there was certain evidence of learning, but little evidence of life.

When, however, a conception becomes dominant there seems to be an inevitable reaction. 'The type of view', observes Dr C. C. J. Webb, 'which makes feeling as opposed to reason the organ of religious experience usually appears as a reaction from some form of what is called Rationalism, and finds a relative justification for its existence upon facts which Rationalism has ignored.'[1]

REVELATION IN THE IMMEDIACY OF EXPERIENCE

Against the sterile rationalism of the orthodox doctrine of revelation there was a protest from two quarters. On the one hand, under the impetus of a rising idealistic philosophy (which from one point of view is only the theoretical expression of religious mysticism), and its stress upon the divine immanence, there was advocated a doctrine of revelation within the immediacy of experience. From an intellectual point of view there was seen to be need for a more personal contact with God than that knowledge about Him embodied in syllogisms. On the other hand, under the preaching of Whitfield and Wesley, there was an emphasis upon the inner

[1] *Problems in the Relations of God and Man*, p. 69.

L

action of the Holy Spirit. Both these views agreed in repudiating the cold propositional rationalism of the orthodox. In some of their statements, those who advocated revelation within the immediacy of experience resemble the present neo-liberalism of the Barth-Brunner school. They were also averse to the Evangelicals, while the latter were little inclined to acknowledge any kinship.

That statement of revelation which found its most vehement expression in Maurice began from the assumption of the immanence of God in every man, whereas the doctrine of the Evangelicals stresses the indwelling of God in believing men. Thus, whilst both maintained the inwardness of revelation, they were, as a matter of fact, really opposed. Only in their insistence upon the inward were they alike, in no other sense were they identical.

That this last observation is true, is confirmed by a comment made by John Wesley on Dodwell's book *Christianity not Founded on Argument*. Dodwell in advocating the inwardness of revelation denies that reason has any place in it. In the context of his remarks Wesley makes it clear that he does not deprecate reason. At the same time it is still a fact that you cannot reason concerning colour if you have no natural sight, 'so you cannot reason concerning spiritual things, if you have no spiritual sight: because your ideas received by your outward senses are of a different kind.'[1] Wesley then goes on to tell us that Dodwell's book was warmly recommended to him as stating the same position 'But', continues Wesley, 'on a perusal of that piece (i.e. *Christianity not Founded on Argument*) notwithstanding my prejudices in its favour, I could not but perceive that the general design uniformly pursued throughout the work, was to render the whole of the Christian Institution to be odious and contemptible . . . the author . . . *makes a shew* of defending an avowed doctrine of Christianity, namely, the supernatural influence of the Spirit of God.'[2]

At the close of our earlier investigation of the idea of revelation as indwelling light, it was pointed out that the followers of George Fox differed from the later school of Coleridge, in the fact that, whereas the former began from an emphasis on the divine transcendence, the latter stressed the divine immanence. For the newer teachers God's indwelling was not thought of as the visitation of an Alien Spirit. By accentuating the kingship of God, the Friends

---

[1] 'An Earnest Appeal to Men of Reason and Religion', *Works*, vol. 12, p. 14.
[2] Op cit., *Works*, vol. 12, ibid.

conceived of God's indwelling as something apart from the human spirit; the residence of a 'Wholly Other'. Those who followed Coleridge stressed, with him, the kinship between God and man, and regarded the divine as immanent in all nature and in all men.

Its advocates were anxious to maintain that the divine and the human existed as one spiritual continuum. Even if it be maintained that they did not lay hold of the true connecting link, it is to their credit that they did see that a revelation is only possible if some 'point of contact' remains. A radical discontinuity renders a revelation impossible, or, at least, useless. If God speaks to men who are in no sense '*capax verbi Domini*', the question may be asked, To what purpose is this waste? Whether indeed the writers with whom we are now to be concerned did overstate their case in their teaching of a continued kinship between God and man remains to be seen. They certainly did stress the idea of the unbroken Fatherhood of God, it is a question if they were equally aware of the fact of the broken sonship.[1] At all events, one thing is clear, their doctrine was conditioned and coloured by philosophical idealism. It was against this background that the understanding of revelation within the immediacy of experience must be presented.

The task, therefore, before us is, first, to give an account of the creative significance of the idealism of Bishop Berkeley, and then, to show how this conception influenced the idea of revelation. The doctrine of revelation which developed as a result will then be traced through representative writers until it reaches its strongest expression in F. D. Maurice.

(i) *The Background of Idealism — Berkeley*

The student of philosophy does not need reminding that it was the purpose of Berkeley to prove that unspiritual matter is non-existent. He resolved to show the immaterialism of the external world. Berkeley was convinced that the notion that brute material substance existed as a reality apart from mind was 'the main pillar of Scepticism'. He thus argued that all that exists are ideas in the mind of God and that human ideas are produced by the direct action of God. This means that all ideas of the human mind are proof of God's existence and being, since all such ideas have their genesis in God.

[1] Cf., H. Wheeler Robinson, *The Christian Doctrine of Man*, p. 91 f.

'It is therefore plain', he writes, 'that nothing can be more evident to any one that is capable of the least reflection, than the existence of God, or a Spirit who is intimately present to our minds, producing in them all that variety of ideas or sensations, which continually effect us, on whom we have an absolute and entire dependence, in short, in whom we live, and move, and have our being.'[1] Berkeley concludes his *Treatise Concerning the Principles of Human Knowledge* with the assurance that God 'is present and conscious to our innermost thoughts; and that we have a most absolute and immediate dependence on him'.[2] Here then is an idealism which is at the same time an immanentalism. It is Berkeley's significance that he does not seek to provide new and novel arguments for the Christian apologist. He would have us see God; he would have us lift up our eyes and behold Him, for He is not very far from any one of us. The words of Acts xvii. 28, 'In him we live, and move, and have our being,' quoted by Berkeley in the passage above, constantly recur throughout his works. While it is not a verse used for any of his sermons, 'it occurs so often in his works', says Canon I. T. Ramsay, 'as to have been called his "favourite quotation." '[3] It is this 'favourite quotation' which is, indeed, Berkeley's real message, for here he finds an assertion of God as actual within. Berkeley's main doctrine was then, as A. D. Lindsay observes, 'an appeal to immediate experience.'[4] It follows, therefore, that he must reject the idea that a knowledge of God comes only as a result of 'resemblance and analogy'.[5] It is, in fact, this very doctrine that he puts into the mouth of an infidel in the *Minute Philosopher*.

Berkeley's Defence of Revelation

It is in *The Alciphron, or The Minute Philosopher*, that we have, what Dr Timothy Dwight describes as 'an able defence of Divine Revelation, by one of the first philosophers of any age and any

---

[1] *A Treatise Concerning the Principles of Human Knowledge* (Dent's edition), p. 191.
[2] Op. cit., p. 195.
[3] A sermon preached at Festival Service in the Chapel of Trinity College, Dublin, July 10th, 1953, by Canon I. T. Ramsay, Nolloth Professor of the Philosophy of the Christian Religion in the University of Oxford, reprinted from *Hermathena*, No. LXXXII, 1953.
[4] *Theory of Vision and other Writings by Bishop Berkeley* (Dent), Preface, p. x.
[5] These words from Archbishop King's sermon on Predestination were taken up and made the thesis of Bishop Browne's volumes.

country'.[1] This enthusiastic estimate of the book is not shared by all. Dean Swift thought it 'too speculative' to have real effect, while Bishop Hoadley spoke of it as 'the most plain attempt to bring obscurity and darkness into all science, as well as to make nonsense essential to religion, that this last age has produced'.

The book consists of seven dialogues in which Lysicles represents the light-hearted worldling. Here is 'refuted' Mandeville's *Fable of the Bees* in which the notion that 'private vices are public benefits' is proclaimed. Whether Berkeley was successful in his refutation is a matter of debate, at any rate, he was ably replied to by Mandeville in a *Letter to Dion*. In Berkeley's work, Alciphron upholds the moral theory of Shaftesbury with the idea of conscience as a form of taste, and the contemplation of the abstract beauty of virtue as its own sufficient reward. Euphranor and Crito announce Berkeley's own views. The main point he makes is that God is not a being whose existence can be proved apart from the world. His thesis is 'faith alone is required'. Since the whole material world is 'illusion' and the only reality IS GOD, it follows that God is nearer than breathing, closer than hands and feet. He does not, however, make faith irrational. He is ready to admit that 'The being of God is capable of clear proof, and the proper object of human reason'.[2] But while the reality of natural religion is open to the light of reason, it is 'limited to those who are capable of such proofs'.[3]

No sharp distinction is allowed between natural and revealed religion. Since God is the common Father of Lights all derived from Him, whether designated natural or revealed, springs from the same source.[4] Berkeley, it seems, was aware that a day would come when Laplace would eliminate the God of deism as an unnecessary preface to the world's history. He therefore resolved to meet the contingency by denying the reality of matter. In this way, he argued, the evidence for Christianity was not by means of logical demonstration. It is essentially moral and probable. The proofs are neither scientific nor demonstrative. The Christian message, in fact, is not directed to the reason, but to faith, although, it is granted, it is not opposed to reason. Revealed religion is not,

---

[1] 'Prefatory recommendation to the first American edition' (1803), by Dr Timothy Dwight, President of Yale College.
[2] Berkeley's *Works*, vol. 2 (Edition A. C. Fraser, 1871), p. 337.
[3] Op. cit., vol. 2, p. 182.
[4] *Minute Philosopher*, p. 183, cf., p. 335.

therefore, a category apart from faith, since faith is a fundamental factor in all our lives. 'Did minute philosopher but reflect, how rarely men are swayed or governed by mere ratiocination, and how often by faith, in the general and civil concerns of the world! how little they know, and how much they believe!'[1] Along with Berkeley's idealism, then, there went the doctrine that revelation was not something that the reason can discover, but which faith must accept. It is the immediate assurance and the direct awareness of God, Who thinks His own thoughts within us.

(ii) *The Rejection of Reason — Dodwell*

The contention of Berkeley that revelation is not addressed to reason but to faith was taken up by H. Dodwell to become the thesis of his volume, entitled, *Christianity not Founded on Argument* (1743). Dodwell contends for a 'constant and particular Revelation imparted separately and supernaturally to every Individual'.[2] It is in this personal and immediate relationship that, according to Dodwell, the true nature of Christian evidence is to be found. He goes beyond Berkeley, however, and maintains that the principle of faith is contrary to reason. 'I am fully persuaded', he writes, 'that the judging at all of religious Matters is not the Providence of Reason, or indeed an Affair where she has any Concern.'[3]

Dodwell advances three main arguments for his view.

1. He first asserts that the intellectual faculty of reason is unable, by virtue of its own nature, to act as the principle to lead into true faith. It was evidently never intended by God to be the method chosen. Infant baptism, he takes as proof that the whole rationalist position is false. Babies cannot rationally accept the terms of salvation, yet, 'they commence true Believers at once, and are made Heirs of Salvation.'[4] This means that salvation is not assent to certain propositions carefully marshalled and investigated. He asks those who would industriously seek for convincing proofs: 'Are you not at this Instant a baptized and covenanted Christian?'[5] In a manner worthy of Luther, Dodwell sees reason as an illustration of human arrogance. Rational religion is a form of pride. Man can take some commendation for having ascended

---

[1] *Minute Philosopher*, p. 258.
[2] *Christianity not Founded on Argument*, p. 112.
[3] Op. cit., p. 7.
[4] Op. cit., p. 9; cf., also, p. 69.
[5] Op. cit., p. 113.

the ladder of his carefully constructed syllogisms to bring God down. Dodwell will not however grant man this ability. For while baptism makes it evident that reason has no place in the commencement of the Christian life, prayer, as an activity in which reason has no real place, assures us that reason has no part in its continuation.

If assent to propositions, after patient investigation, is to be regarded as the faith of the gospel, then the question arises concerning the condition in which people are until the rational avowal be made. A position of indecision must be supposed; a place of neutrality: but is not this very term itself one of horror and detestation in a believer's ear? Even the very notion of examining evidence, suspending judgement, until all is clear to the mind, is an admission of, at least, a temporary disbelief. Then would religion be born out of pious doubt. It would be something we originate by our own fine arguments; except that there is always the difficulty of knowing when the great announcement shall be made. Who can take upon himself the fearful and fateful decision of saying that the last doubtful point has been settled, and no longer does he see through a glass darkly?

During the time of neutrality, when all the arguments are being surveyed, religion, which comes to influence our actions and direct our conduct, is not there. And supposing the conclusion should be reached 'too late', What then? 'As long as we are debating the Genuineness of our Rule, we have no Tie on us as respect its Authority?'[1] During the period of indecision, obedience is not necessary; thus the good works then and there performed are of no value, since, whatever is not of faith is sin. If in this 'Infidel interim', we should be caught unawares, like the fool of our Lord's parable, we should be likewise 'unfurnished of our Passport', we should be without an apology, without a wedding-garment.

Few men are qualified to reason accurately, and God cannot be so unjust as to require of all men that which so many cannot give. It would not become Him to make salvation a matter of such blind chance and guess-work, and to set the precious soul upon the hazard of a random conjecture. In the Gospels the one all-inclusive and the one all-conclusive command is 'to believe'. With clinching emphasis Dodwell asks, 'Will a faith, thus built upon Syllogisms, ever furnish out any of these miraculous Effects, which are described

[1] *Christianity not Founded on Argument*, p. 15.

to attend a just and furnished Belief?'[1] A rational orthodoxy can never administer comfort, never control the passions, never produce holiness of life. The forced acknowledgement of the mind is not the sort that creates heroes and martyrs. It is a warm, believing confidence that will, if occasion demands, strive unto blood, and open up heaven to those who are faithful unto death.

2. As a second disproof of mere rational assent, Dodwell notes that the Scriptures do not picture Christ as presenting His message for leisurely investigation. And His disciples were sent forth, not to argue, but to announce. Indeed, for the former they had neither the qualifications nor the time. Their message was a proclamation which carried its own demonstration and vindication. Christianity was not regarded as a useful scheme for the few who could be led to see how logical and consistent were its doctrines. 'And was it in Truth', asks Dodwell, 'can we suppose, for the sake of any such Conclusion, and to enforce such a Persuasion about his Errand, that the only Son of God, and Partner of the Divinity, could demean this exalted Nature, to struggle through a long course of human Passions and Temptations, and be content to expire at last under such accumulated Circumstances of long Anguish and Horror upon the accursed Tree, and all, as it seems, by this account to recommend his Doctrines only to the Opinions of a Few Men of Parts, who were happily formed with the Faculties to conceive his Proofs?'[2]

3. This leads Dodwell to stress his point that true Christianity is the result of an immediate divine illumination. As a result of which he maintains there is no need of 'mere manuscript authorities and Paper-Revelations'.[3] God addresses Himself to men whose 'will is by nature free', and it is this fact which makes the gospel so unique and urgent. Christianity did not sweep to such early success because of its reasoned advocacy. There were those, in fact, who could not but acknowledge the grandeur of its doctrines and the greatness of its results, and yet they stood still without. The gospel was first welcomed by ordinary people who possessed the minutest portion of human talents. What the philosopher could not penetrate, the pauper could rejoice in. A subtle spirit and an informed genius may be blinded, but he who would be a candidate for discipleship, must first renounce his reason.

---

[1] *Christianity not Founded on Argument*, p. 24.   [2] Op. cit., p. 44.
[3] Ob. cit., p. 59.

The positive proofs marshalled by the learned Dr Clarke in favour of revealed religion have but given birth to as many negative doubts. Argument cannot create faith, and where faith is, it can add nothing. 'For what can Reason's confirmation do for me here, but fix me where I am? and what can her assistance give me in the case more than I have already?'[1] A long comment by Bishop Beveridge on 1 Cor. 2. 14 is quoted to sustain the view that the human reason is at a discount as far as God is concerned. What is needed is a spiritual light within the soul, a divine infilling, an immediate revelation of God. Where this is nothing else is needed; 'however plausibly Christianity may be enforced as a Fact, it can yet never be true, as a Gospel, in Virtue of any Arguments deduced from Reasoning.'[2]

There are not two kinds of Christianity, one for the intelligentsia and the other for the ignorant: one based on reason and the other of faith. He thus concludes 'Be satisfied henceforth that there is a kind of Evidence of Power beyond which Reason can never pretend to Furnish such as brings with it that cordial Peace and Assurance of Mind to which all Conviction by human means is an utter Stranger, such as you can see enable your pious Mother without any of the reputed Advantages of academic Institution to pronounce with so much peremptory Justice on all Religious Causes, and reprove, with so good a Grace, all the well-glossed Heresies of a lettered Clarke.'[3]

It is not easy to estimate Dodwell's book. Wesley, as we have seen, regarded it with disfavour.[4] Leyland, from the standpoint of the rational orthodox saw it as an attempt to ridicule Christianity.[5] Whatever be the truth of the matter, Dodwell's position was undoubtedly an emphatic rejection of the view that Christianity could be disseminated and defended by rational arguments. And it was this very statement which called out the hostility of both the deists and the orthodox, for 'it was monstrous to overthrow that common ground of "reason" where Christian and anti-Christian liked to meet and fight their duels, under a set of rules both sides accepted'.[6]

[1] Op. cit., p. 87.
[2] Op. cit., p. 111.
[3] Op. cit., p. 115.
[4] See above, p. 150.
[5] See the *Oxford Young Gentleman's Reply to Dodwell and Two Letters from Dr Leyland, published together with Christianity not Founded on Argument.*
[6] R. N. Stromberg, *Religious Liberalism in the Eighteenth Century*, p. 108.

(iii) *The Immanence of the Eternal Christ — Law*

The importance of William Law in the development of the doctrine of revelation in the immediacy of experience cannot be overestimated. Insufficient account, we are convinced, has been taken of him. Law stressed the complete inadequacy of the external evidences for Christianity, and 'strikingly anticipates the teaching of the later school of theology, which traces its origin to Coleridge, and has a natural affinity to the mystical elements'.[1] An examination of Law's works will reveal how much Coleridge, Hare and Maurice but re-echo his thought.

Maurice, for example, begins with the same fundamental assumption. He writes to his mother: 'My text is, "Know ye not that Jesus Christ is in you?" . . . not to the faithful Christian or to the unfaithful one, "For in him we live and move and have our being" . . . . Christ is in every man . . . . The truth is that every man is in Christ; the condemnation of every man is, that he will not own the truth; he will not act as if it were true, he will not believe that it is true, except he be joined to Christ, he would not think, breathe, live for a single hour.'[2] This is a mere reiteration of Law's teaching that 'Christ is in every man'. 'Every one has Christ in his spirit, lying there in a state of insensibility and death.'[3] 'Every man hath the Spirit of God, The Spirit is in every soul.'[4]

By maintaining that the presence of Christ is in every man, Law can state categorically that the Church of Christ is therefore not limited to those who are called Christians. We are called upon to 'See here the extent of the Catholic Church of Christ! It takes in all the world'.[5] It is just this view which is further and more fully elaborated by Hare and Maurice.

Fundamental, then, for Law is the doctrine of the divine immanence, especially in the works just quoted where his position is virtually pantheistic.

It is, however, in the volume, *The Way of Divine Knowledge*, that he deals more particularly with the inner revelation of the

---

[1] L. Stephen, *Religious Thought in the Eighteenth Century*, vol. 2, p. 405.

[2] *Life of F. D. Maurice* (by his son), vol. 1, pp. 154, 155.

[3] *The Spirit of Love*, sect. 2, p. 34.

[4] *The Spirit of Prayer*, pt. 1, p. 63. Cf., 'No faith could ever begin, unless every man had Christ in him.' *The Spirit of Love*, pt. 2, p. 34. 'The birth of Christ is already begun in every one. Jesus is already within (whoever thou art,), . . .' *The Spirit of Prayer*, pt. 1, p. 55, 'Poor sinner, Christ dwelleth in the centre, the fund, the bottom of thy soul.' *The Spirit of Prayer*, pt. 1, p. 63.

[5] *The Spirit of Prayer*, pt. 1, p. 56.

indwelling Christ. As this work is specified by its author 'As Preparatory to a New Edition of the Works of Jacob Behmen; and the Right Use of Them', the mystical approach will be readily appreciated. In the form of a dialogue between Humanus, Academicus, Rusticus and Theophilus, Law makes his own position clear. Assent to the whole New Testament can never make one a Christian. True Christian faith is the direct contact of the soul with Christ, in God. It is the rising up within of the Christ-spirit. This is the doctrine that Humanus has been taught by Theophilus; now that he has so learned the truth he will no longer seek to make converts to Christianity by arguments and evidences. Twenty years of debate with the deists has convinced him of this folly. Each new book in the defence of Christianity just brings out new objections. Apologetics is like a lecture on anatomy in which the lungs, the heart, the liver and so on, are indicated in a dead body; but the body is lifeless still.

Academicus must therefore renounce his learning, for it is a mere human thing; 'it has no higher a Nature or Birth than Natural Doubting.'[1] But Christianity is not something learned. Indeed 'the Demonstrators of the truth and reasonableness of Christianity have betrayed their own cause, and left true Christianity un-mentioned'.[2] Academicus will seek in vain to understand Behmen until he sits where the mystic sat. He seeks information, he needs illumination. He would receive good notions, but what is wanting is a new nature.

The experience to which Behmen testifies is only got by re-nouncing reason. The boasted knowledge of the natural man is to be put to death, for 'notional knowledge, the treasure of human reason, is the very builder of Babal'.[3] The man qualified by human learning to publish an edition of Homer with critical notes, may be quite unfit to write comments upon the spirit and meaning of Christ's words. The knowledge of logic does not give a blind man the ability to receive the light of the sun, while skill in Hebrew and Greek cannot open up the soul to the light of God.

When Academicus asked of learned divines the question, What must I do to be saved? he was recommended vast volumes and tedious tomes. He lit his candle early and put it out late. He waded through the literature of seventeen hundred years. And all

---

[1] *The Way of Divine Knowledge*, p. 120.   [2] Op. cit., p. 30.
[3] Op. cit., p. 93.

to fruitless result when he could have stood with the primitive Christians who had none of these packed libraries. Had he stood with them he would have heard these words; he would have learnt that the light and life of God come immediately to the soul. They well up from the depths of one's own being.

Two sorts of people fail to find any help in Behmen. Those who are unregenerate still and those who follow the light of reason. Reason, Law thinks, is rightly called by Behmen, the Antichrist. It leads men from Christ. It is 'the old Serpent called Subtelty, the first and last grand Deceiver of Mankind'.[1] But the true knowledge of God is not got by searching or working. 'The Truth is nowhere to be found by Man, but in a New Birth from above.'[2] This cannot be 'till Christ, who is the one Fountain of Life and Light, be seen in you; it is in vain that you rise up early, and take late rest, in quest of Truth'.[3]

Law repudiates as saving faith a belief in the letter of Scripture. Without the light of God even the instruction of an angel would be fruitless and as the 'dead Paper on which the Scriptures are written'.[4] For Law, as for the school of Barth and Brunner the Word of God is Christ Himself; 'the Word of God which saveth and redeemeth the Soul', he writes, 'is not the Word printed on Paper, but is the . . . ever-speaking Word, which is the Son of God.'[5] The new birth is God speaking and winning a response from the soul. It is the immediate communication, or perhaps, stimulation, within the individual of God's own divine nature.

The personal response of the will to the movements of God is the 'magic power' of which Behmen speaks. But the ultimate fact is the divine will, which, as will, is final 'magic', and is the 'mother of us all'. For Law magic seems to be a synonym for mystery. Yet the human will is in some sense identified with the immanent Christ. It is the 'heavenly Will, which is the only Spark of the Deity in us, given by the Free Grace of God to all mankind, as soon as fallen,

---

[1] Op. cit., p. 164.   [2] Op. cit., p. 134.   [3] Op. cit., p. 133.
[4] Op. cit., p. 137.
[5] Op. cit., p. 164. According to Barth revelation is the '*Deus dixit*' the 'one Word of God within which there can be neither a more or less'. *Church Dogmatics*, 1, i, p. 136. He maintains the two-way equation, 'God's Word is God's Son' and 'God's Son is God's Word'. Op. cit., p. 156. On Brunner's view see, e.g. his *Revelation and Reason*, pp. 118, 119. It may be pointed out that the same idea of Christ's 'contemporaneity' (*Gleichzeitigkeit*) found in Barth and Brunner is clearly taught by Law. For Brunner the idea derives from Kierkegaard. See Brunner's *Revelation and Reason* and the latter's *Philosophical Fragments*, ch. 4, and *Training in Christianity*, ch. 4.

and called in Scripture the inspoken Word of God in Paradise'.[1]
The 'inspoken Word' is the Christ within every man; the Will that
hath the power of salvation in it.

Like Dodwell and Berkeley, Law argues that all men live by
faith. The important thing is the object of this faith; according to
its object it can be divine or devilish, saving or sensual.

The deist who imagines that he follows reason lives in an illusion.
'He may indeed easily enough keep himself free from all Christian
Faith; but whether he will or no, a Faith must do all in him, and
for him, just in the same degree, as it does for the Christian.'[2] But
equally the rational 'Christian' who merely assents to doctrine is
outside saving faith. 'The Delusion of the Deist lies here; He
refuses an Assent to the History of Facts and Doctrines of the
Gospel; and this is *his* proof to himself that he lives by Reason, and
that it is the Principle of his Life. On the other hand, he who
assents to the History of Facts and Doctrines of the Gospel, is, by
the Deist reckoned a Man of Gospel Faith, and lives by it. But this
is all a Mistake on both sides. For this Assent on the one Side, and
Dissent on the other, touches not the Matter of either Reason or
Faith.'[3]

Law asserts that natural religion has been the cause of much
evil. But he comforts himself with the reflection that in every age a
few spiritual writers have witnessed to true 'Gospel faith'.
Notional religion, he contends, was brought forth by a Church
which had lost its life: its elaborate propositions arose from the
contentions of sects. But the Bible is a 'witness' to genuine
spiritual faith; it addresses itself to the heart and the conscience.

Reason having renounced the help of God has made shipwreck.
Learned reason without the Church denies, and learned reason
within builds up some rational interpretation on the letter of
Scripture: but learned reason everywhere is of the earth earthy.

If mystery lies at the basis of all, then it is folly to argue either for
or against. If there is no ultimate understandable premise, there can
be no final sure conclusion. All things were created out of nothing,
thus the possibility of giving a reasoned account of anything,

---

[1] *The Way of Divine Knowledge*, p. 158. Cf., 'When Adam fell, this centre of
his soul became a prisoner in an earthly animal. But from the moment God spoke
Christ in Adam, all the treasures of the divine nature, the light and Spirit of God
came again into man, into the centre of his soul,' *The Spirit of Prayer*, pt. 1, p. 60.
[2] *The Way of Divine Knowledge*, p. 174.
[3] Op. cit., p. 176.

in man's nature or religion, is ruled out. As all things were created out of nothing, then, too, the new creation is not produced out of reason. Where the ground of truth is everlasting mystery the so-called art of disputation on either side is an absurdity. 'Why is not the learned Papist shocked at Transubstantiation,' asks Law, 'or the Protestant at Predestination and Reprobation?'[1] To his own question he makes answer, 'It is because each of them have enough of the Truth of Reason and Goodness of Criticism, to draw the Letter of Scripture to his Side.'[2] Literal learning, as Law calls it, does not lead to the inward knowledge which is the very essence of Christianity. What matters in the renewal of the soul is the immediate awareness of the immanent Christ. Without this all religious forms are inadequate. No specific form of religion is of any consequence if it fails to help towards the opening of the heavenly life in the heart; and no one form of religion is in itself necessary to the Truth. There can, therefore, be full acceptance of Behmen's words, 'A Christian is of no Sect, and yet in every Sect.'

Knowledge of the Christian way can become a snare and a delusion if the enquirer does not 'turn to Christ, as the one Way, the one Truth, and the one Life, and Salvation of the Soul; not as notionally apprehended, or historically known; but as experimentally found, living, speaking, and working in your soul'.[3]

An emphasis like that seen in Law upon the inwardness of Christian evidences was made by Vicesimus Knox, master of Tonbridge School, from 1778 to 1811. Knox felt that Paley's external arguments needed supplementing. However that may have answered the questions of gainsayers, it is, he insists, in the inner witness of the responding heart that we find the most persuasive proof. This is the thesis elaborated in his *Christian Philosophy*. Light and life, he urges, are their own clearest evidence: it is not easy to prove the reality of the first to a blind man, or the reality of the second to a dead one!

(iv) *The Apostle of the Christian Consciousness — Erskine*

Such is the title given to the versatile Thomas Erskine by Principal Tulloch.[4] Erskine, a layman, sided with MacLeod

---

[1] *The Way of Divine Knowledge*, p. 254.
[2] Ibid.
[3] Op. cit., p. 174.
[4] F. W. Cornish, *Quoted in History of the English Church*, vol. 8, pt. ii, p. 192.

Campbell and adopted a soteriology akin to that expounded by his Scottish compatriot, in the latter's book, *The Nature of the Atonement*. He, however, apparently went beyond MacLeod Campbell and asserted a universalist doctrine. All humanity, it seems, is ultimately to be restored to God's favour.[1] Erskine was a friend of F. D. Maurice and his influence upon him was profound. Avoiding, like Maurice, party attachment, he spoke of 'Calvinism as a sheep in wolf's clothing, and Arminianism as a wolf in sheep's clothing'.

It is in his book, *The Internal Evidences for the Truth of Revealed Religion* (1820), that he treats of our subject. At the end of his work referred to, he contends that the standpoint is not novel, but there is much fresh and original notwithstanding. 'The object of the Gospel', he tells us, 'is to bring man into harmony with God; the subject of its operations, therefore, is the human heart in all its various conditions.'[2] With this as the fundamental thesis, the author sets out to consider, what may be called, the 'moral influence' of the Gospel. The value of all the external evidences is repudiated.

The gospel does not address itself to men's reason as something to be leisurely investigated. It comes rather with a moral persuasion to the heart. Several telling illustrations are given to prove that a stirring deed can evoke a response of love and gratitude, and work for a change of life. A mere general amnesty, for example, would not have produced a hatred of sin and a love of God. 'A pardon without a sacrifice could have but a weak and obscure appeal to the understanding and heart.'[3]

God's aim in dealing with men is not to grant them pardon. Had this been so He could have withheld information on the subject until men stood before the judgement seat. God's great purpose was rather to transform men by weaning them from their sins. This is the moral intention of the gospel and the assurance of its truth lies in the attainment of that end. It is this inner transformation, under the moral constraint of the gospel, which is true faith. It is when, with joyous abandonment one gives himself to its influence that there comes 'a new birth'.[4]

The faith of the gospel, then, is not mere knowledge of doctrine. Abstract doctrines have become divorced from their moral biblical

[1] *Dictionary of National Biography*, vol. 6, p. 862.
[2] *Internal Evidences for the Truth of Revealed Religion*, p. 56.
[3] Op. cit., p. 71.
[4] Op. cit., p. 109.

purpose. They are isolated summaries, detached dogmas. In the Bible, doctrine is the source of life. But as for our creeds and articles, 'the doctrines contained in them are not stated with reference to their great object in the Bible — the regeneration of the human heart, by the knowledge of the Divine character.'[1] It is only in 'gospel faith' that the creeds have any value. They give a convenient summary, they act as warnings against danger, and they stand as doctrinal landmarks. But knowledge of them however perfect is not Bible faith. 'The knowledge communicated by revelation is moral knowledge, and it has been communicated in order to produce a moral effect upon our characters; and a knowledge of the Divine essence would have as little bearing upon this subject, as far as we can see, as a knowledge of the elementary essence of matter.'[2]

The moral change effected in us by the gospel is the work within us of the Spirit of God. And because this is so, no external attestation of the gospel is required by an appeal to miracles. Some miracles, like the resurrection of our Lord, belong to the very essence of the gospel and cannot be detached and treated as mandatory labels. 'The belief of the miraculous attestation of the Gospel, then, is just so far useful as it excites our reverence for, and fixes our attention upon, the truth contained in the Gospel.'[3]

Erskine repudiates a religion imposed from without and by authority. True Christian faith must be something rising up within; it must be something to which the conscience can give its assent, for whatever is not of conscience is not of faith. Like Maurice, Erskine regards man as needing the assurance that he is already reconciled to God. 'If the question is asked, "How can I obtain God's mercy?" the reply must be given, "God has already declared himself reconciled through Jesus Christ; so you may have it by believing it." '[4] Like Brunner he regards men as responsible beings committed to decision. 'We feel we are not unconcerned spectators of these things. We are sure that, if there be a principle which can explain and connect them all together, it must be a most important one for us; it must determine our eternal destiny.'[5]

[1] *The Internal Evidences for the Truth of Revealed Religion*, p. 91.
[2] Op. cit., p. 95.
[3] Op. cit., p. 188.
[4] Op. cit., p. 194.
[5] Op. cit., p. 198.

Kant Undermines Rationalism

A new Copernecian revolution in thought was introduced by Immanuel Kant (1722-1804). In his *Critique of Pure Reason* Kant had argued that the ultimate postulates of religion cannot be rationally proved. But in his *Critique of Practical Reason* he allows that what cannot be proved by the pure reason is a necessity of the practical reason. For Kant the ideas of freedom, immortality and God were somehow necessities of a thinking being. It is as absurd by reason to prove there is a God, as to prove freedom, immortality and God to be unreal. 'For we can only say that we know anything by reason when we are somehow conscious that we know it even if it had not been given us in experience; hence rational knowledge and knowledge *a priori* are one and the same.'[1]

Since Kant's day, philosophy generally may be estimated by its agreement or disagreement with him. In the main, it can be said, that he gave rise, on the one hand, to a sceptical intellectualism, and on the other hand, to a practical anti-intellectualism. Reopening the question of knowledge, in an effort to bring men out of the impasse created by Hume's scepticism, Kant postulated an existing 'ego', as more than the sum of sensations. He drew, also, a sharp distinction between the 'thing-in-itself' — the noumenon — which is beyond knowledge, and the thing-in-appearance — the phenomenon — which alone is the object of knowledge. This denial of any knowledge of the noumena led easily to the scepticism of Spencer, to whom God was the great Unknowable, beyond all predications.

But for two reasons Kant's critical philosophy, itself intellectualistic in the extreme, led to the defeat of intellectualism. First, Kant had argued that there was something which reason could not prove, namely, the reality of reason itself. There was thus that which lay outside its scope and criticism. 'Henceforth rationalism must efface itself in the presence of criticism. It has to reconcile itself to the inevitable: reason is losing its empire over objective external reality. Its proved certainties have collapsed. The Scottish David has vanquished the Goliath of dogmatism.'[2] This quotation from Lecerf introduces the second consideration. Kant, it is well known, made an onslaught on the traditional arguments for the existence of God. God could not be rationally

[1] *Critique of Practical Reason* (tr. T. K. Abbott), p. 97.
[2] A. Lecerf, *Introduction to Reformed Dogmatics*, p. 45.

proved to exist. Yet he will grant that the assurance of God's existence arises out of man's moral nature. With Kant then there was begun a new subjective emphasis. All externality is regarded with loathing. Man, for Kant, is essentially an autonomous moral being, and it is that which commends itself to this moral autonomy which is alone of value. Thus Kant can write in a letter to Lavater (24.4.1775), 'I distinguish the *teaching* of Christ from the *report* which we have of the teaching of Christ, and in order to get at the former I try above all to extract the *moral* teaching separated from all precepts of the New Testament. The former is surely the fundamental doctrine of the Gospel, the latter can only be auxiliary doctrine.'[1] For Kant the standard of judging between the 'moral teaching of Christ' and the mere 'report' was to be found within. With him, therefore, begins the rout of reason. 'Since the impressive efforts of Kant', observes W. E. Hocking, 'to mark out a strictly limited province which all our major human interests lie safely outside of, thinkers of the first rank (with exceptions, but with singular accord) have added some strokes to the picture of reason's retirement, representing it as servant to the will, or as a tool and creature of some darker and more primal reality — blind impulse, immediate feeling, the unconscious.... The whole apparatus of reason in religion has retracted in importance in favour of a more substantial basis — which we have agreed to call feeling.'[2]

Immediately, indeed, this side of Kant's teaching was taken up by Jacobi, the 'faith-philosopher' and used as a weapon against Kant's own 'rationalism'. In his book, *Of the Divine Things* we find Jacobi emphasizing 'feelings' as the source of religious knowledge.

The Background of the Theology of Coleridge

The place that Jacobi sought for the 'feelings' was secured in the theological system of Schleiermacher (1763–1834). Schleiermacher defined religion as the immediate feeling of absolute dependence upon God. This 'immediate feeling' he regards as the presupposition of all religions. In this way he announces, what Brunner calls, his 'relativistic conception of religion'.[3] The 'essence of religion',

---

[1] Quoted, S. Körner, *Kant*, p. 170.
[2] *The Meaning of God in Human Experience*, p. 37 f.
[3] *Revelation and Reason*, p. 219.

'the religion within the religions,' that which manifests itself in many historical forms, is this feeling of dependence. It is nothing accidental, but is 'a universal element in life'.[1] It is, in fact, one and the same, with what Schleiermacher calls, the God-consciousness: 'God-consciousness is always ... the feeling of absolute dependence.'[2] This doctrine is, at bottom, the same as that worked out more recently by Otto under his 'Numinous' formula in his *Idea of the Holy*.

Those who become aware of this native God-consciousness need no other argument since 'the recognition of this fact entirely takes the place for the system of doctrine, of all so-called proofs of the existence of God'.[3] The important thing is this immediate or intuitive certainty of God. Indeed this feeling of dependence is nothing other than the immanence of God. This doctrine of 'God-consciousness' is really Schleiermacher's substitute for the Quaker doctrine of the 'inner light'. It is significant that the only English work quoted by Schleiermacher in his *Christian Faith*, is Robert Barclay's *Apology*. While it is true that on each mention of him it is to differ from him (which is understandable since both allusions have to do with the Ordinances, which, of course, Barclay rejected), it is indicative of how strongly was the mystic influence upon him.[4] Barclay, to be sure, sought to safeguard a distinction between the inner light and man's own spirit. But in the final exposition of Schleiermacher's views there is little distinction between the Spirit of God and the spirit of man. For Schleiermacher, the God-consciousness is one and the same with 'immediate self-consciousness'.[5] Even the contention of Otto is not true, the contention, namely, that Schleiermacher argued by inference from the feelings to a God beyond them.[6] He would rather have us assured of a God found within our feelings. For Schleiermacher Dogmatics is 'a statement about our feelings, not about God'.[7] But, ultimately, as any statement about the feelings is a statement about the God-consciousness, then for Schleiermacher, any statement about the God-consciousness as a reality of the feelings, is a statement about God.

---

[1] *The Christian Faith* (tr. from 2nd German edition, ed. by H. R. Mackintosh and J. S. Steward), p. 133.
[2] Op. cit., p. 260. [3] Op. cit., pp. 133, 134.
[4] Op. cit., p. 625: cf., p. 643. [5] Op. cit., p. 5.
[6] *The Idea of the Holy*, p. 10.
[7] H. R. Mackintosh, *Types of Christian Doctrine*, p. 60.

Schleiermacher on Revelation and Scripture

Reference must be made briefly to Schleiermacher's understanding of these two related subjects so as to appreciate the position taken up by Coleridge and his followers. Schleiermacher begins by stressing that revelation is not a human discovery, nor yet, is it something 'excogitated in thought by one man and so learned by others'.[1] Revelation is not an operation upon man as a cognative being; 'For that would make revelation to be originally and essentially *doctrine*.'[2] He views it rather as that which arises within man himself like an heroic or poetic inspiration. It would, he says, 'be difficult to draw any clear dividing line at all between what is revealed and what comes to light through inspiration in a natural way.'[3] This understanding of revelation, is, he contends, illustrated in the Person of Christ. In Him dwelt the God-consciousness in fullest measure. But the indwelling God-consciousness belongs to man, *qua* man. He, therefore, rejects the idea that the divine revelation in Christ was absolutely supernatural. Human nature has within it 'the possibility of taking up the divine into itself, just as did happen in Christ'.[4]

Schleiermacher elaborates his thesis that there is in both the Redeemer and the redeemed a 'supra-rational' element. In both it is a veritable indwelling of God: in Christ in the form of the Logos; in the redeemed as 'a movement of the Holy Spirit'. Yet he will not allow any clear-cut distinction between the supra-rational element and the common human reason. 'For', he says 'the highest goal that is set before these workings of redemption is always a human state which not only would obtain the fullest recognition from the common human reason, but in which also it is impossible always to distinguish, even in the same individual between what is effected by the divine Spirit and what is effected by the human reason. Inasmuch, then, as the reason is completely at one with the divine Spirit, the divine Spirit can itself be conceived as the highest enhancement of the human reason, so that the difference between the two is made to disappear.'[5] This notion, when applied, means for Schleiermacher, that there is nothing strictly supernatural, nor, yet, is there anything specifically rational. The common idea, he contends, that would draw a distinction between natural (rational)

[1] *The Christian Faith*, p. 50.   [2] Op. cit., p. ibid.
[3] Op. cit., p. 61.   [4] Op. cit., p. 64.
[5] Op. cit., p. 65.

and revealed (supra-rational) religion, errs. It is to him obvious that 'this can be no more than a juxtaposition, and that these two kinds of dogma cannot form one whole. Between the rational and the supra-rational there can be no connection. This further becomes pretty clearly evident in all treatises upon Christian doctrine which divide themselves into a natural theology, purely rational and thus valid not only within, but also outside of Christianity, and a positive supra-rational theology, valid only within the compass of Christianity. For then the two are and remain separate from each other'.[1] This division Schleiermacher will not allow, since, in the individual, the element of the God-consciousness is at the same time both divine and human, so in 'one respect all Christian dogmas are supra-rational, in another they are all rational'.[2]

All this means that Schleiermacher's position is, as Brunner does not hesitate to say, semi-pantheistic. 'If a man awakens to the fact that within his single life the Whole is living, that in his personal existence there is beating, vividly, vitally, the pulse of the Infinite movement, then in that man, Schleiermacher teaches, authentic piety is born.'[3] It will be granted that he made man look within for the spirit and the spring of religion. It is a category *sui generis*. God was not the conclusion of a chain of syllogistic reasons. He was there, immediately within the soul — so close that it seemed impossible to separate Him from self-consciousness and contemplate Him objectively. Instructed in Moravianism and influenced by Romanticism, Schleiermacher really gave doctrinal expression to both in his Christian Faith.

In the end the position is that Revelation is not an inbreaking of God, but an upsurging of divine humanity. It is a natural discovery. Such a view of revelation made it too weak to have any creative significance. 'If', says a living author, 'we accept the supernatural only as something too weak and passive to interfere with the natural, we had best call ourselves materialists and have done with it, — we shall gain in honesty what we lose in respectability.'[4] In the context of our period when idealism was in such vogue it would be better to substitute the word 'pantheism' for 'materialism' in the above quotation: with this done, the words are applicable, and the rebuke is warranted.

[1] Op. cit., p. 66.   [2] Op. cit., p. 67.
[3] Op. cit., p. 67. Cf. H. R. Mackintosh, *Types of Modern Theology*, p. 52, from which the quotation above is made.
[4] Joy Davidson, *Smoke on the Mountains*, p. 116.

When we turn to Schleiermacher's understanding of Scripture it will be found that the same subjective principle which runs through all his work is applied. It is that which commends itself to the believer which is of value. The peculiar authority accorded to the Scripture rests upon the faith of the believer in Christ.[1] He condemns those text-books and Confessions which begin with a doctrine of Scripture. He would have us accept the Scripture rather as a witness to the God-consciousness which is expressed in the feeling of dependence. A doctrine does not necessarily 'belong to Christianity because it is contained in Scripture'.[2] Like Tertullian he seems to be saying that the soul is by nature Christian. 'If faith in Jesus as the Christ', he writes, 'or as the Son of God and the Redeemer of men is based on the authority of Scripture, the question arises how this authority itself is to be based; for obviously the thing must be so done as to impress the conviction on unbelieving hearts, so that they too may by this path come to faith in the Redeemer. Now if we have no point of departure but ordinary reason, the divine authority of Scripture, to begin with, must admit of being proved on grounds of reason alone; and as against this two points must be kept in mind. First, this always involves a critical and scientific use of the understanding of which not all are capable; on this theory, therefore only those so gifted can attain to faith in an original and genuine way, while all others would merely have faith at second-hand and on the authority of others . . . . Secondly, if such proof could be given and if faith could be established in this fashion — if, that is to say, faith, given a certain degree of culture, could be implanted by argument — then on such terms faith might exist in people apart from repentance and change of the mind; which means that, having originated in this way, it would not be genuine faith at all. In other words, a conviction of this kind, gained through demonstrative proof,

---

[1] It is worth pointing out that the position adopted by Schleiermacher is the same as that followed by Brunner. Faith in Christ is prior to faith in the Scriptures, is the teaching of Brunner. 'Not because I believe in the Scriptures do I believe in Christ, but because I believe in Christ I believe in the Scriptures,' *Revelation and Reason*, p. 170. That this is a reversal of the historic 'orthodox' position Schleiermacher acknowledges. In a footnote Brunner maintains that M. Kähler was the 'first scholar to point out quite clearly this reversal of ideas'. It is strange that Brunner fails to note that the same line was taken earlier by Schleiermacher. Perhaps his own supposed repudiation of Schleiermacher's theology would not permit the reference. But we are of the opinion that Brunner is closer to Schleiermacher in his view of revelation than he would allow.

[2] *The Christian Faith*, p. 593.

would in itself have no value, for of itself it would not result in true living fellowship with Christ.'[1]

Although we are not concerned here with any criticism of Schleiermacher, it may be apposite to point out that in the passage just quoted, the author seems to argue that because reason cannot be given the supreme place, it cannot be given any. But this conclusion does not follow. At any rate, whether this be cogent or not, it is important to observe that these references to both Kant and Schleiermacher are necessary so as to provide the background for what follows.

(v) The Supremacy of the Subjective—Coleridge

In S. T. Coleridge, there is a strong emphasis upon the subjective element in revelation. Revelation is indeed a subjective matter. As a youth Coleridge had read much Neo-Platonic philosophy. With his friend Wordsworth he studied Spinoza and was greatly influenced thereby. It is recorded by Crabb Robinson that on one occasion Coleridge opened Spinoza's *Ethica* and kissed the portrait of its author, exclaiming, 'This book is gospel to me!' adding, the epexegetical remark, 'his philosophy is nevertheless false.'[2]

For a short time Coleridge joined the Unitarians but soon found himself out of sympathy with their doctrinal tenets. Abandoning them, he declared against all Socinian interpretations, and maintained belief in man's inherent sinfulness, and redemption through the Blood of Christ.

It was, indeed, the burdening reality of sin which conditioned his theological views.[3] A stay in Germany brought him into contact with the Kantian philosophy. Henceforth he forsook his earlier Spinozian necessitarianism and took account of the human will. Anyone who examines his own heart, Coleridge urges, will come to a realization of his own need. He will become aware of the sin for which his own will is responsible. The reality of original sin, he declares, is the primary fact: 'the doctrine of Original Sin gives to all other mysteries of religion a common basis, a connection of

---

[1] *The Christian Faith*, pp. 191, 192.

[2] *Diary*, vol. 1, p. 399.

[3] Cf., '. . . the conviction of sin . . . had for him more than for most philosophic theologians an awful pressing reality and he kept preaching it as the basis of all religion with energy . . . .', A. W. Benn, *History of English Rationalism*, vol. 1, p. 249.

dependency, an intelligibility of relation, and total harmony, that supersede extrinsic proof.'[1]

Kant had placed the origin of evil in the will and at the same time repudiated the Augustinian doctrine of heredity sinfulness and guilt. The same position is adopted by Coleridge. To be account-able man must be free. Positive evil 'follows necessarily from the postulate of a responsible will'.[2] 'Moral evil', he says again, 'is an evil that has its origin in the Will.'[3] Thus 'corruption must have been self-originated'.[4]

Yet an evil common to all must have a ground common to all. This ground cannot be the Divine Will. Coleridge, like Kant, identifies the Divine Will with the law of man's moral being. It is the categorical imperative, 'inasmuch as a Will, perfectly identified with Law is one with the Divine Will, we may say, that in the unfallen rational agent the Will constitutes the Law.'[5] But how man's common sin began in the individual Coleridge, having rejected the traditional doctrine, is unable to say. 'It is a mystery, that is, a fact we can see, but cannot explain.'[6] Coleridge maintains that all that takes place in the noumenal world is outside the range of the understanding. So the Work of Christ is like the origin of sin. Both can only be comprehended by their consequences. 'The mysterious act, the operative cause is transcendent, *Factum est*: and beyond the information contained in the announciation of the Fact, it can be characterized only by the consequences.'[7]

It is when a man feels the need which his own will has originated that he seeks a Saviour. He does not then want demonstrations and evidences. He is after that which can be transacted on the territory of his own spirit. Coleridge will not have this dismissed as 'trans-cendental trash', borrowed from Law and Behmen. He confesses to have read only Law's *Serious Call* and a 'small tract on Prayer'. So close, however, is Coleridge's thought to that of Law that we are tempted to think that he was more influenced by the 'small tract' than he cared to acknowledge. He sees Christianity as a 'divine rekindling'. It is not concerned with formal beliefs for 'religion has no speculative dogmas', he announces in true Schleiermacherian fashion.[8]

---

[1] *Aids to Reflection*, p. 198. [2] Op. cit., p. 189.
[3] Op. cit., p. 192. [4] Op. cit., p. 180.
[5] Op. cit., p. 192. [6] Op. cit., p. 201.
[7] Ibid. [8] *Table Talks*, p. 189.

Coleridge and the Bible

Having indicated Christianity as something essentially inward, Coleridge must inevitably say something about the Scriptures. He condemns out of hand all belief in their infallibility as 'if possible still more extravagant than Papal Infallibility'.[1] In his seven letters published under the title, *Confessions of an Inquiring Spirit*, he elaborates his subjective principle according to which the Bible is to be estimated.

Any identification of revelation with the words of Scripture is to be rejected. In a number of places he announces that the Scriptures 'contain' the Word of God. It is as the Bible 'finds me',[2] he says, that its truth is guaranteed. In the Bible there is 'something' experienced which is absent from every other book: 'the words of the Bible find me in greater depths of my being; and that whatever finds me brings with it an irresistible evidence of its having proceeded from the Holy Spirit.'[3]

Borrowing the term 'bibliolatry' from Lessing, he inveighs against what he regards as 'book worship'. He thinks that the doctrine of the 'verbal inspiration' of Scripture was borrowed from the Jews, who regarded their Pentateuch as so given. 'Now for "Pentateuch" substitute "Old and New Testament", and then I say that this is the doctrine which I reject as superstitious and unscriptural.'[4] Coleridge does not indicate that a doctrine is not necessarily false because it is 'borrowed from the Jews'. The argument could be dangerous if pressed too far, since the basic doctrine of the Gospels is the ethical monotheism of the Old Testament prophets.

There is a sense in which revelation must be understood as truth through history. But for Coleridge it does not seem to matter if the 'history' is a fictitious concoction or an altered sequence of events on the basis of some philosophical presupposition. The word of God is that which speaks, and is only that which speaks. Thus the Scripture is not the revelation; it is for Coleridge, as it is, in our day, for Brunner, the permanent possibility of revelation. Or, perhaps, even less specific than that, the Bible is for Coleridge, as it most definitely is for both Barth and Brunner, a 'witness' to the

---

[1] *English Divines*, vol. 1, p. 154. Cf., 'The idea of an infallible Scripture is to be paralleled only to the Romish tenet of infallibility', *Confessions, etc.*, p. 316.
[2] *Confessions*, p. 286.
[3] Ibid.
[4] Op. cit., p. 299.

actuality of revelation.[1] There is no reliance to be placed upon 'external proofs'. 'The truth revealed through Christ has its evidence in itself, and the proof of the divine authority in the fitness of our nature and deeds.'[2]

Revelation is, for Coleridge the welling up of the divine within, the springing into 'life' of the ever-active God, Who is the in-dwelling Life and Light of every human personality. Everyman shares the divine nature, and 'conversion' is really the rising to conquest of our native God-consciousness. It is just here that there is an interesting contrast between the school of Coleridge which begins with an emphasis on the divine immanence, and that of the neo-liberal school of Barth and Brunner which start with an exclusive emphasis upon the divine transcendence. For Coleridge and his followers, influenced by idealism revelation is really an upsurge of divine life; for the newer school it is an inbreaking of divine life. Revelation is to be characterized as the perpendicular from above, 'das Senkrecht von oben.'

An inevitable consequence of Coleridge's statement must be the obliteration of the distinction between natural and revealed religion. 'I know of no religion not revealed,'[3] he says. Like Kant he sees some of the truth in every religion; a truth according to the measure of God's grace. Coleridge could have used Kant's words, 'There is only one true religion but there can be many varieties of religious creeds . . . . It is therefore, more appropriate to say: this man is of the Jewish, Mahommedan, Christian creed, than, he is of this or that religion.'[4] There is no human soul, Coleridge teaches, unilluminated by the light of God. For the Christian when this light is turned on to the Scriptures, certain passages become radiative: and what becomes so illuminative becomes authenticated — for us.

[1] So many and so important are the parallels between what we may call the Coleridgean School and that of the neo-liberal school of Barth and Brunner that we are tempted to say that they have presented little that is new. This would, of course be too sweeping. The general difference, however, and the one that conditions their varied emphasis is that, while Coleridge gloried in the divine immanence and thus saw a certain 'identity' between God and man, the newer school repudiated Immanence as the 'deadly error of Hegelianism' and put their emphasis upon the 'otherness' of God. Although in the eyes of Barth, Brunner has compromised the position by giving away to 'a new version of Immanence' yet Brunner can still say: 'revelation is still a wonder ". . . that breaks into the world from beyond the world,"' cf., P. K. Jewett, Emil Brunner's Concept of Revelation, p. 18.
[2] Confessions, p. 299.
[3] The Statesman's Manual, Appendix B, p. 266.
[4] Religion within the Bounds of Pure Reason, p. 108.

Coleridge is considered by many scholars to be the real source of those views which found expression in, what has come to be called, the Broad Church. We have seen reason however to go back beyond him for the beginning of those ideas of which he was such a vigorous exponent. At the same time, those who developed his views, as did Arnold, Hare, Thirwall and Maurice, naturally looked to Coleridge as their chief. These men were either his disciples or his admirers. The tradition was continued by Stanley, Jowett, Kingsley and Robertson, 'while for every stage in the development of the school some hint or precedent or germ may be found in the recorded utterance of the master.'[1]

Opposing Theories of Inspiration

Coleridge's attack upon the doctrine of verbal inspiration demands a reference to the two theories which were now brought into conflict. The view of the inspiration of the Bible of which Coleridge was such an ardent advocate, has been suggestively called the 'Illumination Theory'. It is in line with Schleiermacher's view and was later maintained by F. D. Maurice and F. W. Robertson.

The Illumination Theory is an advance on the 'Intuition Theory' as taught by F. W. Newman, and in America by Theodore Parker. In this latter doctrine inspiration is regarded merely as the sharpening of powers possessed in some measure by all men. This statement naturally allies itself with Pelagian and Rationalistic views of man's dependence upon God.

The Illumination Theory is more obviously connected with an Arminian emphasis upon man's natural ability to co-operate with God. The Bible writers, it is said, were inspired as a result of the divine intensification and elevation of their religious preceptions, to a degree beyond that experienced by ordinary believers. This doctrine would limit inspiration to the writers, and refuse it to the writings. Thus the Scriptures are said to 'contain' the word of God; to contain that which their illumination had 'hit upon'.

This theory has the merit of taking account of the human element within the Scriptures. The personal idiosyncrasies of each writer are so obvious that the human individual was not lost in the divine indwelling. It is, of course true that there is an illumination

[1] A. W. Benn, *History of English Rationalism*, vol. 1, p. 282.

of every believing man by the Spirit of God. But there is also a vital difference between the illuminated Christian and the inspired prophet. In the former case the Spirit works to give a vivid apprehension of truth already revealed; in the latter case there is a communication of new truth. This means that there is an activity of the Spirit in each case, not merely different in degree, but also different in kind. So completely dominated is this theory by the subjective principle that it is difficult to acknowledge any part of the Bible as absolutely dependable. As a consequence there is no reliable objective standard of truth and duty. Some canons must be given to detect which parts of the Scripture are to be received, and as these are not provided by the advocates of the Illumination Theory, then, it must be assumed, that that only is allowed which commends itself to the individual conscience and reason. The single individual thus becomes his own authority. The basis then of this Schleiermacherian and Coleridgean teaching is a pragmatist epistemology, which can be certainly valuable as a test of truth, but which is inadequate as an ultimate standard.

On the other side, the doctrine, against which Coleridge pronounced so vigorously, followed from an overstress on the divine transcendence and sovereignty. Here the Bible writers are regarded as passive instruments in the hands of God: His pens, not His penmen. This 'docetic view of inspiration', as Dorner calls it, virtually denies the inspiration of the persons in maintaining that of the writings. Thus we find Hooker saying: 'They neither spake nor wrote any word of their own, but uttered syllable by syllable as the Spirit put it into their mouths.'[1] Hooker's declaration was restated by others in such a way as to convey the notion that the process of inspiration was completely mechanical.

As so stated this theory cannot be made to square with the facts. That there are instances of a communication in a definite form of words cannot be denied.[2] But the exception must not be taken as the general rule. There are obviously 'human elements' in the Bible, in, for example, Paul's anacolutha and the expressions of grief and anger. Had mechanical dictation been the method used there would have been no need of eyewitnesses or the careful researches of a diligent historian like Luke.

While these objections are not of small moment it should be

---

[1] *Works*, vol. 2, p. 383.
[2] Num. vii. 7, 8, Rev. xix. 9, xxi. 7, etc.

observed that, as against the Intuition Theory, the 'Dictation Theory' sought to emphasize that inspiration is not a natural process: and against the Illumination Theory that it is not a partial process. The purpose was to insist that not a part of the Bible, but the Bible in all its parts, is the word of God. In maintaining that the Bible was verbally inspired the interest was not in the method but the result.

Whereas the Illumination Theory was right in stressing the human element, the Dictation Theory was no less correct in emphasizing the divine element. Any true view of inspiration like any true appreciation of the Person of Christ or any correct understanding of Christian experience, must make due allowance for both elements in the final unity. This will mean that inspiration is neither a discovery nor a dictation. It is easy to slide into a conception either too distinctly human or too exclusively divine. Coleridge erred on the one side, those he opposed erred on the other. Inspiration in one sense heightened and in another sense held the quickened powers of the man.

How, in the Person of Christ, the human and the divine were united in one Person is a mystery. So is it with the process of inspiration. It is easier to say what it does NOT involve than to clearly state what it does. The Bible is the most human of books as it is the most divine. And because experience attests this to be a fact, the reality of both the human and the divine elements must be given due recognition in any adequate theory of inspiration. Cogent in this respect are the words of Karl Barth when he writes, 'there is no point in ignoring the writtenness of Holy Writ for the sake of its holiness, its humanity for the sake of its divinity.'[1] At the same time, just as in the Person of Christ, so is it with the Scriptures, it is not easy rightly to unite the human and the divine. There is always the danger of making Christ, and the Bible too, either too much the one or the other, to detract from the human in the interests of the divine, or to accentuate the divine to the detriment of the human.

The old antithesis between the schools of Alexandria and Antioch has returned in the understanding of the doctrine of inspiration. There are some who adopt, what we may not unjustly call, an 'Apollinarian' attitude with regard to the agents of divine revelation. They see the human element, as it were, 'reduced' and

[1] *Church Dogmatics*, I, ii (E.T., 1956), p. 465.

its place taken up by the divine Spirit; only in this way, it is believed, can the Bible be secured from all error.[1]

Others, on the other hand, like Nestorius, set the human and divine in juxtaposition. By thus separating the human from the divine, they feel themselves able to regard the Biblical history and 'Wissenschaft' as subject to the defects of human imperfections.

It goes without saying that an exclusive emphasis upon the divine transcendence leads naturally, if not necessarily, to a 'mechanical' conception of inspiration, while an overstatement of the divine immanence tends to make inspiration little more than a matter of human insight.

No true understanding of the process of inspiration can, we believe, be entertained which does not do justice to the human and the divine in Scripture. There is 'something' in the Bible which can hardly be explained in words; there is an atmosphere, a potentiality, or whatever one may call it, which can, in the last analysis, be referred to only as 'its Divine Character'. This 'Divine Character', which can hardly be denied, must have an adequate cause, a Divine cause, God. But, at the same time, it is quite evident that the divine message was given to men of varying capacities and contrasting temperaments and at different times. What they have given bears the stamp of their personal idiosyncrasies and their own age. The agents of inspiration were clearly no passive instruments, no motionless recipients of the divine word. The individual was himself in the picture as an active participant. This double fact must be fully appreciated if we are to arrive at a true doctrine of inspiration. To ignore one side is, in fact, to invalidate the other.

Following Coleridge we find Archdeacon Julius Hare and F. D. Maurice acknowledge their indebtedness to those who had earlier taken the same line. More particularly, however, they both indicate that they had received much from Coleridge himself.[2] Educated under Vicesimus Knox at Tonbridge School, Hare later became a

---

[1] It was in this way that the Scholastics conceived inspiration, by regarding man as a 'deficient instrument'. This was the position taken by Aquinas, cf., 'In the case of Prophetic Revelation the Prophet's mind is moved by the Holy Ghost in the same way as a deficient instrument is used by the principal agent.' H. Pope, O.P., of the Collegio Angelico, Rome, 'Article on the Scholastic View of Inspiration,' *The Irish Theological Quarterly*, July 1911. (Produced by the Professors in the Faculty of Theology, Maynooth (St Patrick's College.))

[2] *The Mission of the Comforter* (1864), vol. 1, Preface. *The Life of F. D. Maurice* (by his son), vol. 1, p. 175 f.

tutor at Trinity College, Cambridge. The source and substance of
Christianity, Hare argued, in his *Mission of the Comforter*, is in
the inner workings of the Spirit. But His influence is not limited to
the baptized; it is seen in all religions, and wherever righteousness
is found.

(vi) *The Victory of Faith — Hare*

In 1839, Hare preached six sermons before his University, on the
subject of 'faith'. These, with others, given at various times, were
published in 1840, under the title, *The Victory of Faith*. Throughout the discourses he inveighs against the multiplicity of books on
Evidences of Christianity, which have turned the news of the
gospel into a philosophical system or a moral theory. He tells us
'we are inundated with dissertations on the external evidences of
Christianity; in which it was treated like any other historical fact,
and witnesses were sifted and cross-examined; but without regard
to the main witness, the witness in the heart of the believer
himself'.[1]

In a remarkable sermon preached at Hastings, May 19th, 1835,
at the Archdeacon's Visitation, Hare took as his text the words; 'Lo
I am with you always, even unto the end of the world.' The discourse is entitled, 'Christ's Promise, the Strength of the Church.'
In it a contrast is drawn between the outlook of the divines of the
sixteenth and the seventeenth centuries and those of the eighteenth.
The preacher thinks of it like 'the transition in Pharoah's dream
from the fat kine to the lean'. In the former preaching, he says, 'we
find Christ, the Wisdom of God, and the Power of God unto
salvation.' In the newer 'we read about the Infiniteness of the
Divine Attributes, about the Benevolence of the Deity, about the
Judgement evinced in the Dispensations of Providence, about the
demonstrative evidence contained in the Resurrection'.[2] The clergy
of the period 'preacht essays of heathen morality, with no trace of
the Gospel in them, except the name of Christ awkwardly dragged
into a peroration'.[3]

Rejecting all intellectualistic and notional definitions, it is Hare's
purpose to stress the subjective element in revelation. This, he
finds, to be 'faith', which he conceives to be essentially practical.
He makes a similar comment as Dodwell and Law on 1 Cor. i. 7.
Had Paul's purpose, in preaching the gospel, he says, 'been chiefly

[1] *The Victory of Faith*, p. 24.   [2] Op. cit., pp. 341, 342.   [3] Op. cit., p. ibid.

to convince the Understanding, the wisdom of words would have been the very means the best fitted "to accomplish" it.'[1] The God Whom reason constructs, has, however, no power over the heart. It is an arid abstraction, a mirage of the mind. He is not the living God for Whom the soul cries out.

Real faith is not the result of sweeping together the fallen leaves of the past. True faith is that which raises 'our hearts from visible things to the invisible'.[2] The heart is the real hub of religion. In this emphasis upon the inward, Hare claims that he is reasserting the authentic message of Luther. The volume is thus sent out with the prayer that the sermons in it 'might help some in embracing the truth which Luther taught'.[3]

But not only is faith a practical principle, it is also somehow a natural principle of life. It is not to be regarded 'as a totally new quality, a gift of the Spirit',[4] for no man can live without faith. It is in fact 'the ground-work of all that is distinctively human in man, of all his activities, of all his well-being and happiness even in this life'.[5]

To each individual man a special revelation is made. The soul's response to it brings the inner witness of the Spirit. The apostle to the Gentiles did not seek to win men's approval and assent. He sought to capture man's soul. Like Berkeley and Maurice, Hare refers to Paul's Athenian sermon, and says that he 'took occasion from the altar dedicated to the Unknown God, to declare that God to the Athenians, whom they were already worshipping without knowing him, so will every teacher, who has the spirit of St Paul, examine and interrogate the voice in men's heart, until he makes it bear witness to the truth of God's word'.[6]

Rightly does Hare refuse to see an antithesis between faith and reason. The real opposition, he insists, 'is not between Faith and Reason, but between Faith and Sight; or more generally between Faith and Sense.'[7] Faith and reason differ only in the method of their approach to the object. In any complete act of faith the three elements of man's psychical nature, knowing, feeling and willing, must have a place. Faith, therefore, he teaches, 'proceeds from the inmost depths of the soul, from beyond the firmament of Consciousness whereby the waters under the Firmament are divided

---

[1] *The Victory of Faith*, pp. 27, 28.   [2] Op. cit., p. 163.
[3] Op. cit., Preface, p. xiv.   [4] Op. cit., p. 70.
[5] Op. cit., p. 96.   [6] Op. cit., p. 140.
[7] Op. cit., p. 79.

from the waters above the Firmament. It is the act of that living principle, which constitutes each man's individual, continuous, immortal personality.'[1]

Real revelation according to Hare takes place within the individual soul. Whether the Scriptures are to be regarded as an objective standard, an external revelation, *per se*, he does not make clear. He certainly does not think of the Bible as containing truth stated in a formal creed. This, he argues, would be a bondage upon men's minds. He sees the Scripture as giving living examples of men, who, in the development of civilization, sought, through faith, a living personal God. His stress upon the inward seems rather to make him repudiate the authority of the external. 'Lovers of the Bible', he says, 'too easily degenerate into bibliolaters, lovers of the Church into ecclesiolaters'.[2]

(vii) *The Meaning of Revelation — Maurice*

The name of F. D. Maurice holds a secure place in the history of British theology. The son of a Unitarian minister he later became, by conviction, a clergyman of the Church of England. After service in a parish he was appointed Professor of theology in King's College, London. He lost this position as a result of a controversy concerning his orthodoxy. He was then appointed Chaplain to Guy's Hospital and at the same time held a professorship in Cambridge. The erroneous doctrines attributed to him were that he taught universalism and denied eternal punishment. A study of his works does seem to indicate that he did hold the opinions charged against him. According to his biographer, his own son, almost his last words were a comment on the passage, 1 Peter iii, 'the ark', Peter says 'saved the eight souls as a promise that ALL should be saved, so baptism saved those who were baptized, thus figuring God's salvation for all'.[3]

(a) *What is Revelation?*

On this subject Maurice's particular views are set forth in two volumes in which he attacks Dean Mansel's Bampton Lectures of 1859. The first book, entitled, *What is Revelation?*, appeared in the same year as the discourses he opposed. It comprises, first, a

---

[1] Op. cit., pp. 37, 38.
[2] *The Victory of Faith*, p. 321.
[3] *Life of F. D. Maurice*, vol. 2, p. 641.

series of seven Epiphany sermons, and then a number of 'Letters to a Theological Student'.

Maurice in opposition to the 'notional' doctrine of revelation advocated by Mansel, maintains that revelation is an immediate unveiling of God to the soul. Mansel's lectures 'were put forth at the time as the great bulwarks of orthodoxy against all assailants'.[1] But to Maurice their logical conclusion was Agnosticism.

Maurice begins his sermons with a discourse based on Luke ii. 32. He declares that in all men there is an inner feeling after God to which He responds. Revelation is the 'inward beholding' of God within. There can be no substitute for this, be it Scripture, or tradition or Church. 'No book can do it, be it ever so divine, no Church authority or tradition, can do it, be it ever so venerable.'[2] 'To substitute for this practical faith, which rests upon God Himself and His own manifestation of Himself in the Son of God and the Son of Man, a belief in a holy book, is to disobey all the warnings of that Book.'[3]

It is this view of revelation, underlying the theology of Maurice, which constitutes the grounds of his opposition to Mansel. Revelation is the unveiling of Christ within the heart.[4] Mansel has maintained that 'the only way . . . to confute Rationalism, to establish Christianity, is to affirm that God cannot be known, and that man is prohibited by his constitution from seeking such knowledge'.[5] Maurice, in reply, in a sermon on St Paul's words to the Athenians (we have seen this verse used by those who, before him, held the same view of revelation) pressed his idea of revelation as man's immediate awareness of God as reconciled. The apostle, he observes, did not begin with 'clearing the ground of all opinions and speculations'.[6] His method was, not to argue, but to announce. By giving his assent to the declaration of the heathen poet, Aratus, that man is God's offspring, Paul 'endorses the words of the poet'.[7] He confirmed to his listeners that their origin was divine and that God was in 'the strictest and fullest sense, their Father'.[8] They

---

[1] *What is Revelation?*, Preface. *Life*, p. 327.
[2] Op. cit., p. 8.
[3] Op. cit., p. 9.
[4] Cf., *Use of the Word Revelation in the New Testament* (F. D. Maurice), *Present Day Papers on Prominent Questions of Theology* (ed. by the Bishop of Argyle).
[5] *What is Revelation?*, p. 33.
[6] Op. cit., p. 37.
[7] Op. cit., p. 45.
[8] Op. cit., p. 46.

were spiritual beings created and redeemed; their feeling after God is God's revelation to them, the assurance that they would be all gathered to the Father of us all.

Man as God's offspring, redeemed in Christ, is the theme of Maurice's theology. He sees the incarnation as the manifestation of the sinless root of humanity. He expresses disapproval of the Evangelicals who 'still seem to make sin the ground of all theology, whereas it seems to me that the living and holy God is the ground of it, and sin the departure from the state of union with Him, in which He has brought us'.[1] Arising out of this conception we find Maurice proclaiming the gospel to be belief in the ever-present indwelling of God. In a letter to Miss G. Hare he writes: 'The kingdom of God is near you; the kingdom of God is within you. It is what all are longing to hear.'[2]

In his *Theological Essays* he exclaims: 'Thanks be to God for the witness which is borne in our day for the spirituality NOT of a FEW men, but of man as man.'[3] He asserts that the gift of the Spirit is not connected with a society but with the world, seeking to convince the world that has lost its true sociality. The world contains the elements of which the Church is composed, while the Church is 'a human society in its normal state: the world is that same society irregular and abnormal'.[4]

Maurice takes baptism to be a witness to the fact that all men are united by and united in Christ. To the Rev. Isaac Taylor he writes 'do not let us surrender the one great witness which we possess, that a nation consists of redeemed men, sons of God, that mankind stands not in Adam but in Christ; Give up the Prayer Book to an Evangelical or semi-Evangelical commission, and this witness will be eliminated by a thousand little alterations'.[5] Recalling his experiences among the labourers of his first curacy at Bubbenhall and the sick at Guy's Hospital, he says, 'It seems to me that except I could address all kinds of people as members and children of God, I could not address them at all.'[6]

(b) *Maurice and Mansel*

It is in his 'Letters to a Theological Student' that Maurice makes his attack upon Mansel. The thesis developed by Mansel is summarized in a quotation from Sir William Hamilton, made by the

[1] *Life*, vol. 1, p. 450.   [2] Op. cit.. p. 528.
[3] *Theological Essays*, p. 3.   [4] Op. cit., p. 396.
[5] *Life*, vol. 2, p. 258.   [6] *Life*, vol. 1, p. 236.

Bampton lecturer himself: 'the last and higdest consecration of all true religion must be an altar, 'Αγνώστῳ Θεῷ, to the unknown and unknowable God.'[1] If this view were true, as a *Times*' reviewer of the *Limits of Religious Thought* pointed out, then all literature having a mystical tendency must be banished. No longer must Thomas à Kempis be read, and not for the reason that he was a 'Romanist', but because he assumes 'that there is a divine Teacher of Man's Spirit; that it is possible for man's spirit to have converse with that Teacher'.[2] With à Kempis must go Augustine's Confessions, the works of the Jansenists, the Puritans, Bishop Leighton's Commentary and a host of others. Besides, Whitfield and Wesley must be banished from the library of Christians and the Prayer Book will have to be drastically revised. 'All that is expressed in books of divinity by the union of the soul with Christ by living intercourse with Him, is impossible in the very nature of things, if Mr Mansel's mode of confuting infidels is the right one.'[3]

Maurice doubts Mansel's right to claim for his 'notional' doctrine of revelation the authority of Butler. At any rate, Maurice considers Butler useful as a study, or, perhaps, ammunition against the infidel, but he has no value in producing the beginnings of religion in the soul.

In the 'Letters to a Theological Student,' Maurice takes up the Bampton lectures one by one, and point by point. A formidable list of names has come under Mansel's condemnation in the notes to the lectures, as either Rationalists or Dogmatists: included are Schleiermacher, Anselm, Jowett, Priestly, Kant, Coleridge. Maurice retorts that the Bampton lectures themselves cannot be exempt from either charge. Indeed they are at the same time both rationalistic and dogmatic. In fact to be a man one must be both. There is, of course, a false rationalism and a false dogmatism, but to be both in the best sense is desirable and necessary. And we are both in the best sense when the Spirit has awakened us to the divine life within. This does not mean that the gospel must be presented in ponderous propositions and abstruse arguments. The Evangelist, who knows none of the clap-trap of philosophy, can speak and be understood. To put, therefore, faith outside the reason, as Mansel does, is false and fatal.

---

[1] *Limits of Human Thought*, p. 158.
[2] *What is Revelation?*, p. 134.
[3] Op cit., pp. 134, 135.

(c) The Theology of the Conscience

Maurice deals with Mansel's strictures on Schleiermacher. Maurice regards Schleiermacher as honestly reacting from the formal authority of the creeds. He does not, however, he is anxious to insist, accept the 'so-called Theology of the Consciousness'.[1] But his own might be aptly called the 'Theology of the Conscience'. He conceives of the 'conscience' as the light of God within; the divine witness to our natural kinship to God.

Mansel makes much of the Kantian distinction between noumenon and phenomenon. Maurice replies that the distinction is general to all philosophy from the earliest days. He repudiates the attempt to limit knowledge to the phenomenal, to the seen and the felt. Vital religion is not a discovery of God through experience, but a discovery of God in experience. For the fact is, he stresses again, we speculate about that which is distant from us. But the ground assumption of true education is, he claims, 'we are actually united to the Father of All, in His Son.'[2] He argues that 'the relation of the father and mother precedes all consciousness of it; the father and mother have a life of their own besides their relation to us. Their feelings to us are discovered first; then we seek to be acquainted with themselves, to know their minds, character, purposes. That relation to the Heavenly Father which is the ground of our relation to them, is unfolded to us in like manner, amidst the consciousness of disobedience, distrust, wilfulness, forgiveness.'[3]

Arguments for the 'faith' learnt off as if they were of unquestioned authority can lead to fatal results. Away from the class-room and the study they are assailable. In the world they possess no sanctity. Brought to collapse under the criticism of the sceptic, there is nothing left, and the result is a gnawing atheism. But had the lessons been otherwise learned, learned, that is, according to what Maurice understands to be the truth; had men been led to see God in the doubts and struggles of the individual heart, then there would have been no loss of faith when the enemy came in like a flood. Such a faith as this rests, not on 'arguments about the origin of documents', but arises out of life's experiences. Dogma there must needs be. But if there is a living God, 'surely to speak of Him is better than to speak of my notions about Him; or even my convictions which will be feeble or vital in proportion as they

[1] *Theological Essays*, p. 128.　　[2] *What is Revelation?*, p. 352.
[3] Op. cit., p. 210.

are or are not divorced from that which calls them forth.'[1] True
preaching, he thinks, begins with the Spirit, whereas the creeds
begin with the Father.

(d) 'Realized Eschatology'

For Maurice the Incarnation reveals the 'sinless root of humanity'. It is the assurance of 'Regeneration as the restoration of human
beings to their true filial position in Christ, of mankind to its
unity in Him'.[2] This regeneration has to do with 'society': 'Phrases
have been used by all parties', he writes, 'which seem to imply,
that it is simply an operation of the individual.'[3] Christ is the
'regenerator' of society, and revelation is the awakening of society
to that fact. In consequence of this teaching, Maurice anticipates
the more recent doctrine of 'realized eschatology'. With humanity
restored in Christ, a tribunal of judgement can no longer be placed
in a distant future: 'it is one before which we in our inmost being,
are standing now.'[4] It was for this reason that Maurice was
charged with denying the doctrine of eternal punishment. Eternal
life is likewise not something delayed to a future time but is
discovered in the present.

(e) Where the Bible comes in

In the context of a doctrine of revelation as taught by Maurice
the question naturally arises, What place has the Bible in all of this?
In Letter xiv in the *Sequel to What is Revelation*, Maurice makes
answer. The Bible apparently is a witness for him to this conception
of revelation. Throughout its unfolding story, God was unveiling
Himself, and every crisis of Israel's history is 'a day of the Lord'.
In every event God was revealed, rebuking those who forgot Him,
and assuring those who followed Him. The Bible is not to be
equated with the revelation. Mansel had argued that the Bible
must be taken as a whole or not at all. This Maurice takes as an
indication 'that the book, merely, as such was taking the place in
his mind of the Revelation whereof the book speaks'.[5]

He accepts the Bible, like Coleridge, because, as he puts it, 'I
have heard Christ for myself, speaking to me out of this book, and
speaking to me in my heart.'[6] He draws the now familiar distinc-

---

[1] *Sequel to What is Revelation*, p. 3.　　[2] *Theological Essays*, p. 226.
[3] Op. cit., p. 232.　　[4] Op. cit., p. 299.
[5] *Sequel to What is Revelation*, p. 280.　　[6] *Theological Essays*, p. 340.

tion between the words of the Scripture and the Word of God in the Scripture. 'More and more' observes his son, 'he had come to look upon all expressions implying that the letter of the Bible is the word of God as denials of the living "Word of God" of Whom the Bible speaks.'[1]

In a letter to Charles Kingsley on the subject he writes: 'Why was it you received the Old Testament? Not because you heard stories about inspiration or cared a farthing for them, but because the Book spoke to you of a deliverer of the people, which no Greek myths spoke.'[2] He protested against a declaration by a group of clergy who maintained that the Bible not only contained, but that it IS the word of God. 'The Word of Truth, I believe, as St John taught and as George Fox taught, to be very much ABOVE Scripture, however, he may speak by and in the Scripture.'[3]

In F. D. Maurice the understanding of revelation which we have traced throughout this chapter may be said to have reached a climax, although, as indicated, the whole view has been revived again in a new context, by the neo-liberal school of Barth and Brunner. Maurice, however, emphatically does not belong to the modern period, although much of what he has to say is characteristically so. It was for him to insist more 'dogmatically' than those who preceded him, that religion is a matter of life and revelation has its 'locale' in the inner spirit. Maurice, above all, emphasizes the free Spirit of man, and he thus deprecates all unproductive disputes and subtle causistries. In his defence of his case, however, Maurice makes sweeping generalizations and pointless exaggerations, and, as a result, he does not carry conviction.

'Maurice', observes Professor A. K. Rogers, 'is not himself a controversialist, but the outcome of his case is perhaps even more dangerous in its ultimate tendency. It leads him, that is, to deprecate any disposition to put the issue sharply, or to allow the mind to range beyond what makes for religious edification. It is this dislike of facing issues, rather than any unavoidable obscurity in his positive beliefs, that is responsible for Maurice's pervading cloudiness. Thus his own views were strongly in the direction of the new and freer conception of the Scriptures. But instead of coming to the aid of Colenzo he takes the side of his enemies, not because Colenzo's criticisms are mistaken, but because the moral lessons of the Bible are so greatly more important than questions

[1] *Life*, vol. 2, p. 452.   [2] Op. cit., p. 267.   [3] *Life*, vol. 2, pp. 499, 500.

of literary accuracy, that doubts about the letter ought to be kept
as much as possible in the background.'[1]

There is, of course, much in the statement of revelation we have
just traced which is of practical moment and relevance. It was right
to direct attention to the living Personality of Christ, and it was
vital to stress the fact that the Christian Faith is more than mere
assent to doctrines however authoritatively conveyed; and more
than belief in writings however divinely revealed they may be
conceived to be.

But, although our primary concern in this study is with the
tracing out of developments, rather than with the criticism of
theories, there is, nevertheless, one point above several others
which could claim attention, which calls for special reference. In
their understanding of revelation as an inward unveiling of the
indwelling Christ, the 'Coleridgeans' (if we may coin a word to
cover all those doctrines we have had in review) failed to make
clear what, on their view, is the position of the Scripture. Dodwell
scorns, what he called, a 'Paper-Revelation', Law condemns pre-
occupation with the 'letter of the Scripture', and all of them
repudiated a 'book-religion'. Yet they all appear to be left with a
Bible on their hands with which they are not too sure what to do.
To get rid of it seemed inadmissible, to hold on tightly to it seemed
impossible. As far as the 'Coleridgeans' are concerned there was no
satisfactory reply to the question, Where does the Bible come in?
and especially none to the related question, What is the nature of
its authority?

Having identified 'verbal inspiration' with a dictation or
mechanical process, the idea of a verbally inspired book is rejected.
It is not clear, however, whether the Bible is to be regarded as an
inspirational book or as an inspired Scripture. If it is the former
then the problem of the nature of its authority (if authority it has),
remains. If, on the other hand, it is somehow regarded as an
inspired Scripture then the problem of the relation of inspiration to
the words of Scripture has to be faced. God has chosen human
words to be, what Brunner calls, the 'locale of revelation'. He has
not chosen music or painting. And if human words are the selected
vehicle then it is required to be shewn how the assertion that God
was not interested in the 'words' of Scripture is to be understood.
It is trite to observe, as has been done, that Luke's words are

[1] *English and American Philosophy since 1800*, p. 119.

specifically, 'Lucan', and Matthew's are 'Matthean'; no one doubts that this is so. But Luke and Matthew and the rest had what Rudyard Kipling calls, in another context, 'the magic of the necessary word.' How they 'hit upon' the 'necessary word' to indicate and to illustrate that which is indeed almost beyond words is not told to us. These issues are not raised here to press any particular point of view, but because they are questions forced upon any thoughtful reader confronted with the doctrine of revelation as the immediate unfolding of the indwelling Christ.

Maurice, it may be observed, condemned Mansel for quoting a passage of Scripture at the opening of each of his Bampton lectures because these ornamental prefixes had no immediate and necessary connection with what followed. Maurice himself in his own sermons is at pains to point out the importance of every phrase in any true exposition of the Scripture. He uses his text, as historically it was meant to be used, as that which gives force and authority to his words. But it is not evident what force and authority the Scriptures he quotes are intended to give. The 'Coleridgeans' refer to certain passages, which, they hold, sustain their view of revelation. But suppose the one to be convinced and converted to their doctrine answers, 'Such passages have not "found me" ', — What then? Is it not obvious that something more than this subjective criterion is needed? For the rightness of this doctrine of revelation is made to depend upon the Scripture, upon the rightness of which, in its turn, we cannot depend.

One is aware of a zigzag of thought throughout the whole of the writings with which we have dealt. On the one hand, there is an appeal to Scripture as if it were considered sufficient. To those who are to be assured of the correctness of the position of the 'Coleridgeans' it is quoted as the word to silence all doubts and settle all controversies. It is enough that, 'It is written.' It was certainly enough for Christ, Who opposed His foes, whether Satanic or Sadducean, with the identical formula. But on the other hand, for all that, the Scripture which is quoted in this sufficiently authoritative way, is not to be regarded as the word of God. From whence, then, does its authority spring? The answer which seems to be in the thought of these writers is, that it gains its authority when it *becomes* the word of God within experience. But apart from the fact that the 'Coleridgeans' appear to deny their own thesis in the way they use the Bible, there is a difficulty which they failed to meet. Since, *ex hypothesi*, there is a sharp divorce between revelation, which is a coming to a knowledge of the Christ within, and Scripture as a record, a 'witness', perhaps, to this view of revelation, it would then appear that the divine revelation can well take place apart from the Scripture. This is indeed allowed as a possibility. But let the possibility be admitted, and it will not be long before the actuality be claimed. This means that we are thrown back (in theory at least) into all the vagaries of enthusiasm, in which each can assert the validity of his own private revelation.

The vehement rejection by the 'Coleridgeans' of the whole idea of a 'propositional' revelation is only possible on the basis of the assumption that revelation is illumination, never communication. Its concern is with 'light' rather than with 'truth'. But if there is a relation between the two: if, that is, the written word does not merely indicate the possibility of revelation, but in some way brings revelation to us, then there is a sense in which Scripture is revelation because therein God speaks in, by and with the written word thus bringing us into relation to His initial revealing acts. If the Scripture does not merely indicate where 'light' is to be found but does so 'in truth' then it is not easy to escape the fact that, in so far as revelation comes through 'the word as truth', it cannot be without 'propositional' form. 'We speak disparagingly about mere assent to propositions. But do we mean mere assent, or assent to mere propositions? Mere assent is possible and ignoble. Assent to a mere proposition is a monstrosity which cannot occur. For if assent is real, the proposition has done its work, and it is the ontological reality itself, whose nature the proposition has described to us, that we acknowledge.'[1] Let us be agreed that the Bible holds what Dr Temple calls an 'interim position'[2]; yet the fact remains that there is still a real relation between the words and the Word. It is this 'real relation' the 'Coleridgeans' did not, and, we think, on their premises could not, make clear.[3]

[1] Alan Fairweather, *The Word as Truth: A Critical Examination of the Christian Doctrine of Revelation in the Writings of Thomas Aquinas and Karl Barth*, p. 14.

[2] See *Nature, Man and God*, pp. 116–18.

[3] On several occasions throughout the previous exposition it has been suggested that much of what is being said by Barth and Brunner (with, of course, important qualifications) was already said by the 'Coleridgeans'. For this reason it has been thought to be useful in this footnote to indicate the main features taking Brunner as an example.

Brunner, like Coleridge, begins by insisting upon the identity of revelation with Christ the Word as subjectively apprehended. (Cf., *The Christian Doctrine of God*, p. 63.) He goes on to insist upon a vital point, the complete separation of Christ as the Word of God from the Bible as human testimony, or 'witness' (*Hinweis*) to that revelation. The divine Word of God, incarnated and unveiled (yet still veiled) in the human heart, which is properly revelation, belongs to the sphere of 'Thou-Truth' (*Du Warheit*), in contrast with the witness to that revelation, the Scripture, which is 'It-Truth' (*es Warheit*). For Brunner, too, the tragedy of all tragedies is to identify the two. This is the folly of the 'orthodox', the greatest and gravest of its manifold sins originating from the absurd doctrine of verbal inspiration. Brunner excells himself in his condemnation of this 'fundamentalist' error. As a witness to revelation the Scripture is mainly doctrines and revelation is not concerned with doctrine, for revelation itself is God's in-breaking in the personal divine Word of God, Jesus Christ. This is the revelation to which the Bible 'points'. But not every part of the Scripture bears witness with equal clarity: 'we cannot maintain that everything that is Biblical — not even everything in the New Testament — is in the same way, or to the same extent, the "bearer" of the word of God' (*Revelation and Reason*, p. 129). Some passages, indeed, but 'stammer' out His name (*The Philosophy of Religion*, p. 153). That which is on the 'rim' of the New Testament has little 'witness' value. While there are passages, like 2 Pet. ii. 4, which fall outside the 'rim'. For all that the Scriptures have an 'instrumental authority', although when it comes to matters of 'world-knowledge' what they have to say, has 'no doctrinal authority,' cf., *The Christian Doctrine of God*, p. 57.

Brunner has made the idea of 'verbal inspiration' the focus of his ridicule, but when he comes to find some authority for the Scripture, he cannot do so apart from the words. The human word can bear testimony to the divine Word because of the similarity between the two (cf., *The Christian Doctrine of God*, p. 184). God's revelation, in the last, must come through human language. 'Hence the Word of God is there in the form of revealed human words, not behind them . . . , but in direct identity, in a complete correspondence of man's word and God's word' (*The Christian Doctrine of God*, p. 26). This seems very much a falling back into a doctrine he has repudiated. He agrees that the idea of 'verbal inspiration' is the 'classical' doctrine, but it is an error withal, yet it is an error 'most comprehensible'. It would indeed be better to 'hold fast to it, than on account of its incorrect form, cast off its precious content, which is the Christian Church's principle of Scripture' (quoted by P. K. Jewett, *Emil Brunner's Concept of Revelation*, p. 159). Brunner's difficulty is that he desires to draw a sharp distinction between the Word and the words and yet he cannot maintain it. He observes, 'the written record is part of this revelation, it is not the whole' (*Revelation and Reason*, p. 12) and yet he says, 'Holy Scripture therefore does not only speak of revelation; it is itself revelation' (op. cit., p. 21). This is no isolated reference; 'In theory' he remarks again, 'there is no particular need to bring the Word of God and the written word into a specially close connection; quite the contrary' (op. cit., p. 125). Yet for all that, 'It is only through the written word that the testimony of Christ of the first witnesses has been maintained in its original and distinctive form' (p. 126). This means that 'the written Scripture, is the medium in which the word of God comes to us, since it alone contains the Apostolic word of revelation' (ibid.). These sort of statements could be multiplied, and they are not easy to harmonize. The same pendulum swing of ideas which we have seen in the 'Coleridgeans' is to be observed. Appeal is made to the Scripture because it contains, in its words, the revelation of God, on the other hand, no decisive appeal can be made to it just because the revelation of God in the Word is not 'connected' with the words of Scripture. In his little book '*Our Faith*' which appeared in 1936 Brunner likens the Voice of God in the Bible, 'His Master's Voice', to a voice heard on a gramophone record. It is the real voice of the singer which is heard, but there are noises and scratchings besides which are not the master's voice (cf., op. cit., p. 10). That is good as far as it goes. But there are two questions which arise. How can we be sure that the voice we hear is indeed the master's voice? When it appeals to me as such, and when it 'finds me'. Such answers are not too obvious. Again, How can we be sure that the voice heard was indeed the voice recorded? And especially how can we be sure if we accept that

Important, then, is, we believe, the question we have raised concerning the relation of revelation and record. The revelation is, of course, prior to the record. First the life then the literature which embodies and secures the original revelation for subsequent generations. If there were no adequate record then would each new age need again the revelation. Bethlehem and Calvary would need to be repeated to bring God to men. But the records become for the ages subsequent to the original revelation the vehicle of objective truth about Him of Whom was the disclosure. From this it follows, as Dr W. R. Matthews says, 'we are not free to construe our conception of God in abstraction from history. . . . Our starting point is a creative experience which comes to us mediated through human testimony.'[1] The record is necessary if the revelation is to be preserved. The revelation of God in Christ would not have been guaranteed to those who followed unless He completed it in an adequate medium of transmission. It would have been tragically still-born if it were not permanently safeguarded. The securing of this result will be assured 'either by a continuous Apostolate supernaturally secured in the *Charisma veritatio*, as Rome claims, or by a book which should be a real successor of the Apostles, with a real authority on the vital matters of truth and faith. But we discard the supernatural pope for the supernatural book'.[2] But not all that was revealed has been recorded. The apostle John refers to many things that Jesus did which have not been written down. In this sense, it must be allowed that there is a distinction between the revelation and the record, but, at the same time, all that is recorded has been revealed, and what is not recorded is as a matter of fact unknown to us. This fact means that no cleavage can be made between history and interpretation. It is impossible on

God was not active in the recording? The problem becomes more complicated when it is stated that the Bible is a 'witness' to a revelation, and more difficult still when so much is allowed as apparently incapable of ever 'becoming' the word of God; as ever being a 'bearer' of God. In this case the demand for some criterion to separate the voices on the record from the voice of the master becomes urgent. It is the impossibility of finding any such standard, other than one's own subjective appreciation of the 'one voice' that has made men like the ex Bishop of London, Dr Wand, write off the whole attempt to make such distinctions as folly. In his book on *The Authority of the Scriptures*, he writes, 'the title, Word of God, if it is to be used at all, as we hold it must, applies to the whole Bible and not to mere parts of it, however supreme their value may be.' It is impossible, he argues, to distinguish some short sentence out of the whole as having a divine character above the rest. 'The Word of God', he concludes, 'is heard both in the events themselves and in the record of them,' op. cit., p. 83.

[1] *God in Christian Thought and Experience*, p. 44.
[2] P. T. Forsyth, *The Person and Place of Jesus Christ*, p. 171.

certain philosophical presumptions to alter the facts and retain the interpretation. They belong together. So in the New Testament, the facts are not to be separated from the interpretation of those facts within the New Testament itself. 'In the actual history (it is said) God was at work revealing; but in the record, or commentary, it was man construing. In the transfer to writing much of the reality has vanished; and the living plant is even dried between the leaves of the book. So it is said. And thus our very exaltation of the personal revelation in Christ has led to a fatal depreciation and neglect of the Bible, as being a mere record, which we may use for our satisfaction but need not for our life.'[1] But, as we see it, the revelation in Christ is only final and full when it is seen not in this act or that, but in every deed and word and the application and interpretation of every deed and word: that is, in the whole Christ of the whole New Testament. Thus we learn from the New Testament of the Revelation incarnate, and we see in the New Testament Revelation interpreted, and we have in the New Testament Revelation preserved. The Bible in a real sense presents us with God-given facts and God-inspired valuations. Here we have the seamless coat of fact and value woven into a pattern so close that it is not possible to sever them. The Bible contains 'the record, the interpretation, and the literary reflection of His grace in history'.[2] The real message of the Christian gospel is not a bare fact but a revealed fact and an inspired interpretation. It is the whole record of facts and interpretations which constitute the story of redemption and which become saving history.[3]

This means that the authority of the Bible lies within its own sphere, namely, that of a redemptive relation with God. It is, at the same time, the avenue, the dynamic and the touch-stone of genuine Christian experience. This does not mean that the Bible is placed, obstructively, between the soul and God, and thus becomes a sort of 'paper pope'. The authority of the Bible, we have asserted, relates to the redemptive experience, and like all truth, to be of value it must be subjectively realized. Thus the correlative of

[1] P. T. Forsyth, *The Person and Place of Jesus Christ*, pp. 148, 149.
[2] A. B. Bruce, *The Chief End of Revelation*, p. 280.
[3] The point we make here is simply that God's final self-disclosure is not to be regarded as a single isolated 'event', as such, and on its own. The full and final revelation of God, for example, is not the 'event' of the Incarnation *per se*, but the incarnated life in its totality. But the incarnated life is the life of Christ as lived, and known to us by His words spoken and His deeds done as these were from the first interpreted and applied.

revelation is faith: of the Bible is the Holy Spirit. It is as Calvin says 'the secret testimony of the Holy Spirit', which seals the authority of Scripture to the believing heart. There must be the '*testimonium Spiritus Sancti internum*'. 'Let it therefore be held as fixed that those who are inwardly taught of the Holy Spirit acquiesce implicitly in Scripture; that Scripture, carrying its own evidence along with it, deigns not to submit to proofs and arguments, but owes the full conviction with which we ought to receive it to the testimony of the Spirit.'[1] This is a different thing from cold assent to external writings. The telescope before the eye of the astronomer is not a means of obstruction: it is a means of observation. By it the glories of the otherwise unknown sky are revealed. By it he learns what is there, and what without it he could never see. So is it with the written word, when once focused by the eye of faith: by it God is seen.

[1] *Institutes of the Christian Religion*, vol. 1, p. 72.

CHAPTER VIII

THE TEACHING OF THE EVANGELICALS

At this point it would seem that an enquiry is demanded into the understanding of revelation held by those who were described as the 'Evangelicals'. It will have been clear from the earlier pages that those who have been referred to as the 'orthodox', as well as their opponents who emphasized the subjective doctrine of revelation, both repudiated the title. The Evangelicals, therefore, stood apart from each of these two sections. They maintained, in opposition to both, their own doctrine of a divine disclosure which may be summarized under the heading:

REVELATION IN THE WORD THROUGH THE SPIRIT

It is, of course, only in what follows that this summary statement can be clarified and its adequacy justified. But to seek into the doctrine of revelation taught by the Evangelicals, two tasks are involved. On the one hand, it is necessary to find its origin since no special view comes into being, so to speak, overnight. The Evangelicals certainly did not think of their teaching as something new. They were emphatic that they were in line with the past. It will consequently be part of our present investigation to trace out the lineage which they claim. On the other hand, since the Evangelicals, though not without real scholars, were not specially interested in creating theological systems, we shall have to find from among them a teacher who shall best state their position. The first, then, of the two purposes of the present section is to seek:

(i) *The Background of their View*

The Evangelical party of the eighteenth century was the spiritual heir of the Puritans in their understanding of Revelation and the Scripture.[1] The concern of both was to declare the Biblical message

---

[1] 'Evangelical Churchmen trace their pedigree to the Puritans; and the Reformers . . . ,' G. R. Balleine, *A History of the Evangelical Party in the Church of England*, p. 1.

rather than to justify the ways of God to man. For this reason there
is not, particularly among the former, much discussion concerning
the necessity and nature of revelation. For both, the best proof of
the existence of a special disclosure of God was the possession of
the Scriptures. There was no great need to justify that which was
so evidently and creatively existing. God had communicated His
revelation which was confirmed by the presence and confined
within the covers of the Bible, the Written Word of God.

It was this conviction which was the assurance and strength of
the Puritans. To them is to be attributed that habit of Bible reading
which became so characteristic of British Protestantism. By their
example and teaching 'England became the people of a book, and
that book was the Bible'.[1] The Puritans found in the Bible the
source of their inspiration, and by laying stress upon the right of
every man to its use they gave vitality to 'a wide spread "Bible
religion" as distinct from a "Church religion" '.[2]

(a) The View-point of the Puritans

The Puritan literature is not, however, without reasoned statements concerning the very basis of their faith. There is, for
example, the brilliant treatise by the learned John Owen, entitled,
The Divine Original of the Scripture. The argument which he here
sets out is extended in his *Reason of Faith*. A similar line of
thought is developed in the appendix of Thomas Halyburton's
posthumous work, *Natural Religion Insufficient and Revealed
Religion Necessary*.[3] Chalmer's in his preface to his *Institutes of
Theology* pays a high compliment to Owen's work. He declares
that the Puritan theologian has given to those who desire a
'satisfactory conviction of the claims of the Bible', 'the most solid
and indubitable proof.' Great as were the contributions of Leslie,
Lyttleton, Dodderidge, Bates, Baxter, that of Owen was even
greater, since, continues Chalmers, 'we hold Dr Owen to have
rendered a more essential service to the cause of divine revelation,
when, by his clear and irresistible demonstrations, he has proved
that the Written Word itself possesses a self-evidencing light and
power for manifesting its own divine original, superior to the
testimony of eyewitnesses, or the evidences of miracles, or those

[1] J. R. Green, *A Short History of the English People* (1891), p. 460.
[2] D. C. Somervell, *A Short History of our Religion*, p. 239.
[3] Halyburton was made Professor of Divinity in St Andrews in 1710, but died
in 1712, at the age of thirty-eight.

supernatural gifts with which the first teachers of Christianity were endowed for accrediting their divine mission.'

In his treatise Dr Owen sets out to prove that 'the whole authority of the Scriptures in itself depends solely on its divine original'.[1] The argument runs as follows: God, it is asserted, spoke IN the prophets, psalmists and preachers whose messages we have. What they had to say was not the result of their own insight and discovery. 'God was with them, and by the Holy Ghost so spake in them — as to their receiving of the Word from him, and their declaring of it unto others by speaking or writing — as they were not themselves enabled by any habitual light, knowledge, or conviction of truth, to declare his mind and will, but only acted as they were immediately moved by him.'[2] Accordingly the divine inspiration had reference, not simply to the men, but also to their words.

The inspired men were not left to record their message in any words they pleased. 'They invented not their words themselves, suited to the things that they learned, but only expressed the words they received.'[3] As regards matter and form they were under the influence of the Spirit, thus the whole product is the Word of God. This being the 'divine original' of the Scripture, its authority is assured. All God's revelations are self-evidencing. Nature, for example, 'declares itself to be from God by its own light and authority.'[4] In like manner do the 'innate light of nature, and principles of conscience of men'.[5] This fact is, however, more true and more obvious in the case of the Written Word which God has magnified above all else.[6] From the revelation of the Bible the authority of God speaks out clearly and convincingly. As authority can only operate is the sphere of personal relations, the authority of the Scripture, which is none other than the authority of God, means that it is to be acknowledged and obeyed. Those who profess to accept the authority of the Bible are compelled by that very profession to receive it as the Word of God. The Scripture declares itself to be Θεόπνευστος, and it is therefore to be attended to in the same manner as any person who was divinely inspired.

Our Lord reminded the rich man of the parable that his surviving brethren had the written word as the only and adequate ground of assurance. He indicates 'that those who will not own or

[1] *Works of Owen* (edited by W. H. Goold, 1853), vol. 16, p. 297.
[2] Op. cit., p. 298.
[3] Op. cit., 16, p. 305.
[4] Op. cit., p. 311.   [5] Op. cit., p. 310.   [6] Op. cit., p. 311.

o

submit to the authority of God in the Word, would not be moved
by the most signal miracles imaginable'.[1] The apostle heard the
voice of God on the mount, yet that same apostle 'tells us that,
comparatively, we have greater security from and by the written
Word than they had *in* and *by* that miraculous voice'.[2] Thus is the
word of prophecy made more sure.

Owen proceeds to specify the 'innate arguments in the Scripture
of its divine original and authority'. They are its 'light' and its
'power'. Light manifests itself. It needs neither argument for its
presence nor witnesses to its existence. It is declared of the written
word, as it is of God Himself, that it is the light. Scripture is the
story of man's salvation. It is power — '*vis, virtus, Dei*'. The saving
word is not only δύναμις θεοῦ in itself; it is also δυνάμενος, 'able
and powerful' in respect of us. The Scripture therefore shares that
property which belongs to God.

Owen adds what he calls, 'the consequential considerations, for
the confirmation of the divine authority of the Scriptures'.[3] These
are the suitableness of its doctrines for the needs of all men and the
harmony existing between its several parts.

The final assurance, however, that the Scripture is the word of
God, is the testimony of the Spirit. The Spirit never 'speaks to us
of the Word, but *by* the Word'.[4] 'That the Scripture be received as
the word of God, there is required a twofold efficacy of the Spirit.'[5]
On the one hand he acts upon the individual's mind. He communicates spiritual light, gives wisdom, and creates a spiritual
sense and taste. On the other hand the testimony of the Spirit has
reference to the Word itself. Here Owen has in mind the effectiveness of the word in other hearts because of the effectiveness experienced by the individual. In reference to the word, the testimony of the Spirit is 'a public testimony, which, as it satisfies our
souls in particular, so it is, and may be, pleaded in reference unto
the satisfaction of all others to whom the Word of God shall
come'.[6]

This double testimony of the Spirit is, however, only formally
distinguishable. In all grounds of assent, Owen argues, there
unite in one the authority of testimony and the self-evidence of
truth. So is it in reference to the Scriptures. 'In the same Word,

---

[1] Op. cit., p. 317.   [2] Op. cit., p. 317.
[3] Op. cit., vol. 16, p. 337.   [4] Op. cit., p. 326.
[5] Op. cit., p. 325.   [6] Op. cit., p. 328.

we have both the authority of the testimony of the Spirit and the self evidence of the truth spoken by him; yea, so that both these are materially one and the same, though distinguished in their formal conceptions.'[1] For Owen, the testimony of the Spirit is no 'private whisper, word or voice, given to individual persons',[2] but, 'the public testimony of the Holy Ghost, by and in the Word, and its own divine light, efficacy and power.'[3]

A less usual attitude to the Scriptures is taken by John Goodwin, who, although generally reckoned among the Puritans, yet, in this respect, as in others, stands outside the main stream.[4] Daniel Neal refers to John Goodwin as 'a learned divine and a smart disputant, but of a peculiar mould'.[5]

In his *Divine Authority of the Scripture Asserted* Goodwin takes up a point made in his earlier *Hagiomastrix, or Scourge of the Saints*, which had laid him open to the charge of denying the Scriptures to be the Word of God.[6] Goodwin had stated that the word of God was something different from the written Scripture. It is the purpose of his *Divine Authority of the Scripture Asserted* to amplify and justify his position. He therefore maintains that the divine word is not to be identified with the written record. It certainly cannot be equated with any one translation, since there is no translation without defects. Translations are, after all, as Jerome long ago remarked 'muddy streams or rivulets, in comparison with the Originalls'.[7] Neither can the word of God be identified with the original manuscripts themselves. These are unknown, and even among the oldest and best there are variations.

The real word of God, on the other hand, is incorrupt and incorruptible, consequently, observes Goodwin, 'the true and proper foundation of the Christian Religion, is not inke and paper, not any book, or books, not any writing, or writings whatsoever, whether Translations, or Originalls; but that substance of matter, those gracious counsells of God concerning the salvation of the World by Jesus Christ, which indeed are represented and declared, both in Translations, and Originalls, but are effentially and really distinct

---

[1] *Works of Owen*, vol. 16, p. 328.   [2] Op. cit., ibid.
[3] Op. cit., ibid.
[4] Goodwin's strong Arminianism to which Wesley acknowledges his debt puts him also outside the general Puritan tradition. Cf., J. R. Mersden, *The Early Puritans*, p. 348 f.
[5] *History of the Puritans*, vol. 3, p. 362.
[6] *Hagiomastrix* (1647), sect., 28.
[7] *Divine Authority of the Scripture Asserted* (1648), p. 7.

from both, and no waies, from their natures and beings, depending on either of them.'[1]

According to Goodwin, then, here is the authentic Word, the true Scripture, which like water in a cup is to be distinguished from the vessel which contains it. This is the Scripture, the divine authority of which can be established by two modes of arguments, the 'intrinsical' and the 'extrinsecall'. The former of these is of two types, the one 'which respects the planning, phrase, language, and manner of indighting or framing the Scripture'. The other 'which respects the matter or substance of them'.[2] The 'extrinsecall' is likewise of two sorts; '1. such remarkable passages or acts of Divine Providence, whereby God plainly owns the Scriptures as his, and from himself. 2. Into such doings, or sayings of men, which were so far confederate with those Providences of God, as to joyn in testimonies with them on the behalf of the Scriptures.'[3]

This sharp divorce between the Word of God and the written Scripture was vigorously and vehemently opposed. It ran counter to the prevailing view. The doctrine generally accepted was that, although the method of inspiration might not be explicitly stated, it nevertheless resulted in language which was rightly to be designated the 'word of God'.

In such a manner did men like Matthew Henry, the commentator son of Philip Henry, understand the Scripture to be the revelation of God. He states in his Ordination Confession, 'I believe: "that this book of Scripture was given by the inspiration of God, holy men speaking and writing as they were moved by the Holy Ghost," "And that this foundation of all revealed religion, is a perfect, sufficient rule of direction for all the children of men." '[4]

In his *Commentary on the Scriptures* the same understanding of the written record is maintained. He observes in reference to 2 Tim. 3. 15–16 that, 'Those who would acquaint themselves with the things of God, and be assured of them, must know the Holy Scriptures, for these are the summary of divine revelation.'[5] He

---

[1] *The Divine Authority of the Scripture Asserted*, p. 17. Cf., 'I conceive the matter of the Scriptures, I mean those glorious and Divine Truths, those holy and righteous commands, those great and precious promises, those astonishing and dreadful threatenings, conteined and expressed, as well in Translations, as in the Originalls were of greatest pregnancie and power both to discover and assert their royall Parentage, and descent from God.' Op. cit., p. 16.

[2] Op. cit., p. 31.

[3] Op. cit., ibid.

[4] May 9th, 1687, cf., J. B. Williams, *Life of Matthew Henry*.

[5] Matthew Henry's *Exposition of the Old and New Testament*, ad. loc.

goes on to say that the excellency of the Scriptures lies in their divine inspiration. The Bible is therefore 'a divine revelation, which we may depend upon as infallibly true. The same God that breathed reason into us, breathes revelation among us'.[1]

In another comment on 2 Peter 1. 19–21, he is more definite and explicit concerning the activity of the Holy Spirit in the inspiration of the Scriptures. His words on this point may be taken as representative of the general view. 'The prophets and penmen of the Scripture', he writes, 'spake and wrote what was the mind of God, and though, when under the influence and guidance of the Spirit, it may be well supposed, that they were willing to reveal and record such things, yet it is because God would have them spoken and written. . . . That the Scriptures are the word of God, is not only an article of the Christian's faith, but also a matter of science and knowledge. . . . As a man not barely believes but knows assuredly, that that very man is his peculiar friend, in whom he sees the proper, peculiar, distinguishing marks and characters of his friend; so the Christian knows that *book to be the word of God*, in and upon which he sees the proper marks and characters of a divinely inspired book. He tastes a sweetness, and feels a power, and sees a glory, in it truly divine . . . . To call off our minds from all other writings, and apply them in a peculiar manner to these as the only certain and infallible rule, necessarily requires our being fully persuaded that these are divinely inspired, and contain what is truly the mind and will of God.'[2] He goes on to refer to the Holy Spirit as the 'Supreme Agent' in inspiration. The writers were 'but his penmen'. They were His 'instruments'. 'The Holy Ghost', he declares, 'inspires and dictates to them what they were to deliver of the mind of God . . . so that the very words of Scripture are to be accounted the words of the Holy Ghost.'[3] The Bible is, therefore, to be esteemed and reverenced as the book of the Holy Ghost, its very words proceeding from God.

The same estimation of the Scripture is declared in the context of controversy, by one of the earlier Puritans, William Whitaker (1547–95), who was Regius Professor of Divinity in Cambridge for sixteen years.[4] In his *Defence of the Authority of the Scriptures* he

[1] Matthew Henry's *Exposition*, ibid.
[2] Op. cit., ad. loc.
[3] Op. cit., ibid.
[4] Whitaker was honoured by the degree of Doctor of Divinity by the University of Oxford, for his learning.

maintained against Bellarmine, the divinity and sufficiency of the
Bible as the rule of Protestant faith.

The Puritans, therefore, did not regard the Bible as a mere
record of revelation. It is itself the revelation of God in which and
through which God comes savingly to the soul.

John Arrowsmith, who at a later date than Whitaker, occupied
the Regius chair of divinity at Cambridge, writes: 'The Scripture
is of divine authority: Holy men of God (saith Peter) spake as they
were moved by the Holy Ghost. They wrote accordingly. All
Scripture, saith Paul, was given by inspiration of God . . . they
have God for their author . . . . It is a thing wherein the Son of God,
who indited the Scripture gives abundant satisfaction on the
spirit of goodly men, as to make other arguments, though not useless, yet to them of less necessity; He alone bearing witness to the
divinity of holy writ, and to the truth of his own testimony, so
putting a final issue to that controversie.'[1]

Henry Palmer, who in 1644 became master of Queen's College,
Cambridge, like Arrowsmith equates revelation with the Scripture.[2] He asks in his catechetical fashion '29 Q. From whence must
we learne to know God and serve him rightly?' He gave the reply,
'29 A. To know God, and serve him rightly, wee must be taught of
God's word.' '30 Q. Which book is God's Word?' '30 A. The
Bible or the Scriptures of the Old and New Testament is the very
word of God.'[3]

In a sermon on 1 John 4. 1, A. Burgess observes, 'That therefore
we may not split ourselves upon inevitable Rocks: God hath left us
his word as a Rule, *by which all revelations and operations* of his
Spirit are to be tryed. All the Scriptures are Θεόπνευστοι, by
divine inspiration; and therefore the breathings of God's Spirit are
to be expected in this Garden: and those commands of *attaining to
the Scripture only* and to observe *what is written*, are a plain demonstration that God hath tyed to the Scriptures onely.'[4]

John Ball was held in high esteem by the Westminster divines.
He asks the question, 'What is it to be immediately inspired?' He

---

[1] *A Chain of Principles* (1659), pp. 103, 104. Cf., 'The Scriptures in like manner
contain the minde of Jehovah . . . . Somewhat of *his nature* we may learn from his
creatures, but should have known little or nothing of *his will*, had not the
canonical *Scripture* revealed it,' op. cit., p. 86.

[2] Benjamin Brook, *Lives of the Puritans*, vol. 3, p. 76.

[3] *An Endeavour of Making the Principles of Christian Religion . . . plaine and
easie, etc.* (1644), p. 7.

[4] Sermon xxiii, *Spiritual Refining* (1652), (2nd edition, 1658), p. 132.

answers, 'To be immediately inspired is to be, as it were, breathed, and to come from the Father by the Holy Ghost without all means.' He goes on to assert that in this fashion the original Scriptures 'were inspired both for matter and form'.[1]

One of the most important, as well as one of the most interesting writers of the Puritan period was William Bridge. His three sermons on 2 Peter 1.19 are of major importance for an understanding of the prevailing doctrine of revelation and the Scriptures. The purpose of Bridge in these sermons, is to set forth the sufficiency and supremacy of the Scripture. In comparison with the voice that spoke from the excellent glory, 'the Word of God written is surer than that Voice they heard in the mount (whereof he spake in the former verse). More sure is the Written word, than the Voyce of Revelation; not *ratione veritatis*, not in regard to the truth uttered, for that Voyce was as true as any word in Scripture; but more sure, *ratione manifestationis*, more certain, more settled, and established.'[2] Like John Owen he sees the Scripture as a self-manifesting light. It is more sure, more pleasant, and satisfying than all those claims to light advanced by men. The light of the Scripture is perfect. It is therefore more to be relied upon than immediate revelations, than dreams, than visions, than direct impressions made upon the heart whether with or without the Word, than experience, than the law and light within, than 'Judicial astrology'. 'The written word of God is our appointed Food, our daily Food.'[3]

While Bridge puts the Bible above the 'law', the 'light' and the 'Spirit' within, he does not mean it to be understood that he gives no place to the testimony of the Spirit. The reverse is the truth. The need of the Spirit to enlighten both the mind and the book is insisted upon. At the same time he maintains that the Spirit never by-passes the Scripture. The Holy Spirit is 'sent to open the Scripture to you, not to take away the Scripture from you'.[4] He points out that our Lord, in the days of His flesh, referred to and deferred to the written word. He argues that as a consequence 'Christ in us, is not more privileged than Christ without us; but Christ without us, was tied by the Scriptures, therefore Christ within us much more'.[5]

---

[1] *A Short Treatise, etc.*, pp. 7, 8.
[2] William Bridge's Works (Twenty-two several books of Mr William Bridge ... collected in two volumes), 1657 Scripture Light, the Most Sure Light, Ser. 1, vol. 2, p. 4.
[3] Op. cit., p. 23 (Sermon 2).   [4] Op. cit., p. 29.   [5] Op. cit., p. 30.

Bridge will not allow the application of the term 'the word of God' to be applied to Christ exclusively, and as a pretext for refusing its application to the Scriptures. 'Some there are', he writes, 'who say, That Christ only is called, the Word, or the word of God; and that the Doctrine preached or Written, is not the Word or the Word of God, But though Christ is called the Word, John 1, yet I do not find in all the New Testament, that he is called the Word of God in the present.'[1] This designation, Bridge contends, is for Him when the kingdoms of this world become the kingdoms of our God and His Christ. Then shall He be King of Kings and Lord of Lords, 'the Word of God'.

This means then that the Scripture is to be regarded in itself as the very word of God. It is therefore necessary 'to hold fast the very letter of it'. At the same time it has to be made clear that the true Scripture is not the letter by itself, since the 'Letter with the true sense and meaning of it, is the Word'.[2] The letter and the sense belong together as do the body and the soul. Does not the sense lie 'wrapped up in the Letters and Words thereof'?[3] The words of 2 Cor. 3. 6 may be quoted against him. But Bridge replies that in this passage the contrast is not between the letter and Spirit of the Scriptures, but between the law and the gospel. The apostle calls 'the Ministration of the Law, the Letter; and the Ministration of the Gospel, the Spirit'.[4] Thus to preach from the letter of Scripture is not to preach the letter, or to be ministers of the letter.[5] For this understanding of revelation and Scripture, Bridge claims the authority of Luther.

Yet the Puritan divines, in their teaching that the Bible was, *in toto*, the word of God, differed from the non-Puritan Churchmen only in the extent of its application. The Puritans considered that all matters relating to the worship, constitution and discipline of the Church were set down in its pages.[6] Their opponents, on the other hand, were ready to admit that there was much in the

---

[1] *Scripture Light, the Most Sure Light*, Ser. 3, p. 40.
[2] Op. cit., p. 46.
[3] Op. cit., ibid.
[4] Op. cit., p. 47.
[5] It is surely in this way that the famous saying of Luther is to be interpreted. The Scriptures, he declared, are the crib that contains the Christ. But to separate the Christ from the crib is to fall a victim to, what a later period spoke of as 'enthusiasm'. Whereas to give attention to the crib (mere intellectual assent to the propositions of the Scripture) and miss the Christ is but another species of rationalism. Crib and Christ, letter and sense, word and Spirit belong together.
[6] J. R. Green, *A Short History of the English People*, p. 460.

Church's life for which the Scripture had made no provision. Tradition and convenience were therefore a sufficient justification in these cases. For the non-Puritan, the Scripture, as far as it went, was still the word of God; both its message and its words being given by the Holy Ghost. So certain is this that Archbishop Parker could deprive a vicar of his benefice for denying the verbal inspiration of the Bible.[1]

(b) The Work of the Westminster Divines

The Puritan attitude to the Scriptures found expression in the work of the Westminster Assembly. This statement finds justification, not only from the fact that Arrowsmith and Bridge, whose words have been quoted above, belonged to the small committee which prepared the material and sketched the outline of the Confession, but also from an examination of the work produced and a comparison of it with the Puritan literature.

The opening section of the Confession, 'Of the Holy Scriptures', declares them to be the 'written word of God', and 'divinely inspired'. For a 'full persuasion and assurance of the infallible truth, and divine authority thereof', there is, however, needed the inner witness of the Holy Spirit.[2] It is declared that there is no appeal from the Scripture. The Larger Catechism asks the question, 'What is the word of God?' The answer given is, 'The holy Scriptures of the Old and New Testament are the word of God, the only rule of faith and obedience.'[3]

The Westminster divines maintained that the Bible was authoritative and infallible because it was inspired. Only because it is a product of the Spirit's action can the Scripture be regarded as possessing the authority of God. Because it is born of the Spirit's inspiration it needs no certificate of approval from any man or Church.[4]

In their declarations on this subject the Westminster divines felt themselves to be expressing the attitude of the Protestant churches as a whole. More particularly, however, as Professor Benjamin Warfield writes: 'the chief source of the Westminster doctrine of the Holy Scripture is the general teaching of the Reformed

[1] Op. cit., p. 471.
[2] Confession, ch. 1, v.
[3] The Larger Catechism, Q. 3 and Answer.
[4] Cf., J. Macpherson, The Westminster Confession of Faith, with Introduction and Notes, p. 35.

theology.'[1] The Puritans did, in fact, believe that their doctrine of revelation and the Scripture, which gave birth to the Westminster Confession, was itself based upon that of the Reformers. They considered themselves to be stating essentially, although, perhaps, more formally, the teaching of Luther, Calvin and the rest.

Warfield gives an extended quotation from Heppe's profound study of the doctrine of the Scripture in the Continental Reformers in his *Die Dogmatick der evangelisch-reformirten Kirche* (1861). Heppe has shewn that they regarded the Bible as authoritative and infallible because of its divine inspiration. 'Since the authority of Scripture coincides with the authority of God, it is absolute authority.'[2] No sharp distinction was allowed between Scripture and the Word of God. The canonical Scriptures, it was held 'not only contain the word of God, but are themselves God's written word; for their penning was brought about by special and immediate agency of the Holy Spirit, who incited the authors to the writing, suggesting to them thoughts and words which should be penned, and guarding them from every error in the writing — that is, the canonical books were *inspired* by the Holy Ghost to the authors, in both form and content'.[3]

(c) The Position of the Reformers

The legitimacy of the belief of the Puritan and Westminster divines that their understanding of the subject was a true interpretation of the Reformers, is a matter of importance. That they DID consider themselves to be continuing their teaching is beyond question. The whole subject is however confused by the desire of

---

[1] *The Westminster Assembly and Its Work* (O.U.P., New York), p. 161. Cf., 'No reader of the Puritan literature of the seventeenth century will fail to observe how hard it leans upon the great Reformed divines of the Continent — freely appropriating from them lines of argument, forms of expression, and points of view. While also, no doubt, freely adapting them to their own purposes. The consequence is that the sources of several sections of the Confession of Faith can with almost equal readiness be found in Ball or Du Buc, in Cartwright or Calvin, according as we choose to look near or far for them. There is scarcely a leading divine of the first three-quarters of a century of Reformed theology, who wrote at large on the Scriptures, from whom statements may not be drawn as to make it appear to be the immediate source of the Westminster sections.' B. Warfield, op. cit., ibid. Cf., also, 'Undoubtedly the English Puritans owed their heaviest debt to the theology, political theories, and principles of ecclesiastical polity that were based upon the continental reformers in Geneva, Zurich, and the Rhineland cities.' P. W. Dawley, *John Whitgift and the Reformation* (1955), pp. 133, 134.

[2] Quoted from Heppe, B. Warfield, *Westminster Assembly and its Work*, p. 166.

[3] Op. cit., p. 164.

opposing parties to claim the Reformers as their Fathers. Contradictory statements are consequently made under the supposed authority of Luther or Calvin. Each is made to speak the language of controversial necessity. The truth of this last observation can be seen from statements made by recent writers. Referring to Luther, A. L. Lilley says: 'No Christian doctor of the front rank ever disparaged the revelational role of the Scripture more consistently than the great reformer.'[1] On the other side, F. R. Barry, putting Luther and Calvin together, asserts, 'In their zeal for the newly discovered Scriptures . . . the Reformers allowed themselves to be intoxicated with a crude and fanatical bibliolatry.'[2] He goes on to maintain that their Bible worship has led to disastrous results; 'the authority of an infallible Scripture has proved to be more sterilizing in morals than the autocracy of an infallible pope.'

Here we have two writers — and their number could be multiplied[3] — attributing to the Reformers opposing doctrines. On the one hand there are those who believe that the Fathers of the Reformation rejected all external authority in the rediscovery of the freedom of the Spirit. On the other hand, there are those who stigmatize them because they substituted a new authority — an infallible Bible for an infallible Pope. They are thus supposed to be, at the same time, the creators of a new subjectivism and a new scholasticism. They are commended by some because they were 'liberal' in their attitude to the Bible; and they are condemned by others because they were 'bibliolaters'.

Of one fact, however, we may be certain, namely, that the Reformers rediscovered the doctrine of divine grace by which, through faith, the ungodly are justified. It was the experience of this new found truth which was the grounds of Luther's rejection of the authority of the Church. But while he did turn away from the Church as the umpire in the things of the soul, it is not true

[1] A. L. Lilley, *Religion and Revelation*, p. 79.

[2] F. R. Barry, *The Relevance of Christianity*, p. 24.

[3] Cf., e.g. Dr Schaff who declares that the Reformers did NOT believe in the theory of a literal inspiration and an inerrant Bible. (See Warfield, op. cit., p. 261.) On the other side, W. Herrmann regrets that they did. (See *Communion with God*, p. 40 f.) Brunner vacillates. He begins by claiming that his own position was that of the reformers. But in his *Revelation and Reason* he attributes the notion of verbal inspiration and Bible infallibility to the second generation reformers. But in his later *Dogmatics* (vol. 1) he allows that Luther held the view along with his other 'liberal' doctrine. The 'orthodox' doctrine is indeed the 'classic' one. The false idea of the words of Scripture as 'revelational' he sees already taking place within the New Testament itself, especially in the Pastorals. The passage 2 Timothy iii. 16. he quotes as illustrating this regrettable process.

that he thereby introduced a subjective regulative principle. It was his own personal experience of new life in Christ which gave birth to the Reformation and which became for Luther a fact of prime importance. As a reaction from the cold intellectual acceptance of certain credal propositions on the authority of the Church, it was inevitable that Luther should make the principle of justification by faith the standard by which all else was to be tested. So it came about that in his enthusiastic proclamation of the doctrine of 'sola fide' he should view with disfavour anything which seemed to call its truth in question. It was this fact, which, for example, made him refer to the Epistle of James as 'a perfect straw-epistle'.

It was also this fear of compromising the absoluteness of God's grace which led Luther to hurl his invectives against the place given to reason in the Roman system. Aquinas had made natural religion an essential preface to revealed, without which the latter could not be really understood. Not only was this, in the thinking of Luther, a failure to appreciate the true effects of the 'Fall', but it was a compromise of the fundamental Biblical principle, that a man has no merit to plead before God; not even that he is able to grasp Him by his unaided reason. Reason is, therefore, for Luther 'blind and dark'; it is 'contrary to faith', and so forth.[1] Yet Luther's strong words are to be understood as a vigorous repudiation of the native ability of man, either to find out God of himself, or to originate saving faith.[2]

It is considerations such as these which have led some to conclude that Luther abandoned all external authority, and that his 'repudiation' of reason, meant the enthronement of feelings. This is not, in fact, the case. It is certain he did emphasize, it may be did over-emphasize, the 'material' principle of the gospel, justification by faith. So vivid was the experience of it to him that he came to consider it to be the sum and substance of revelation. From this point of view Luther would have the whole Bible interpreted, according to the 'analogy of faith'. Every part of Scripture was to

[1] Much more, in language less choice, is collected by Martiain, e.g. 'You are to abandon your reason; knowing nothing at all, annihilate it completely or you will never enter heaven', 'Aristotle (is) the godless bulwark of the papists,' etc., etc. J. Martiain, *Three Reformers* (E.T.), p. 30 ff.

[2] Yet Luther in a passage in his *Table Talks*, has made it clear what is involved in his repudiation of reason. 'The natural wisdom of the human creature in matters of faith, until he be regenerate and born anew, is altogether darkness, knowing nothing at all in divine cases. But in a faithful person, regenerate and enlightened by the Holy Ghost, through the Word, it is a fair and glorious instrument, and work of God.' *Table Talks*, Hazlitt's translation, ccxciv.

be read in the light of this principle. The less vital sections got their validity here.

Setting out, therefore, from his own experience, Luther did strongly assert the 'material' principle, and from that stand-point did 'judge' the Scriptures,[1] but he also maintained the 'formal' principle, the exclusive authority of the word of God. 'Luther', observes Dorner, 'clearly discerned, and succeeded in exhibiting, in the most pregnant manner, *justification by faith in Christ*, and the *sole divine authority of the Holy Scriptures*, i.e. the *so-called material and formal sides of the Evangelical principle*, each in its independent worth and title, but both also in their inward inseparable connection.'[2]

While Luther spoke of the 'word of God' as the gospel of justification by faith, whether written or preached, it remains true that 'the identity of the Holy Scriptures with the Word of God is generally assumed by Luther and occasionally expressed in explicit language'.[3] In fact the opening words of his Table Talks run thus: "That the Bible is God's word and book I prove thus . . . .'[4]

The position is less equivocal with Calvin. Although giving strong emphasis to the doctrine of the *testimonium Spiritus Sancti internum*, Calvin was even more emphatic than Luther concerning the 'formal' principle, the authority of the Scriptures. His main view on the point is found in the opening sections of his *Institutes of the Christian Religion*.[5] There, having shewn the necessity for Scripture to embody the revelation of God, he goes on to deal with its authority. Faith in Scripture as the Word of God is assured by the 'secret testimony of the Spirit'. The Scriptures are declared to be divinely inspired. Herein is the ground of their infallibility and authority.

[1] Yet Luther can say: 'We ought not to criticize, explain, or judge the Scriptures by our mere reason, but diligently, with prayer, meditate thereon, and seek their meaning,' *Table Talks*, iv.

[2] J. A. Dorner, *History of Protestant Theology*, vol. 1, p. 220 (words in italics are in italics in the original). Cf., 'During the preceding period,' writes K. R. Hagenback, referring to the period prior to 1700, 'Protestant theology had been accustomed to call the Sacred Scriptures themselves the Word of God; in the course of the present a distinction was made between the *word of God contained in the Holy Writ* and the Sacred Scriptures.' *Compendium of the History of Doctrine*, vol. 2, p. 406.

[3] G. P. Fisher, *History of Christian Doctrine*, p. 280. Cf. (on the same point), W. P. Patterson, *The Rule of Faith*, p. 405. M. Reu, *Luther and the Scriptures*, pp. 17, 24, 35, 55, 63, 92, etc. Julius Kostlin, *The Theology of Luther*, 2, p. 252 (tr. Charles E. Gray).

[4] *Table Talks*, ad. loc.

[5] *Institutes of the Christian Religion*, bk. 1, chs. vi to x.

In his work, *The Theology of Calvin*, Wilhelm Niesel, makes a statement which calls for comment. Niesel contends that Calvin did not accept either a 'literal inspiration' of Scripture or its 'inerrancy'. He writes: 'There would be no need to add to them (i.e. the arguments of a book by Peter Brunner) if recently the opinion had not been expressed that Calvin taught a literal inspiration of Holy Scripture. . . . We might point out that in the Scriptural exegesis of Calvin there is nothing to suggest a belief in literal inerrancy.'[1] This is, we believe, not a fair statement of the facts.

It may be replied, first of all, that there was no need to set out in any detail the idea of a 'literal interpretation' of the Bible, because there was none other considered, at the time, among the generality of Christians. It was only men like Castellio, the Humanist and Rationalist, against whom Calvin strove so hard to maintain the absolute authority of the Word, who denied it. At the same time it is not really exact to say that Calvin had nothing to teach about a 'literal inspiration' of the Bible, and to conclude, therefore, that he did not believe it. He speaks, for example, of Moses as the amanuensis, or secretary, of God; and he tells us that 'the Holy Spirit so governed the language of Paul that not a superfluous word escaped him'.

Niesel points out that in the chapter in the *Institutes* dealing with the Scriptures, Calvin has nothing to say about the 'method' of inspiration. This is to be admitted, since Niesel means that Calvin does not set out in detail a 'mechanical-dictation' theory. But it is enough for Calvin to insist upon inspiration as extending to the whole Bible; and on that there is little room for doubt.

At the same time, it may be observed, that Niesel notes that there are three places outside the *Institutes* where Calvin writes with definiteness on the subject of the inspiration of the Scriptures. One of these is a comment on 2 Tim. 3. 16, which, as a matter of fact, Niesel does not quote. The passage is given here because it is, we believe, of the greatest importance and does not confirm the dogmatic statement of Niesel.

'In order to uphold the authority of Scripture,' writes Calvin, 'he (i.e. the Apostle) declares that it is *divinely inspired*; for, if it be so, it is beyond controversy that men ought to receive it with reverence. This is a principle which distinguishes our religion from

[1] W. Niesel, *The Theology of Calvin* (tr. Harold Knight), p. 31.

all others, that we know God hath spoken to us, and are fully convinced that the prophets did not speak at their own suggestion, but that, being organs of the Holy Spirit, they only uttered what they had been commissioned from heaven to declare. Whoever then wishes to profit in the Scriptures, let him, first of all, lay down this as a settled point, that the Law and Prophets are not a doctrine delivered according to the will and pleasure of men, but *dictated* by the Holy Spirit.'[1]

Turning back to the *Institutes* we find Calvin saying, 'But since no daily responses are given from heaven, and the Scriptures are the only records in which God has been pleased to consign his truth to perpetual remembrance, the full authority which they ought to possess with the faithful is not recognized, unless they are believed to have come from heaven as directly as if God had been heard giving utterance to them.'[2] Quoting the first half of this passage only, Dr A. Mitchell Hunter of New College, Edinburgh, in his able and accurate study observes; 'The logical concomitant of such a view was the assertion of the inerrancy of Scripture.... For the assurance of faith, it was necessary to be able to trust the accuracy of every word of the record. The inerrancy of the letter was the corollary of its exclusive and inclusive inspiration.'[3]

That Calvin then did accept the view held generally by Christians of the period, that the Bible was authoritative and infallible, because its words were given by the Holy Ghost, may be regretted, but it must be allowed. True he did not go into detail regarding the method of the Spirit's action. His concern was, after all, with the fact of inspiration since it was necessary to the very existence of the Reformed faith to proclaim the sole divine authority of Scripture over against the claims of the Roman Church. The time for a full statement of the method of inspiration was not yet.

Warfield, we believe, has correctly stated the position, when he observes that 'The Reformers, though using the language conformable to, or even suggestive of, the theory of dictation, do not formally present that theory, as do the Systematists of the seventeenth century as the fixed ground-work of their doctrine of the

[1] *Calvin's Commentaries* (tr. W. Pringle, 1948), ad. loc. Cf., 'in the *dogmatic formulation* of the authority of the Bible he (Calvin) was already entirely under the sway of the orthodox view of literal divine inspiration,' E. Brunner, *Revelation and Reason*, p. 275.
[2] *Institutes*, vol. 1, ch. vii, (1), p. 68.
[3] *The Teaching of Calvin* (2nd edition), p. 72.

Scripture'.[1] It will be seen therefore why the Puritans regarded themselves as the interpreters of the Reformers: and why they and the Westminster divines believed themselves to be merely formally stating the doctrine of revelation and the Scripture proclaimed by the great Protestant Fathers of the Church.

(d) A Statement on the Evangelicals

The Puritans certainly identified revelation and the Scriptures. They regarded the words of the Bible as given by the Holy Spirit and therefore infallible and inerrant.

This exactly expresses the understanding of revelation of the Evangelicals of the eighteenth century. For this reason Bishop J. C. Ryle can declare concerning such men as Grimshaw, Venn, Berridge, Harvey and others of their company that 'the spiritual reformers of the last century taught constantly *the sufficiency and supremacy of the Holy Scripture*. The Bible, whole and unmutilated, was their sole rule of faith and practice. They accepted all its statements without question or dispute. They knew nothing of any part of Scripture being uninspired. They never allowed that man has any 'verifying faculty' within him by which Scripture statements may be weighed, rejected or received. They never flinched from asserting that there can be no error in the Word of God; and that when we cannot understand or reconcile some parts of its contents, the fault is in the interpreter and not in the text. In all their preaching they were eminently men of one book. To that book they were content to pin their faith, and by it to stand or fall.'[2]

This brings us to the second task specified at the beginning of this section, the task, that is, of finding someone who can best express the teaching of the Evangelicals. A reading of Bishop Ryle's book just quoted, will show that the Evangelicals were not as avowedly Calvinistic as their Puritan forerunners. They tended to modify, in some measure, what were regarded as the harsher elements of that system. But, at the same time, many of them as convinced Churchmen loyal to the articles of their Church, found it impossible to go on to a full Arminian position.[3] We thus find them, on the one hand repudiating Calvinism, or more accurately, repudiating what was popularly regarded as Calvinism, namely a

---

[1] *The Westminster Assembly and Its Work*, p. 262.
[2] *The Christian Leaders of the Last Century* (1873), p. 26.
[3] Cf., 'The Evangelicalism which developed within the Church of England had more in it of Whitfield than of Wesley. . . .' G. Faber, *Oxford Apostles*, p. 85.

strict necessitarianism. On the other hand, it is equally evident that they were in general agreement with the Reformers. While they considered themselves to be uniting, what they believed to be the truth in the two rival systems of Calvinism and Arminianism, their leanings were certainly towards the former.

It is this consideration, as well as the almost universal acknowledgement of his scholarship, which has led us to select Charles Simeon as

(ii) *The Exponent of their View*
CHARLES SIMEON

It has been said that, what theologians divide preachers unite. There is some justification for this remark, as there is some illustration of it in the message of Charles Simeon. In the 'Preface' to the twenty-one volumes of his works — *Horae Homileticae* — Simeon refuses to be placed in any one party. The true system of the Scriptures, he is persuaded, is not the exclusive possession of either Calvinism or Arminianism. His own position is clear-cut. He 'takes his religion from the Bible and endeavours, as much as possible to speak as that speaks'.[1] The distinctions brought into such sharp opposition in the different systems of theology are in the Scriptures set side by side. The verses, for example, of John 5. 40 and 6. 44 are drawn into antagonism by various writers; but he will not think of the one as opposed to the other.[2] He will dwell with equal pleasure upon both. It is, he thinks, 'better to state these apparent opposite truths in the plain unsophisticated manner of the Scriptures than to enter into scholastic subtleties, that have been invented for the upholding of human systems.'[3]

Such a position, he is aware, will be deemed inconsistent. But he is content to 'rest the vindication of his conduct, simply on the authority and example of the Inspired Writers'.[4] Since God has not given or required the reconciliation of these antitheses, he will

[1] *Works* (*Horae Homileticae*) (3rd edition, 1838), 21 vols., vol. 1, Preface, p. xiv.

[2] Cf., 'Some imagine, that if our salvation, depends wholly on the free and sovereign grace of God, there can be no need for exertion on our part. Others, on the contrary, argue, that if our salvation lie to be effected by means of our own free endeavour, it cannot be dependent on Divine Grace. But these apparently opposite assertions are not made only in different and detached passages, but oftimes in the very same passage,' vol. 10, p. 33.

[3] Vol. 1, Preface, p. xv.

[4] Ibid., cf., 'The Author is no friend of systematizers in Theology, He has endeavoured to derive from the Scriptures alone his views of religion: and to them it is his wish to adhere, with scrupulous fidelity,' 1, Preface, p. xxiii.

P

not have them imposed. Experience unites what systems divide. Thus, each knows himself a free moral agent, and, yet, every redeemed man testifies to the fact that he is saved by grace alone through a faith which is not self-originated.

Simeon 'bitterly regrets that men will range themselves in converting the Inspired Writings into friends and partisans of their peculiar principles'.[1] Both Calvinists and Arminians are guilty of attaching more weight to passages which lend colour to their special views. Simeon believes that there is 'not a determined votary of either system, if he had been in the company of St Paul, whilst he was writing his different Epistles, would not have recommended him to alter one or other of his expressions'.[2]

Yet both Calvinists and Arminians are one upon their knees. There the former acknowledges his responsibility and the latter his dependence. It is this union of the two systems, evident in the attitude of prayer, which Simeon wishes to express in his expositions.[3]

He desires to avoid, too, what he calls 'an ultra-Evangelical taste',[4] which would read into certain passages the doctrine of salvation where such was foreign to the author's intention. Where practical teaching is found, it is to be given in the conviction 'that lessons of morality are, in their place, as useful and important as the doctrines of grace'.[5] Simeon is anxious to seek out the plain meaning of Scripture. He will not read into a passage that which is not there. Exegesis must never become eisegesis. He remarks: 'We must not be deterred from speaking of the principles of Christianity, because some despise them as *evangelical*; nor must we omit the practical parts of our religion, because others discard them as *legal*.'[6]

Although Simeon can repudiate certain 'refinements of Calvin (which) have done harm in the Church',[7] he can still declare emphatically, 'I am no Arminian.'[8] He speaks with much more definiteness upon the 'evils of Arminianism'.[9] The fact is that

---

[1] Vol. 1, Preface, p. xxii.

[2] Op. cit., Preface, p. xxiii. Cf., vol. 15, p. 39; vol. 18, p. 436, 494 f.

[3] Cf., 'What both these individuals are upon their knees, it is the wish of the Author to become in his writings. Hence it is that he expects to be alternatively approved by both parties, and condemned by both,' op. cit., 1, Preface, p. xxiv.

[4] Op. cit., Preface, p. xxv.

[5] Op. cit., Preface, p. xxv. Cf., 'Some place all their piety in contending for doctrine, in opposition to morals; and others, in exalting morals, to the disparagement of doctrine,' vol. 14, p. 518.

[6] Vol. 5, p. 65.   [7] Vol. 2, p. 202.   [8] Ibid.   [9] Vol. 18, pp. 493–9.

Simeon really represents the standpoint, in the period, of the Evangelical within the Established Church. Men of such outlook, as late as 1815 were dubbed 'Church-Methodists' by their opponents.[1] Methodists they undoubtedly were in their faith and fervour, but in doctrine they tended more to the side of Calvin. On this account they were more inclined to stress the formal aspect of faith, the objective Word, than those who emphasized the human response. These naturally accentuated the material aspect, the principle of faith. Both the Evangelical Churchman and the Methodist proper were agreed as to the need for the Word and the Spirit, but whereas the former was more anxious to stress the place of the Word, the latter was concerned with the activity of the Spirit. The experience and teaching of Charles Simeon and John Wesley abundantly confirm this observation. It is for this reason that the present and following sections have been entitled, respectively, 'Revelation in the Word through the Spirit,' and, 'Revelation by the Spirit through the Word.'

Charles Simeon can rightly be taken as typical of the doctrine of the Evangelical Churchman of his day. Details of his life do not concern us here, except to say that he was a convinced Churchman.[2] At the same time the sympathies of Simeon extended far beyond the bounds of his own communion. He was as catholic as he was evangelical. He thus represented a wider body of opinion than that of the 'Church-Methodists'. As the most profound scholar amongst them he was naturally regarded as their leader and spokesman. 'If you knew what Simeon's authority and influence were,' wrote Lord Macaulay to his sister, years after Macaulay had graduated from Cambridge in 1822, 'and how they extended from Cambridge to the most remote corners of England, you would allow that his real sway in the Church was far greater than that of any Primate.'[3]

Concerned as we are here with Simeon's general views on revelation, we purpose, as far as possible, to let him speak for himself.

(a) Natural Religion

Although Simeon was supremely a preacher and an expositor, he

[1] W. L. Mathieson, *English Church Reform (1815–1840)*, p. 11.
[2] Cf., Series of Sermons preached before the University of Cambridge on the Excellency of Liturgy, vol. 2, Nos. 191, 192, 193, 194. Also *The Churchman's Confession*, vol. 16, pp. 406–21.
[3] Sir G. O. Travelyan, *Life and Letters of Lord Macaulay*, one vol., ed. Silver Library, p. 50 n.

was, no less, a scholar and a theologian. Above all he was a 'Biblical theologian' whose theology may be described as the Theology of the Word of God. It was, as has been indicated, his avowed purpose to discover and declare the meaning and message of the Bible.

It is obvious, however, that no one can expound the Christian Scriptures without some reference to those beyond to whom its revelation has not come, since the books themselves contain such references. How Charles Simeon understood, what is termed, Natural Religion, cannot but be a matter of deep interest.

Beginning with his comments upon Romans, chapter 1, it will be seen that he strongly emphasized the Pauline declaration that the Gentiles are 'without excuse', although not possessing the 'oracles of God'. 'The Gentiles', he observes, 'have in every age had sufficient opportunities of attaining the knowledge of God.'[1] True, the heathen were ignorant of those items 'exclusively made known in the book of revelation', but, in the works of creation they had sufficient evidence of God's existence. Theirs was the possibility of building up an idea of God, and of tracing everything up to a 'First Cause'. God's self-existence and eternity they could have deduced from what their observation could have assured. The excellency of His works should have made them aware of God's power and godhead. Here were the possibilities for the heathen, but they remained possibilities only. They 'did not improve these possibilities aright' and, as a result, they entertained the 'most unworthy conceptions of the Deity'.[2]

By allowing passion to override reason, the heathen failed to observe the signature of God on the spacious universe. Thus were the Gentiles 'altogether ignorant of God and unconcerned about him. They did not regard the notices of him which were visible in all the works of his hands'.[3] Even the most erudite of the ancients were unable to decipher the writings of God upon ordered nature. 'The most learned philosophers could not absolutely determine whether there were a God, or, if there were, whether there were one or many.'[4] And as 'all the principles of the greatest philosophers were involved in doubt and uncertainty, so were they altogether destitute of any sanctifying influences'.[5]

[1] Vol. 15, p. 16.   [2] Vol. 15, p. 17.
[3] Vol. 15, p. 395.   [4] Vol. 13, p. 436.
[5] Vol. 14, p. 164.

Yet while the Gentiles could not read the indications of God in the stars, they could not banish altogether the intimations of Him in their own souls. They were not completely destitute of an inner witness, since 'there is even in the minds of heathens some idea of a superintending Providence'.[1] There are none so ignorant 'as not to acknowledge the existence of a Supreme Being'.[2] He assures us that nothing 'can be more clear, than that the most uncivilized savages have an idea of a Supreme Being, whom they conceive themselves to have offended and whom they wish to propitiate'.[3] The Gentiles, therefore, had light sufficient, but they allowed themselves to be blinded. They have involved themselves in 'wilful ignorance'. Having put out their own spiritual eyes, they are brought to a just judgement and condemnation.[4] It is the witness to God in every heathen heart which becomes the basis of God's dealings with them. 'Belshazzar of old knew little of God, but was judged in the light of what he knew.'[5]

There was a day when God 'winked at' the ignorance of men. But that day has now passed since the night of darkness has gone and the Day Star has arisen. God has given a sure word to which men must take heed. 'He no longer leaves men to indulge their own vain reasonings and empty speculations. He has now revealed his will, which he has made known, not as a deduction from uncertain premises, or as a recommendation of doubtful expediency, but with an authority which supersedes all reasoning, and a plainness that dispels all doubt.'[6]

Simeon seems to teach that it is only within the light of Revelation that natural religion has any significance. It is from this vantage point that the writing of God on the universe becomes clear. Natural religion, apparently, has no practical value for the natural man. Whether on this point Simeon is in line with Calvin, those who have followed the discussion between Brunner and Barth on 'Natural Religion' will be ready with their 'Ja' or their 'Nein'. At all events, Simeon states emphatically that, 'in reading the book of creation, we, by means of our superior advantages, are enabled to see much that was hidden from' the heathen.[7] We only

---

[1] Vol. 14, p. 591.   [2] Vol. 11, p. 325.   [3] Vol. 7, p. 304.
[4] Cf., 'We need only open our eyes and survey the visible creation to be assured of his eternal power and godhead. In this respect the most stupid heathens, in respect of neglecting the worship of him, are without excuse,' vol. 6, p. 126.
[5] Vol. 9, p. 504.   [6] Vol. 14, p. 468.   [7] Vol. 15, p. 19.

rightly read the book of creation in the light of revelation. Thus 'the most ignorant amongst us excels the greatest philosophers of Greece and Rome'.[1]

Whether Simeon regards a direct appeal to nature, in these days, as of value in creating a belief in God, is not easy to decide. He does say that 'the variety and beauty of the things existing in this terraquous globe, all so adapted to their respective offices and uses, and all subservient to one grand design, the glory of their Creator, evince that his wisdom and goodness are equal to his power'.[2] He uses the illustration of the watch,[3] borrowing it, perhaps from Paley, whose works we know he had read,[4] to convince his hearers of the need for a designer. 'In the works of creation', he declares, 'somewhat of God may be discerned.'[5] He thinks there are clear and convincing proofs of God shown in the world. 'It seems astonishing to those who have ever considered the evidences of Christianity,' he says, 'that anyone should hesitate to embrace it or to acknowledge any one of its fundamental truths'.[6]

All this, however, he realizes, the partisans of natural religion will be ready to hear. All this agrees with man's pride in his own reasoning capacities. There is a sense of satisfaction in being able to ascend the ladder of syllogistic constructions and to have reached so worthy a conclusion. But such a result has no practical value. It has no dynamic significance for the life. 'There are those ready to hear somewhat of God as manifested in creation. But of his manifestation in redemption they will not hear.'[7]

In the first sermon preached before his university in 1785 on, 'The Only True and Sufficient Grounds of Glorying,' Simeon asserts that there is a knowledge of God in which to glory. It is not, however, 'the knowledge that there is a God; for this is common to the evil angels as well as the good. It is not a knowledge of God from the works of creation: for that comes as much under the observation of heathens as Christians. But it is a knowledge of God as revealed in the inspired writings.'[8]

It would therefore appear that it is only for the believing man that natural religion has any real value. Nature must be read from

<hr>

[1] Vol. 15, ibid., cf., pp. 53, 54.
[2] Vol. 6, p. 126, cf., There is sufficient evidence of a Divine agency in the world 'as will be abundantly sufficient to remove all doubts upon the subject of God's existence', vol. 13 p. 226.
[3] Vol. 13, p. 226. [4] Vol. 6, p. 484. [5] Op. cit., p. 313.
[6] Vol.13, p. 567. [7] Vol. 5, p. 234. [8] Vol. 9, p. 106.

the standpoint of grace. This comes out in a sermon on the 'Christian's Delight in God'. 'In all the works of creation,' he there asserts, 'in all the dispensations of Providence, and in all the wonders of redemption, he sees the glory and excellency of his God.'[1] Yet while the material world, at most, displays 'the *natural* perfections of God', 'not even the angels in heaven can set forth his moral perfections.'[2] This disclosure of God, Christ alone can make and has made.

There are those who have not the ability to follow a chain of argument, who cannot see the cogency of the theistic proofs. But these are not thereby any the less certain of God. There are those 'incapable of entering into abstract views of the Divine perfections: but this representation of the Deity they are as capable of comprehending as the most learned upon earth can be: yea; he knows both the existence, and the omnipotence of the Deity, as much from inward experience, as he possibly can do from the visible creation; because he feels himself to be a living witness of them'.[3]

(b) Reason — Natural and Enlightened

Those who, in the era of Charles Simeon, made natural religion the only reality, and who rejected revelation as both unnecessary and impossible, regarded reason as the only organ by which the religion of nature can come to be known. For them reason was omnipotent. But such a high estimate of the value of reason was refused by Simeon. Although he considered the possession of a rational faculty to be that which raised man above the animal, it is, at the same time, so vitiated by sin that its power is nullified.

'The endowment of reason', says Simeon, 'elevates us far above other creatures. They have instinct: man the capacity to comprehend things of spiritual and eternal import, and an ability to know, to love, to enjoy and to glorify our God.'[4] Religion is therefore a possibility for man as distinguished from the animals. Reason, indeed, is the remnant of the divine in man. It is that which puts him in a category by himself. Rationality is of the very essence of personality, and as such can never be completely eradicated. 'As *rational* beings', he observes, 'we have yet a considerable portion of the Divine image upon us; but as *moral* agents we are very far

---

[1] Vol. 6, p. 461.   [2] Vol. 14, p. 141.
[3] Vol. 5, pp. 502, 503.   [4] Vol. 6, p. 283.

from original righteousness.'[1] This 'original gift of understanding is our Creator's gift.'[2] And as such it is 'certainly the richest endowment of the human mind'.[3] This means that man can be addressed as a being capable of rational response. Appeal can be made to him as a creature able to appreciate the reason for things. 'Man is a rational being: and though, prone to abuse his reason for his evil ways is capable of judging when sound argument is proposed for his consideration.'[4]

But reason is, however, not the sovereign power the deists conceive it to be. It is now a corrupted organ, and an impotent instrument. Man is totally depraved; vitiated, that is, in the totality of his personality. There is no part which is not touched and tainted by sin. By the 'Fall' all the constituents of man's psychological make-up have been stained and strained. This means that reason can never be entirely disinterested. It is never impartial. Man, in fact, is 'capable of becoming so warped by specious reasonings, and selfish considerations, as to become an agency of Satan'.[5]

It becomes consequently a truism for Simeon that reason is no longer an adequate agent for the apprehension of spiritual truth. This conclusion is inescapable when once its incompetence within its own sphere is seen and acknowledged. Reason, therefore, 'is by no means a certain guide, even in the things which come within its proper and legitimate sphere; it is too frequently biassed in its decisions, even when the person itself is unconscious of any undue influence upon his mind.'[6] Being then an imperfect instrument where it should have been sufficient it follows that reason cannot be adequate in a sphere outside its operations. This is the fallacy of those who style themselves 'rational Christians'.

The truth is that the 'natural man neither does nor can understand spiritual truths'.[7] In a sermon entitled, 'Divine Knowledge Most Desirable,' Simeon stresses the point, which is basic to his whole teaching, that 'Reason is very inadequate to guide our steps'.[8]

---

[1] Vol. 8, p. 144.   [2] Vol. 3, p. 493.
[3] Vol. 11, p. 221.   [4] Vol. 5, p. 470.
[5] Vol. 11, pp. 221, 222. Cf., 'Reason can never suggest motives sufficient to counteract the passions,' vol. 14, p. 61.
[6] Vol. 13, pp. 667, 668. Cf., 'Reason in those things that are *within* its sphere, is a useful, though not an infallible guide . . . beyond its sphere . . . it ceases to be a guide indeed' (vol. 16, p. 121).
[7] Vol. 13, p. 390.
[8] Vol. 7, p. 198. Cf., 'We must confess the insufficiency of reason for the understanding of the sublime truths of Christianity' (vol. 16, p. 238).

We are to be thankful for the light reason sheds upon our ways in the affairs of every day. But it is the first principle of spiritual understanding, according to Simeon, to recognize that in the realm of the spirit 'unenlightened reason is not competent'.[1] Failure to understand this fact is the beginning of error. It was because the deists were unaware of reason's inability that they ended up in the self-deception that they could of themselves know God. But let the proper sphere of reason be observed and all will be well. Simeon says; 'while we acknowledge with gratitude the powers of reason in the investigation of speculative or temporal nature, we must be very jealous of its conclusions in matters that are purely spiritual and practical. In whatever relates to God and the soul, its decisions are apt to be biassed by prejudices, or interest or passion; and it yields, or withholds, assent, not so much according to the weight of evidence adduced, as according to the dispositions which are called forth into exercise'.[2]

This means that divine knowledge is not the discovery of natural reason. In a sermon on the 'Way of Attaining Divine Knowledge', Simeon makes the point that 'The heart is the proper seat of divine knowledge: other knowledge is seated in the head: it is acquired by deep study, and by the force of intellect: nor in whatever degree it is attained, does it at all satisfy and renew the soul. But the truth of God enters the soul'.[3]

For those who would understand the things of God, the reason must become enlightened. The believing man, to be sure, is not given a new faculty for spiritual apprehension. 'A natural man has the same faculties and powers as the spiritual man: his understanding is capable of comprehending common objects, or to investigate the depths of human sciences. . . . A spiritual man has no advantage over him in these respects.'[4] The difference is, however, that the natural man 'does not comprehend or enjoy what is spiritual'.[5]

Yet there is a sense in which the spiritual man does possess another means of knowing. The natural man would have all his reasons clear, he would believe only what he can comprehend. But the spiritual man knows by faith. 'It is not to human learning or to strength of intellect that the discovery of Christ is

[1] Vol. 15, p. 91, cf., vol. 6, p. 265, vol. 10, p. 161, vol. 11, p. 408.
[2] Vol. 13, p. 511.   [3] Vol. 7, p. 10, also pp. 12, 17, 19.
[4] Vol. 14, p. 53.   [5] Ibid.

made, but to faith.'[1] All the learning in the world, Simeon declares, will not give a spiritual understanding, just as a knowledge of the bodily mechanism does not furnish us with any additional corporeal organs.[2]

Does this mean that reason has to be renounced? Is it to be repudiated as a thing of no worth? Simeon will not allow us to think so. True religion does not cripple reason. God has assured to his people, not a 'spirit of delusion', but 'of a sound mind'. The prodigal's return to his father's house, was, he observes, his first proof of his sanity.[3] In all that the gospel declares, he is sure, that 'reason also is no less on our side than revelation'.[4]

Reason and Revelation

What then is the relation of reason to revelation? This is a question dealt with by Simeon in a discourse entitled, 'Means of Attaining True Wisdom.' The main point is that it is reason's office to judge whether revelation is credible. 'The only use of reason as applied to revelation', he tells us, 'is to ascertain whether the revelation, purporting to be from heaven, be indeed of Divine authority, and what is the true import of that revelation in all its parts.'[5] This is no isolated remark, elsewhere there is the same idea: 'reason must judge whether there be sufficient evidence of its (revelation's) divine origin,'[6] and that once satisfied there its activity ends. That which revelation discloses is for faith to receive.[7] Reason can no longer question that which revelation has brought. It is not at liberty to reject that which it cannot fathom or repudiate that which it cannot reconcile. 'If it be thought, that to expect a rational being so to submit to the authority of revelation is to require a sacrifice that is unworthy of him, I answer, that THIS is the very way in which all human knowledge is acquired.'[8] The

---

[1] Vol. 7, p. 507. Cf., 'There is an essential distinction between divine and human knowledge, so is there a very great difference in the ways by which each of them is to be obtained, the one being attainable only by rational investigation, the other only by faith' (vol. 13, p. 245).

[2] Vol. 7, p. 507, cf., p. 609.   [3] Vol. 9, p. 180.
[4] Vol. 14, p. 580.   [5] Vol. 16, p. 121.
[6] Vol. 6, p. 439. Cf., vol. 16, p. 121.

[7] Vol. 6, p. 439 f. Cf., 'Reason will presume to sit in judgement upon the truth of God. But this is not its province. Its proper office is to judge whether the Scriptures are a revelation of God: but when that is ascertained, faith is then to apprehend whatever God has spoken: and the highest dictates of reason is, to submit ourselves to God with the simplicity and teachableness of a little child' (vol. 16, p. 358).

[8] Vol. 6, p. 439.

child must first accept on trust, although later he discovers that what he accepted agrees with experience: 'so receiving the mysterious truths of God, we first take them on the authority of our Divine Teacher; then, gradually, we find that they correspond with our own experience, we see that they are precisely as they have been presented to us.'[1]

Simeon however will not have it that there can be any ultimate disharmony between reason and revelation. Paul spoke to Agrippa the words of truth and soberness, and what he declared he regarded as the very truth of God. But he spake with the conviction that 'unbiassed reason must approve of all that he taught'.[2]

This is a point Simeon labours to establish in a discourse before his university, 'An Appeal to Men of Wisdom and Candour.' 'There is no part of religion (he is referring, of course, to the Christian revelation) repugnant to reason, nor any part which enlightened reason must not highly approve.'[3] The idea is more strongly emphasized in an earlier section of the same sermon: 'though revealed religion is neither founded on human reason, nor makes its appeal to it; yet it is perfectly consistent with reason and approves itself to the judgement of everyone whose mind is enlightened by the Spirit of God.'[4]

Yet the highest knowledge of God that man possesses 'is always *negative*'.[5] We have no positive knowledge of Him at all. We call Him, Spirit, but we know as little what Spirit is now, as the day we were born.[6]

The teaching of Simeon, under this heading, which has been illustrated from his works, may, then, be briefly summarized. He regards reason in its 'proper sphere' as uncertain, outside of that sphere, in the realm of the spiritual, as useless. It can assure the credibility of revelation, but it is helpless to secure its contents. The ideas of religion are not contradictory of revelation, although revelation is not discovered by reason. To gain true wisdom a man must become 'a fool'. His final position is, that if we would have divine knowledge we must have; 'First, a consciousness of the

---

[1] Ibid.
[2] Vol. 14, p. 580. Cf., 'The truth of God though elevated above reason, is in perfect accordance with reason' (vol. 15, p. 252).
[3] Vol. 16, p. 230.
[4] Op. cit., p. 229. Cf., 'You do not condemn reason because some pervert it to the support of error and assume to themselves the title *rational* Christians' (vol. 16, p. 422).
[5] Vol. 3, p. 373.   [6] Vol. 16, p. 194.

weakness and fallibility of our reason in the things relating to God: and, secondly, a willingness to submit our reason to the teachings of God's word and Spirit.'[1]

(c) Revelation and the Scriptures

Natural reason cannot find out God; this, then, is the burden of Simeon's message. Even the very wisest of the philosophers of Greece and Rome could not gain any real knowledge of God and of the things that make for religion. Of God's existence and essence they could speak only hesitatingly.[2] They had no confident verdict about the immortality of the Soul; what 'faint conceptions' they had, were mere matters of conjecture — 'of surmise or opinion only, not of knowledge'.[3] Such uncertain views could never become a creative creed; they were powerless to move the soul or change the life. They had no message for the sin-oppressed soul. 'Go even to the wisest philosophers of Greece and Rome', he bids us, 'and see how vain were their expedients for pacifying a guilty soul, or purifying a polluted soul.'[4]

The position is, then, that unless God comes forth in self-revelation there can be no knowledge of Him. Divine knowledge is not a discovery by man but a disclosure from God. 'We know nothing of God or his ways, any further than he sees fit to reveal himself to us.'[5] Simeon bases the necessity for revelation upon the fact of man's inability to come to any meaningful knowledge of God.[6] A redeemed understanding of Him must be a revealed understanding of Him. The saving truth of God must remain forever in the realm of impenetrable obscurity unless God draws aside the curtain and comes forth in self-disclosure upon the stage of human history. The necessity of revelation arises from the fact that 'no man could possibly know God's will, unless God should be pleased to communicate information respecting it from above'.[7] It is the assurance of Simeon that this required revelation has been made. There has been an unveiling of the divine plan and purpose: 'we are not left to the uncertain deductions of reason.'[8]

---

[1] Vol. 16, p. 121.
[2] Vol. 16, p. 194.
[3] Vol. 19, p. 11.
[4] Vol. 4, p. 561.
[5] Vol. 6, p. 94.
[6] Cf., 'Divine truth is manifestly beyond our comprehension; and we must receive it simply on the authority of God' (vol. 16, p. 194).
[7] Vol. 5, p. 149.
[8] Vol. 1, p. 1.

The Revelation Confirmed

This revelation, according to Simeon, has all the marks of authenticity. He thinks that there are good reasons for studying the evidences of our religion.[1] An understanding of the facts concerning the faith will deliver us from becoming an easy prey to scepticism. The infidel's effort to shake our faith will be vain and impotent if the reasons for our religion were taught from early youth.[2] If indeed the unbeliever were to give impartial consideration to these evidences he could not but acknowledge their cogency and see the truth of what they are adduced to approve. The tragedy is, however, that he cannot be thus impartial and consequently he rejects the truth on the pretence that proof is wanting. 'Infidels pretend that their doubts arise from want of evidence: but they in reality arise from an indisposition of heart to weigh with candour the evidence before them.'[3]

Miracles and prophecies Simeon regards as the supreme proofs of the truth of Christianity as the revealed religion. 'It has pleased God', he says, 'to give us every evidence of the truth of our religion, that the most scrupulous mind could desire. The proofs arising from prophecies and miracles, are such as carry irresistible conviction to every candid enquirer.'[4]

Prophecy, he believes to be the most satisfactory evidence of the truth of Christianity. This is not because of the mere number of things foretold, but because of their content. Prophecies are not the result of lucky guesses or of human insight. They are in fact contrary to all human expectations.[5] They are of such a nature that human wisdom could not have devised them nor human power accomplished them.[6] Yet in number the prophecies are not meagre. It is by reason of its 'fulness', 'minuteness' and 'consistency' that prophecy can be regarded as a 'sure word'.[7] Simeon boldly states that the 'declarations of the prophets were so numerous and minute that a history of our Lord might be compiled from them, fuller, in many respects, than is contained in the Evangelists'.[8]

[1] Vol. 3, p. 327.
[2] Ibid.
[3] Vol. 14, p. 221.
[4] Op. cit., p. 351.
[5] Vol. 8, pp. 247–8.
[6] Vol. 18, p. 487.
[7] Vol. 20, p. 323.
[8] Vol. 14, p. 221. Cf., 'Every minute circumstance relative to the Gospel has been foretold by one or other of the prophets; in so much, that, if we understood perfectly every part of the prophetic writings, we might extract from them as complete an account of the person and work and offices of Christ . . . as from the New Testament' (vol. 14, p. 189).

No man, he asserts, can remain an unbeliever concerning the truth of Christianity if he examines the prophecies with a candid mind.[1] The agreement of event with prophecy will induce the strongest conviction. Anyone who sees how prediction is followed by fulfilment, sometimes after the lapse of a period, when none of those who had heard the declaratory word were alive, and could not therefore have engineered events as a pious fraud, must be convinced of the truth of Christianity.[2] The observation of fulfilled prophecy cannot be lightly set aside. It is the divine attestation of the genuineness of the gospel. It sets the seal of God upon it. Simeon therefore urges the study of prophecy, among other reasons, for the sake of its evidential value. Even if 'intellectual amusement' were our only desire, he tells us, 'we can scarcely conceive a richer feast to the mind than a study of prophecy.'[3]

Prophecy is to be understood as the unfolding of the purpose of God.[4] It is consequently not of human devising. It 'springs not from man's conjectures but from a divine revelation. The prophets, so far from being the source of their own predictions, could not even understand them, any further than they were illuminated by that very Spirit by whose immediate agency they were inspired'.[5] It is God Who has predicted and fulfilled. Thus prophecy is a proof that 'Christianity must be of divine origin'.[6]

For all that, the value of the evidence of prophecy is in some sense limited. The ability to compare event with fulfilment is not with everyone. It is a hard and hazardous task. Simeon thinks therefore that the proof from miracles is more direct and conclusive. Christ's claim is vindicated by both prophecies and miracles. But the 'completion of prophecy was indeed a decisive proof of his Messiahship to those who could compare the prophecies with the events; but that was a long and arduous process; a work which a few were competent to undertake: whereas the working of miracles afforded a short, compendious, and irresistible evidence, to the eyes of all who beheld them'.[7]

Simeon defines miracles as 'works contrary to the common

[1] Vol. 20, p. 322.
[2] Vol. 14, p. 202, cf., p. 300.
[3] Vol. 20, p. 327.
[4] Vol. 3, p. 243.
[5] Vol. 14, p. 327. Cf., The prophets were instructed 'by the immediate inspiration of God' (vol. 8, p. 759, cf., vol. 20, pp. 148, 151).
[6] Ibid.
[7] Op. cit., p. 224.

course of nature, works which God alone is able to perform'.[1] He is
certain that the miracles of Christ have evidential value. Christ
Himself appealed to them in this way.[2] They are to be regarded as
testimonies to His divine mission.[3] They are intended for us to be
acted parables, vivid demonstrations of God's saving mercies.
They 'shadow forth the spiritual blessings which he came to
bestow'.[4]

The miracles of the gospel are to be taken then as God's more
dramatic authentication of His revelation since it is not possible to
suppose that He would permit the working of miracles to establish
falsehood.[5] It is noted that God did allow Pharoah's magicians to
imitate some of the miracles of Moses. This leads Simeon to
qualify, in some measure, the stress he has placed upon the evidence of miracles. 'I am not prepared to say', he writes, 'that a
miracle is of itself, independent of all its circumstances, a sufficient
proof that the person performing it comes from God.'[6] There are
impostures. There are those who can work wonders. But the
miracles of Jesus are beyond doubt not of this type. He is such an
One Who could only work that which is good.[7]

Since miracles have ceased they can be appealed to now only on
the basis of their record. 'We cannot work miracles in confirmation
of doctrine but we appeal to the miracles by which it was confirmed
in the days of Christ and of his apostles.'[8] The record of the
miracles he believes to be 'not one whit less satisfactory than
ocular demonstrations'.[9] This point is made on more than one
occasion. 'But when the miracles of our Lord were recorded by
persons who were eyewitnesses of the same, and these records
were speedily circulated amongst myriads who also had been spectators of them; and when in these writings an appeal is made to the
bitterest enemies of our Lord, who would have been glad to contradict these assertions of the Evangelists on the supposition that
they would have been disproved; these records come down to us
with an evidence not at all inferior to ocular demonstration: and if

[1] Vol. 14, p. 223.
[2] Op. cit., p. 181, also, p. 376. Cf., 'That the miracles that Jesus did, were
intended to convince the Jews of his Divine mission, and that they were sufficient for that end, is manifest from the appeal which he himself made to them
in this very view' (vol. 14, p. 224).
[3] Vol. 13, p. 492.
[4] Vol. 14, 181, cf., p. 291 and vol. 13, 368, also, p. 373.
[5] Vol. 14, p. 224.   [6] Vol. 13, p. 367.
[7] Op. cit., p. 368, cf., vol. 14, pp. 367, 368.
[8] Vol. 13, p. 466.   [9] Vol. 14, pp. 224, 225.

any man rejects the testimony which is thus sanctioned both by friends and enemies, he is wilfully blind, and would reject any other evidence that could be given him.'[1]

Yet there is a demonstration of the truth of Christianity which has come to us, but was not given to those who witnessed the miracles. This particular proof is the resurrection of our Lord from the dead. 'The divine authority of the Christian religion', he declares, 'was chiefly to be proved by the resurrection. Hence our Lord gave his Disciples the most unquestioned evidence of the resurrection during the space of forty days previous to his ascension into heaven.'[2]

Simeon makes mention of other proofs by which Christianity is authenticated. He declares that 'no species of evidence is wanting to confirm it'.[3] He refers to the doctrines and morality of the gospel as beyond anything the greatest philosophers could invent.[4] There is further a compelling harmony and unity in all that which has been revealed. Of the several references to the conversion of Paul, he says, 'It seems to have been intended by God as a strong evidence of the truth of our religion.'[5]

Simeon does not ignore the place of internal evidences. 'It may well be supposed', he says, 'that any revelation purporting to come from God, should in addition to all external evidences, have internal proofs also of its divine original.'[6] The fitness of the revelation for fallen men and the gospel which gives all the glory to God are such convincing evidences.[7]

Simeon divides religion into two kinds, the theoretical and the practical. 'In the term *theoretical*, I include', he says, 'everything that is necessary to prove the truth of Christianity: and under the term *practical*, whatever is required of those who embrace it. To understand the theoretical part is desirable: to perform the practical is necessary. The two kinds, however, are not necessarily united: the theoretical may exist where the practical is disregarded; and the practical may exist, where the theoretical is unknown. Thousands of pious souls have neither time nor talent for collating MSS, or for weighing the evidences that may be adduced in favour of particular hypotheses: and to say that these cannot be religious, because they are wanting in critical acumen, would be as

---

[1] Vol. 13, p. 66.
[2] Op. cit., p. 162.
[3] Vol. 18, p. 487.
[4] Vol. 15, pp. 471, 499.
[5] Vol. 1, pp. 315, 316.
[6] Vol. 14, p. 352.
[7] Vol. 15, p. 83.

absurd as to say a man cannot be honest, because he has not suffi-cient knowledge of the laws to be a judge.'[1] The good results which Christianity produces must indicate the validity of the faith. With regard to this proof he comments, 'If this be not a proper test of our religion, whereby shall the superior excellency of Christ be known? If the Bible produce no better effects than the Koran, I do not hesitate to say that it is no better than the Koran.'[2]

Both external and internal evidences are, then, to be given their full weight. If this is done, Simeon is certain that the truth of Christianity cannot be long denied. He thus concludes, 'The divine authority of our religion is fully established. Its external evidences demonstrate God to be the author; nor are the internal evidences less convincing.'[3]

Revelation and Mystery

Simeon was well aware of the reiterated dictum of the deists that, where mystery begins, religion ends.[4] He meets the conten-tion in a manner reminiscent of Butler. He points to the presence of mystery within our own being and without our own selves.[5] As far as nature is concerned, ''Tis mystery all'. He therefore boldly declares 'that Christianity is altogether a mystery'.[6] The central truth of the gospel, Christ crucified, is the greatest mystery of all.[7] Simeon will not have Christianity reduced to a set of rational propositions. Its majesty lies in its mysteries. In a sermon on the passage, Great is the mystery of godliness, he makes the comment, 'It has often been said by infidels, that, where mystery begins, religion ends. But if this were true there would be no uniformity or consistency in the works of God. All his works of both creation and providence are full of mysteries: there is not any one sub-stance of which we know all the properties, or any one event, for which we can assign all the reasons. If there were nothing in religion above the comprehension of man it would afford a strong presumption that our religion was not from heaven: for why should it be revealed if man could have devised it without revelation?'[8]

That Christianity contains mystery is, then, both natural and

---

[1] Vol. 9, pp. 5, 6.   [2] Ibid.
[3] Vol. 20, p. 250.   [4] Vol. 2, p. 105, also vol. 18, p. 250.
[5] Cf., 'On whatever side we look we are surrounded by mysteries; yea, we are a mystery to ourselves. The works of creation, and providence, and redemption are all mysterious' (vol. 15, p. 456).
[6] Vol. 2, p. 105.   [7] Vol. 18, p. 210.   [8] Op. cit., p. 504.

Q

necessary. It follows from the fact that man's reason is unable to reach the saving truths of the gospel and that the doctrines that are to be most surely believed have been revealed by God. The presence of mystery in things which concern our redemption follows from analogy with the things of creation.

The mystery which around us and within us lies has to be accepted. Those within Christianity should be likewise accepted as part of the divine order. 'There are many things revealed to us in the Gospel which are contrary to any generally prevailing opinion of mankind . . . . In order to understand them aright we must receive them simply on the authority of God; and conclude them to be true, because he has revealed them.'[1]

Revelation within the Record

For Simeon, the revelation which God has so graciously given and so certainly authenticated is contained within the Scriptures. He regards the Bible, not as the permanent possibility of revelation, but as its permanent actuality. Objectively, and in themselves, they are the word of God. Although, as we shall see later, Simeon makes much of the inner witness of the Spirit, he never, like Maurice, thinks of the Bible becoming the 'word of God' in the context of experience. Simeon, therefore, considers the revelation and the record to be for all practical purposes one and the same. God's early revelation to man was, he observes, 'merely oral,' but it was preserved in a guarded tradition until it could be put in writing. He considers the Mosaic era as of special significance because God then 'for the first time vouchsafed to man a *written record*'.[2] The continuation of the revelation in an oral tradition he regarded as impracticable. 'If there were no written documents of the things transmitted,' he says, 'we could not have been sure that our information respecting them was correct; seeing that many variations must inevitably happen in traditions handed down through so many succeeding ages.'[3]

The result therefore for Simeon is that, because the Bible contains the revelation of God we are confined to it as providing the source and limiting the scope of our knowledge of God. 'Of God we know nothing, but from his word.'[4] This does not mean that other books are utterly useless. They have their place; but their

---

[1] Vol. 14, pp. 165, 166.   [2] Vol. 15, p. 452.
[3] Vol. 14, p. 224.   [4] Vol. 6, p. 438.

value depends upon the measure of their accord with the Scriptures. In so far as they are borrowed rays from the Bible, they will be of help. 'From human writings', he observes, 'you may learn *something* of God, but from the Scriptures alone can you acquire such knowledge of him as it is your privilege and duty to possess.'[1] This means for Simeon that the Bible, *in toto*, is to be regarded as the Word of God. It is throughout an inspired volume, 'with nothing superfluous or defective,' and, consequently 'may be wholly and exclusively, called "the Word of God" '.[2]

For such a doctrine of Scripture certain assumptions are necessary and from it certain conclusions follow.

With regard to the first, a very strict view of inspiration must be held. In this connection Simeon had no hesitations. He consequently declares that the Bible is the Word of God written by men 'who wrote only what God by his Spirit dictated'.[3] The 'whole Scripture was as much written by the finger of God, as the laws were, which he inscribed on the two tables of stone, and delivered to his servant Moses'.[4] In a reference to the apostolic writings, he says that the Holy Spirit kept the apostles 'from error of every kind: so that which they have spoken must be regarded as the Word of God, no less than if their very words had been dictated from above, yea, in all that they revealed, they were kept from error of every kind and every degree'.[5]

It must not be supposed, however, that Simeon regarded the Biblical writers as passive instruments in the hands of God. He has no 'docetic' doctrine of inspiration. The activity of the writer was not lost in the action of God. Whilst the matter of the biblical writers was inspired of God, and in the manner of their expression 'they were preserved by the same Spirit from any mistake and error', they still 'express themselves in their own way'.[6]

Simeon's conception of revelation as contained within the divinely-inspired Scriptures leads to some very definite conclusions. They are, first of all, to be received as an unerring and infallible body of revealed truths.[7] As such they are to be believed implicitly.[8] Because the Scripture contains 'the *whole* revealed will

---

[1] Vol. 5, p. 35.   [2] Vol. 17, p. 497.   [3] Ibid.
[4] Ibid.   [5] Vol. 14, p. 216.   [6] Vol. 19, p. 72.
[7] Cf., vol. 3, pp. 172, 385; vol. 4, p. 7; vol. 8, p. 122; vol. 9, p. 341, etc. 'There is no reason for questioning the divine authority of the sacred oracles, for God is as immutable in his word, as he is in his nature' (vol. 15, p. 56).
[8] Vol. 3, p. 230, cf. The Scriptures must be 'received implicitly in whatever they declare and be obeyed in whatever they command' Sermon on Christ's

of God',[1] it must be taken as the one rule of faith and practice.[2] Simeon constantly refers to the Bible the words of Isaiah 12. 3. It is a 'well of salvation from which we are to draw water with joy'.[3] It is a 'sure directory'.[4] It is a 'kind of map, whereby we find our way through this tractless desert and arrive safely at our Father's house'.[5]

In a comment on the parable of the Rich Man and Lazarus he notes that the former in his anxiety for his brethren was reminded that they had the Scriptures. They are the guide to heaven wherein 'there is no instruction wanted, which is not contained in the sacred volume, and conveyed, too, in the most edifying manner. Its warnings are most solemn, its invitations most earnest, its expostulations most affectionate, its promises most enlarged'.[6]

In a sermon on Psalm 138. 2, he tells us that God honours His word above everything else, and 'magnifies it above all his name'. A little concerning God may be gathered from creation, but 'the mysterious transactions' which took place in the 'council-chamber of the Most High', are made known only here.[7]

The last sermon but one of the *Horae Homileticae* is entitled, 'The Perfection and Sanctity of the Holy Scriptures.' Here the point is made that the Mosaic dispensation ended with the injunction, 'ye shall not add unto the word which I command you, neither shall ye diminish ought from it.' In like manner the Christian dispensation is concluded with the solemn declaration that nothing is to be added to or taken from the things written in the book, not merely the book of Revelation itself, for 'as this book completes and closes the sacred Canon, I consider the warning as extending to the whole of the New Testament Scriptures'.[8] The Bible is the perfect revelation of God within which His glorious perfections and eternal purposes are set forth. 'It is at our peril to change or modify any part of that system which God has revealed in his word.'[9]

It need not be thought that God should have given specific rules for every possible case, for then 'the Scriptures would have been so voluminous, that a whole life of study would not be sufficient to

Appeal to the Scriptures, preached before the Society of Scripture Readers, Dublin, 1830.

[1] Vol. 3, p. 516 (cf., vol. 6, p. 152).   [2] Vol. 2, p. 334; vol. 3, p. 190.
[3] Vol. 6, p. 152; vol. 7, p. 560, etc.   [4] Vol. 6, pp. 304, 366.
[5] Vol. 8, p. 421.   [6] Vol. 12, p. 565.
[7] Vol. 6, p. 437.   [8] Vol. 21, p. 278.
[9] Vol. 21, p. 280.

make us acquainted with them'.[1] By supplying us with 'a few general principles, and embodying them in living examples, God has given us all the information we need'.[2]

The Reformers, he declares, stood for the authority of Scripture. But many at the present time instead of 'submitting to be taught of God' adopt their own sentiments. Simeon urges his hearers and readers 'to regard the Scriptures' with the veneration that is due to them.[3]

It will be clear from what has been said that Simeon makes the relation between Christ and the Scriptures to be an absolute one. 'The body of Scripture', he writes, 'is penetrated by a soul, which though invisible, really pervades every part; and that soul is Christ.'[4] Yet we are not to think of Christ as imprisoned within the pages of a book. Christ lives for us, in and through the Word. He observes, 'in ascribing our salvation to the knowledge of the Scriptures we do not derogate from the honour of Christ; since it is only by revealing his work and offices to us, and leading us to depend upon him, that they become effectual for this blessed end. But at the same time we must put an honour on the Scriptures to which no other book has the smallest claim. Other books may be the channels for conveying divine knowledge; but the Bible alone is the fountain from which it flows.'[5]

The Bible is, however, no mere record of past events. It is not simply a dated document, an account of transactions passed. 'The history of the Jews is not a mere record of times and persons far distant from us, but a display of the Divine procedure towards others, as a pledge of a similar procedure towards us.'[6] Any occasional declaration, any insignificant ordinance, any personal promise can come livingly into the present and be God's word for us. 'There is not a precept that is not binding upon us as on those to whom it was delivered: there is not a threatening, at which *we* have not cause to tremble; nor a promise, on which *we* are not warranted to rely if only we believe in Jesus Christ.'[7]

(d) The Scriptures and the Spirit

Although Charles Simeon regarded the Bible as a book of divinely communicated truths to be accepted and believed just

---

[1] Vol. 21, ibid.   [2] Op. cit., p. 279.   [3] Op. cit., p. 282.
[4] Vol. 16, p. 481.   [5] Vol. 19, p. 69.   [6] Vol. 6, p. 64.
[7] Vol. 17, p. 409.

because they were revealed, it is not to be concluded that he considered faith to be mere assent to these truths. He states emphatically that to believe in Christ is 'much more than a bare assent'.[1] If there were one point more than another emphasized by Simeon, it was this; mere speculative knowledge of the Scriptures is useless. The words are almost a refrain throughout the 2,526 sermons. The references given below, although by no means complete, will give some impression of how constantly the point was made.[2]

The acceptance of doctrine was not therefore sufficient of itself. Indeed Simeon repudiates such a view as mere 'notional' faith as of no value to the saving of the soul. 'The mere report, as contained in the written word, is not of *itself* sufficient to bring to a saving knowledge of these sublime truths: Christ must be revealed *in* us, as well as *to* us.'[3] It is, as a matter of fact, just here that Simeon finds the distinction between the so-called 'orthodox' and the Evangelical.[4] The former like to pass by the 'name of rational Christians'.[5] For Simeon, however, the true seat of religion is the heart not the head. It is not primarily the assent of the human mind but the activity of the Divine Spirit.

Simeon emphasizes again and again that without the inner working of the Spirit, the Bible is a 'dead letter'. 'Even the Scriptures themselves will be a "dead letter" and "a sealed book" unless the Spirit of God open the understanding to understand them.'[6]

Simeon consequently gives an important place to the work of the Spirit. No man is to imagine that faith in the Bible, as such, is of saving value. If the question is asked, Can such faith save him? The answer returned by Simeon is an unhesitating, No. This is brought out in an important passage in a sermon in volume 10; 'First, then, it is not the word that does good; but the Holy Ghost by the Word. If the word wrought anything, its operations would be uniform and universal, or, at least, in a much greater degree than it is now, and people would be benefited by it in proportion

---

[1] Vol. 13, p. 358.

[2] Vol. 4, p. 142; vol. 5, pp. 5, 7, 151, 312; vol. 6, p. 108, 'A speculative knowledge of the Gospel is possessed by many who have no personal interest in it, and no desire after its blessings . . . .'; vol. 6, pp. 176, 261, 448; vol. 7, p. 12; vol. 8, pp. 152, 445; vol. 9, p. 238; vol. 11, pp. 42, 60, 70, 149, 153, 344; vol. 12, p. 313; vol. 13, pp. 315, 447, 496, 540, 541, 568; vol. 14, pp. 350, 549; vol. 15, pp. 54, 242, etc., etc.

[3] Vol. 6, p. 94.

[4] Vol. 20, p. 524.

[5] Vol. 20, p. 146.

[6] Vol. 5, p. 373, also vol. 6, p. 309; vol. 7, p. 506; vol. 8, p. 30; esp. vol. 16, pp. 450–61, 477–81; vol. 17, p. 500; vol. 18, p. 319.

to the strength and clearness of the intellect . . . . Next, it is not the knowledge of the word that benefits, but the knowledge of Christ in the record. We might be able to repeat the whole Bible and perish at the last. Christ must be known by us; and that not speculatively but experimentally.'[1]

It is not, then, to be imagined by anyone that because God has revealed His secrets in the written word, 'that we need no further revelation of it to the soul.'[2] All need this divine influence to improve the revelation already given.[3] A mere critical study of the Bible cannot give spiritual understanding. Some may burn the midnight oil and labour all the day long to investigate the meaning of the letter of the Scripture, but such a knowledge may leave the person entirely ignorant of God.[4]

For Simeon then, a knowledge of God comes by the Word and the Spirit.[5] Anyone who has studied Simeon's works cannot fail to see that he made much of the place of the Spirit in the things of the soul. There is hardly a page in all the twenty-one volumes of the *Horae Homileticae* in which there is not some reference to the Holy Spirit. So abundant are these allusions that it comes as a surprise to learn of the criticism that 'Charles Simeon and his friends said little of the Paraclete'.[6] It is worthy of note that at the very time Irving was proclaiming that Pentecostal miracles were being revived in London, Simeon was giving his balanced discourses in St Mary's on 'The Offices of the Holy Spirit'.

It was Simeon's conviction that the Word without the Spirit was of no saving value. He illustrates his point like this: an object which is obscure may be made visible either by reflecting stronger light upon it, or by strengthening the organs of vision. God's methods of instructing us are analogous to these, 'in that he brings home with power to our souls the truths which we hear, and inclines our hearts to embrace them.' The telescope and the microscope, he observes, make no difference either to the organ or to the object of

[1] Vol. 10, pp. 284, 285. Cf., 'A man might commit to memory the whole Bible, and yet not understand one spiritual truth in it, if he trusted in his own spiritual powers, instead of looking up to God for the teaching of his Spirit' (vol. 7, p. 7).
[2] Vol. 5, p. 169.
[3] Vol. 5, p. 149, cf., vol. 21, pp. 232, 233.
[4] Vol. 6, p. 309, 374; vol. 7, p. 562, etc.
[5] Cf., 'In the Scriptures nothing is wanting. It is God's rod of strength to quicken and to sanctify . . . . Yet all that is wanting to render the word effectual is to get it applied to our hearts by the Spirit of God' (vol. 12, p. 565, cf., vol. 17, p. 506, etc., etc.).
[6] See H. C. G. Moule, *Charles Simeon*, p. 82.

vision. 'So there is no difference in the truths which are heard by different persons, or in the capacity of those by whom they are perceived: the difference is in the manner in which the truths are presented to the mind: and if we, by instruments of human contrivance, are able thus to bring to the sight of men things that are invisible to the naked eye, we may well suppose that God is able to bring home to the souls of men truths which the unassisted mind is unable to comprehend.'[1]

The Spirit and 'Enthusiasm'

By his continual insistence upon the necessity for the illumination of the Holy Spirit, Simeon had to guard his hearers and readers against the excesses of 'enthusiasm'. He was well aware of its evil, on the one hand, whilst, on the other hand, he realized how easy it was to go to the other extreme and so to repudiate any warmth and zeal in religion as to make it a cold rational affair. To this extreme, he believed, had gone those who styled themselves 'rational Christians'. 'A supreme delight in God is by many deemed enthusiasm, whereas the religion that exists in speculation, theory, and forms, is supposed to be exclusively entitled to the appellation of *Rational*.'[2]

To fall into the excesses of enthusiasm was the one fear of many throughout our period. To avoid this pitfall they seemed to find it necessary to reject altogether any doctrine of the inner working of the Spirit.[3] They limited His activity to the apostles in whom He worked miracles and to whom He communicated divine truths. Since this body of doctrine has now been given it was the business of the modern Christian to give it his assent and not to look for any extraordinary action of the Spirit. Consequently, as Simeon notes, any reference to the divine influence of the Spirit was considered as enthusiastic and absurd.[4] Any warmth in religion was therefore regarded with loathing. Any strong expression of faith or burning

---

[1] Vol. 10, p. 274.
[2] Vol. 4, p. 10.
[3] Cf., 'The error of modern times *within* the pale of faith is a spiritual error, as well as that without: I mean enthusiasm: So clearly is this such that we are continually suffering our jealousy and fear of it to keep our tempers back from that spirituality, to which belongs the kingdom of heaven', J. Miller, *The Divine Authority of the Holy Scripture*, p. 45.
[4] Cf., 'They believe that the Holy Ghost was given formerly to the Church for the working of miracles; but they will not believe that he is continued to the Church for the purpose of guiding, comforting and sanctifying the soul,' vol. 20, p. 405.

manifestation of devotion was written off as enthusiastic deceit.[1]

But however much those whose hearts have been strangely warmed are derided as deluded, Simeon is convinced that there is a real place for enthusiasm. Where earthly things are the objects of pursuit, he observes, the affections are not only approved but applauded, 'but when the soul is attracted by heavenly objects, the livelier emotions of the mind are deemed enthusiasm.'[2] This is for Simeon an impossible position. As he sees it, a religion without warmth is a religion without worth. It may be orthodox, but it cannot be operative. He therefore declares that 'Lukewarmness in religion is as odious to God as an utter neglect of it'.[3] There must be a true zeal like that for which Phineas was commended.[4]

The Sadducees of old 'ridiculed as enthusiasm' whatever opinion was contrary to theirs.[5] Even the joyous exuberances of the children singing their glad Hosannas was disapproved as the effusion of weak and uninformed minds. Those who would give vigorous voice to their faith and praise are regarded as likewise deficient. A religious zeal is however a necessity of true faith. Without it religion becomes a form without a life and worship an association without an inspiration, and Christian living a duty without a devotion. Of our Lord it was said, His zeal consumed Him, 'but remember', adds Simeon, 'it was *himself* it consumed, not others.'[6] Therefore, 'a man's own heart is the first sphere for the exercise of zeal.'[7]

Such an attitude, he believes, will not be understood by those who are strangers to all spiritual joys.[8]

While, however, Simeon insists on the place of the feelings in religion, he is far from giving sanction to the eccentricities and contentions of many who suppose themselves inspired of the Spirit. In a series of sermons on David dancing before the Lord, he says, 'I will not say that the body is not to participate in the emotions of the mind . . . . But there is a delicacy and refinement in Christian feelings, so the less they savour of the *animal* the better.'[9] Feelings are not therefore to be undervalued. Yet they are not to

[1] Cf., 'The world may represent us as enthusiastics because we believe that in the end all will be well,' vol. 5, p. 297. 'Some represent the preaching of God's anger upon sin as nothing better than gloomy enthusiasm,' vol. 5, p. 201. 'I cannot wonder that the world should cry out against the people of the Lord as enthusiastic and absurd . . . .' vol. 6, p. 37.

[2] Vol. 13, p. 68.   [3] Vol. 7, p. 250.   [4] Vol. 6, pp. 225–35.
[5] Vol. 11, p. 442.   [6] Vol. 3, p. 523.   [7] Vol. 14, p. 499.
[8] Vol. 11, p. 501.   [9] Vol. 3, p. 251.

be taken as the criteria whereby the existence of true religion is to
be judged. If there were not more substantial evidences of piety
than passing feelings the result would be perpetual uncertainty. He
makes the point that it is 'not by vain conceits, or transient
impressions that we judge, but by practical results .... Beware
then how you substitute the reveries of enthusiasm for the holiness
of the Gospel'.[1] The truth and the genuineness of our faith and
profession are to be judged, not by occasional feelings but by our
abiding taste, by a life redeemed and regulated by the word of
God.[2]

For those who deny the influence of the Spirit, regarding such a
doctrine as opening the way for all sorts of enthusiastic excess,
Simeon retorts, 'It would be enthusiasm to tell men that their own
reason is sufficient for every purpose of spiritual instruction.'[3]

Simeon did not wish to escape the opprobrious title of 'enthusiast' by denying the inner workings of the Spirit. The rational Christian might make the charge, but he could retort with a *Tu Quoque*.
It would seem a far greater evidence of vain conceit to regard
religion as the discovery of man's own unaided reason. He is ready
to give place to the Spirit, and if he is derided as a poor enthusiast,
he will accept it. He can point out, however, that the 'necessity of
Divine Teaching, in order to a spiritual acquaintance with the
truth of God, is by many denied, and all expectation of the Spirit's
influence for this end is denied as enthusiasm'.[4] There are those
who 'value themselves on the opposition they give to what they
call enthusiasm',[5] but they are, in fact, really rejecting the true
emphasis of the primitive and reformed Church.

If to insist upon the inner witness of the Spirit is the reason why
so many would brand him an 'enthusiast', Simeon is content to be
so branded. At the same time, he is aware that there is a claim to
the witness of the Spirit which is false and fatal. 'There is such a
thing as enthusiasm: and it is by no means uncommon for persons
to mistake some feelings or conceit of their own for the sanctifying
influences of the Spirit of God.'[6]

[1] Vol. 14, p. 38.
[2] Vol. 6, p. 479. Cf., vol. 3, pp. 518, 519; cf., also, 'Lay not too great a stress
on some transient emotions: but judge yourselves by the most certain test of a
willing and unreserved obedience' (vol. 1, pp. 413, 414).
[3] University Sermon, 'Means of Attaining True Wisdom,' vol. 16, p. 1.
[4] Vol. 6, p. 306.
[5] Vol. 7, p. 137.
[6] Vol. 1, p. 491.

This mistaken enthusiasm arises from two main errors. Firstly, it is false to suppose that because the Holy Spirit gave the early disciples powers to work miracles, therefore, His presence, in these days, will produce the same results. According to Simeon the miracles are finished. They have fulfilled their purpose in authenticating the gospel and in vindicating Christ's claim to be the Messiah. We have now the abiding testimony to these facts in the inspired records so that the need for continued miracles has passed. It is a fallacy into which some have fallen to conclude that the possession of the Spirit means the performance of extraordinary works. 'We willingly concede', he writes, 'that it would be enthusiastic and absurd in us to expect the miraculous influences which were vouchsafed to the early disciples.'[1]

A clear distinction must consequently be drawn between the miraculous activity of the Holy Spirit in the early Church and the illuminating action of the same Spirit in the present Church. In the one case the Holy Spirit came as an occasional visitant: in the other He comes as a continual resident. 'We are not to expect the miraculous aid of the Holy Spirit, but a gracious influence we may expect.'[2]

Then, secondly, trouble arises when the influence of the Spirit is made to, or better, perhaps, is thought to operate apart from the word. It may be ideally true to assert that God can act without the word. Taken in the abstract it may be right to say, 'It becomes not us to restrict God in the use of means.'[3] God may, if He see fit, speak directly to man by dreams and visions. He has done so in the past.[4] There is, however, no reliable evidence that He does so now. Simeon confesses that he is not partial to the claim to the activity and guidance of God's Spirit arising from such means. It can only lead, he thinks, to certain delusion.

There is no reason, Simeon teaches, why God should speak in this special way. He has given His word to the world, and all that is needed now is for the Spirit to illuminate that word. He thus

[1] Vol. 13, p. 84.
[2] Vol. 20, p. 569. Cf., 'To have the Spirit is not to have those miraculous powers, which were given in the apostolic age . . . but . . . those special influences of the Spirit, whereby men are enlightened and transformed into the divine image' (vol. 15, pp. 205, 206).
[3] Vol. 20, p. 37.
[4] Cf., vol. 1, p. 482; vol. 20, p. 37, cf., 'We can place no confidence in any special manifestations which are professedly derived from such sources. We may also say that nothing certain can be known from any direct impression of the Spirit of God upon the mind' (vol. 5, p. 482).

says emphatically, 'It is by the Scriptures that the Holy Spirit speaks to men.'[1] This for Simeon is the safeguard against all false enthusiasm. Let this be understood and all occasion for wild excesses and fantastic claims has been taken away. Of one thing we are to be sure, not only does the Spirit not speak contrary to the word, but He does not really speak apart from it. By other means He may indeed call attention to the word, but it is in and by the word only that the Spirit bring us to the knowledge of God.[2]

The conclusion is this: 'We are therefore to submit to the teaching of God's word and Spirit. To this advice it may be objected, that we promote an enthusiastic dependence on divine impulses . . . We should indeed promote enthusiasm, if we exhorted anyone to follow impulses that were independent of the written word: but if we recommend all persons to regulate their sentiments *solely* by the written word, and to rely on the influence of the Holy Spirit *no further than they accord with that*, then neither we, nor they, are in any danger of enthusiasm: because the sacred oracles are an unalterable standard to which every thought and action may be brought, and by which its quality may be infallibly determined.'[3]

It is a false enthusiasm, then, to go beyond what is written. Some have laid claim to a revelation of which even the apostles knew nothing. They have attributed to the influence of the Holy Spirit that which has been the very antithesis of His presence. They have sometimes credited to the Spirit of God actions which are the very work of the devil. 'A person of warm imagination and a confident mind can easily be wrought upon by that subtle spirit, so that he shall appear both to himself and others to be eminently distinguished by manifestations from God, whilst yet he is only under the influence of a Satanic delusion.'[4]

It is an evidence of a false enthusiasm to assert that God has communicated a truth in some special manner, by a dream, for example, or a vision, when that truth is already made known in the written oracles of God. What is so written is sufficient; and, since the canon of Scripture is now closed, there is no reason for, as there is no possibility of, such special information to be made known to select individuals. God has nothing further to add to His word.

[1] Vol. 21, p. 499.   [2] Vol. 20, p. 38.
[3] Vol. 16, p. 131.   [4] Vol. 5, p. 482.

'There are enthusiasts in the world' he writes, 'who will persuade themselves that they are God's people, because they have had a revelation of it from heaven or a dream whereby it has been made known to them . . . I will not say that God *may* not reveal to man as he pleases: but I will say, that we have no reason to expect that God will make known to us by revelation anything, which without such a miraculous interpretation, may be easily and safely deduced from his blessed word.'[1]

It is true enough that with some the inner witness of the Spirit is more strongly realized than with others. Their experience is so vivid that it might almost seem as if the Spirit of God acted directly. So dramatic is His action, in some cases, that it appears to those to whom it comes, as if the Holy Spirit brought a new and personal revelation. Even in the case of one's own experience, one receives an 'immediate impression', 'imparted in a more instantaneous manner, and in a higher degree at some times than at others.'[2] However true this may be, Simeon is quite sure that the Spirit's testimony is not given without any reference to the Scriptures.

There is therefore a true and a false enthusiasm. In that which is true Simeon will rejoice since therein lies that which completes within the individual the revelation which God has given. It is by the inner action of the Spirit that the outward revelation of the word is realized. Thus a mere assent to objective doctrines is inadequate. It may lead to 'orthodoxy' but it is not the true 'fiduciary' faith of the New Testament.

On the other hand, the claim to the leading of the Spirit apart from the word results in a false enthusiasm. This is both a delusion and a vain conceit.

This means that there must be certain criteria whereby the true can be distinguished from the false. In one passage the special characteristics of both are drawn together. 'I grant', he says, 'that there are enthusiasts who pretend to such impulses and such communications as the Scriptures do not warrant us to expect . . . but we must not despise those manifestations which God does vouchsafe to his people, because there are enthusiasts who profess to have experienced more.'[3] 'We apprehend then' he goes on to state later, 'that the genuine experience of communion with Christ

---

[1] Vol. 13, pp. 455, 456, cf., p. 494.
[2] Vol. 15, p. 284.
[3] Vol. 13, p. 167.

may be distinguished from enthusiastic pretentions to it, both by its rise, and its operations on the mind. Enthusiasts found their pretentions on some visions or dreams, or on the word of God coming in a peculiar manner to their minds.'[1] As a result they are elated to presumptuous confidence and spiritual delusion.[2]

It is of the greatest importance then, both for the individual and for the Church, to be able to clearly understand the nature of false enthusiasm. The difference between this and the true is worked out by Simeon under three headings. First, by 'what preceded it'. In the case of true enthusiasm there is a conviction of 'our lost estate'. Then, secondly, by 'what accompanies it'; it is the very essence of the true to inspire humility. Thirdly, by 'what follows it'. 'Manifestations of God to the soul always produce zeal in his service; victory over sin; and a longing for the enjoyment of him in heaven; but supineness, subjection to evil tempers, and a "forgetfulness" of the eternal world, generally characterize the self-deceiving professor.'[3]

Simeon has, then, a very definite doctrine of revelation. He finds it contained and confined within, what he constantly refers to as the 'oracles of God', or the 'inspired volume'. Yet complete as the word is in itself, it is not sufficient by itself. There must be, in addition to the objective revelation in the word, the subjective illumination of the Spirit. Mere assent to the doctrines of the objective revelation in the word is not the faith of the gospel, while a claimed impression of the Spirit, apart from the word, is only an enthusiastic conceit. Thus, for Simeon, revelation is to be found IN the word THROUGH the Spirit.

Two main criticisms have been directed against the doctrine of revelation just outlined. Some have felt that by confining revelation within the Bible there is a consequent detraction from the absolute and unique self-disclosure of God in Christ. Revelation, therefore, it is maintained in opposition, is not found in written words but in the Word absolutely, that is, in the living Person of Christ. It has been seen that in the case of the 'orthodox' there was a real danger of making revelation a matter of propositions and of missing the

---

[1] Vol. 13, ibid.

[2] Cf., 'Enthusiasts put their vain conceits in the place of the word and have presumed to call their own feelings or fancies by the sacred appellation of a promise,' Funeral Sermon for Hon. the Rev. Wm Bromley Cadogon, late St Giles, Reading, Jan. 29th, 1797.

[3] Vol. 15, p. 285.

divine Person of Christ. Simeon, however, it must be acknowledged, was at pains to stress the absoluteness and uniqueness of
Christ. His theme was, as Dean Howson suggests, the pre-
eminence of Christ. On the other hand, as we have seen, he was
aware of the uselessness of a mere knowledge of the letter of
Scripture. The Bible was, of course, for Simeon, objectively and
fully the word of God, yet it was only as one encountered, through
the illumination of the Spirit, the living Word within the written
word that the divine revelation was completed within the soul.
This is well brought out in a passage quoted earlier, but here
repeated because of its relevance to the question; the words are a
summary of his point of view. 'First, then,' he declares, 'it is not
the word that does good; but the Holy Spirit by the Word . . . .
Next, it is not the knowledge of the word that benefits, but the
knowledge of Christ in the record. We might be able to repeat the
whole Bible and perish at the last . . . .'[1] He sees Christ as the 'soul'
of the Bible. Simeon would, we think, agree with the idea of
revelation as the action of God within history. As he sees it God
did act dramatically and revealingly in the history of Israel and in
the events of Christ's life. But for Simeon these acts of God in
history, of which we have the divinely inspired record become
God's saving acts in individual experience by the action of the Holy
Ghost in and through the word.

The other criticism, later directed against the view-point of
Simeon was that he was ignorant of the newer understanding of
biblical history. He lived at a period when what later came to be
called 'higher criticism' was in its infancy; when, indeed, it was
really operative amongst those outside the Church. Had Simeon
lived later, would he have modified his position regarding the
Scriptures? The question is, of course, purely a hypothetical one.
But we think the answer would be emphatically, No. There is
evidence throughout the twenty-one volumes of his works that he
was not unacquainted with the direction in which things were
moving. There are passages, indeed, in which he specifically rejects the criticism of Bible history, which, in his day, was mainly
associated with deistic scepticism. He will not admit to the altering
of the 'events' of the history to fit into preconceived philosophical
principles. Event and interpretation belong together. If the interpretation is to be taken as valid then, too, the history must be

[1] Vol. 10, pp. 284, 285.

regarded as authentic. This seems to be the point of view taken by Simeon; and it does mean for him, as it did mean for all those who followed the same understanding of revelation, that the biblical events are divinely given and that no human reconstruction of them is admissible.

CHAPTER IX

THE DOCTRINE OF A LEADER

U nder this heading, 'The Doctrine of a Leader,' attention is to be directed to John Wesley's understanding of revelation. It is neither necessary nor fitting for us to enter upon any details of a life the influence of which is stamped indelibly upon the passing centuries. Account will be taken, therefore, of his character and career only in so far as they may illustrate and illuminate the subject with which we are concerned. Wesley's particular understanding of revelation may be placed under the caption

REVELATION BY THE SPIRIT AND THROUGH THE WORD

Stating it in this way it will be seen that Wesley's doctrine is in harmony with, and yet contrasts with that of Charles Simeon. Both Wesley and Simeon equated revelation with the Scriptures. They were agreed that the Bible alone contained the revelation of God. Yet, whereas Simeon put the emphasis upon the adequacy of the word used by the Spirit, Wesley placed it upon the action of the Spirit Who uses the word. Thus while they were alike in their estimate of the Scriptures, they differed in their emphasis upon the Spirit.

Coming then to Wesley's own statement of his position, it will be our first concern to refer to

(i) *The Source of Wesley's Faith*

A similar attitude to the Scriptures prevailed throughout the eighteenth century amongst those who have been described as 'orthodox Churchmen' as well as those designated Evangelicals. Although the Evangelicals gave expression to what has been called a 'Bible-religion' as distinct from the 'Church-religion' of the orthodox, the place given to the Scriptures was in each case the same.

John Wesley was, in his early life, a 'high Churchman' and as

R

such was ordained to the ministry. Yet even before his conversion
he is to be found proclaiming the sufficiency of the Scriptures and
warning against adding to them.[1]

Such then was the understanding of the Bible to which Wesley
was heir and to which he remained faithful. His opponents
imagined, however, that by stressing the action of the Holy Spirit,
he was somehow undermining the authority of the Bible. This is
clearly indicated in his letter to the Rev. Mr Potter. In his criticism
of Wesley, Potter had written: 'But the Scriptures are a complete
and a sufficient rule. Therefore to what purpose could any further
inspiration serve? All further inspiration is unnecessary: the supposed need of it is highly injurious to the written word. And the
pretension thereto, (which must be either to explain, or to supply it)
is a wicked presumption with which Satan hath filled their hearts
to lie to the Holy Ghost.'[2]

Wesley replies that his teaching about the Holy Spirit is in no
way detrimental to the Scriptures. Be the Scriptures, he says, ever
so complete they will not save your soul. There must be, therefore, in
addition to the revelation in the book, a revelation within the breast.

After the experience in Aldersgate Street, Wesley's attitude to
the Bible did not change. What did change was his understanding
of the action of the Spirit. It is to be observed that in the sermon to
which reference has been made, 'On Corrupting the Word of God,'
preached before that decisive day, there is no allusion to the Spirit
of God. It is, perhaps, idle to discuss the source of this second
emphasis. Allowance must necessarily be made for Wesley's
earlier contact with the Moravians. It is well known that they spoke
much about the 'witness within'. It may be that Wesley naturally
borrowed their phraseology. But when every acknowledgement has
been made, is it not more to the point to see Wesley's later expressions concerning the action of the Spirit as an interpretation of
the experience which came to him on that momentous day when his
heart was 'strangely warmed'?

(ii) *The Statement of Wesley's Teaching*
(a) *Reason and Revelation*

In his statement concerning the place of reason in life and re-

---

[1] 'On Corrupting the Word of God,' cxxx, vol. 11, p. 93 ff. (*The Works of the
Rev. John Wesley*, edited by Joseph Benson, 15 vols., 1809.)
[2] Quoted by Wesley in his Letter to Rev. Mr Potter (sect. 17), vol. 13, p. 80.

ligion Wesley was aware of the contrary extremes of deism and mysticism abroad in his day.

Nothing, he believed, was so contradicted by the facts of experience as the Cartesian assumption that reason is equal in all men. Knowledge is obviously, in some measure, conditioned by geographical location. The condition of some people is such that 'to compare them with horses or any of our domestic animals would be doing them too much honour'.[1] The dispensations of God's grace, like His providence, have resulted in the light of civilization having come to some and not to others. The realities of experience give no justification to the deist's optimism. The fact of inequality follows from the operation of God's mysterious ruling and cannot be used as an objection against revelation. Pressed as an argument, it would tell with equal force against natural religion, and the result would be 'flat Atheism'. 'It would conclude, not only against the Christian Revelation, but against the Being of God.'[2] The inequalities of life are not its injustices, since the reason for them lies in the mysterious purposes of God. The sure fact is that times and seasons are in His hands.

But while the deist exalts reason to the throne as the absolute monarch, mysticism abases it to the dust and will not even recognize it as an unprofitable servant. 'Among them that despise and vilify reason, you may always expect to find those Enthusiasts, who suppose the dreams of their own imagination to be revelations from God.'[3]

The Golden Mean

Wesley seeks a *via media* between these two extremes. Reason must be neither overrated nor undervalued. 'So much easier is it to run from East to West, than to stop at the middle point!'[4] It is Wesley's purpose in the sermon from which quotation has been previously made to prove that we know in part.[5] The desire for knowledge is universal, but the possession of it is a different matter. There are limits beyond which none can go however much he may wish to do so.

With this premised Wesley goes on to specify these limits. He sees man as a half-blinded spectator in a universe of mystery. The

[1] 'The Imperfections of Human Knowledge,' lxxiv, ii, sect. 7, vol. 9, p. 318.
[2] Ibid., iii, sect. 2.
[3] 'The Case of Reason Considered,' lxxv, Intro., sect. 2, vol. 9, p. 324.
[4] Ibid, sect. 3.
[5] 'The Imperfections of Human Knowledge.'

depths of the earth, the bounds of the world, the distance of the stars, are all beyond his penetration.[1] The true 'esse' of things familiar is unknown. What is it that makes a metal to differ from a stone? or one metal from another? or gold from silver? or tin from lead? 'Are microscopic Animals, so called, *real* Animals or not?'[2] Do not these things 'elude our utmost diligence?'[3]

When from the sentient world we turn to the spiritual our knowledge is infinitely less. How can we grasp such high realities? Here, for example, we can raise questions concerning the soul but we cannot answer them, What is it? Where is it? Such problems as these none can solve. 'Here we are at a full stop.'[4] What about God's works of providence; 'It is a childish conceit to suppose chance governs the world.'[5] Yet when we come to contemplate the superintending activity of God what insoluble problems are on our hands. There is the fact of inequality arising from education and civilization. There is apparent partiality. Who can explain such mysteries as these? And then God Himself in the reality of His being and essence is beyond the discovery of human knowledge. 'How astonishingly little we know of God! How small a part of His nature do we know! of His essence and attributes!'[6] The deist talks glibly about knowing God through nature, when he hardly knows nature. ''Tis mystery all.'[7]

And man himself is a mystery. The ancients counselled us, 'Know thyself.' But who can understand the secrets of his own being? Here is a mechanism too intricate for us to trace out. Within our own being there are depths we can never plumb. 'How shall we comprehend the ever-blessed God, when we cannot comprehend ourselves?'[8]

While, however, knowledge is thus partial and imperfect, Wesley, like Butler, will not 'vilify reason'. He will not go to the other extreme. He acknowledges with some shame his earlier attachment to Luther's *Commentary on the Epistle to the Galatians*,

---

[1] Cf., 'How small a part of this great work of God (i.e. creation) is man able to understand!' 'God's Approbation of His Works,' lx, Intro., sect. 2, vol. 9, p. 132. Again, 'As to the internal parts of the earth, even to this day, we scarcely have any knowledge of them,' op. cit., i, sect. 3.
[2] 'The Imperfection of Human Knowledge,' i, sect. 11, p. 314.
[3] Ibid.
[4] Op. cit., i, sect. 13, p. 315.
[5] Op. cit., i, sect. 1, p. 316.
[6] Op. cit., i, sect. 1, p. 309.
[7] Op. cit., i, sect. 11, p. 314.
[8] *Thoughts on Memory*, vol. 15, p. 389.

which he now finds 'deeply tinctured with mysticism throughout'.[1] Referring to Luther, Wesley adds, 'How does he (almost in the words of Tauler) decry *reason*, right or wrong, as the irreconcilable enemy of the Gospel of Christ! whereas, what is reason, (the Faculty, so called) but the power of apprehending, judging, and discovering? which power is no more to be condemned in the gross, than seeing, hearing or feeling.'[2]

Wesley deals with those who 'overvalue' reason. There are those who 'extol it to the skies', and consider it to be 'the highest gift of God'.[3] Such believe that this 'all-sufficient Director of all the children of men' can guide into all truth and lead into all virtue.[4] With these 'overraters' of reason, Wesley links 'men of eminently strong understanding, who because they know more than most men, suppose they can know all things'.[5] It is on this ground that they reject the Christian revelation and repudiate the Scriptures as the oracles of God.[6]

To these 'overraters' and 'applauders' of reason, Wesley has some decisive points to make. 'Reason', he urges, 'cannot produce faith.'[7] He tells us that he himself drew together from the ancients and moderns the strongest arguments for the existence and being of God, but they had not carried conviction to his heart. They had left him bewildered; and instead of creating faith, actually led to unbelief.[8] Hobbes was, without question, a man of strong understanding; 'But', asks Wesley, 'did it produce in him a full, a satisfactory conviction of an invisible world? Did it open his understanding to see

"Beyond the bounds of this diurnal sphere"?'[9]

To these questions Wesley returns an unhesitating, 'No!' Not only is reason helpless to produce faith, it is equally useless in creating hope, or love, or happiness. Such then being the inadequacy of reason there is no ground left for boasting in its supremacy.

This does not mean, however, that reason is therefore to be undervalued. It is a 'precious gift of God'.[10] For Wesley, as for the Cambridge Platonists, it is the candle of the Lord.[11] Wesley was, in

---

[1] *Journal*, June 15, 1741.   [2] *Journal*, June 15, 1741.
[3] 'The Case of Reason Considered,' lxxv, Intro., sect. 3.
[4] Ibid.   [5] Op. cit. sect. 4.
[6] Ibid.   [7] Op. cit., ii, sect. 1.
[8] Op. cit., ii, sect. 2.   [9] Op. cit., ii, sect. 4.
[10] Op. cit., ii, sect. 10.
[11] Ibid.

fact, reproached from two sides. Those who stressed 'faith' believed
he made too much of reason. In a passage in his *Journal* he refers
to those who demanded belief without solid reasons. They say of
him, 'Your carnal reason destroys you. You are for reason: I am for
faith.' Wesley answers, 'I am for both: for faith to perfect my
reason: that by the Spirit of God not putting out the eyes of my
understanding, but enlightening them more and more, I may be
ready to give a clear, scriptural answer to every man that asketh me
a reason of the hope that is in me.'[1]

On the other hand, those who stressed reason condemned
Wesley as irrational. In a letter to the Regius Professor of Divinity
at Cambridge, Wesley denies the charge. 'You go on: "It is a
fundamental principle of the Methodist school that all who come
into it must renounce their reason." ' 'Sir,' replies Wesley, 'are you
awake? Unless you are talking in your sleep, how can you utter so
gross an untruth? It is a fundamental principle with us that to
renounce reason is to renounce religion, that religion and reason go
hand in hand, and that all irrational religion is false religion.'[2]

The Sphere in which Reason Operates

It is within the sphere of revelation that reason operates. It is the
means whereby the truths of God are apprehended and assured.
Man's rationality is the 'point of contact' for the divine revelation.
This means that faith will be 'always consistent with reason'.[3] This
is the assumption of his *Earnest Appeal to Men of Reason and
Religion*. Anyone who departs from true and genuine reason,
Wesley asserts, departs from Christianity. He is willing, indeed, to
join with those 'desiring a religion founded on reason and every
way agreeable thereto'.[4]

If reason in this context means 'the nature of things' then we
may be assured that Christianity is in complete harmony with the
essential rationality of existence. The Christian man is therefore
the really rational man. On the other hand, if by reason is meant
'the faculty of reasoning, of inferring one thing from another',[5]
then he can still address himself to men of reason. It is 'those who
are styled mystic divines'[6] who would renounce the use of reason.

[1] *Journal*, Nov. 27, 1750 (Thurs.), (In 'Letter to an Old Friend').
[2] *Selected Letters of John Wesley*, edited by Frederick C. Gill, No. 126.
[3] 'The Case of Reason Considered,' ii, sect. 1.
[4] *An Earnest Appeal*, sect. 28, vol. 12, p. 11.
[5] Ibid.   [6] Op. cit., sect. 30.

But there is no authority for such renunciation in Holy Writ.[1] After Christ, the apostle Paul was the strongest reasoner.

At the same time Wesley insists that reason must have its ποῦ στῶ. It must have material upon which to work. He accepts the epistemology which holds that knowledge comes by the way of the senses. 'For many years it has been allowed by sensible men, *Nihil est in intellectu quod non prius in sensu* .... All the knowledge which we naturally have, is originally derived from the senses.'[2] There are no innate ideas. In his Remarks on Mr Locke's *Essay on the Human Understanding* Wesley makes it clear that he agrees with Locke's doctrine of the '*tabula rasa*'.

But if the human reason works upon data provided by the human senses to give human knowledge, then, by analogy, it is only a divinely enlightened reason working upon the material provided by the 'spiritual', or as Wesley also calls them, the 'internal' senses, which give us spiritual knowledge. A 'new set of senses (so to speak) is opened in our soul'.[3] Wesley illustrates his point by what he calls a 'trite instance'.[4] It is only those who have the sense of sight who can reason about colours, 'so you cannot reason concerning spiritual things if you have no spiritual sight; because all your ideas received by your outward senses are of a different kind.'[5]

The external senses cannot provide the spiritual material upon which the reason can operate. This material is furnished by the internal senses only, and when so supplied there can be no limit to the activity of reason. 'We therefore not only allow', says Wesley, 'but earnestly exhort all who seek after religion to use all their reason which God hath given them in searching out the things of God.'[6]

It is in this context that Wesley repudiates Dodwell's *Christianity Not Founded on Argument*. It was maintained by Dodwell that Christianity is contrary to reason. For Wesley nothing could be further from the truth. It is the very glory of the gospel to liberate and elevate man's natural faculties. Those whose minds were darkened have been enlightened by the gospel. They have new spiritual 'matter' upon which to work. Faith gives the new

[1] Ibid.
[2] 'On the Discoveries of Faith,' cxiv, Intro., sect. 1, vol. 10, p. Cf., no. 8 'Difference of Walking by Sight and Faith,' cxv, sect. 7, vol. 10, p. 381; O '3 Faith,' cxxiii, sect. 18. Vol. 11, p. 37.
[3] 'On Faith,' cxxiii, sect. 18, vol. 11, p. 37.
[4] *An Earnest Appeal*, sect. 34.
[5] Ibid.　　　　　　　　　　[6] Op. cit., sect. 31.

spiritual content and the enlightened reason makes the new constructions. Reason consequently becomes the handmaiden of faith and the servant of revelation. 'God did not take away your understanding but enlightened and strengthened it.'[1] At the same time the understanding of faith is not the discovery of even the enlightened reason. God sheds His light into the native darkness of the mind, 'and we then see, not by a chain of *reasoning* but by a kind of *intuition*, by a direct view.'[2]

Reason in the Natural Man

The unenlightened reason of the natural man, however, is helpless within the spiritual sphere. 'For his soul is in a deep sleep. His spiritual senses are not awake: they discern neither spiritual good or evil. The eyes of his understanding are closed; they are sealed together, and see not. . . . Hence, having no inlets for knowledge of spiritual things, all the avenues of the soul are shut up, he is in gross, stupid ignorance of whatever he is most concerned to know. He is utterly ignorant of God, knowing nothing concerning him as he ought to know. He is a total stranger to its true, inward, spiritual teaching.'[3]

In a sermon, 'On the Education of Children,' he goes further and denies that there are any innate ideas of God at all: 'it does not appear, that man has naturally any more idea of God than any of the beasts of the field: he has no knowledge of God at all: neither is God in all his thoughts.'[4] Apart from early instruction, he elsewhere asserts, children 'would have no more knowledge of God than the beasts of the field, than the wild ass's colt. Such is natural religion! abstracted from traditional, and from the influences of God's Spirit'.[5] We are by nature, he tells us, 'ἄθεοι, Atheists in the world.'[6]

There are declarations of man's natural helplessness with which the most extreme Calvinist could not quarrel. In spite of his 'boasted reason' man has 'no pre-eminence over the goats'.[7] He is

[1] 'The General Spread of the Gospel,' lxviii, sect. 11, vol. 9, pp. 236, 237.
[2] 'The End of Christ's Coming,' lxviii, sect. 11, vol. 9, pp. 236, 237.
[3] 'Spirit of Bondage and Adoption,' ix, i, sect. i, vol. 9, p. 230. Cf., 'The Circumcision of the Heart,' xvii, Intro., sects. 2, 3, vol. 7, pp. 241, 242. 'The New Birth,' xxi, ii, sect. 4, vol. 7, p. 297, etc., etc.
[4] 'On the Education of Children,' c, sect. 5, vol. 10, p. 208.
[5] 'On Original Sin,' xx, ii, sect. 4, vol. 7, p. 284.
[6] 'On Dissipation,' lxxxiv, sect. 7, vol. 10, p. 3. Cf., 'On Original Sin.' ii, sect. 3.
[7] 'On Original Sin,' ii, sect. 9.

'totally corrupted'.[1] The original likeness to God has been de-stroyed. Man has 'lost both the knowledge and the love of God, without which the image of God could not subsist'.[2] Every single individual has 'totally lost, not only the favour, but likewise the image of God'.[3]

The result of all this is to make the natural man completely impotent. This is a point continually stressed. 'Our nature is altogether corrupt, in every power and faculty. And our will de-praved equally with the rest, is wholly bent to indulge our natural corruption.'[4] We are 'so utterly dead, that "in me dwelleth no good thing", that I am inclined to all evil, and totally unable to quicken my own soul'.[5] 'No power by nature, and no merit in man'; this was the grand principle with which the Oxford friends set out, Wesley declares in his funeral sermon on the death of Whitfield.[6]

In spite of these uncompromising statements, however, Wesley insists that there are truths of natural religion which the heathen are required to believe. He makes this point, for instance, in a sermon on 'Salvation by Faith'. 'Now God requireth a heathen to believe', he says, 'that God is: that he is a rewarder of them that diligently seek him; and that he is to be sought by glorifying him as God, by giving him thanks for all things: and by a careful practice of moral virtue of justice, mercy, and truth towards his fellow-creatures. A Greek or Roman, therefore, yea, a Sythian or Indian, was without excuse if he did not believe this much: The Being and Attributes of God, a Future State of Rewards and Punishments, and the Obligatory Nature of Moral Virtue.'[7]

Notwithstanding this 'black-out' of man's reason by the light-quenching power of sin, Wesley believed that there remained in human nature that which could respond to God. He maintained that man *qua* man is *capax Dei*. In one sermon, for example, he

---

[1] Op. cit., ii, sect. 2, etc.

[2] 'The New Birth,' xxi, i, sect. 2, vol. 7, p. 294.

[3] 'The Heavenly Treasure in Earthen Vessels,' cxxv, Intro., sect. 2, vol. 11, p. 49.

[4] 'On Self-Denial,' li, i, sect. 3, vol. 8, p. 359.

[5] 'On the Discoveries of Faith,' cxiv, sect. 5, vol. 10, p. 382. Cf., 'On Working out our own Salvation,' xc, iii, sect. 2, vol. 10, p. 82, etc., etc.

[6] 'Funeral Sermon on the Death of Mr Whitfield,' Sunday, Nov. 18, 1770, lvi, iii, sect. 2, vol. 9, p. 13.

[7] 'Salvation by Faith,' i, i, sect. 1, vol. 7, p. 8. Cf., 'Some great truths, as the Being and Attributes of God, and the difference between moral Good and Evil, were known, in some measure, to the Heathen world, the traces of these are found in all nations.' 'On Working out Our Own Salvation,' xc, Intro., sect. i, vol. 10, p. 75.

refers on several occasions to man as 'a creature capable of God'.[1]
It is this capacity for God which calls forth God's response in self-
disclosure. Reason is so utterly incompetent that man can only
know God as God draws aside the curtain and comes forth to be
known in the apprehension of faith. Little of the visible world is
known to the natural reason; less of the invisible. But the 'Author
of both worlds' has given us more than could be discovered by
natural reason: 'without Revelation how little certainty of the
invisible things did the wisest of men obtain! The smallest
glimmerings of light which they had were merely conjectural. At
best they were only a faint, dim twilight, delivered from uncertain
traditions; and so obscured by heathen fables, that it was but one
degree better than utter darkness.'[2]

But God has met the crying need of the human heart. He has
made a sufficient revelation of Himself and set it forth in secure
form in the Oracles of God. Here are the data for the spiritual
senses, and material for the enlightened reason.

Enlightened Reason not Absolute

Yet the reason enlightened by the Holy Ghost does not assure
complete knowledge. Wesley stresses this in a sermon on 'Christian
Perfection'. Christians are not perfect in knowledge, 'they know,
with regard to the world to come, the general truths which God
hath revealed.'[3] They know they are loved of God, and they are
aware of the working of the Spirit in their hearts, and the duties
God requires of them. 'But innumerable are the things they know
not.'[4] It is beyond them to fathom the perfection of God, the inner
nature of the Trinity, the mystery of the Incarnation, the workings
of the divine providence. Christians cannot say when God having
'accomplished the number of the elect, will hasten his kingdom'.[5]
There is much concerning God, like His omnipresence, 'too vast to
be comprehended by the narrow limits of human understanding.'[6]

The Christian is not only not free from ignorance, he is also not
free from error.[7] However the Christian may rise in the scale of

---

[1] 'The Great Deliverance,' lxv, i, sects. 2, 5, iii, 6, 11, vol. 9, pp. 192, 193, 200,
202. Cf., 'The Deceitfulness of Man's Heart,' cxxiv, i, sect. 2, vol. 11, p. 42.
[2] 'On Faith,' cxxiii, sect. 15, vol. 11, p. 36.
[3] 'Christian Perfection,' xlii, i, sect. 1, vol. 8, p. 215.
[4] Op. cit., sect. 2, vol. 8, p. 215.
[5] Op. cit., sect. 2, vol. 8, p. 215 1.
[6] 'God's Omnipotence,' xlvii, i, sect. 2, vol. 8, p. 304.
[7] 'Christian Perfection,' i, sect. 4.

spiritual experience he never becomes all-knowing. 'The highest perfection which man can attain, while the soul dwells in the body, does not exclude ignorance and error, and a thousand other infirmities.'[1] But this acknowledgement of the presence of ignorance and error does not mean that there is no confidence or certainty, since 'the children of God do not mistake, as to the things essential to salvation'.[2] This means that there can be difference of opinion in many things. None can claim to possess all the truth. In things essential knowledge is sure, but in things unessential to salvation Christians can and do err frequently.

There are even different interpretations of the Scripture among those who are, without doubt, 'born of God'. Such difference of opinion, however, is no proof, 'that they are not children of God on either side. But it is a proof that we are no more to expect any living man to be *infallible*, than to be omniscient.'[3]

It is impossible for all men to think alike. There are differences due to education and environment; to capacity and to country. Still 'though we cannot think alike, may we not love alike?'[4] Here, indeed, 'is the sum of Christian Perfection; it is all comprehended in that word, Love.'[5]

(b) Revelation and Scripture

For Wesley God's special revelation is equated with the Bible which he regards as the oracles of God.[6] 'I really believe the Bible to be the Word of God,' he says with evident emphasis.[7] 'According to the light *we* have, we cannot but believe the Scripture is of God; and, while we believe this, we dare not turn aside from it, to the right hand or to the left.'[8]

By implication and by declaration Wesley leaves no doubt concerning his acceptance of the Scriptures, in their entirety, as the Word of God. There was none so bound by the Bible as Wesley.

[1] 'On Perfection,' lxxxi, i, sect. 3, vol. 9, p. 399. Cf., 'The Catholic Spirit,' xli, i, sects. 3, 4, vol. 8, p. 202.
[2] 'Christian Perfection,' i, sect. 4.
[3] Op. cit., sect. 5.
[4] 'The Catholic Spirit,' xli, Intro., sect. 4, vol. 8, p. 200.
[5] 'On Perfection,' lxxxi, i, sect. 4, vol. 9, p. 300.
[6] Cf., e.g. 'On Laying the foundation Stone of the New Chapel, Ap. 21, 1777,' liv, ii, sect. 2, vol. 8, p. 399. 'The Mystery of Iniquity,' lxvi, sect. 31, vol. 9, p. 217. 'The Signs of the Times,' lxxi, ii, sect. 10, vol. 9, p. 275. 'On Obedience to Pastors,' cii, ii, sect. 7, vol. 10, p. 234. *An Earnest Appeal*, sects. 6, 13, 46. *Further Appeal*, sect. 10.
[7] 'On Dissipation,' lxxxiv, sect. 16, vol. 10, p. 7.
[8] *An Earnest Appeal*, sect. 27.

He speaks of it 'as the History of God'.[1] Within its pages is set down 'a clear, concise and perfect account' of God's divine ordering. To preach Christ is to be linked and limited to the written word. '*To preach Christ*, is To Preach what God hath revealed either in the Old or New Testament.'[2]

Adherence to the divine record, is, he declares, the essential Protestant position. 'The faith of the Protestants, in general, embraces only those truths necessary to salvation which are clearly revealed in the Oracles of God. Whatever is plainly declared in the Old and New Testament is the object of their faith. They believe neither more or less, than what is manifestly contained in and proveable by the Holy Scriptures.'[3]

In reference to our Lord's parable of Dives and Lazarus, Wesley asserts, on the authority of the Bible, that there is everlasting torment for the unrepentant. 'I warn you in his name,' he says, 'that the Scriptures are the real word of God.'[4] Some, like the rich man, may demand a dramatic event to bring to a knowledge of God. Such a startling demonstration Wesley argues would be useless. Anyone wakened at night by what appeared the touch of a vanished hand and the sound of a voice that is still; awakened, that is, by one purporting to have come from beyond the grave, would, in the morning, dismiss the experience as a dream. Such happenings can have no faith-inspiring effect. The event would, possibly, leave no abiding influences. The Scripture, on the other hand, remains, 'That standing Revelation', it 'is the best means of rational conviction: far preferable to any of those extraordinary means which some imagine would be effectual. It is our wisdom therefore to avail ourselves of this; and to make a full use of it, so that it may be a lantern to our feet and a light in all our paths'.[5]

All through his ministry, Wesley emphasizes that his attitude to the Bible has not changed. He refers to the time when, at Oxford, four young men united together 'each one of them was *homo unius libri*, a man of one book'.[6] It was, in fact, this allegiance to the Bible which made them the object of derision. 'They were constantly reproached for this very thing; some terming them in

[1] 'On Divine Providence,' lxxii, Intro., sect. 4, vol. 9, p. 279.
[2] 'The Law Established through Faith,' xxxvii, i, sect. 2, vol. 8, p. 149.
[3] 'On Faith,' cx, i, sect. 8, vol. 10, p. 343.
[4] 'Dives and Lazarus,' xlviii, iii, sect. 2, vol. 8, p. 321.
[5] Op. cit., xlviii, iii, sect. 7, vol. 8, p. 322.
[6] 'God's Vineyard,' cxi, i, sect. 1, vol. 10, p. 349.

derision *Bible-bigots*; others, *Bible-moths*: feeding, they said, upon the Bible as moths do on cloth.'[1] Even before the event in Aldersgate Street he declared his purpose to abide by the Scriptures alone. After a conversation with Peter Böhler, on the nature of saving faith, he records, 'The next morning I began the Greek Testament again, resolving to abide by the Law and the Testimony.'[2] The passing years only confirmed him in his position. He was unshaken in his belief in the Bible as the embodiment of God's revelation. 'I will speak for one,' he says, 'after having sought for truth, with some diligence, for half a century, I am, at this day, hardly sure of anything, but what I learn from the Bible. Nay, I positively affirm, I *know* nothing else for certain, that I would dare to stake my salvation upon it.'[3]

God, then, has given to man certain information about the way to heaven. 'He has written it down in a book.' Thus the cry of Wesley's soul is, 'O give me that Book! At any price give me the book of God.'[4]

Such a position accorded by Wesley to the Bible means that it is for him an inspired and infallible volume.

Wesley, as far as we know, does not specify the method of inspiration. He is, however, very definite about the fact. A short article is boldly entitled: '*A Clear and Concise Demonstration of the Divine Inspiration of the Holy Scriptures.*' Miracles, prophecies, the goodness of its doctrines and the moral character of its penmen, are 'the four grand and powerful arguments which strongly induce us to believe that the Bible must be of God'.[5] Wesley sets out, what he conceives to be the only possibilities about the origin of the Scriptures. The Bible must be, he contends, the invention of good men or angels, bad men or devils, or of God. Good men or angels would never have prefaced their own statements with, 'Thus saith the Lord.' Bad men or devils, on the other hand, would not have originated a book which commands duty and forbids sin, and which, indeed, condemns their soul to eternal perdition. Thus the only possibility remaining is that the

---

[1] Ibid.
[2] *Journal*, Thurs., March 23, 1738. Cf., Fri., June 22, 1739. 'Second Letter to the Author of The Enthusiasm of the Methodists and Papists Compared,' vol. 13, pp. 37–8.
[3] 'The Good Steward,' xlvi, ii, sect. 7, vol. 8 ,pp. 292, 293.
[4] Preface to the *Works of John Wesley* by Joseph Benson, vol. 1, p. iv.
[5] *A Clear and Concise Demonstration of the Divine Inspiration of the Holy Scriptures*, vol. 15, p. 351.

Bible must be of God. 'Therefore, I draw this conclusion', Wesley adds, "That the Bible must be given by Divine Inspiration."[1]

This inspired book is, consequently, infallible. Wesley makes this point uncompromisingly in a passage in his *Journal*. He tells how on reading 'Mr Jenyng's admired tract, on the "Internal Evidences of the Christian Revelation" ', he was at a loss to know the writer's theology, 'whether he is a Christian, deist, or atheist.' He continues: 'If he is a Christian, he betrays his own cause by averring, that, "all Scripture is NOT given by inspiration of God; but the writers of it were sometimes left to themselves, and consequently made mistakes." Nay, if there be any mistakes in the Bible,' retorts Wesley, 'there may well be a thousand. If there be one falsehood in that book, it did not come from the God of truth.'[2]

But highly as Wesley regarded the Bible he still did not conceive of the faith of the gospel as a mere assent to its truth. Faith is, he teaches, more correctly to be defined as 'fiduciary'.[3] As such it is 'abundantly more than assent to the truth of the Bible'.[4] The devils, in fact, believe all that is written in the Bible.[5]

It is just here that Wesley sees the difference between his own position and those styled the 'orthodox'. But 'a man may be orthodox in every point', he may be zealous in the defence of right opinions, he 'may be almost as orthodox as the devil', and yet have no true religion.[6] Wesley refers to a time when he was himself ignorant of the nature of saving faith. He had then fondly imagined that it meant no more than a 'Firm assent to all the propositions contained in the Old and New Testament'.[7] Such a concep-

---

[1] Op. cit., ibid. Cf., 'In matters of Religion I regard no writings but the inspired . . . . In every part I appeal to the Law and the Testimony, and value no authority but this.' A 'Letter to Rev. Mr Law,' vol. 13, p. 340.

[2] *Journal*, Wed., July 24, 1776.

[3] *An Earnest Appeal*, sects. 58, 59.

[4] 'Second Letter to Mr Church,' vi, sect. 5, vol. 12, p. 396.

[5] Ibid. Cf., 'The Almost Christian,' ii, iii, sect. 5, vol. 7, p. 26, 'Marks of the New Birth,' xviii, i, sect. 2, vol. 7, p. 255. 'It is not, as some have fondly conceived, a bare assent to the truth of the Bible, of the articles of our creed, or all that is contained in the Old and New Testament,' 'The Way to the Kingdom,' vii, ii, sect. 10, vol. 7, p. 100. See also, 'Salvation by Faith,' 1, i, sect. 4, vol. 7, p. 9.

[6] 'The Way to the Kingdom,' vii, i, sect. 6, vol. 7, p. 92. Cf., 'A religion of Opinions or what is commonly called Orthodoxy . . . ,' 'On the Unity of the Divine Being,' cxvi, sect. 15, vol. 10, p. 404. Also '. . . right opinion, assent to one or ten thousand truths is not true religion'. 'On the Trinity,' lix, Intro., i, vol. 9, p. 123. Cf., further, 'Difference between Walking by Sight and Faith,' cxv, sect. 18, vol. 10, p. 397. 'The Danger of Riches,' xcii, ii, sect. 1, vol. 10, p. 109.

[7] *A Further Appeal*, 6, sect. 1, vol. 12, p. 122.

tion he came to see was false to the New Testament itself. Faith is a
relationship with a living Person and not allegiance to a set of
doctrines. Like Charles Simeon, Wesley sees the possibility of the
Bible becoming 'a dead letter'. The sacred oracles, he says, 'are a
mere *dead letter*, if they are "not mixed with faith in those that
hear them." '[1] There is no magic in the words of Scripture as such.
The power belongs, not to the volume, as a volume, but to the
actuating Spirit. 'We know', he says, 'that there is no inherent
power in the words that are spoken in prayer, (or) in the letter of
the Scripture read.'[2]

On the other hand, this must not be taken to mean that Wesley,
in any way, despised the very letter of Scripture. No one was at
more pains than he to seek out the specific meaning of every
word.[3] In a conversation with a woman in Birmingham who repudiated the need for sacraments, Wesley asked, 'Is the word of
God your rule?' She replied, 'Yes; the word made flesh: but not the
letter. I am in the Spirit.'[4] The notion was completely anathema to
Wesley. He had little regard for those who thus loosed themselves
from the divine revelation. Consequently, while he denounces
mere assent to the words of Scripture, he stresses the need for
those very words. 'I have declared again and again, that I make the
word of God the rule of all my actions: and that I no more follow
any "secret impulse" instead thereof, than I follow Mahomet or
Confucius.'[5]

(c) Scripture and the Spirit

True Christianity is, then, no mere speculative belief; it is
rather a 'feeling possession of God in the heart, wrought by the
Holy Ghost'.[6] This was one of the most important emphases of
Wesley. He insisted constantly upon the need for the inner operation of the Spirit of God. This was true heart religion in contrast
with the rational religion of the orthodox. So strongly did Wesley
feel on this point that he bluntly calls 'Anti-Christ' anyone who
denies the inspiration of the Holy Spirit or who would limit his

[1] 'On the Discoveries of Faith,' cxiv, Intro., sect. 4, vol. 10, p. 381, cf.,
'Marks of the New Birth,' xviii, i, sect. 5, vol. 7, p. 257. 'On Charity,' xcvi, ii,
sect. 2, vol. 10, p. 161.
[2] 'The Means of Grace,' xvi, sect. 3, vol. 7, p. 225.
[3] Cf., *An Address to the Clergy*.
[4] *Journal*, Sat., March 24, 1753.
[5] *Answer to Mr Church's 'Remarks'*, sect. 5, vol. 12, p. 318. Quoted again in a
Letter to the Bishop of London, sect. 5, vol. 12, p. 408.
[6] 'Free Grace,' lv, sect. 14, vol. 8, p. 413.

influence to the Apostles.[1] It was in this context that Wesley was induced to speak of the Montanists as the 'real, Scriptural Christians'.[2]

The correct question to put to anyone is not, Are you in agreement with the propositions of the Bible? or the doctrines of the Church? but rather, 'Hast thou the witness in thyself?'[3] In a number of passages he stresses that it is the Spirit's action that makes revelation inward and spiritual.[4]

Accordingly, he teaches, there is, in addition to the revelation of God in the Scriptures, need for a further revelation of Christ in our hearts. This demand for a dual unveiling of God he sets forth in a powerful sermon preached before his University.[5] Those who are under the influence of the Holy Spirit have 'the witness in themselves'. Such have little need, for what Wesley calls, a 'distant witness'.[6] While the manner of the Spirit's witness within cannot be understood, there is 'a revealing, unveiling, discovering to us' which can be 'known and felt'.[7] In addition to the 'outward call', there is besides, what Wesley refers to as an 'inward call, by (God's) Spirit applying his word'.[8]

In one of his discourses on the 'Law Established through Faith', Wesley declares that 'God by His word and His Spirit, is always with us'.[9] How far the two, the Word and the Spirit, associate, Wesley does not make clear. He is not as definite on this point as Charles Simeon. On the one hand, we find Wesley making a severe comment on Count Morsay, whom he regards as a thorough 'enthusiast'. He was guided 'in all his steps, not by the written word, but by his imagination, which he calls the Spirit'.[10] On the other hand, in a sermon on the 'Witness of the Spirit', he declares, 'The testimony of the Spirit, is an inward impression on the soul,

---

[1] 'Awake, Thou that Sleepest,' iii, iii, sect. 7, vol. 7, p. 39.
[2] *Journal*, Wed., Aug. 15, 1750. Cf., 'The Mystery of Iniquity,' lxvi, sect. 24, vol. 9, p. 213. 'The Witness of God's Counsels,' lxxiii, sect. 9, vol. 9, p. 297.
[3] 'Awake, Thou that Sleepest,' iii, ii, sect. 8, vol. 7, p. 35.
[4] Cf., 'The Privilege of the Children Born of God,' xix, iii, sect. 2, vol. 7, p. 277, 'On the Trinity,' lix, sect. 17, vol. 9, p. 131, 'Letter to Rev. Mr Potter,' vol. 13, p. 81, etc.
[5] 'The Circumcision of the Heart,' xvii, i, sect. 7, vol. 7, p. 245.
[6] *An Earnest Appeal*, sect. 61, vol. 12, p. 25.
[7] *Further Appeal*, sect. 6, vol. 12, p. 56.
[8] 'On Predestination,' lxii, sect. 12, vol. 9, p. 159.
[9] 'The Law Established through Faith,' xxxvii, i, sect. 6, vol. 8, p. 161.
[10] *Journal*, Tues., July 4, 1775. Cf., comment on the 'Life of Mr Morsay', Sat., July 4, 1778, 'he was a consummate enthusiast: not the word of God, but his own imaginations, which he took for divine inspirations, were the sole rule both of his words and actions.'

whereby the Spirit of God directly "witnesses to my spirit, that I am a child of God." [1] Twenty years later he repeats the point in almost identical words. There he speaks of the direct and immediate testimony of the Spirit. [2]

Such declarations as these, in which Wesley seemed to regard the Holy Ghost as acting apart from the Word gave apparent substance to the charge made against him that he was himself the real enthusiast. He certainly does appear to regard the Spirit's influence and inspiration as operative in a direct and immediate way. Putting the matter psychologically, it may be said that in this sense Wesley was an 'introvert'. We are, in fact, guilty of no anachronism in thus classifying him, for it may come as a surprise to some to find Wesley himself using the terms 'introversion' and 'extroversion', which Karl Jung has brought into such vogue. [3]

Wesley makes no apology for his insistence upon the inwardness of true religion. He therefore, for example, makes a spirited reply to Mr Shinstra who condemns his witness as fanaticism. According to Wesley Mr Shinstra would condemn true heart religion which is the working of the Spirit within. To repudiate inward feelings as his critic would, is to reduce religion to a dry, dead carcase. [4]

Wesley's constant references to the Spirit's influence, action and leading made him an easy target for those who, regarding themselves as correctly orthodox, dreaded anything that savoured of the zealous and the enthusiastic. Right from the moment when his heart was 'strangely warmed' John Wesley found himself a centre of controversy on the score of 'enthusiasm'. The news of his 'conversion' perplexed his relations and friends. It was received by his brother Samuel with a sense of bewilderment, not a little tinged with anger. He regarded John as having being smitten with a fatal attack of enthusiasm. He confesses fear of it, and adds, 'I heartily pray God to stop the progress of this lunacy .... What Jack means by his not being a Christian till last month I understand not.'

Straightaway his experience was written off as an excess of

---

[1] 'The Witness of the Spirit,' x, i, sect. 7, pp. 137, 138.

[2] 'The Witness of the Spirit,' xi, ii, sect. 2, vol. 7, p. 148.

[3] According to Wesley the words were used by the mystics. ' — the attending to the voice of Christ within you, is what they call, INTROVERSION. The turning of the eye of the mind from him to outward things they call, EXTROVERSION.' 'On Dissipation,' lxxxiv, sect. 21, vol. 10, p. 9.

[4] *Journal*, Mon. Aug. 12, 1771. Cf., Thurs., Aug. 24, 1780, Sun., Ap. 25, 1784, Thurs., May 13, 1784.

S

enthusiasm. Throughout the following years John Wesley found it necessary, again and again, to refute what he came to refer to as this 'thread-bare charge'.[1] His brilliant reply to Bishop Lavington shows how seriously he regarded the calumny. Lavington was a bishop of the typical Hanoverian style, 'fat, drowsy, contented, and as destitute of spiritual sense as a block of wood.' He looked upon the 'revival' with anger and terror, and released against Wesley a torrent of bitter accusations, each one of which Wesley patiently answered, with short, packed sentences, the best medium for his swift logic and lofty emotions. But Lavington was one only of a host who took up the cry. The mere appellation, 'Enthusiast', was considered sufficient reason in itself for discrediting Wesley and his message. Wesley, however, believed that he was only giving the rightful place and prominence to the operations of the Holy Spirit. He quotes extensively from the homilies of the Church to show how the emphasis upon the immediate inspiration of the Spirit is the official doctrine of the Church.[2]

What he has to say on this head is, he believes, common to all Christians in all ages. He confesses himself at a loss to understand how for so many years the charge of 'enthusiast' is trumped up. Its usage, he thinks, 'generally spares the objector the trouble of reasoning, and is a shorter and easier way of carrying his cause.'[3] Yet he only insists upon the need for the inner witness and revealing of the Spirit. The one who has no such emphasis is unable to refute the proposition from Scripture and antiquity: 'What then shall he do? Why, cry out, Enthusiasm! Enthusiasm! and the work is done.'[4] Those who oppose him 'have a cant word for the whole religion of the heart, They call it Enthusiasm'.[5] But it is, Wesley asserts, 'no enthusiasm to teach that the unction from the Holy One belongs to all Christians in all ages.'[6]

Thus what many would dismiss as mere enthusiasm, Wesley sees as the very essence of true Christianity. Scriptural Christianity, he says in a sermon with this title, is a supernatural work of the Spirit in the soul.[7] This is the 'extraordinary work' which men like Dr Gibson, the late Bishop of London, affirms to be 'no better than

---

[1] 'A Letter to the Rev. Mr Downes,' sect. 14, vol. 13, p. 97.
[2] Cf., *A Further Appeal*, i, sects. 24, 25, 26, etc.
[3] Op. cit ii, sect. 27.
[4] Ibid.
[5] Op. cit., ii, sect. 20.
[6] Op. cit., iv, sect. 14.
[7] 'Scriptural Christianity,' lv, iv, sect. 10, vol. 7, p. 60.

down right enthusiasm'.[1] Wesley, in justification for his emphasis, contrasts the attitude to religion brought about by his preaching and that which earlier prevailed. Some sixty years ago, he observes, 'People in general were wonderfully cool about that trifle, Religion.'[2] It is different now. To-day there is a zeal and an earnestness not unbecoming for such an important issue as the salvation of the soul. Only a warm religion is a worthy religion. It is by an emphasis such as this that Wesley maintains that Christ has been brought into human lives. God is no longer conceived as having emigrated from His world. He is dramatically alive therein. He is not 'an idol compounded of fragments of tradition and of frozen metaphysics'.[3] Wesley was a true iconoclast. He had indeed annihilated a multitude of shrines and brought God back into His temple. Thus the century which opened with a cold formalism ended with a warm faith. 'Our light looks like the evening of the world' such was the description of the moral and spiritual condition of the people given in the *Proposal for a National Reformation of Manners*, published in 1694. Under Wesley the light had flamed afresh. God, it seemed, had given to the country another chance.

The contrast, for example, between the theological atmosphere of Warburton and Wesley is immense. Warburton's theology has not been unfairly summarized by Leslie Stephen as 'a supernatural chief justice whose sentences were carried out in a non-rational world; a constitutional monarch who had signed a constitutional compact and retired from the active government of affairs'. Such was Warburton's 'God'. For Wesley it was, 'Immanuel', 'God with us'. The love of God shed abroad in the heart by the Holy Ghost.[4] 'True Christian zeal' is therefore, 'no other than the flame of love.'[5] Such a religion as this is not to be dismissed as a mere excess of enthusiasm.[6]

[1] 'On Laying the Foundation Stone of the New Chapel, City Rd., Ap. 21, 1777,' liv, Intro., sect. 3, vol. 10, p. 170.
[2] 'On Zeal,' xcvii, Intro., sect. 3, vol. 10, p. 170.
[3] Leslie Stephen, *History of English Thought, etc.*, vol. 2, p. 338.
[4] Cf., Enthusiasm is usually regarded as 'something evil: and this is plainly the sentiment of all those who call the Religion of the heart Enthusiasm'. 'Nature of Enthusiasm,' xxxix, sect. 10, vol. 8, p. 171.
[5] 'On Zeal,' xcvii, i, sect. 3, vol. 10, pp. 171, 172.
[6] Cf., True religion is often dismissed as enthusiasm 'a word just fitted for their purpose, because no man can tell either the meaning of it, or even the derivation. If it has any determinate sense, it means a species of religious madness. Hence, when you speak your experience, they immediately cry out "much religion hath made thee mad", and all that you experience, either of the invisible or of the

Wesley allows that there is a false enthusiasm and he is not slow to unmask this 'many-headed monster'.[1] It is his purpose in a sermon on Acts 26. 24 to make clear the dreadfulness of a false enthusiasm. He discusses the meaning of the term, and rejects the etymological derivation of it from ἐν θεῷ, as 'unnaturally forced'. He observes that the term, as now generally used has a bad connotation, and accepting this he goes on to contrast the 'enthusiast' with the 'rational Christian'. Enthusiasm is then described as 'a religious madness arising from some falsely imagined influence of God'.[2] Such are those who are deluded by the notion that they possess in a special manner God's grace and gifts when in fact they do not. They affect a personal infallibility and imagine 'that God dictates the very words they speak: and that, consequently, it is impossible they should speak anything amiss, either as to matter or manner of it'.[3]

Their real error lies in their disregard for the means which God has given for the perfecting of the saints. They rely on sudden impulses and give no attention to the united testimony of the people of God and the written word. 'One general end of enthusiasm', he says, 'is expecting the end without the means, and expecting knowledge, for instance, without searching the Scriptures, and consulting the children of God.'[4] 'God has written all the Scriptures on my heart', say some, 'therefore I have no need to read them.'[5] For Wesley this was lamentable folly.

This discussion of 'enthusiasm' in relation to Wesley, is, we believe, of importance as it indicates how great was his emphasis upon the subjective aspect of revelation. From what has been said previously it will be clear that few would have called Charles Simeon an 'enthusiast'. His emphasis was, as we have seen, upon the objective aspect of revelation. The contrast, then, which was earlier indicated, has, we think, been sustained. For Charles Simeon, revelation is in the Word through the Spirit; for John Wesley, revelation is by the Spirit through the Word.

Wesley certainly will be behind no one in his emphasis upon the activity of the Spirit. He is ready to insist that there is no work of

eternal world they suppose to be only the waking dreams of a heated imagination'. 'Difference of Walking by Sight and Faith,' cxv, sect. 19, vol. 10, p. 397.
[1] 'The Nature of Enthusiasm,' xxxix, sect. 32, vol. 8, p. 180.
[2] Op. cit., sect. 12, p. 171.
[3] Op. cit., sect. 19, p. 175.
[4] A Plain Account of Christian Perfection, Answer to Question, 33.
[5] Ibid., cf., 'Nature of Enthusiasm,' xxxix, sects. 22, 27, vol. 8, pp. 176, 178.

God except by the Spirit. Yet, there is, he maintains, no private revelation given to any man; there is no secret disclosure of special information. God saves and sanctifies, liberates and leads by His Spirit, but it is by His Spirit through the Word. This for Wesley is the full and final revelation of God to man.

CHAPTER X

THE NEED FOR A UNIFICATION

(i) *Objective and Subjective*

In the foregoing review of developments in the understanding of Revelation from 1700 to 1860, several clear-cut and sometimes mutually hostile doctrines have been shown to emerge. Broadly, an opposition can be seen to have been introduced between the objective and subjective views. The exclusive stress on the objective aspect which characterized the 'orthodox' doctrine gave rise to a sterile notion of revelation. Revealed religion was conceived as either adding a few extra ideas to natural religion, or as a body of disclosed truths to which assent had to be given. Those who thus repudiated the subjective aspect were especially concerned to guard the transcendence of God. He was viewed consequently as a Being completely different from man; a Being nevertheless Who had declared His existence and attributes by leaving sufficient evidence of His power and godhead on the universe of His creating. It was such accentuation of the divine transcendence which pushed the orthodox apologists close to the deists whom they sought to oppose.

On the other side, the subjective doctrine, starting with an insistence upon the divine immanence, renounced and ridiculed the objective aspect, and made revelation to be the unveiling within of the ever-present God. Pantheism was consequently the perpetual danger of this view; and the charge was in fact made, not without justice, in some cases. It was this emphasis upon the subjective, at first under the influence of Hegelianism and later under that of Existentialism, which was destined to hold the field throughout the following decades. For Hegel, God is the All-inclusive Absolute. This meant, according to Hegel's teaching, that

> '*All are parts of one stupendous whole,*
> *Whose body nature is, and God the soul*'.

These two lines from Pope's *Essay on Man* admirably summarize Hegelianism and show it to be a philosophy of sheer immanence.

From this there developed in the succeeding years a type of pantheistic doctrine which found voice and vogue in the so-called, *New Theology*, which had such eloquent advocacy in the writings of R. J. Campbell.

On the other hand, Kierkegaard, from an existentialist point of view, put an emphasis upon the idea of God as 'infinite Subject', and upon the individual in his subjective reality and actuality. Kierkegaard was, to be sure, exasperated with Hegel whom he harangues for failing to take account of the existing individual. As a traditional 'Herr Professor', he declares, Hegel has gone to the extreme of absentmindedness and actually forgotten his own existence, the real subject of thought. It is in this way that Hegel has obliterated the individual by submerging him in the Absolute. He has thus, according to Kierkegaard, given a false subjectivity which it is Kierkegaard's purpose to correct. Had Hegel been content to add to his massive work a footnote declaring it to be but a 'thought-experiment', he would have gone down into history as a great thinker.[1] The trouble is that he wanted his system to be taken seriously; to be actually accepted as truth. And yet it is precisely his system which does not take seriously, what is the most serious reality of all, the actual self, the single individual. For Hegel, then, the single individual is submerged in the uncharacterizable Whole, the so-called Absolute. It is Kierkegaard's business to bring about his re-emergence; to call the existing individual from the grave of death to which Hegel had assigned him. And Kierkegaard will do this, not by any denial of subjectivity, but by an assertion, of what he claims, is true subjectivity, for 'the passion for the infinite is precisely subjectivity ... and thus subjectivity becomes truth'.[2] Yet, at the same time, Kierkegaard will not have God mixed up in

---

[1] Bretall, *A Kierkegaard Anthology*, p. 191.

[2] *Concluding Unscientific Postscript* (trs. Swenson and Lowrie), p. 181. Cf., 'the polemic against Hegel must not blind us to the great characteristic of the age which Kierkegaard shares with Hegel in philosophy and Schleiermacher in theology. All three are children of the Romantic revival and revolt against the Enlightenment. In their different ways all three are apostles of subjectivity. "The absolute is subject not substance," said the philosopher. "Religion is the intuition of the infinite, the feeling of absolute dependence," said the theologian. It remained for Kierkegaard to correct what he found false emphasis in both teachers. "The passion for the infinite is ... subjectivity, and thus subjectivity becomes truth." Against Hegel he says, "Your absolute Subject has swallowed up the individual, and so has become indistinguishable from the absolute Object; subjectivity has vanished in a boundless objectivity." Against Schleiermacher we can imagine him saying, "Your subjectivity has not sufficiently allowed for the specific quality of the 'object' in Christianity, where it is present to faith as paradox. Hence its true analogy is not aesthetic feeling but an activity

man's subjectivity. There is an infinite distance between God and man. God is the Wholly Other. For Kierkegaard the fundamental error in Hegelianism was its emphasis upon 'Immanenz'. Hegel dared to assert an existing continuum between God and man in such a way as to make it possible for man to arrive at a knowledge of God by his own innate abilities. He was led to this error by conceiving of Christianity as but a development, albeit the highest, in the religious consciousness of the race.

For Kierkegaard this 'historicizing identity-philosophy' (which, it may be noted, received a theological emphasis by Schleiermacher) was the abandonment of true Christianity, which would be restored only by the proclamation of an absolute qualitative difference between the divine and the human. There is, therefore, Kierkegaard asserts, 'an endless yawning difference between God and man,'[1] so much so, that, 'if God exists, and consequently is distinguished by an infinite difference of quality from all that it means to be a man, then neither can I nor anybody else, by beginning with the assumption that He was man, arrive in all eternity at the conclusion, "therefore it was God." '[2]

It is this accentuation of the 'Otherness' of God which has been specially stressed by Barth and Brunner, to give rise to, what may be called, a *neue Sachlichkeit*. It is referred to here as a 'new objectivity' in the sense that revelation is not thought of by these writers as an upsurge of the divine either latent or lively within the human. Indeed it is asserted, more particularly by Barth, '*Finitum non est capax infiniti*,' therefore, revelation comes to man 'in an irrational way, from without'. Revelation comes within the divine-human encounter. But the initiative is with God; God confronts man. Revelation is, therefore, supremely an activity of God. Here we see a new insistence upon the idea of the divine transcendence, with the result that, while the Kierkegaardian 'absolute qualitative difference' between God and man is stressed, man is in no way *capax Dei*. The question could, therefore, be raised, Has not the other aspect of Kierkegaard's teaching, namely, that upon the uniqueness of the single individual, been somehow compromised? We merely raise the question here: it is not within our purpose to

combined with a passivity which together constitute a passion which is the highest energizing and supreme manifestation of subjectivity." ' James Brown, *Subject and Object in Modern Theology*, pp. 35, 36.

[1] *Training in Christianity*, p. 67.
[2] Op. cit., p. 31.

seek an answer. By declaring 'immanence' to be the presence in the
world of transcendence, and by conceiving of revelation to be the
intrusion of the divine into the human, there does appear with these
writers a new sort of 'objectivity'; an 'objectivity' in the sense that
revelation is altogether from without, although it is to be added,
'and from above.' It would appear that for Barth and Brunner,
however, the notion of 'objectivity' is not much more than the
repudiation of the idealistic identification of the human and the
divine. In the last analysis, knowledge of God comes in the revelational encounter. The 'objectivity', then, of Barth and Brunner
is really an emphasis on the 'otherness' of God. There does not
seem to be any objectively existing revelation. It is this specific
teaching which A. C. Knudson had in mind, when, in a review of
Brunner's *The Divine-Human Encounter*, he referred to the 'chief
scandal of present day theology' as 'irrationalism and mystery
mongering'.[1] Although, therefore, Barth and Brunner do lay emphasis upon the idea of God as objectively existing as the Wholly
Other, their view of revelation seems to be a continuation of the
Kierkegaardian existential subjectivity.

These facts reveal how the two broadly opposing doctrines of
revelation, which we have seen coming into vogue in the period
from 1700 to 1860, remain. The divorce has persisted throughout
the following years; sometimes the objective and sometimes the
subjective aspect received exclusive accentuation. What seemed to be
needed was a remarriage of the two, but the succeeding ages do not
reveal any sufficient attempt being made to achieve an adequate
union of the objective and subjective elements.

But not only did the period uncover this broad opposition between objective and subjective, but it revealed, as a consequence,
other divorces which have only in the last decade come into sharp
focus. The present period shows a revived interest in the question
of revelation. This fact can be seen from the spate of books which
have appeared in the last quarter-century with the word 'Revela-

[1] While we have ventured here to refer to Barth's and Brunner's emphasis on
the 'otherness' of God as a 'new objective' insistence, it should be noted that in
an earlier section a similarity was indicated between the doctrine of the Friends
and this modern school. Cf., above, p. 72 (note). Cf., 'the conclusion must be
stated that the theologian who has spent his life in an effort to free Christian
theology from entanglement with mysticism and with philosophy has in his own
theology developed a perspective which embodies a philosophical mysticism
whose classic exponent is a philosopher who does not depend upon the New
Testament.' Daniel Williams, 'Brunner and Barth on Philosophy,' *The Journal of
Religion*, vol. xxvii, No. 4, p. 251, Oct. 1947.

tion' in their titles,[1] not to mention the numerous works with other titles in which the subject is discussed. It is however the antitheses indicated by or latent in the understanding of revelation from 1700 to 1860 which are now receiving serious attention. In the broad context of the opposition already noted, the opposition, that is, between the subjective and objective doctrines of revelation, there are further divorces to be observed between the mediate and the immediate; between the Scriptures and the Spirit; between the words and the Word. Here were initiated divisions and separations which the theology of revelation, since, has not been able successfully to unify.

(ii) *The Mediate and the Immediate*

The objectivists tended to make revelation something altogether mediate. God Himself is not known: there are truths about Him set forth in propositions which are to receive our assent, but God Himself is still afar off, secluded behind syllogisms. On the other hand, the subjectivists placed emphasis upon the immediate and direct knowledge of God. But in their statements, the mediatory nature of revelation was either denied, ignored, or obscured.

It seemed impossible in the period for these two opposing doctrines to come to any sort of terms. There were those who maintained that revelation is mediated and is therefore not direct, and there were those who claimed it to be direct and therefore not mediated.

At the present day, the neo-Thomists who advocate an exclusive 'propositionalist' doctrine of revelation, are opposed by the Barthians whose exclusive emphasis is upon what may be called an 'activist' view. A large section of Protestant theology insists that God's self-disclosure is in terms of saving acts; revelation consists of divine events. Those who proclaim this doctrine are critical of any conception of revelation in terms of doctrine. Some take an extreme position and maintain that revelation contains no doctrinal

[1] The following titles will illustrate the point: F. W. Camfield, *Revelation and the Holy Spirit; Revelation: A Symposium*, edited by John Baillie and Hugh Martin; Etienne Gilsôn, *Reason and Revelation in the Middle Ages*; H. Richard Niebuhr, *The Meaning of Revelation*; H. Wheeler Robinson, *Redemption and Revelation*; H. Wheeler Robinson, *Inspiration and Revelation in the Old Testament*; Herbert Cunliffe-Jones, *The Authority of Biblical Revelation*; E. Brunner, *Revelation and Reason*; L. S. Thornton, *Revelation and the Modern World*; E. P. Dickie, *Revelation and Response*; E. Lewis, *A Philosophy of the Christian Revelation*; J. Y. Mackinnon, *The Protestant Doctrine of Revelation*; J. Baillie, *The Idea of Revelation in Recent Thought*.

element at all. Others believe the Biblical doctrinal statements to be inferences made by Christians under the influence of the Spirit — inferences, that is, made from the knowledge of God's saving acts in history. Dr William Temple, for example, says emphatically 'there is no such thing as revealed truth'.[1] He grants, however, that there are 'truths of revelation'. These, he goes on to say, are 'propositions which express the results of correct thinking concerning revelation'. But in all these views, however 'doctrine' is understood, it is insisted that revelation in the proper meaning of the term is to be conceived of in terms of divine activity.

The question here is not, as Barth seems to think, simply that between those who regard the divine Spirit as a *datum* or as a *dandum*. Let it be granted, as we think it must, that the divine Spirit is always *dandum*, for the Spirit of God is God in action. At the same time the Scriptures themselves declare that the 'word of God' given in former days is the 'word of God' for us. The God Who spoke in the circumstances of a prophet's or an apostle's life was not simply declaring His interest in the individual to whom He addressed His word. He was speaking to the prophet for the sake of the people; to one man for the sake of other men. God's purpose in declaring His word was to speak to human needs; it was not merely to correct, console or constrain a single individual. What was immediate to the prophet or the apostle were his own personality and environment. But he spoke God's word indirectly to his contemporaries and to those who would follow after. In this sense, therefore, revelation as a disclosure of God must be mediated, and yet, How is it possible for mediate experience of God to become immediate? How can past and distant information become present and dynamic instruction? The question may not be easy to answer, but the fact remains that it can and it does. 'In any appropriation of the dramatic saving events of the Bible I meet not a doctrine about God, not a special type of religious experience, although these are secondary products of the encounter, but I meet God himself.'[2]

The problems raised by an exclusively propositional doctrine of revelation on the one hand and by a completely dynamic one on the other are many and far-reaching. Those who maintain the former

---

[1] *Nature, Man and God*, p. 317. The whole chapter entitled, 'Revelation and its Mode,' (Lecture xii) is important.
[2] W. J. Wolf, *Man's Knowledge of God*, p. 83.

can be asked, Does not a revelation in terms of mere propositions tend to obscure the divine Person? Would not this mean that there would be no knowledge of God Himself but only knowledge about Him? Does such knowledge, it might be further asked, meet the needs of the human spirit? And must not 'faith', in this context, be defined in exclusively intellectualistic terms as purely assent to doctrine? On the other side, to those who maintain that revelation is to be understood as divine action, another set of questions arises. The first is: Is such a view in line with the general teaching of the Church throughout the ages? Does not a revelation in terms of divine action alone leave open the question where is an adequate objective authority to be found? Is not the purpose of revelation the disclosure of some knowledge of God as well as the bringing of the human individual into fellowship with God Himself?[1] Is it sufficient to define revelation as God's saving acts in history and to exclude its application to the biblical significance given to those events?[2] While those who advocate this view of revelation are right to reject the notion that saving faith is faith IN doctrine, May not the truth be faith THROUGH doctrine? These are but a few of the questions which can be raised on each side. The point we stress however is this: Is there any need for this opposition? Can revelation not be both propositional and dynamic at the same time? This is the problem with which the theology of revelation may have to be concerned for some time to come. The point has been made by E. G. Homrighausen when he writes: 'Whether the Christian revelation is only personal and not to some extent propositional is another question, for if God reveals Himself adequately, man's mind must be satisfied.'[3]

It was the writers of the period 1700 to 1860 who brought into opposition the propositional and dynamic views of revelation. The

[1] G. Ernest Wright in his book, *God Who Acts*, denies that the Bible contains any 'static, propositional' statements of doctrine. See, e.g. pp. 35, 36. But is not such a declaration as 'Hear, O Israel: the Lord our God IS one Lord' (Deut. 6. 4) a doctrinal, indeed a metaphysical statement? Cf., E. J. Young, *Thy Word is Truth* (1957), p. 224 f.

[2] Cf., 'In so far as there is revelation of God there is something timeless and of enduring validity; yet this timeless element is mediated through a historical moment and historical circumstances,' H. H. Rowley, *The Faith of Israel*, Intro., p. 21. Also, 'The Bible is throughout based upon the belief that God has unveiled to men something of his own character and will, and that he has spoken through men, in whose mouth he has put his own word,' ibid.

[3] E. G. Homrighausen (Princeton Theological Seminary) Review of Brunner's *The Divine-Human Encounter*, Theology Today, vol. 1, No. 1, April 1944, p. 135 f. Cf., *A Philosophy of the Christian Religion*, Ed. J. Carnell, p. 29. Even Emil

hostility we believe need not be allowed to continue. To deny the mediate in the interests of the immediate, or vice versa, appears to ignore the experience of a multitude of believing people who attest the fact that a revelation which is mediated does become immediately direct and creatively real in the living experience of Christian faith. In the truths revealed, as, for example, God as active, as incarnate, as redeeming, and so forth, there is somehow found an experience of God Himself. The remark of Louis Berkhof is justified by the facts. 'Special revelation', he writes, 'does not consist exclusively in word and doctrine, and does not merely address itself to the intellect. This is more clearly understood at present than it was formerly . . . . The view once prevalent, that revelation consists exclusively in a communication of doctrine, was clearly one-sided. At present, however, some go to the other extreme, equally one-sided, that revelation consists only in communication of power and life.'[1]

(iii) *The Scriptures and the Spirit*

Another aspect of the same general problem left by the discussion of revelation from 1700 to 1860 concerns the relation between the Scriptures and the Spirit. We have seen how the divorce was brought about and the opposition created in the period of our review. It was then asserted by some that all that was needed for faith was assent to the propositions of the Scriptures: the activity of the Spirit was restricted to those of the early Church, or more particularly to those whose commission it was to draw up the things which were to be most surely believed. There was no need for any further action of the Spirit immediately to inspire or illuminate. Men had reason which was adequate to weigh, impartially, the 'evidences of Christianity' and to see how superior were its ethics

Brunner allows the significant word to escape him that 'A Church . . . can do justice to her commission only when she recovers the unity of the *Logos* and the *Dynamis*, of the word and the act of God, which is the distinctive element in the Biblical revelation,' *Revelation and Reason*, p. 164.

[1] *Reformed Dogmatics*: Intro., Louis Berkhof, p. 144. Cf., 'We can understand that man may have some sense of God's majesty and power through Creation or through the processes of history, that he may have some inkling of God through his natural reason or through the sense of the sacred which is part of the human constitution; even so, "behold these are the outskirts of His ways, and how small a whisper do we hear of Him!" But all such knowledge of God is mediate and indirect . . . . The Christian as much as any other is a mediated revelation. We see God in Christ, the Mediator between God and man. Yet Christians have maintained as the very essence of their faith that Jesus Christ is in some sense God Himself incarnate. Thus the revelation of God in Christ is different in kind from every other revelation', N. Micklem, *What is Faith?* pp. 44–6.

and doctrines to all other systems, whether religious or philosophical. And being thus convinced, it was their business and duty to avow the truth of that which was so evidently of divine origin. Revelation is therefore in the context of this conception, a matter of *truth* only.

On the other hand, in the sections, in which the doctrines of revelation as indwelling light and revelation as immediate experience were reviewed, we saw, in the first case in its extreme form, in the second in a modified form, the emphasis upon the place of the Spirit. In the first of these two views revelation is understood as an intrusion into man of the divine Spirit, which is totally distinct from anything human. Revelation is consequently the residence within of an Alien Spirit. In the second view the human and the divine are merged and revelation is conceived to be the upsurge within man of his own essential divinity. It is the coming to authority within of the 'Spirit' which is always there. Whereas in the one case, revelation is thought of as the incoming of an Alien Spirit, in the other it is thought of as the emergence of a Resident Spirit. Both views, however, are concerned to teach that revelation is a matter of *Spirit* only.

In this way there was set up an antithesis between 'Spirit' and 'Truth'. It is this divorce which has proved troublesome in the present era. Here indeed is one of the problems created by the earlier age in which modern theology has become specially interested. The school of Barth and Brunner, for example, as has been shown throughout the foregoing pages, has revealed a tendency to emphasize the place of the Spirit. Barth makes the Bible a 'witness' to the activity of the Spirit. Like Brunner he denies that revelation has or can ever be given in the form of truth. He insists that the will of God can only be known in the present moment. Revelation is God confronting and challenging in the 'now'. It is not a belief in something He has spoken long ago. It is to this immediate and direct activity of the Spirit of God that the written Scriptures bear witness. They attest the possibility of revelation, whenever God chooses to use them in this way.[1] Revelation, therefore, cannot ever be anything written; it cannot consist of truth presented to the minds of men as a static or propositional *datum*.[2]

[1] *Church Dogmatics*, i, i, pp. 57 f., 125 f.
[2] *The Word of God and the Word of Man*, pp. 46, 56, etc. Cf., D. M. Baillie's, *God Was in Christ*, pp. 36–8. Baillie notes Barth's lack of interest either in the historical personality of Jesus or in His teaching. Neither is any revelation of God, but rather a 'veiling' of Him. Cf., also, pp. 51, 52.

Is there not, however, a need for, and a possibility of, rewedding these two views, and thus bringing into an acceptable unity the idea of revelation as 'Spirit' and the idea of revelation as 'truth'? A less one-sided relationship between the Scriptures and the Spirit needs to be thought out, a relationship, indeed, more akin to the historic Evangelical position. The Scriptures themselves on their side, give witness to the reality and actuality of the Spirit: they give the assurance that the Holy Spirit has come. And they proclaim further that the Spirit will verify to our understandings the truth of that which the Scriptures themselves declare. On the other side, the Spirit makes authentic to us the reality of the Christ Who has come. But it is through the record that we learn that He has come: it is from its pages we are taught the reality of the Incarnation, 'Emmanuel', 'God with us'. The Spirit gives witness to the truths which are already declared in the Scriptures. It is, as William Cowper suggestively states, when the Spirit breathes upon the Word that the truth comes to sight. A more intimate relationship would seem to be demanded between the Spirit and the Scriptures than the protagonists of these opposing views appear to permit.

There were those, as we have seen, who denied the inner activity of the Spirit and maintained Christian faith to be belief in the Scriptures, while, in opposition, there were those who proclaimed divine revelation to be the direct and immediate inspiration of God and who denied the need for the Scriptures, or who saw them merely as a witness to this idea of revelation. But a Scripture without the Spirit makes for a fruitless faith, while the Spirit without the Scriptures gives an undisciplined faith. The one makes for a dead orthodoxy, the other for an unrestrained enthusiasm. The first gives lifelessness to the Church, the second licence to the individual.[1] There is, we believe, need for a more perfect under-

---

[1] Cf., the statements by Bishop Martensen on this point. Martensen thinks that the 'older Protestantism' which gave 'prominence to salvation as solely and exclusively the reference and design of Scripture' tended to a too individualistic use of the Scripture. But as the Scripture contains much more than the individual needs to know for his own salvation, he believes that emphasis must be put on the place and purpose of the Scripture within the Church. But even there, he declares, the Holy Spirit acts by means of the Scripture. 'The necessity of Scripture is not *principally* for the individual, but for the Church; and its full import and design is stated rather in the assertion, that it contains all truth necessary for the preservation of the Church, and for its progressive development towards its final consummation. This again is to say, that by means of Holy Scripture, under the guidance of the Holy Spirit, the Church not only may be kept in purity of doctrine and true worship, but that in the whole course

standing of the relation between the Scripture and the Spirit. It is
the necessity for this understanding which lies behind some remarks made by G. W. Bromiley concerning the Barthian theology.
He asks: 'Ought we to think that the Bible is trustworthy merely
because we can demonstrate its historical accuracy? Ought we to
think it authoritative merely because we have come to know the
truth of its message through the Holy Spirit, and irrespective of
the historical reliability or otherwise? Ought we not to seek the
authority of the Bible in the balanced relationship of a perfect
form (the objective Word) and a perfect content (the Word applied
subjectively by the Holy Ghost) — the form holding the content,
the content not applied except in and through the form?'[1]

(iv) The Words and the Word

There is one further and final point to be made. The writers of
the period 1700 to 1860 developed another antithesis which in
recent days has become an issue of importance. The 'orthodox' and
the 'evangelical' writers were agreed in their view of the Scriptures.
To both, they were, *in toto*, the 'Word of God'. For those whom we
have referred to earlier as the 'Coleridgeans' the term 'Word of
God' was regarded as misapplied to the written word.[2] For

of her development there can be no new practice or law established, be it in
relation to doctrine or to life, which she cannot abolish by means of the eternal
principle of truth and life laid down in the Holy Scripture: moreover, that on the
one hand, all critical and cleansing activity in the Church, and on the other hand,
all building up, edifying and strengthening activity (taking this expression in its
widest sense), must find its governing type for all times in the Holy Scriptures.
Maintaining as we do that the Holy Ghost guides the Church into all the truth
by means of the Scripture, we attribute to the Scripture perfect sufficiency and
clearness (*sufficientia et perspicuitas*); in so far, that is, as the Church is given
through Scripture the revelation of the Spirit concerning what is advisable or
useful for *any particular time*, while Scripture itself must be looked upon for *all
times*, much that it contains not being perfectly accomplished until the latter days.
Experience, moreover, teaches that whenever a true reform has been accomplished in the Church, the word, *It was not so in the beginning*, has been spoken
with telling power against a lifeless ecclesiasticism, because it has been spoken
in the strength of the Holy Scripture. This holds good not only of the great Reformation of the sixteenth century, but of the many successive protests which have
been made both in the Middle Ages and in modern times. For as the Church has,
in every age, triumphed over that false *gnosis*, which resolves Christianity into
merely human reason, by the Word of Scripture, this same word has been a
safeguard against a barren orthodoxy, which has built up ecclesiasticism at the
expense of Christianity; and it has continually led back to an illumination inseparable from edification, because the apostolic illumination is in its essence an
enlightenment which leads on to salvation.' H. Martensen, *Christian Dogmatics*,
pp. 405, 406.
    [1] *The Evangelical Quarterly*, vol. xix, No. 2, April 1947, p. 136.
    [2] Cf., e.g. 'the word of God which saveth and redeemeth the soul is not the
word printed on Paper, but is the . . . ever-speaking Word, which is the Son

Coleridge and his followers there was some justification for their eagerness to reserve the title 'Word of God' exclusively for Christ Himself. It was, they believed, a necessary protest against the orthodox notion of revelation as a body of divinely communicated truths to which assent was to be given. An influential body of theological opinion in these days maintains the same position. The 'Word of God', it is proclaimed, is the living person of Christ. The 'Word of God' is a Person, and it is inappropriate if applied to the written Scripture, which is regarded as the record of revelation, of God's saving acts in history.

It is a question however whether this divorce between the Scriptures and the 'Word of God' to which it bears witness can be maintained in view of the testimony of the Scriptures themselves. The phrase, for example, 'Thus saith the Lord' or its equivalent, occurs nearly 4,000 times in the Old Testament alone. In the New Testament, too, there are several passages where the phrase the 'word of God' undoubtedly refers to the spoken or written word.[1] There are other places in the New Testament where a life-giving quality is attributed to the 'Word', but it is not altogether clear whether the reference is to the Incarnate or the Written Word.

In Philippians 2. 16, for example, there is the expression 'the word of life' (λόγος ζωῆς); the title is here evidently applied to the written word. But the same description is given in John 1 of Christ Himself (ὁ λόγος . . . ἐν αὐτῷ ζωὴ ἦν, ii, 4). Thus are the Incarnate and Written Word so identified that we are not always sure to which reference is made: yet the same attribute of 'liveliness' is applied to each. The fundamental resemblance lies in the fact that both are a tangible expression of the invisible God. As the written or spoken word expresses, for the purpose of communicating to another, the invisible and inaccessible thought, so Jesus Christ as the Incarnate Word and the Scriptures as the Written Word, express and communicate knowledge of the invisible and inaccessible God. It is this life-giving attribute of the Bible which

of God'. W. Law, *The Way of Divine Knowledge*, p. 137 (see above, p. 160). 'More and more he (F. D. Maurice) had come to look upon all expressions implying that the letter of the Bible is the word of God as denials of the living "Word of God" of whom the Bible speaks,' *Life of F. D. Maurice*, by his son, vol. 2, p. 452 (see above, p. 187).

[1] See Matt. vii. 13; Luke viii. 21; Acts iv. 31, vi. 7, xii. 24, xiii. 5, xiii. 7, xiii. 44, xviii. 11, xix. 20; Rom. ix. 6; 2 Cor. iv. 2; 1 Thess. ii. 13; 1 Tim. iv. 5; 2 Tim. ii. 9; Titus ii. 5; Heb. xiii. 7; 1 John ii. 14, etc. The Scriptures are called also 'the oracles of God', Rom. iii. 2; 'the word of the Lord', Acts xiii. 48; 'the word of Christ,' Col. iii. 16; 'the word of truth', Eph. i. 13, etc.

indicates that there is a unique relation between it and Him Who is rightly called the 'living Word of God'.

In Hebrews 4. 12 there is the statement, 'For the word of God is living ($\zeta\hat{\omega}\nu$ $\gamma\alpha\rho$ $\dot{o}$ $\lambda o\gamma o s$ $\tau o\hat{v}$ $\theta\epsilon o\hat{v}$), and active, and sharper than any two-edged sword' (R.V.). Commentators are not agreed as to whether the reference is to the Incarnate or the Written Word. On the whole, it seems to suit the writer's thought better to take it to mean the written word. Yet the very next verse unites the Incarnate Word, Who searches human hearts, with the action of the written word.

In 1 Peter 1. 23, there is another of these passages in which it is difficult to decide whether the Incarnate or the Written Word is in view. Peter speaks of 'the word of God which liveth . . .', or literally, 'the word of God living' ($\lambda o\gamma o v$ $\zeta\hat{\omega}\nu\tau o s$ $\theta\epsilon o\hat{v}$). It is more probable that here the reference is to the written word in view of the quotation from Isaiah 40. 6–8. In all these passages the attribute of 'liveliness' is applied to the Written Word in the way in which it is applied to the Incarnate Word. This point gives the right to Dr J. K. Mozley to observe 'it is finally true that it (the Scripture) is the Word of God, just as it is finally true about Christ that He is the Word of God'.[1] Certainly the conclusion to be drawn from the data provided by the Scripture itself is, as H. R. Mackintosh says that 'the tie between the Word of God and the Bible is an absolutely vital tie'.[2] It is this relationship between Christ and the Scriptures which the writers of the period 1700 to 1860 seem to have been unable to discern.

There was another distinction introduced in the period 1700 to 1860 which has become of importance in recent discussions on the problems of revelation and its record. Writers of the school of Coleridge and Maurice spoke of the Scriptures, sometimes as 'becoming' and sometimes as 'containing' the word of God. The statements of Coleridge and Maurice and the others were made as a conscious repudiation of the notion that the Bible is a divinely communicated volume in which the human instrument was so obliterated as to leave no room for the human element. To Coleridge and Maurice who had learnt from Kant that man must not be used as a means to an end, this idea was repugnant. The 'Coleridgeans' were anxious to show that the Bible contained

---

[1] *The Christian Faith*, edited by W. R. Matthews, p. 85.
[2] Quoted from the section by H. R. Mackintosh, in Charles Gore, *The Doctrine of an Infallible Book*, p. 57.

human elements, and in so far as it did so, such elements, they declared, were necessarily fallible and in some cases, at least, were definitely erroneous.

It is well known that in these days writers are divided in the same understanding of the 'word of God' in relation to the Scriptures. There are those who take the 'Coleridgean' position and maintain, as did the writers of this school, that the Scripture becomes the word of God in the context of experience. Many recent writers are insistent that the Bible is not in itself, in its totality, the Word of God, but is the vehicle of the divine word. Something of this teaching can be illustrated by reference to C. H. Dodd's book, *The Authority of the Bible*. Dodd says that 'in the expression "the Word of God" lurks an equivocation',[1] and he goes on to assert it is a 'metaphorical expression'.[2] The Bible really mediates the 'Word of God' and therein lies its authority.[3] Ultimately it is that which 'finds' me most, reveals God best. That which arouses and commends itself to the awakened moral consciousness is more certainly the 'word of God'. 'The criterion lies within ourselves, in the response of our own spirit to the Spirit that utters itself in the Scriptures.'[4] This means, therefore that 'Nowhere is the truth given in such purely "objective" form that we can find a self-subsistent external authority'.[5]

On the other side theologians of such diverse views as E. J. Young and J. K. Mozley reject completely all ideas of the Bible as either 'containing' or 'becoming' the 'Word of God'. Mozley, to illustrate, regards the distinction between the Bible and the Word of God as valueless both from the 'apologetic' and the 'dogmatic' points of view. On the apologetic side, Mozley argues that the idea that the Bible 'contains' the Word of God, destroys its unity and leaves us with no answer to the question of the sceptic or the doubter. From whence comes the Bible? On the dogmatic side he finds the 'usefulness' of the Bible compromised. Many of those who maintain that the Scriptures merely 'contain' the Word of God are ready to admit that Jesus Christ is objectively and in Himself, the Word of God. But what is true of Christ, is true also, Mozley maintains, of the Scriptures. He writes: 'So it is with the Bible; its nature as the word of God, as the book in which the deeper tone of the one divine voice is heard through the many changing tones of

---

[1] *The Authority of the Bible*, p. 16. [2] Ibid.
[3] P. 289. [4] P. 296. [5] P. 289.

the human voices, is not open to demonstration; but, in the Christian view of the Bible, it is finally true that it is the Word of God,
just as it is finally true about Christ that He is the Word of God. In
neither case would the substitution of the expression "contains" or
some similar term be an adequate embodiment of Christian faith.'[1]
The necessities of a sound theological system demand that the
whole Bible should be so designated, he urges. 'Whatever place
belongs to the Bible in Christian theology belongs to it as a whole.
If in any sense at all the thought of the Word of God may be
brought into connection with the Bible it will be fatal to the main-
tenance of that wholeness, if in the course of the development of the
dogmatic scheme it were necessary to enquire whether allowance
were being made for the possibility that at such and such a point
reference to the Bible might be illegitimate, since in that particular
context there was no certainty that the Bible was containing the
Word of God.'[2]

The advocates of each of these opposing views will require
answers to certain important questions from the other. Those who
maintain that the Bible 'contains' the Word of God will demand of
their opponents: What precisely is the significance of the word 'is',
in the proposition, 'The Bible *is* the Word of God?' Can the
'contradictions' within the record be reconciled with the assertion
that the Bible is throughout the 'Word of God'? Is the statement,
it is further asked, true to experience? Can it be maintained, for
example, that the list of names in the book of Numbers is as much
the Word of God as the Epistle to the Romans? And in the Epistle
to the Romans itself, are the last two chapters as 'divine' as the
earlier sections? Is Joshua as important for the spiritual life as
John? What is to be said about such passages as the *Pericope
Adulterae* and the last verses of Mark's Gospel? If the Bible is the
'Word of God', does not this mean that its several injunctions are

---

The Christian Faith (edited by W. R. Matthews), p. 55.
   [2] This carefully worded statement of Mozley needs to be pondered for it is an
exact statement of the position. Were it the purpose in these pages to follow
through the implications of what is being disclosed by our study, this is the
conclusion which we would maintain. In spite of all the problems which beset
the doctrine that the Bible *is* the Word of God, the designation more truly than
any other expresses its precise nature. The more thoroughly the doctrine of
Scripture is studied in its isagogic and practical contexts the more unhesitatingly
may it be referred to as the Word of God. The assertion that the Bible merely
'contains' the Word of God or that it is a 'witness' to a possible revelation, when
made, as it now is, to repudiate the proclamation that it is itself the Word of God,
is not only misleading but is clearly false.

all equally binding? In this case, is not the word concerning women not praying with uncovered head of as permanent force as the moral requirements of the redeemed life?

On the other hand, those who insist that the Bible in its totality and essence is the Word of God ask of their opponents: If the Bible only becomes or contains the Word of God, When can we declare that it is so? Does not the assertion that the Bible 'becomes' the Word of God, mean that it becomes in us what it is not in itself? Does not this mean that truth is made by experience? Is there no objective standard of truth by which the varying claims to have heard the voice of God may be tested? Does not the subjective method which this view expounds make the ultimate authority in the things of the Spirit to be the individual's own conscience? Did not Jesus frequently refer to the Old Testament Scriptures as the 'Word of God' although He was aware of the difficulties for faith which were involved? Is not all that is required for the subjective appreciation of divine revelation, not a denial that the Bible is the Word of God, but a clear understanding of what is meant by the inner testimony of the Spirit?

These are certainly important questions asked by one side of the other. The question, however, arises as to whether there should not be a union of the two ideas in any final statement of the meaning and significance of the Bible. Martensen, at any rate, seems to think so, although he expressed preference for one statement as against the other. Martensen notes that those who maintain that the Bible 'contains' the Word of God are anxious to safeguard its human element; while those who state that it IS the Word of God emphasize its divineness. But there must be asserted, he observes, as in the Person of Christ, 'not only the union of the divine and human in Scripture, but at the same time the distinction between the two. The old proposition, *the Scripture is the Word of God*, expressed the union; the modern dictum, *the Scriptures contain the Word of God*, expresses the distinction. The first proposition is clearly preferable to the second which is vague and indistinct, and may be applied to many writings. The first, however, is untrue, if it be taken so to affirm the union, as to exclude all distinction of the divine and human elements in the Bible . . . . The opposite pro-position, which does not venture to assert that scripture IS the word of God, but that it only CONTAINS the Word of God, con-siders only the distinction between the divine and human elements, and overlooks the all-pervading, obvious, and typical union of these in scripture, the sacred, all-pervading, apparent, and fundamental truth, which in unsullied clearness enwraps and even subdues the temporal and human narrowness.'[1]

Fruitful use has, more recently, been made of another distinction indicated by the 'Coleridgeans' between revelation and its record. The important truth marked out by the distinction is that there is a real and objective revelation in divine works and words prior to, and independent of, any written word. Revelation, in the present era, is said to be God's activity in human history and experience. The question, however, needs to be asked; Is it possible to abstract this activity from its historical circumstances? Professor C. R. North refers to what he calls 'the modern Marcionite attitude to the Old Testament'. The error in it, he then goes on to say, 'is that we unconsciously tend to lay the emphasis upon certain *ideas about* God, which we assume to be true, or untrue, independently of history. It is a concession we make, quite needlessly, to Lessing. We grant that the ideas have been mediated through history, and we are scrupulously careful, when we expound them, to place them in their historical setting. We fail to see that the historical circumstances are an integral part of the revelation. Instead, we are inclined to treat them as so much husk to the pure grain of truth. The historical occasion, once it is past, is more or less irrelevant except for the purposes of illustration. It has served its purpose as a matrix for the truth, and may now, without much loss, be ignored. In point of fact, the historical occasion is an essential element in the revelation.'[2]

If it is allowed that 'the historical occasion is an essential element in the revelation', then we should go further. The 'historical occasion' of the divine act, it is argued, is known to us only as it is recorded. Revelation then, it must be maintained, may be conceived as God's divine actions in history, but these 'actualities' of God in history are as if they had not been, apart from their preservation in records. This must mean, in the last analysis, that 'the line between revelation and its record is becoming thin, and that, in another true sense, the *record*, in the fulness of its contents, *is itself for us the revelation*'.[3]

---

[1] *Christian Dogmatics*, p. 403.
[2] C. R. North, *The Old Testament Interpretation of History*, p. 153.
[3] J. Orr, *Revelation and Inspiration*, p. 159.

In this connection it is of interest to observe how a number of writers, who are most anxious to avoid any identity of revelation with its record are found unwittingly to make it.[1] The question then is, should the idea of revelation be extended to include, not only the acts of God in history, but the history of those acts, and the interpretation and application of those divine activities as they are preserved for us? This is the conclusion which seems to be demanded. It certainly is true that as 'soon as we try to abstract the values from their concrete embodiment, we evacuate them of all reality and become sentimentalists. The spiritual must always be embodied to be known and faithfully served; the eternal must clothe itself in temporal form to enter effectually within our horizon.'[2]

CONCLUSION

The historical study of the subject of revelation which has been our theme has shown how certain periods in the history of the Church are marked by specific interest in special ideas. The period 1700 to 1860 was concerned with the problems of the divine self-disclosure. But in this closing section it has been shown how in the present period of revived interest in the doctrine of revelation, it is the problems which the earlier period left unsolved which are demanding attention. There has been, of course, no exhaustive attempt made here to solve these problems. The question has, however, been raised whether the opposing doctrines which then came into conflict, and which still persist, are ultimately hostile. It is suggested that the full truth concerning revelation may be somehow a synthesis of the views indicated and illustrated. God's self-disclosure, we believe, cannot be reduced to any neat formula.

Varied, and sometimes opposing, as were the doctrines of revelation between the years 1700 and 1860, the one belief common to all was that there was a revelation of God. This is the certainty which men still require. They would know that God has disclosed Him-

---

[1] Cf., e.g. Brunner, 'the written record is part of this revelation it is not the whole,' *Revelation and Reason*, p. 12. 'Holy Scripture therefore does not only speak of revelation, it is itself revelation,' op. cit., p. 21. Dodd, 'The Church . . . offers the Bible . . . as the authoritative record of the divine revelation in history,' *The Bible To-day*, p. 15. 'The Church offers this book as a revelation of God,' p. 12.
[2] H. Wheeler Robinson, *Redemption and Revelation*, p. xliv, cf., p. 186. Cf., 'The Bible contains the record, the interpretation and the literary reflection of His grace in history,' A. B. Bruce, *The Chief End of Revelation*, p. 280.

self, and that the revelation given is adequate to and available for the deepest needs of every man as a rational and spiritual being.[1] And, just because man is both, revelation will be both. What may, therefore, become divided by the necessities of theory can become united in the realities of experience.[2] Because man is 'spiritual', revelation must come as 'Spirit', and because he is 'rational', revelation must come as 'Truth'. This means that, as a final fact, revelation will be, not one to the exclusion of the other, but at the same time both. Revelation, that is, will be not 'Spirit' only, and, not 'Truth' only; but revelation will be, at once, 'Spirit and Truth'. The experience of the apostle Peter illustrates the point. For him faith was not belief in 'truths' based upon the occular demonstrations of 'signs and wonders': and for us, faith is not belief in 'truths' reared on the strength of historical evidences. Peter's confession was the result of a divine illumination; for us, likewise, there must be the inner witness of the Spirit. 'And yet it remains true that the revelation came to Peter as an inward witness to the Jesus whom he knew in the flesh, and it comes to us as a witness to the Jesus whom we know as an historical personality through the Gospel story.'[3] God's full and final self-disclosure is in the Christ declared to us in and through the pages of the New Testament and

---

[1] It should be pointed out, however, that it is to Greek thought, not to the Biblical writings, is due the definition of man as a rational animal. 'The classical view of man, comprised primarily of Platonic, Aristotelian, and Stoic conceptions of human nature . . . is to be understood primarily from the standpoint of the uniqueness of his rational faculties. What is unique in man is nous.' (Reinhold Niebuhr, *Human Nature*, p. 6). The Scripture, on the other hand, presents man as a sentient being whose chief end is to worship and glorify God. Latent, perhaps, in the Greek doctrine, which it was not possible for its philosophers, clearly to indicate, is the idea of man as a worshipping being, since it is rational creatures alone who are qualified for the high purpose which the Scripture presents. Yet the Biblical literature which reveals man as a worshipping creature, most certainly assumes that he is a rational creature. He is addressed as a responsible being called 'to reason together' with God. An exclusive Greek conception results in the view of man whose best powers are seen in the perception of rational connection to formal syllogisms and revelation is consequently considered to be merely a disclosure of truth in logical propositions. But when the truth in the Scholastic view and the truth of the Scripture view are united it will give an understanding of revelation as at the same time a communication and a communion. There will be information for the sake of fellowship. In a final synthesis therefore, our understanding of revelation must unite the ideas of Greece and Galilee.

[2] Cf., 'An antimony simultaneously admits the truth of two contradictory, logically incompatible, but ontologically equally necessary assertions. An antimony testifies to the existence of a mystery beyond which the human reason cannot penetrate. This msytery nevertheless is actualized and lived in religious experience. All fundamental dogmatic definitions are of this nature,' Sergius Bulgakov, *The Wisdom of God*, p. 116, note.

[3] D. M. Baillie, *God Was In Christ*.

made known to us by the Spirit. Herein is a revelation adequate and available to all as 'Spirit and Truth'.

The modern understanding of revelation, it is claimed, has, on the one hand, made impossible a doctrine of a verbally inspired Scripture. The books of the Bible can no longer be regarded as written down by 'private secretaries of the Holy Ghost' as John Donne, for example, maintained. On the other hand, the protagonists of the modern view contend that their 'activist' doctrine of revelation has made obsolete the older liberalism which was obsessed with problems of the text and authorship of the books of Scripture in an effort to upset the accepted doctrine of the Bible as the Word of God. This type of liberalism, it is now asserted, is no longer valid. It missed the point because, by concerning itself with questions of introduction, it failed to focus attention upon the content of the Scripture itself. It was thus blind to the significance of revelation which is to be regarded not as a word spoken long since or as a doctrine once and for all given, but as an event, a divine activity. By casting out the idea of Scripture as itself the Word of God the older liberalism lost all idea of any Word of God.

The newer liberalism claims to have retrieved the situation. Now 'the term "Word of God" has been reconceived. As a word in inter-personal relations is a means of personal self-disclosure, as speech is a revelation or disclosure of personal life, so the "Word of God" is understood by analogy as the whole process of divine self-disclosure. It was in this sense — so runs the claim — that the Word of God was originally used in the Bible. Barth has spoken of a threefold process of divine self-disclosure, (1) God encounters and speaks to man, (2) man speaks or proclaims God's Word, and (3) someone writes down the record of these events.[1] Thus the emphasis is taken from the written word, which becomes simply a written record of revelation, and is placed upon an event or experience in which God is alleged to reveal or disclose himself to man. What others have called religious experience is viewed as a "divine-human encounter." [2]

Stressing the Kierkegaardian emphasis upon the autonomy of the single individual, there is to-day, under the influence of Martin Buber, importance placed upon the 'I-Thou' relationship of religious knowledge in contrast with the 'I-It' relationship of

[1] K. Barth, *The Doctrine of the Word of God*, p. 98 f.
[2] John A. Hutchinson, *Faith, Reason, Existence* (O.U.P., New York), p. 112.

scientific knowledge. More recently there has been a declared effort to explain revelation in still more personal terms. This is shown, for example, in William Nicholls' book entitled, *Revelation in Christ*. It is acknowledged, of course, that the writers of the more immediate past have succeeded 'in the shifting of the locus of revelation from literature to history, and from the propositional to the personal'.[1] At the present, a firmer declaration that Christ is the only proper 'locus' of revelation is being called for. In some quarters this view is linked with the idea of the Church as an extension of the Incarnation and with the conclusion drawn that there may be more knowledge of Christ still to be disclosed. It is in this way that the wheel has come full circle and the very effort to safeguard revelation as final in Christ is consequently jeopardized.

It is a matter of astonishment to find it being constantly asserted that the idea of revelation in Christ is the special discovery of recent years. Such claims can be made only by a total disregard of historical facts. It is true, of course, that the older orthodox apologists did obscure the Person of Christ and did conceive of revelation as the communication of doctrinal propositions. Brunner has some justification for his remark that the idea early arose in the Church under the influence of Greek philosophy that divine revelation was the communication of doctrinal truths which were otherwise inaccessible to human reason, and that faith consisted in holding these supernaturally revealed doctrines for truth.[2] Brunner is perhaps too confident about the earliness of the influence: but, however this may be, it is a fact that there did come a time when there was the influence with the results as stated for the idea of revelation. The preceding pages will have made clear, however, that it was among the orthodox anti-deistic apologists where this idea prevailed. And they were merely carrying on the scholastic tradition. But the same charge cannot be sustained against the Evangelicals. They certainly held to an exalted view of Scripture; but their high view of Scripture was coupled with the highest view of Christ's Person. The very exaltation of the Bible, in their case, far from detracting from Christ, worked rather the other way. The investigation of the works of Charles Simeon and John Wesley will have made it clear that their profound view of the Person of Christ was not the summary of ideas derived from their own personal

[1] William Nicholls, *Revelation in Christ* (S.C.M., 1957), p. 9.
[2] E. Brunner, *The Divine-Human Encounter*, p. 12.

encounter with God in Christ. Their conception of Christ was based upon the Scriptures through which the experience was mediated. To begin with the personal encounter seems to be in the last analysis a falling back upon the view of Schleiermacher which makes *Dogmatics* to be the summary of the pious feelings. It is such ideas which account for the contradictions inherent in the newer liberal approach.

In its reactions from the 'Jesus of History' cult of the older school the newer emphasis upon the 'super-historical' Christ makes the Scriptures even less vital for faith. The historical picture is, after all, of little value, since revelation does not belong to the Christ Who lived and taught and died. It is the Christ Who is outside the historic process, the exalted Christ, Who is revelation. The Synoptic gospels have to do with the historic human Jesus and, it is said, it matters little for faith how factually correct they are. John's gospel, on the other hand, is a construction of faith and is therefore not historical. We are thus informed that, 'Faith presupposes, as a matter of course, *a priori*, that the Jesus of history is not the same as the Christ of faith.'[1] Professing to renounce Schleiermacher's views (for who is a more violent critic of him than Brunner?) this newer liberalism ends up by adopting his attitude to the biblical basis for faith.

The older liberalism has shown how difficult it is to accept the highest view of our Lord's Person when once the foundations upon which it rests have been undermined. It is certainly not as a result of a personal encounter that we learn that the Word became flesh and that the Word was God. The 'becoming' flesh is, to be sure, an event indeed, the divinest event of all. But it is declared as a doctrine. The statement that the 'Word was God' is unquestionably a doctrinal statement.

This means as a final result that the proclamation Christ is revelation, or Revelation is in Christ throws us back upon Scripture. It is not any Christ Who is revelation. Those who say, Lo, here is Christ, or, Lo, there, are not to be believed unless the Christ Whom they declare is the Christ of the New Testament. It is not the Jesus of History or the Christ of Faith as if there were two distinct beings. The Christ Who is final revelation is not the Christ of subjective experience, nor the Christ of personal encounter, nor the Christ of Church declaration, except in so far as these are identical

[1] E. Brunner, *The Mediator* (E.T.), p. 184.

with the Christ set forth in Scripture. The Christ Who is revelation is the Biblical Christ; no more and no less. This is the Christ Who Himself authenticated this conclusion when 'beginning from Moses, and from all the prophets, he interpreted to them in all the Scriptures the things concerning himself'.[1]

[1] Lk. 24:27 (R.V.)

ALPHABETICAL LIST OF
BOOKS MENTIONED

ALPHABETICAL INDEX TO
WESLEY'S WORKS QUOTED

PRINTED IN GREAT BRITAIN BY ROBERT MACLEHOSE
THE UNIVERSITY PRESS, GLASGOW

ALPHABETICAL INDEX TO WESLEY'S WORKS QUOTED

PRINTED IN GREAT BRITAIN BY ROBERT MACLEHOSE AND CO. LTD
THE UNIVERSITY PRESS, GLASGOW